FIREBRAND

FIREBRAND

The Life of

DOSTOEVSKY

By

HENRY TROYAT

Translated by Norbert Guterman

Woodcuts by S. Mrozewski

WILLIAM HEINEMANN LTD
LONDON   ::   TORONTO

FOREWORD

THE LIVES OF MANY FAMOUS MEN ARE LESS COLORFUL THAN their works. Faced with these sedate careers, the biographer is tempted to become a novelist, to supplement, interpret and invent, more concerned with his own art than with the truth, with himself than with his hero; and, instead of serving a great man, he uses him as a subject.

But with Dostoevsky, it is easier to sin by understatement than by overstatement. His story is so rich in spectacular despair and miraculous joy that the temptation is not to fictionize but to shade off. It is as though Dostoevsky had arranged his life in the style of his novels and made his own story the most captivating of them all. Its truth seems more incredible than the most fantastic legend, and to tell it with scrupulous honesty is enough to arouse the distrust of most readers. I wish I could take the reader by the hand and show him the police reports with the emperor's signature in the margin, the love letters, or the notebooks in which epileptic fits are noted beside sketches of Gothic cathedrals and plans for cloudy novels.

There is not a single detail in this book that is not confirmed by the documents I have consulted. When I write that Dostoevsky stood before his window to admire a white night in the sky of St. Petersburg, it is because actually on that date a white night was observed in the Russian capital. When I say that Dostoevsky and his friend drove by a fire between Semipalatinsk and Zmiev, it is because on that very day, ac-

5

cording to Baron Wrangel's *Memoirs*, the peasants burned weeds at the side of the Siberian road. If I state that the general who read the verdict to the plotters on Semenovsky Square had a defect of speech, it is because actually, according to many contemporary reports, this personage was known for his fits of stammering.

Indeed, I have not permitted myself any literary inexactitude, however slight. I would have been embarrassed to embroider with easy inventions a reality so terrible, beautiful and generous as that which I got to know through the memoirs and letters of contemporaries.

There does not exist, even in Russia, a complete and definitive biography of Dostoevsky. This one does not claim to present new facts; its only merit is that it was written in a spirit of absolute sincerity and great love.

HENRY TROYAT

CONTENTS

1. THE FAMILY

IT WAS COLD. THE SNOW HAD DRIFTED HIGHER THAN THE windows, and ravens flapped above the white plain, like rags of disaster blown by the wind. Maria ordered the servants to heat the furnace and told her husband to take his bath. He obeyed her, either because he loved her or because he, himself, felt that he urgently needed a bath. This hygienic desire proved fatal. For as he left the frame cabin which served as the master's bathhouse, he was attacked by Yan-Tura, some man hired by his wife, who wounded him with a shot. He let out a fierce groan, and rushed toward the house. By order of Maria, the door had been barricaded. The unfortunate husband banged his fists against it, but Yan-Tura overtook him and finished him with a blow from the back of a saber.

"Take him to the devil," said Maria to those who brought her the corpse.

The dead man was placed on a bier and covered with an old blanket. Near the entrance there were puddles of blood that dogs and pigs were licking avidly. Maria's eldest son took refuge in a neighbor's house and started court proceedings against his mother. The shrew, who had remarried in the meantime, was sentenced to death. . . .

The heroine of this story, which could have been the central episode of a novel by Dostoevsky, was Maria Dostoevsky, an ancestress of the writer. It took place in 1606, but this is not the first appearance of the name of Dostoevsky in Lithuanian chronicles. A century earlier on October 6, 1506, it is recorded that the prince of Pinsk presented the boyar Daniel Ivanovich Irtishevich with several villages, including Dostoevo. The descendants of Daniel took the name of Dostoevsky.

A certain Feodor Dostoevsky was an intimate of Prince Kurbsky, the celebrated hero of Russian poetry, who had to escape the wrath of Ivan the Terrible, and seek refuge in Lithuania while writing to the czar letters remarkable for their intense hatred and injured dignity. At about the same time one Raphael Ivanovich Dostoevsky was indicted for swindling and embezzlement of public funds. Other Dostoevskys were judges, priests and captains. A kindly Dostoevsky led a reputedly holy life in the Lavra of Kiev. In 1624, Stepan Dostoevsky escaped from the dungeons of the Turks and hung silver chains before the icon of the Holy Virgin in Lwow. In 1634, Shashny Dostoevsky and his son took part in the murder of a military commander. In 1649, Philip Dostoevsky was called to account for looting expeditions and bloody raids upon his neighbors' estates. Thieves, murderers, magistrates, visionaries and pettifoggers—this ancestry, in which good and evil were wedded through successive generations, seems to herald the work of Dostoevsky.

After the middle of the seventeenth century a branch of the family settled in the Ukraine, where they fiercely resisted Polish Catholic influences, and most of its members became Orthodox clergymen. They were monks or priests, but their existence is little known to us. Fallen from their ancient splendor, deprived of their estates, attached to the service of God, they seem to have lived out their lives in unassuming honesty and fallen into oblivion—thus proving once again that virtue does not make history.

Following the example of his ancestors, the father of Mikhail Andreevich Dostoevsky was a priest and could not conceive that any other vocation might appeal to his son's imagination. He was shocked when the boy, then fifteen years old, declared his intention of studying medicine and, secretly aided by his mother, left the family home and went to Moscow.

Mikhail Andreevich did not know a soul there. He had little money and even less experience. Nevertheless, he set himself to studying fiendishly, was admitted to the School of Surgery and Medicine, treated the wounded during the campaign of 1812, and finally was promoted to the rank of major in the army.

Regiments, garrisons, promotions followed one another; on March 24, 1821, Mikhail Andreevich was appointed attending physician at the Hospital of the Poor. Mediocre honorary distinctions were the landmarks of this career, begun in a surge of revolt and quietly spent in the mild serenity of an administrative office—the cross of St. Vladimir

4th class, the cross of St. Anne 3rd class, the modest title of
assessor. The major had also put his name on the register of
the hereditary nobility of Moscow.

In 1819, Mikhail Andreevich married Maria Feodorovna
Nechaev, the daughter of a merchant, who brought him a
considerable dowry, a sincere love, and good practical sense.
She was sensitive, gentle and self-effacing, with a beautiful,
aristocratic and somewhat tired face. A pastel drawing by
Popov shows her dressed in the fashion of 1820; silk head-
bands frame her short face with its large dreamy eyes and un-
smiling lips. The same artist made a portrait of Mikhail
Andreevich Dostoevsky. It reveals a coarse peasant face
with eyebrows raised near the temples, a strong mouth and
heavy chin. Carefully clipped sideburns reach to the middle
of the cheeks. The rigid gold-embroidered collar of his dress
uniform rises to his jaws, and he has the fixed look of a
bird.

This difficult start in life and mediocre success had embittered Mikhail Andreevich. He was harsh toward himself
and others, but even in his severity he lacked greatness. Ill-
tempered, suspicious, meddlesome, the petty tyrant insisted
on well-regulated schedules, the solemn observance of family
precedences, domestic discipline and bigotry—he was the
master next to God. And yet this chieflet suffered from excessive sentimentality and sudden fits of sadness that sometimes shook him to his very depths. He poured out his heart
to his wife: "A deadly ennui has taken possession of me. I
don't know what to do with myself. God knows what ideas
haunt me both in daylight and in dreams!"

She was frightened when she saw him so dejected, and he
swallowed her candid panic with pleasure. "My heart is
heavy," she wrote him during a brief separation, "when I

imagine you so sad. I beg of you, my angel, my God, take care of yourself, at least for my love's sake; remember that from far away I worship you, and that I love you more than my own life, you, my only friend."

Thus the unfortunate woman attempted to restore the unbearable self-confidence of her beloved little tyrant. And relaxed, pitying, grumpy, he let himself be treated. But once the crisis was over he climbed again upon his ridiculous pedestal.

Actually he was not fundamentally bad, indeed, he was *not even bad*. He loved his wife because she adored him. He did not inflict corporal punishment on his children, although they would have preferred it to his terrible fits of anger. He valiantly refrained from drinking during his wife's lifetime, and when he yielded completely to drunkenness, he had the honorable excuse of being a widower and utterly desperate. As for his stinginess, some biographers have attempted to justify it on the grounds of his mediocre income and the slowness with which promotions came to him. True, his salary of one hundred rubles in notes—at that time, one silver ruble was worth three and a half rubles in notes—was low; but his wife's dowry, the income from his private practice, the subsidies he probably received from his extremely wealthy relatives, such as the Kumanins, enabled him to make ends meet easily enough. It seems exaggerated to speak of Mikhail Andreevich's poverty, since his rent was paid by the government and he had seven servants attached to the hospital, as well as four private horses for his own use.

Furthermore, in 1831, he bought a property one hundred and fifty versts from Moscow, in the government of Tula. It comprised 1,350 acres of land and the villages of Darovoe and Cheremashny with about one hundred "souls."

Despite all this, the new country squire's letters to his wife, who was in the country with their children, are always full of complaints: "I have received everything except two flasks of liqueur which, according to Grigory, were broken. I wonder, my beloved, whether they broke of themselves or whether they were not first emptied and then broken. . . ." Or: "At home everything is quiet, although Vasilisa has aroused my suspicions on several occasions; but at present I am constantly keeping an eye on her. Write me, my beloved, and tell me how many bottles and flasks of liqueur you still have in the cupboard." In other letters he asks his wife to give him a detailed list of the silver, not omitting the odd pieces. "You write that I should have six tablespoons, but I find only five. You also write that there is one broken spoon in the chiffonnier; I could not find it there, are you not by chance mistaken?"

He enjoined upon her to send without delay an exact list of his wrappers and nightcaps. And throughout the correspondence of this couple, these miserly details alternate with lyrical outbursts of marital passion.

In Moscow the Dostoevskys lived in an annex of the Hospital of the Poor. The façade of this hospital, adorned with majestic Doric columns and surrounded by an iron fence with pilasters bearing lions, was on the Bozhedomka, the Street of God's Houses. The approaches of the Bozhedomka were lined with educational and charitable institutions: orphanages, asylums for the poor, and the Alexander and St. Catherine institutes for young ladies of the nobility. It was a district of administrative niggardliness, frank ugliness, poverty that begged for charity—the district officially reserved for misery and boredom.

The house occupied by the Dostoevsky family was a small one-story private dwelling, built vaguely in Empire style and surrounded by a garden, behind which began the grounds of the hospital with its barrackslike buildings, its imposing linden trees and private chapel. It was a mysterious and painful world out of bounds for the children.

In the apartment of the Dostoevskys there were two rooms and an entrance hall. A makeshift board partition cut the vestibule in two, making a ramshackle room for the sons. It had no windows and its walls were painted in dark gray. Farther on, there was a large room painted in canary yellow, and finally the parlor in cobalt blue. Later, another room was added to this apartment. The furniture was simple and practical—in the parlor two game tables, one dining table and a dozen chairs upholstered in green leather; in the other room the parents' beds, a washstand and two immense linen chests. The ceilings were high, the furniture was of respectable size, and the seats, stuffed with horsehair, preserved like wax the imprint of the respectable backsides that had sat upon them.

It was in this apartment that the major's second son spent his childhood. He was born on October 30, 1821. On November 4, in the Peter and Paul chapel of the Hospital of the Poor he was baptized Feodor, after his maternal grandfather.

Day followed day with healthful monotony. A strenuous schedule without any diversion destroyed the very idea of time in this family, which, all in all, considered itself happy. They rose at six in the morning. At eight o'clock the father left to visit his wing of the hospital. The servants took advantage of his departure to clean the apartment and heat the stoves. He returned at nine o'clock, and immediately left again to visit his patients in the city. After lunch he locked

himself in the parlor to take a nap for an hour and a half or
two hours on the old leather sofa. In summer, one of the children had to sit by Mikhail Andreevich and chase away the
flies with a linden tree branch. If an insect succeeded in fool-
ing the sentry and awakened the sleeper by sitting on his
nose, the cries and scoldings were enough to ruin one's appetite for supper. "Woe to him who let a fly pass," Andrey
Dostoevsky later wrote in his memoirs. All the family dili-
gently applied itself to protecting this patriarchal siesta. In
the adjoining room, seated at the round table, they spoke in
low voices, smothered their laughs, and trembled at the
slightest grumbling of the dozing tyrant.

The clandestine murmur of these gatherings filled Feodor's
childhood. Maria Feodorovna loved to tell a thousand strange
memories of her parents. Her father had fled Moscow when
the French entered it. As he crossed a river his carriage
plunged into the water and the bank notes in the luggage
were so wet that they stuck together and could not be
pulled apart. Maria's voice was sweet, her eyes were tender and mysterious. Life was pleasant when the major was
asleep.

The children, however, preferred their nanny's fairy tales
to their mother's stories. This nurse, Aliona Frolovna, held
an important position in the family. She was an enormous
woman, swollen with diseased fat, and her belly, according
to Andrey Dostoevsky, touched her knees. She dressed very
neatly, and always wore a white net cap. Her appetite was
insatiable. Yet this comfortable mastodon was in the last
stages of consumption, a fact which greatly amused the
doctor: "You write me that this woman of forty-five pouds
is wasting away, and that on the other hand you had a hard
time loading and unloading the carriage; I conclude that

there is no disaster without some profit, for I imagine that she lost at least twenty pouds [sic]. This reduction in weight will be greatly appreciated by the horses and the carriage."

Mikhail Andreevich liked to make fun of the poor woman's fancies, some of which were curious. Aliona Frolovna maintained, for instance, that God demanded of every Christian that he eat a mouthful of bread between each two mouthfuls of meat, fish or vegetables. Only porridge could be swallowed without an "escort." "First chew a piece of bread, my dear, and then take food into your mouth. The Lord God has decreed it that way."

Her only weakness was that she took snuff. A filthy and hideous merchant visited her at regular intervals. The major used to declare that they were engaged but she would reply indignantly, "Fie, may heaven forgive you! It is the Lord who is my fiancé, not an ordinary tobacco merchant."

At night Aliona Frolovna occasionally roared like a beast, and the children would awaken frozen with fright. Then the major would jump down from his bed and shake her till she came to. "I warn you," he used to say, "that if you yell once again I will order that you be given a bloodletting of three pounds." Actually, she was bled almost every day, without results.

The doctor also advised her to eat less at meals, but she claimed that if she fell asleep on an empty stomach she always dreamed of gypsies, which was very unpleasant. So for the sake of peace and quiet Mikhail Andreevich gave in to her whims. Indeed, Aliona Frolovna was the only person who could hold her own against this tyrant; often she even protected the children against his fits of anger. She was a "citizen of Moscow," and was proud of it. She was intimate with the children, and when she spoke to her master she omitted the usual title of *barin*, and addressed him as Mikhail Andreevich, as though she was not a servant. Finally, she kept the keys of the cellar and pantry, and this was an unquestionable distinction.

The family took tea at four o'clock, and spent the evenings at the round table lighted by two suet candles—the wax candles were reserved for anniversary dinners. The father, mother, and later the children, read in turn from Karamzin's *History of Russia*, Derzhavin's *Odes*, Zhukovsky's *Poems*, a novel entitled *Poor Lisa* or certain poems of Pushkin. Mikhail Andreevich was fairly cultivated for a man of his profession, and—one should do him justice—wanted his sons to respect arts and letters.

Dinner was at exactly nine o'clock. As soon as they left table, the children kissed their parents, knelt before the holy images for their evening prayers, and returned to their dark, windowless, silent room, where the furniture seemed suddenly to loom up before them, dangerous and magical. Feodor was afraid of shadows and his brother Mikhail was not much more courageous than he. But they fell asleep quickly, their eyes fixed on the little flame of the icon, which throbbed like a living thing against the wall.

Diversions were rare in the Dostoevsky family. Twice a year, the children's wet nurses (Maria Feodorovna had nursed only her son Mikhail) came from their villages to visit their former charges. "Lukeria has come," Aliona Frolovna would announce to her mistress. And Lukeria would enter the parlor, with ribbons on her head and linden bark shoes on her feet. In the doorway she made the sign of the cross, bowed gravely, and distributed to the children homemade pancakes that she had brought in a bright kerchief. Then she returned to the kitchen. But after nightfall she slipped into the room where the little ones waited for her and sat by their side. There, in the dark, when anything can happen, she told them in a low voice about the adventures of Prince Ivan, Bluebeard, the Firebird, or Aliosha Popovich. She spoke the old peasant language, slow and racy, stressing the syllables that contained the vowel "o." Slightly frightened but charmed the children listened to her read: "And the boyar stopped at the crossroads. . . ." Afterward, the boys discussed the respective merits of the nurses. Which one knew the most beautiful stories—Varenka's or Feodor's?

Feodor's parents received few visitors. The major was rather unsociable and liked to go to bed early. He took his children to the theater only two or three times, on special occasions. After seeing *Yako, or the Monkey of Brazil*, Feodor spent several weeks imitating the actor who played the monkey. And, too, he lost sleep over Schiller's *Robbers* interpreted by Machalov. Walks were patriarchal and approximately dull. On summer days, at the same hour, the whole family went to the Maria meadow, near the hospital. As they passed the sentry on duty before the Alexander Institute, father dropped a coin at the feet of the soldier who surreptitiously picked it up. The walk was an opportunity for lofty and edifying conversations with his offspring concerning arithmetic or geometry. . . . The children were forbidden to run on the grass, because a well brought-up boy, Mikhail Andreevich explained, could not sink so low as to scamper like a hare. They were forbidden to make friends with "unknown children" or play such games as horse, ball, and *lapta*, which were only for plebeians. On Sundays and holidays the family went to church for vespers. On gala occasions they played "kings." And for their father's birthdays, the little fellows wrote compliments in French on

special paper tied with ribbons. Later they even recited
poetry for him: Pushkin, Zhukovsky, and—inexplicably—
fragments of the *Henriade!*

Within this little clan, Feodor Mikhailovich Dostoevsky
grew up completely sheltered from all contact with the
external world, deprived of friends, experience or freedom.
This lonely childhood, this artificial development of his
sensibility, left an indelible mark on him: "We are all un-
accustomed to life," says one of his heroes. Dostoevsky himself could never become accustomed to it.

Feodor, however, was no gloomy and priggish child. His
vulnerable honesty did not prevent him from being wild,
irascible, mischievous and sometimes authoritarian. When
playing cards with his parents he managed to cheat, to the
major's great confusion. Drives in the carriage put him in a
feverish state of excitement. The slightest diversion threw
him into a state of ecstasy. Having seen a runner at a fair, he
began to trot back and forth in the garden, with a handkerchief between his teeth and his elbows at his sides, till he was
completely exhausted. "I am not surprised by Feodor's mischievous deeds, they are always to be expected from him,"
wrote Maria to her husband. Once the major scolded his son
in these prophetic words: "Ah, Fedya, quiet down; you
won't come to any good. One day you'll end up wearing the
red cap." This red cap, the headdress of simple privates,
Feodor Mikhailovich was actually to wear after his release
from prison.

A fence separated the garden of the Dostoevskys from the
vast hospital grounds. Despite the doctor's ruling Feodor
liked to talk with the patients, dressed in beige wrappers and
cotton caps, who came out to breathe the fresh air. The

lonely little boy sought the company of these timid, defeated, miserable people rejected by a world of which he knew nothing. What wretched dramas, what humble misfortunes had wrecked their lives? And why were they so close to him, despite the difference in age and social position? When the major caught his son talking with a patient, he scolded him severely. Mikhail, his oldest son, was calm, a bit dreamy perhaps, but on the whole docile; the youngest, Andrey, gave him entire satisfaction. But Feodor! "He is a real firebrand!" his parents used to say.

To quiet the boy's neurotic wildness, the doctor explained to him in detail how poor they were, how difficult it would be for them to "make a career," how moderate must be their expectations. This dark picture of the future terrified the children and doubtless developed in Feodor that fear of all social life, that excessive suspiciousness and those sudden apprehensions from which he suffered till his death.

"Follow my example," the father used to say. If only he had known how his son feared being like him! Was it not because of his father's avarice that he was so generous, because of his parents' severity that the boy demanded complete indulgence toward everyone? Thus he proved to himself that he had nothing in common with his father. He seems to have experienced toward his father uncertain and contradictory feelings. He feared him, occasionally hated him, and even had a kind of physical repugnance for him. "Who has not desired his father's death?" exclaims Ivan Karamazov. But sometimes Feodor was shaken by fits of compassion, and was indignant at being so far away from him.

"How I pity my father! What a strange character!" he

wrote to his brother Mikhail. And the doctor's death struck him all the more forcibly, because he was not sure that he had ever loved him as a father.

In 1831, the purchase of Darovoe relieved the drab existence of the family. Now Maria Feodorovna took her children to the country as soon as spring came. The major whose duties kept him in the city joined them only in July, and his visits never spoiled the vacation for more than two days—at a time.

The trip which took two or three days was an adventure. A serf named Simon Shiroki came for them from the village with draft horses, and the old coach was loaded with trunks and bundles. Fedya climbed onto the seat beside the driver, and the equipage trotted off, crossed the city, and took the country roads cut by dry crusty ruts, passing fields of rye, young birches with leaves of shivering silver, thatched huts with frame porches, little barefoot children in smocks who raised their hands and shouted something unintelligible. Milestones appeared and disappeared. There were smells of dust, dung and moth-eaten cloth now to the right and now to the left of the carriage. The horses' shoes made a noise like a tongue smack against the palate. The wheels creaked, the bells rang. Fedya implored Simon to let him hold the reins. "Do I drive well?"

At the first stop Fedya ran to see the village, wet his shoes in the grass and finally climbed up again on his seat intoxicated by the air, impatient and enchanted. The whip cracked, and again the coach lumbered on.

The house at Darovoe was a dilapidated little pavilion of three rooms, with rough chalked walls and a thatched roof set in the shadow of century-old linden trees. A narrow

meadow extended to a birch wood cut by ravines. At nightfall the wood was sinister, infested, it was said, with wolves
and snakes. Because Feodor particularly loved to venture
into it secretly, this corner was called "Fedya's forest." The
estate also had a vegetable garden. Later the doctor had a
pond dug near the house. Mikhail Andreevich sent a barrel
of live carp from Moscow, which were released in the
water. Then the priest headed a procession which walked
around the pond, carrying icons and holy banners.

Today the grove has been cut down, cabbages grow on
the dried bottom of the pond, and a new, clean and anonymous house has replaced the Dostoevsky pavilion. But the
villages of Darovoe and Cheremashny have not changed.
They are tiny hamlets, of about twenty huts each, inhabited
by primitive peasants famous for their ability to steal horses.

Maria Dostoevsky spent the whole summer at Darovoe.
She managed the chicken yard, the vegetable garden, the
fields of wheat, oats, potatoes and flax. With charming
candor, she wrote to her husband: "The serfs are all in good
health, except those of Fyodor's family whom I found close
to death; but at present, thank God, they are better. Only
three among them are still refraining from plowing. The
cattle, thank God, is in good health." And in another letter:
"God has given me a couple of new serfs. Nikita had a son,
Igor, and Fedot a daughter, Lukeria. The sow had a litter of
five, the duck is quietly brooding on her eggs, and as for
the geese, they do not give anything. . . ."

While the mother managed the household and supervised
the health of her peasants and beasts with equal solicitude,
the children enjoyed their new freedom. On this miserable
little estate, which seemed to them a world of feasts and
miracles, they organized games. Fedya invented the game of

savages. The boys built a cabin under the linden trees, undressed, smeared their bodies with paint and put on hats
decorated with leaves and goose feathers. Then, armed with
bows and arrows, they attacked the woods where the village boys and girls were entrenched. The prisoners were led
to the cabin and released only upon payment of a generous
ransom. Fedya also invented the game of Robinson Crusoe.
Later the children bathed in the pond.

The young city dwellers were popular among their serfs,
especially Fedya, who spent entire days in the fields watching the little muzhiks, bearded, dirty, with childlike eyes, and
heavy calloused hands. He harried them with questions,
asked them to let him drive a horse harnessed to a harrow or
a plow, or to let him handle the scythe. One day, at harvest
time, he saw a peasant woman who had upset her jug and was
wailing because her baby was thirsty and threatened with a
sunstroke. He walked a mile on foot to bring her some water
from the village.

These peasants attracted him as had the patients of the
Hospital of the Poor. He felt at ease with these simple,
frugal, countless people, and all his life preserved a passionate
love for them. It was to them that he returned when he
wanted to renew his faith in Russia's holy mission—not to
the gold-braided officials, not to the refined aristocracy,
but to them, to their soiled faces, their arched backs, their
soft, blank expressions. Even when he was in prison, isolated
and despairing, he found his first comfort in their memory.
"I recalled that month of August in the country. The
weather was dry and clear but somewhat cool, for there was
much wind. The summer was drawing to its end, and I
was soon to return to Moscow, to bore myself all winter
long studying French; and I was heavy-hearted at the

thought that I was about to leave the countryside. . . ."

He plunged into the woods. He cut hazel branches to lash frogs. Around him the woods were silent. Ruddy lizards studded with black spots slithered along the stones of the path. May bugs hung from the low leaves. The air smelled of mushrooms, peeled trunks, rotten grass. One day he suddenly heard a terrifying cry: "Wolf!" He fled shrieking, crossed the thickets and came to a glade where a muzhik was plowing.

"It was our peasant Marey . . . a man of about fifty, robust, fairly tall, with a ruddy disheveled beard streaked with gray. I knew him, although I had never spoken to him. Hearing my cry, he stopped his mare, and as I came close to him and gripped his plow with one hand, and his sleeve with the other, he saw my fright. 'Wolf, wolf!' I breathed, panting.

"He raised his head and cast an involuntary glance around him. For a moment he almost believed me. 'Where is the wolf?' he said.

" 'There was a cry. . . . Someone cried: Wolf!' I stammered.

" 'Come on, there is no wolf, you have been dreaming. What would a wolf be doing here?' he murmured to reassure me.

"But all trembling I clung more insistently to his blouse and I think my pallor must have been extreme.

" 'Ah, how frightened you are, aie, aie!' he said, shaking his head. 'Come, it's all over, my little one. Look how brave he is!'

"He stretched out his hand and suddenly stroked my cheek. 'Come, it's over. May Christ be with you. Make the sign of the cross.'

"But I did not make the sign of the cross. My lips were clenched. He noticed this and placed his thumb with its black nail, dirtied by the earth, on my convulsed lips. . . .

"And twenty years later, in Siberia, I suddenly recalled this incident in every detail. I saw again the tender maternal smile of the poor peasant, our serf. I recalled the signs of the cross he made, the shaking of his head when he said: 'You are frightened, my little one.' And most of all, that thumb, dirtied by the earth, with which, gently, almost timidly, he grazed my mouth. And suddenly, moving away from my bunk and casting a glance around me, I felt that I could look at these unfortunates with different eyes, and that all hatred and anger, as though by magic, had vanished from my heart."

Each new ordeal, each new assault of his religious doubts made him turn again to the peasants, to implore their immutable presence, their simple calm strength, and they would answer with the words: "Come, come, there is no wolf. . . . I won't let the wolf take you. . . . May Christ be with you."

Marey actually did live at Darovoe. He was a muzhik, a great expert on horses, whom Maria Feodorovna held in great esteem, so much so that she forgave the liberties of his tongue. Likewise, it was at Darovoe that Dostoevsky met the girl Smerdiashaya of *The Brothers Karamazov*. Her real name was Agafia Timofeevna; she was considered a moron, wore only a shirt all year round, and slept in the cemetery. The village of Cheremashny figures in the same novel. And as for Aliona Frolovna, Dostoevsky immortalized her name in *The Possessed*.

And how Aliona Frolovna deserved this reward! One day, in Moscow, when Dostoevsky was nine years old, the door of the parlor opened, and Grigori entered, coming straight from the village. "And now instead of the wealthy administrator, dressed in the German style, we saw a man in an old blouse and canvas shoes. 'What is the matter!' cried my father, frightened. 'The estate has burned down,' Grigori answered in a hoarse voice."

The fire destroyed the peasant huts, the barns, the harvested crops and the cattle. Even Father Arkhip died in the flames. The family imagined that the ruin was complete. They fell to their knees. Maria Feodorovna sobbed. Then Aliona Frolovna came to her and touched her shoulder. "If you need money," she said, "take mine." She had saved five hundred rubles. Fortunately the damage could be repaired without the servant's help.

Feodor never forgot Aliona or Marey. "Do not judge the Russian people," he wrote, "by the infamies it often happens to perpetrate, but by the great and sacred things for which it is unceasingly yearning from the depths of its ignorance. . . . These things give a light which illumines the road before us."

The education of the Dostoevsky children began early. Maria Feodorovna herself assumed the task of teaching her son Feodor the alphabet. She taught it to him in the old-fashioned way, giving each letter its Slavic name: *az, buki, vede.* . . . Feodor, then four years of age, was bewildered by this procession of strange syllables.

The first book he read was *Four Hundred Stories from the Old and New Testament*, illustrated with faded lithographs of the creation of the world, Adam and Eve in Paradise, the deluge. . . . Years later when Dostoevsky was forty-nine, he found a copy of this book of his childhood, and preserved it in his library as a precious relic.

When the children were able to read the stories of the Old and New Testament, Mikhail Andreevich engaged a learned deacon who taught them Biblical history. He was a teacher at the Catherine Institute and his eloquence charmed the whole family. Maria Feodorovna often listened to the stories he told the children as they sat around the game table, their hands on their cheeks, and their feverish eyes following in imagination the birth, Calvary and death of Christ.

Soon another teacher was engaged to give the Dostoevsky children the rudiments of French. He had been born in France and his name was really Souchard, but he had obtained the emperor's permission to Russify his name into Drachusov. Later the children were sent to this same Drachusov as part time boarders.

This little, round, illiterate man who strongly rolled his R's gave them lessons in French; his two sons taught them mathematics and Slavic history and Russian grammar, and his wife, everything else. As no one knew Latin in this humble establishment, the major undertook the task of teaching it to his sons himself. Every night he got them together, and their torture began.

Mikhail Andreevich was a fierce teacher. All his schoolmaster instincts blossomed in the presence of his pupils. He not only forbade them to sit during the lesson which lasted more than an hour, but if any of them, overcome by weariness, leaned against a piece of furniture, he was immediately reprimanded in a thunderous voice. The pupils stood motionless, frozen by fright, crippled by fatigue, declining and conjugating: *mensa, mensae . . . amo, amas, amat. . . .* The slightest mistake brought shouts and bangs of the fist on the table. Sometimes furious the teacher would close

Bantyshev's grammar and leave the room with a heavy step, slamming the door behind him. Mikhail Andreevich, however, never compelled his pupils to kneel for any length of time, nor did he stand them in the corner with their faces to the wall.

Dostoevsky's parents refused to send their children to the Gymnasium where corporal punishment was a matter of course. In 1834, they, like many other families who for the same reason disliked the Gymnasium, decided to entrust their children to private boarding schools and sent the brothers Mikhail and Feodor Dostoevsky to Chermak's school, a venerable and expensive institution.

Chermak was a worthy pedagogue, meticulous and honest, and although he was a man of mediocre education, managed to surround himself with a good staff. The atmosphere at the school was patriarchal and good-humored. The boarders ate at the table with the Chermak family, and Madam Chermak herself took care of their little cuts and bruises. When one of his pupils deserved encouragement, Chermak summoned him to his office and gravely handed him a little piece of candy. And the boys of the upper grades accepted this reward with the same rapture as the little fellows of the lower classes.

On Saturdays, Mikhail and Feodor went home to be treated to a holiday meal of their favorite dishes, but before touching their food they were expected to tell all about their new life—the marks they received, the homework they had to do, the pranks of their comrades. The major who would not forgive the slightest infringement upon his own authority was greatly amused by the stories of the schoolboys' escapades. Was he maliciously enjoying this revenge against the world as he listened? Or did he despise these academicians, too weak to inspire respect in their charges? "Ah, the scamps! Ah, the little rascals!" he would utter with obvious satisfaction.

After dinner, the children read every book that fell into their hands. At first they were limited to the monthly publications of the *Reading Study*, thin volumes, of which each issue had a cover of a different color. But Feodor was also an ardent reader of *Waverly*, *Quentin Durward* and travel books. He dreamed of visiting Venice or Constantinople, of oriental luxury, of dangerous conquests and noble missions. He swallowed Walter Scott, Dickens, George Sand and Hugo, pell-mell, and digested them as best he could between lessons of arithmetic or grammar.

Mikhail was even degenerate enough to write verse in secret. Both brothers memorized poems by Pushkin and Zhukovsky and recited them to their mother who, stretched out on the sofa, emaciated and undermined by consumption, arbitrated their debate with a smile. Pushkin was then a young writer, and his reputation did not equal that of Zhukovsky. Usually Maria Feodorovna favored the latter, and Feodor was indignant that the *Count of Habsburg* should even be compared to the admirable and cruel *Death of Oleg*.

One day, Vania Umnov, the son of one of the few friends of the family, taught Feodor a literary satire by Voeyekov, entitled *The Madhouse*. Feodor recited it to his father who decided that it was indecent because "it contained sallies against well-known writers, particularly Zhukovsky."

This Vania Umnov was the only boy of their own age whom Mikhail and Feodor were allowed to receive in their home. The major, however, was not entirely responsible for his children's lonely life. Feodor would have liked to make friends among Chermak's other pupils but his exces-

sive pride, suspiciousness and morbid timidity kept his schoolmates at a distance. He had a burning desire to confide in
almost anyone, but withdrew into himself whenever he was
approached. He was afraid to live.

What was there in common between his simple cheerful
schoolmates and this boy, whose existence was darkened by
a carefully nurtured melancholy? What was there in common between his romantic aspirations, his vague yearning
for fame, his literary enthusiasms and the rough games of
his companions? Their vulgar jokes disgusted him. The
friendship of a young girl might have cured him of his
irritability and shyness, but the doctor jealously supervised
every move of his sons. Until the age of sixteen they received no pocket money. Further, they were always brought
back to Chermak's boarding school in the hospital carriage,
so that they would not be tempted to dawdle in the city. As
for their leisure hours on Sundays and holidays, Mikhail
Andreevich decreed that Feodor and Mikhail should spend
them giving lessons to their younger brothers, Andrey and
Nicolai, and their little sisters.

Maria Feodorovna's illness grew more serious, and in the
winter of 1836 she was confined to her bed. This did not
prevent her husband from harboring ridiculous suspicions
against her and accusing her of having betrayed him.

"My friend," she wrote him in May, 1836, "I wonder
whether you are not again torn by doubts as to my faithful-
ness, which are as terrible for me as they are for you. If this
is so, I swear to you, by God, by heaven and by the earth,
that I have never betrayed you and never will betray the
sacred oath I made to you at the altar."

Only the complete exhaustion of the wretched wife finally

appeased her husband's jealousy. Maria Feodorovna became
so weak that she could no longer comb her hair. And since
she considered it indecent to allow strangers to arrange her
coiffure, she had her hair cropped close. In the hospital
pavilion, the visits of relatives and friends succeeded one
another at an ever swifter tempo. Several physicians tried
to help their colleague's wife, but her illness was incurable.
Dostoevsky's mother died on February 27, 1837, after giving
her blessings to her children and husband and her last instructions to the whole household. She was thirty-seven
years of age.

This death was a terrible blow to the family. Feodor and
Mikhail were utterly crushed. The major, crazy with grief,
knocked his head against the walls. He ordered a funeral
stele for his wife, and on one of its facets had engraved the
following quotation from Karamazin: "Rest, beloved ashes,
till the joyous awakening."

A month earlier Pushkin had been killed in a duel with
Baron d'Antes, but Feodor and Mikhail learned of this event
only after their mother's death. The news deeply affected
them. Feodor declared that he would have worn mourning
for the poet if he had not been wearing it for his own mother.
This feeling was not excessive considering the stunned sorrow
with which all Russians received the news of the disaster.
They felt vaguely that Pushkin's end heralded a new and
fearsome era. Not only had a gifted individual perished at the
height of his powers; an idea, a way of being, had disappeared
with him.

"My God! Russia without Pushkin, how strange it is. . . .
My life, my supreme joy have died with him. A very great
man is no longer," wrote Gogol.

Lermontov, then a lieutenant of the Hussars, wrote *Death of the Poet* and was exiled to the Caucasus. Everybody contributed his expression of grief.

The poet is no longer. Fate has done its work.
The national Parnassus is deserted. Pushkin is dead. . . .

These mediocre verses by an unknown author fanned the despair of Feodor and Mikhail.

Life at home became unbearable. The widower was now disgusted with his work and thought only of burying himself in his estate at Darovoe. He decided to send his sons to the Military Engineering School at St. Petersburg, which seemed to him an excellent idea, because the graduates of this institution could become either officers of a guards regiment or engineers. Nevertheless, their departure for the capital was postponed because of Feodor's sudden illness. He suffered a loss of voice, and the various remedies employed proved of no avail. A specialist recommended a trip in good weather, and the experiment was successful. But for the rest of his life Dostoevsky spoke in a strange, low and "artificial" tone, which made his hearers uncomfortable.

The separation was a solemn one. Ivan Barchev, the hospital chaplain, officiated at the services for the travelers. The family, according to custom, sat around the table, rose again, and made the sign of the cross; then the father and the two sons climbed into the hired carriage which was waiting for them.

The trip took almost a week. The horses proceeded at a walk. At each relay there was a delay of three hours. The travelers ate in village inns, and visited the stables where the grooms harnessed the new horses. Then they resumed their journey, at a funeral pace, along a slippery road that lay between flat fields stained here and there by black woods and swamps.

The monotonous landscape wearied the gloomy major, but the boys were intoxicated with a thousand vague hopes. A new life was beginning for them. They were going forth to "serve the great and the beautiful!" according to their favorite formula. True, they would have to study mathematics, but poetry would illumine their intimate life. Mikhail wrote verses at the rate of three poems a day; Feodor composed cloak-and-sword novels against a background of Venetian palaces. They recited to each other Pushkin's latest works. As soon as they arrived in Petersburg they would visit the scene of the duel, then they would go to see Pushkin's house and the room where he had died. Then . . .

An ugly incident interrupted their reverie. At a relay in the Tver region, while the Dostoevskys were waiting for their horses to be changed, a troika stopped before them. A governmental courier stepped down, with a plumed three-cornered hat, a coat with narrow flaps in back and a face as purple as a rotting sausage. He gulped down a glass of vodka while a fresh carriage was brought to him, and then climbed into it. No sooner had this carriage started than the courier rose from his seat and began to belabor the driver's neck with his fists. The driver staggered forward and began to whip the horses with all his strength. The more blows he received, the more blows he dealt out himself. . . .

"This nauseating image remained engraved in my memory for the rest of my life," wrote Dostoevsky in *A Writer's Diary*. In this incident he found the explanation of the brutality with which certain people reproached the Russian peasants. Stop ordering them about, shouting at them, beat-

ing them, thought Dostoevsky, and they will straighten their
backs, and be the gentle and thinking human beings that at
bottom they always are.

In *Crime and Punishment*, Raskolnikov dreams of a horse
that died under the blows of the beastly Mikolka: "the
mare, under the impact of the blow, staggers, totters; she still
tries to pull, but another blow of the crowbar on her back,
and she founders on the ground as though all her four limbs
had been broken."

In his *Diary* Dostoevsky mentions Nekrassov's poem, *The
Gentle Eyes*. It describes a muzhik who lashes the eyes of
his horse: "You cannot pull, but you will pull just the same.
Die, but pull."

Dostoevsky was obsessed by the idea of suffering. Every
crime is explained, redeemed, magnified by suffering. Suffering is our great reason for being. His father had been cruelly
tried by fate, and his distress justified his severity toward his
children. Each man throws upon his neighbor the burden of
his own despair, hatred and fear. Nothing begins in ourselves, nothing ends in ourselves. All of us are caught in the
same neurotic net, and a single gesture of any one of us
causes our fellow men to feel a painful twitch.

"Feodor Mikhailovich liked to evoke his peaceful happy
childhood," declared Anna Grigorievna Dostoevsky. But
Dr. Yanovsky, who was a friend of Feodor's, answers her:
"It was in his childhood that Feodor Mikhailovich experienced those dark and painful emotions which pass only with
time and which predispose the individual to nervous illness,
epilepsy, hypochondria and mistrust."

The pious visits to Pushkin's house, the exciting walks
on the quays of the Neva, the conquest of "the beautiful

and the great" were postponed by the major who, immediately upon their arrival in St. Petersburg, placed Feodor
and Mikhail as boarders in the home of Koronad Philipovich
Kostomarov. This officer with the booming name undertook
to prepare the boys for the examination they were to pass before being admitted to the school. He was a portly character,
and his big black mustache and icy stare terrified the new
pupils, though they soon discovered, as he spoke to ·them,
that beneath his soldierly appearance he was gentle and kind.

Fully reassured as to the future of his sons the doctor
left for Moscow. The two brothers, impressed by this fore-
taste of studious solitude, fell to work with a will.

"Our affairs are following their prescribed course," wrote
Mikhail to his father. "We study geometry and algebra, we
draw plans of fortresses, redoubts and bastions, we trace the
profiles of mountains. Koronad Philipovich is quite satisfied
with us and has shown himself exceptionally kind toward us;
he has bought us thirty rubles' worth of instruments and
twelve rubles' worth of paints." And: "Our teacher thinks
we have better chances than the eight other pupils who are
studying with him."

The day of the examination came at last. Feodor passed
and was admitted, while Mikhail was declared unfit for
reasons of health and sent to the annex of the school at
Reval. The joy of wearing a uniform and of being treated as
a *conductor* could not make up Feodor's despair at the
thought of having to be separated from his brother. Feodor
knew that no one could replace this confidant, this affec-
tionate comrade and exalted poet who could understand him
at a glance and whose own most secret thoughts he could
always guess. Nevertheless he pretended to be enthusiastic
when he wrote to his father: "At last I have been admitted

to the Engineering School, at last I have donned the uniform and entered the service of the state!" But later on, he said what he really felt: "With my brother Mikhail, at the age of sixteen, I was sent to the Engineering School in Petersburg, and thus our future was ruined."

The Engineers' Castle, as the school was sometimes referred to, had been built by Emperor Paul I for his personal use. It was in the most beautiful part of the city where the Moika and Fontanka rivers met, and it was separated from the Summer Garden by a drawbridge with a massive tower. Here, indeed, the monarch was assassinated on March 11, 1801, at midnight, by orders of his protégé, Count Pahlen, the military governor of St. Petersburg, with the silent acquiescence of his son Alexander.

"It has pleased the Lord to call unto Himself our beloved father, Emperor Pavel Petrovich, who died suddenly as a result of an apoplectic stroke," wrote Alexander in his manifesto issued the day after the regicide.

In 1819, the castle was restored and given to the Military Engineering School. It had spacious, lofty, bright halls with whitewashed walls. A dormitory, a refectory and classrooms were installed in the former imperial apartments. The pupils, boys between the ages of fourteen and nineteen, numbered one hundred and twenty-six and formed a corporation with solid traditions: they cherished honesty, respected the *veterans*, protected the weak, laughed at danger and had a special fondness for dancing. An oath administered upon admission filled the *conductors* with a sense of responsibility.

The curriculum was strenuous: algebra, geometry, ballistics, physics, architecture, fortifications, topography, geography; and, of course, also literature, history and military training. The pupils drew impeccable plans, carefully shaded their wash drawings, and meticulously traced their sections. They discussed their future careers, brilliant connections, carriages, parties and parades. They fomented rebellions against the oppression of the *veterans*. Then, upon the recommendation of a *chief conductor*, the two enemy classes would embrace and vow eternal manly friendship.

The discipline was extremely rigid. Its purpose was to tame the young and make them hardy, and for this end any means was good, but above all the whip. One pupil of this school later wrote in his memoirs: "There were cases in the regiment of the nobility, when for a simple error made in the exercises, the pupils were whipped so severely that they had to be carried out of the riding hall on a blanket, half-dead."

Feodor went into this small, naïve, but brutal and over-stimulating world straight from a sheltered family existence. He was at that time a thickset boy, round-faced, snub-nosed, with a pale, freckled complexion. His light chestnut hair was close cropped. His wide, high forehead surmounted deep-set gray eyes, embarrassingly intense in their gaze. His eyebrows were thin, his lips thick, his face sad, drawn and worried. He did not wear his uniform well. He was nicknamed Photius, after the inspired heresiarch who founded the Orthodox Church.

The first contacts with his comrades were painful.

"How stupid they looked," he writes, in his *Notes from the Underground*. "In our school the expression of the boys' faces degenerated into brutishness. Children who had entered it beautiful and healthy became monstrous after a few years. At the age of sixteen I looked upon them with somber surprise. I was amazed by the pettiness of their thoughts, games, conversations and occupations. They respected only success.

Everything that was just, but humiliated and persecuted, aroused their cruel and infamous mockery. In their eyes, titles replaced intelligence. At the age of sixteen they already spoke of good little lucrative posts. They were vicious to the point of repulsiveness."

He hated these young beasts for being so simple, so healthy, for suffering so little, for taking pleasure in such little things. Here, even more than at Chermak's boarding school, he tasted the bitterness of isolation.

"My life here is repugnant," he wrote to his brother. "Only that which is freed from earthly materialism and happiness is beautiful." And the conversations of his schoolmates constantly recalled him to these *earthly* things—make a career, be promoted. Was he thinking of making a career? "I think that the world has taken a negative direction and that high and beautiful spirituality has become a satire. It is dreadful. How cowardly is man! Hamlet! Hamlet!"

Like a budding Hamlet, somber, despairing and solitary, he roved the corridors with a book in his hands, avoiding his teachers and stopping short those of his companions who tried to address him. But he did not refuse to work; on the contrary, he was diligent in his tasks. Nor did he protest when Professor Plaksin declared that Gogol was a talentless author who indulged in cynicism and dirt. He accepted everything, bowed to everything—he bore his cross. "A being who becomes accustomed to everything, that I think is the best definition one can give of man," he wrote later in his *The House of the Dead*.

Gradually he became accustomed to his new life and organized his isolation.

"He preferred to keep apart," writes one of his school-mates. "Was he unhappy or did he imagine that he was? How can one know? The handling of weapons, group exercises, the old soldierly customs, coarse but frank, were never to his liking. His morbid pride, his moral refinement and physical frailty confined him to his own company."

During the brief and noisy recreation periods Feodor took refuge in a recess of a window that looked out on the Fontanka. He opened a book and read, leaving the world of petty worries and hideous scholarly preoccupations behind him. The pupils came back from the yard, formed ranks, passed by him on their way to the refectory and then returned, noisy and laughing. Feodor Mikhailovich did not hear or see anything. He put down his book only when the drum beat the retreat. But often in the dark of the night, we are told by General Saveliev, superintendent of the school, Dostoevsky could be found at his little working table in the "round room." He sat barefoot, a blanket around his shoulders, writing by the light of a candle end stuck in a tin candlestick.

The school director's own appreciation of Dostoevsky has been preserved. "What are his gifts? Good." That is all. Yet it is not impossible that he was even then preparing his first novel, *Poor Folk*.

The strange personality of this *conductor* who despised the handling of weapons, games, dancing and the sacred hours in the refectory could not fail to arouse the curiosity of his comrades. A few of them befriended him and were soon charmed by his lyrical enthusiasm. Four or five young boys formed a circle to discuss poetry and even ideals. Feodor dominated his schoolmates and guided their first readings. Some of them owed to him the revelation of Gogol's *Overcoat* and the novels of Dickens and Walter Scott.

Under the pretext of some light illness these conspirators of "the beautiful and the great" gathered in the dormitory, and Dostoevsky recited poetry or prose to them in his dull, low panting voice. Then he commented on the selection. At the slightest objection his tone rose, and invectives rained like blows. Often the boys in the adjoining room saw the objector take to his heels. Dostoevsky would run after him, with a book in his hand, still trying to convince him. "When our school tasks were done and we were just chatting," writes one of his schoolmates, "Feodor Dostoevsky entered our room and at once won our attention by his inspired words. By midnight we were dead tired, but Dostoevsky, leaning against the door, would still be speaking with a kind of nervous fervor. His choked voice electrified us and attached us to him."

Dostoevsky's lyrical ardor, however, did not help him in his military duties. One day, as he reported to Grand Duke Mikhail Pavlovich, he forgot to introduce his report with the formula: "To His Imperial Highness," and the Grand Duke exclaimed: "What fools they are sending me!"

The maneuvers at Krasnoe Selo or Peterhof were every year the most difficult period for Dostoevsky because he was almost penniless. In hot weather he had no money to buy himself a cool drink; in the rain he could not buy a glass of hot tea or a suit of dry clothes. Meanwhile, Dostoevsky's father, now retired on his estate, drank and despaired. He refused to see anyone or hear about anything.

"Send me something, as soon as possible," Feodor wrote him, "thus you will help me get out of an inferno! Oh, it is horrible to be in need." Or: "My dear, good father, do not imagine that your son in asking you for money is asking for something superfluous. . . . I have a head and a pair of hands, and if I were on my own I would not ask for a kopek, I would become accustomed to poverty. . . . But, dear father, remember that at present 'I am serving' in the full meaning of this term. Willy-nilly I must conform to the rule of the society in which I live. . . . At present, life in camp costs at least forty rubles per pupil. (I am writing all this because I am speaking to my own father.) I do not include the cost of tea and sugar in this sum, although they are indispensable. When one is drenched by rain under a canvas tent or when one returns from exercises tired, shivering from cold, and one has no tea, one can fall sick—and this happened to me last year at maneuvers. Nevertheless, considering your straitened circumstances, I will do without tea. I ask you only for the indispensable—enough money to buy two pairs of ordinary boots."

Dostoevsky's father had land, a steady income and a fat bundle of notes reserved for the dowries of his daughters. He spent practically nothing in his remote village. He could not fail to see that his son's requests for money were justified. Nevertheless, the answers of the old miser were masterpieces of petty trickery, trembling indignation and sanctimonious benevolence.

"My friend," he wrote, "you should know that it is blameworthy and even criminal to grumble against a father who sends you all he can afford. Remember what I wrote to both of you concerning the wretched wheat harvest. Last year, too, I wrote you about the bad state of our crops. . . . And now are you going to rebel against your father because he does not send you enough money? I myself have nothing to wear, I have not had a new suit for four years, and my old one is completely worn out. I have not a penny for myself. But I will wait. I am sending you thirty-five rubles in notes, which, at the Moscow rates, should give you forty-three rubles and seventy-five kopeks. Spend this money with caution, for, I repeat, I shall not be able to send you any more for a long time."

Feodor was in despair. He wrote to Mikhail on August 9, 1838: "You complain of your poverty, my brother, but I am not rich either. Will you believe that I had not a kopek during the entire period of the maneuvers? On the way I caught cold—it rained continually and we were without shelter—and was ill from hunger too, for I had not enough money to buy a little hot tea. . . . I do not know whether my melancholy ideas will ever be dispelled. . . ." And in a postscriptum he added: "I have a plan: to go insane."

On October 31 of the same year he wrote again: "It is sad to live without hope, my brother. I look before me, and my future frightens me. I am surrounded by an icy, polar atmosphere, without a ray of sun. It is a long time since I have felt the assaults of inspiration; but I have often relived the experience of the prisoner of Chillon in his cell, after the death of his brothers. . . ." This rhetorical lamentation is interrupted by a hint concerning the most recent books he had read: "You congratulate yourself for having read a great deal. But do not imagine that I envy you. I have read at least as much as you."

And true enough, he read all of Hoffmann, in Russian and in German, almost all of Balzac ("Balzac is great," he wrote in a letter), Goethe's *Faust* and lyric poems, and Victor Hugo's works except *Hernani* and *Cromwell.* Victor Hugo, he wrote, was "purely angelic," but the French did not appreciate him at his proper value. As for Nisard who dared to criticize the author of *Odes et Ballades,* "he lies, although he is intelligent." Schiller made a great impression on Dostoevsky: "I memorized Schiller, I spoke Schiller, I dreamed Schiller. . . ." And Racine! "You claim that Racine contains no poetry? But have you read *Iphigénie?* Can you say it is not sublime? And *Phèdre?* My brother, you would be the least of men if you said this was not the loftiest of nature and poetry! And Corneille? Have you read *The Cid?* Read it, you wretch, read it and fall on your knees before Corneille. You have sinned against him!"

The recipient of these letters was at least as romantic as their sender. Mikhail read and wrote verses night and day. "Ah, little father," he wrote to the major, "rejoice with me, I think I am not lacking in poetic gifts. I have written quite a number of short poems. . . . At present I have begun a play." The same letter began with a declaration that must have made the doctor choke with rage: "Let them take everything from me, let them leave me naked, but let them give me Schiller, and I will forget the world!" Mikhail's poems filled his brother with enthusiasm. "I have read your verses. They brought tears to my eyes and shook my soul for a long moment." And to confirm his good opinion he quoted their young friend Shidlovsky.

This Shidlovsky was a strange young man. "He looks like a martyr" so Feodor wrote, "he is emaciated, and his cheeks are hollow and his eyes dry and ardent." The two brothers had met him the day of their arrival in Petersburg at the inn where they were stopping. When they learned that this young man who had come to the capital in order to obtain a position in the Ministry of Finance was a real poet and planned to publish his works, their enthusiasm was boundless. The major himself was seduced by this eloquent youth, as cultivated and somber as Byron. Shidlovsky showed his young friends the

capital and later, traveling between Petersburg and Reval, he
served as the messenger of the two brothers.

"Thanks to Shidlovsky's friendship, I have had numerous
hours which I count the happiest of my life. Oh, what a sincere and pure soul! Tears come to my eyes when I awaken
these memories." Indeed both Feodor and Mikhail were
charmed, fascinated by this poet who wrote: "Yes, I am a
volcano. Fire is my element," and believed what he wrote.

Shidlovsky was in love with a certain Maria who was married to another man. "Without this love he would not be the
just, pure, lofty priest of poetry that he is." But that was not
all. Religious doubts haunted this poet. He believed alternately that he was elected and accursed, and oscillated between blasphemy and faith. At night, he worked on his history of the Russian church. But he could not endure the
Petersburg climate, and retired to his mother's country
house. In this solitude he was seized by a profound mystical
exaltation and sought to remedy his anxiety by following a
monastic rule of life. But it was of no avail. To recover his
peace of mind, he went on a pilgrimage to the Lavra at Kiev
where a certain saintly man advised him—as the *starets*
Zosim was to advise Aliosha Karamazov—to seek salvation in
the world.

Shidlovsky returned to his estate, but continued to wear
the frock of a novice. He often took the road and stopped at
village inns to preach the gospel to peasants who listened with
bared heads. He died in 1872.

There is no doubt that this character, torn between the
Christian humility of an Aliosha and the satanic negations of
an Ivan Karamazov, haunted Dostoevsky in all his works.
He was a creature "of fire and ice," like most of Dostoevsky's heroes, like Dostoevsky himself.

Failure to pass a certain examination postponed Feodor's promotion. He wrote to his brother, "I have not been admitted to the next grade. Horror! Another year, a whole year of work!" He blamed his professor of algebra for having unfairly failed him. This professor detested him, he thought. Everybody detested him. "I would like to crush the universe." He sent his father his notebook to prove to him that the examination jury had been motivated by the darkest malice. "Oh, God!" he wrote. "What have I done to arouse your wrath? Why do you not dispense your favors to me, so that I might gladden the heart of the most loving of fathers? Oh, how many tears I have shed! Pupils who answered less well than I were admitted, thanks to their connections."

Feodor's grief was so great that he fell ill and was compelled to stay in bed for several days. His only comfort was the books his brother sent him, and the letters awaited with the impatience of a lover. He postponed unsealing them and increased his pleasure by carrying them around unopened for hours.

But sometimes he was bitterly disappointed when he opened the envelope. Mikhail was no longer the same. He now spoke of clothes, asked Feodor whether he wore a mustache and alluded to a young lady who was not a shining creation of his poetic genius but existed in the flesh. She was named Emilia von Ditmer, lived in Reval and Mikhail planned to marry her. To be sure, this decision did not prevent him from writing, and he wallowed in his own lyricism just as enthusiastically as before. To be infatuated with a real woman, not even to have the excuse of an unhappy love, like Shidlovsky, was to be unpardonably sentimental.

Feodor awakened to love much later—and in a wretched way. For the time being he tried to understand and soberly judged others. But he felt lost and miserable.

"I am alone, and so are all men," he writes in *Notes from the Underground*.

Soon an event occurred which brought his emotional confusion to a climax.

With Mikhail and Feodor settled in St. Petersburg, the father sent his two younger sons to Chermak's boarding school and established himself at Darovoe with his two youngest daughters, Vera and Alexandra.

The seclusion of Darovoe was unbearably gloomy. The major drank so heavily that he suffered from dizziness and hallucinations. Aliona Frolovna, the nurse, reported that he occasionally held conversations in a loud voice with the ghost of his wife. He asked the questions and gave the answers, changing his voice and using his departed wife's favorite expressions. At night he would suddenly rush into his daughters' room and look under their beds to make sure that no lovers were hidden there. Then he wandered from room to room lamenting his wasted existence, his undeserved sorrow and the ennui of his life. To beguile his grief he took one of his servants, a certain Catherine, as a mistress. He also played with the idea of marrying a wealthy neighbor of his, Alexandra Lagvenov, but could not bring himself to propose.

The harvest was but fair, and the major was unable to avoid the financial collapse which threatened him. Whenever it was suggested that by investing some money he could improve the yield of his acres, he grew panicky, hesitated and finally decided against the expense. He had become fantastically tight-fisted. His daughter, Barbara, inherited this disease. After her husband's death, despite her considerable wealth, she dismissed her servants, refused to heat her apartment and lived exclusively on bread and milk in order to economize. When she heard the news of her father's death, she remarked: "A dog should die like a dog." In 1893, she was murdered and her body burned by thieves.

At Darovoe, idle and desperate, Mikhail Andreevich took out his ill-temper on the peasants. One day, Fedot, a muzhik, neglected to salute him—he had not seen the major coming.

"Go, get yourself whipped at the stable," cried the master. This punishment was carried out on the spot.

In wintertime, the serfs were in a difficult predicament. If they saluted, he shouted, "Scoundrels, I believe you remove your caps on purpose in order to catch cold and thus be unable to work." If they did not salute, they were inevitably lashed.

In 1839, the peasants plotted the murder of the "bad master." One June morning when the major gathered all the peasants together to cart away the dung, three of them, men from Cheremashny, did not answer the roll call.

"Why aren't they here?" asked Mikhail Andreevich.

"They're sick," explained the *starosta*.

The major foamed with rage and brandished his iron-pointed club. "I'll cure them with this!"

The driver was one of the plotters, but frightened he almost gave the game away. "Don't go, *barin*," he exclaimed, "something might happen to you!"

The old man stamped his foot. "You don't want me to cure them? Harness the horses, and hurry!"

The driver shrugged his shoulders and prepared the carriage. Upon his arrival at Cheremashny, the doctor found his three "patients" loitering in the street. "Why didn't you come this morning?" he asked.

"We're tired," one of them said.

The major struck him with his club, and they fled into a deserted courtyard. When their master followed them there, one of them, Vasily Nikitin, a giant of a fellow with a brutish face, seized the major's arms from behind, but the others, afraid, did not budge.

"What's the matter? Did we take an oath or didn't we?" cried Vasily.

The muzhiks rushed upon the unfortunate man, tied him and stretched him out on the ground, but they did not strike him for fear of leaving marks. They unclenched his mouth with a knife and poured alcohol down his throat despite his jerking and gagging. Then they tied up his mouth in order to smother him. But the major was hard to kill, so one of the wretches crushed his genitals in his fist. The body of the tortured man twisted, grew rigid and then relaxed. Dying, he was hoisted into his carriage. The panic-stricken driver lashed the horses and the carriage dashed across the fields.

The murderers were beset by religious scruples—one does not let a Christian die without giving him an opportunity to make his confession. So they took the major out, placed him at the foot of an oak tree and went to look for a priest. When he arrived, Mikhail still breathed but could no longer speak. The priest accepted his silent confession and witnessed his last gasp.

"What did you do to him?" he asked the driver.

"It was a stroke," answered the peasant.

The subsequent investigation failed to reveal anything. The major's family actually intervened to hush up the scandal, for if the court had discovered that there had been a

murder, almost all the peasants of Cheremashny would have
been indicted and sent to Siberia. This would have ruined the
family without giving them any moral satisfaction.

Feodor Mikhailovich learned about this death when he was
at the Engineering School. A month earlier he had sent his
father a sharp letter asking him for money. On the very eve
of the murder he had perhaps cursed the major's miserliness
and lack of understanding. At the very moment when the
elder Dostoevsky had given up the ghost, his body writhing,
his eyes dilated by terror, his son had rebelled and reproached
him for senile egoism. The crime of the muzhiks fell upon
Feodor Mikhailovich, and he assumed responsibility for a
murder which he had not committed. He was guilty in a
sense inaccessible to human laws—and this revelation dazzled him with all the cruelty of an obvious fact. A dreadful
spasm shook him, and threw him to the ground, foaming at
the mouth and raling. This may have been his first epileptic
attack. He never mentioned the event in his correspondence.

The admission of Feodor's moral and emotional confusion
can be found in his works, above all in *The Brothers Karamazov*. Smerdyakov kills the father of the Karamazovs, but
he is less guilty of this murder than the oldest son, Ivan, who
dreamed of it without committing it.

"The principal assassin is you and not myself, although I
did the killing," said Smerdyakov.

"Have I then wished for my father's death to that extent?"
asked Ivan Karamazov.

In *The Possessed* Pyotr Stepanovich orders the murder of
Stavrogin's wife, but Stavrogin accepts the responsibility for
an act he had secretly wished for.

"I didn't kill her," he said, "I was even opposed to this
project." But silent agreement, an unnoticed withdrawal of

affection are enough to make us accomplices. The strange power of thought over matter, the transcendence of matter by thought, obsessed Dostoevsky. The well-defined laws of nature, the astute deductions of natural science, the cold constructions of mathematics add up to form a "wall of stone." "To be sure, I cannot break this wall with my head; but I won't resign myself just because it is a stone wall."

Dostoevsky did not resign himself. He tried to break through. And once he had broken through, he found himself in the domain of the irrational which is the real home of his heroes.

Following the tortured corpse of Mikhail Andreevich he entered that strange region which is no longer reality but is not nothingness, where those innocent according to earthly laws are guilty according to other unwritten laws, where a given act no longer depends upon its author, where feelings replace proofs, where ideas evaporate, where nothing is certain, fixed or decided in advance. And at each new blow of fate he moved farther away from evidence and closer to mystery. "There are things that one fears to reveal even to oneself. . . ."

2. THE WRITER

Having passed the necessary examinations, Dostoevsky was promoted to the rank of second lieutenant. With his comrade, Totleben, he rented first a small apartment, then an immense one with only one room furnished, for which he paid twelve hundred rubles in assignats. But he liked the landlord's face, and that was sufficient. Similarly, Simon, his orderly, was too worthy a fellow to be scolded.

"Let him steal from me," he said, "that won't ruin me." Actually he was always short of funds, although his pay plus the subsidies he received from Karepin, his brother-in-law who had become the support of the family, gave him a steady income of five thousand rubles a year.

Dostoevsky's life then was extraordinarily restless and

empty. Every morning he attended courses given for the officers of the school. In the evening he sought entertainment —he had a passion for the plays given in the Alexander Theater, the ballet, the recitals of Ole Bull and Liszt. In the afternoon, he locked himself in his room and worked in the thick, blue smoke of cigarettes. His complexion was cadaverous. The glands of his neck were swollen. He coughed and spoke haltingly in a hoarse, rasping voice. Dr. Riesenkampf, a friend of the two brothers, sometimes visited him and brought him medicine which Dostoevsky refused to take.

In 1840, Mikhail arrived in St. Petersburg to take his examinations and he remained there until February, 1841. On the eve of his departure for Reval he gave a party for his friend at which Feodor Mikhailovich recited the two plays he had composed: *Mary Stuart* and *Boris Godunov*. The manuscripts of these plays have been lost, but according to witnesses, the author had drawn freely from Schiller and Pushkin.

Once back in Reval, Mikhail, despite the opposition of his guardian, married the young Emilia von Ditmer whom he had so often mentioned in his letters. Several months later Dostoevsky received his brother Andrey, who came to St. Petersburg to continue his studies. Feodor disliked this obtuse and pedantic boy.

"His character is so neutral that everyone avoids him," Feodor wrote to Mikhail. Fortunately, in December, 1842, Andrey was admitted to the School of Architecture, and the older brother could again enjoy his solitude.

Dostoevsky's money went fast. He lost enormous sums at billiards and complacently allowed his servants to rob him. When he came to Reval to stand godfather to Mikhail's first son, his brother and sister-in-law were frightened by his wretched appearance. They bought him linen and suits, and asked Dr. Riesenkampf to stay in Dostoevsky's apartment in order to supervise his expenditures. Riesenkampf agreed to do this.

This association, however, did not help to balance Feodor's budget. Whenever a seedy-looking patient came to visit the doctor, Dostoevsky drew him into a corner, questioned him about the details of his intimate life, and rewarded him with money for his frankness. Riesenkampf wrote to Mikhail, "He is constantly poor while his entourage lives in clover. They are pitilessly stripping him clean."

One day Dostoevsky entered the doctor's room and said with confidence, "I just received a thousand rubles from Moscow." The next day he came again, and humbly asked his friend to lend him five rubles. He had lost part of his thousand at billiards and the rest had been stolen from him by a tailor.

Some time later, not a bit discouraged, Feodor befriended a man of German origin and an obvious failure. He invited him for dinner and tea and questioned him, taking notes, all against payment, of course. The prudent Riesenkampf was in despair, but a new remittance of a thousand rubles came just at the right moment. Overjoyed by this turn of fortune, Dostoevsky ordered a dinner at Dominique's. After dinner he agreed to play one game of dominoes with one of the habitués of the establishment. He played twenty-five games and lost the rubles down to the last kopek.

All these indiscretions forced Feodor to take loans at usurious rates of interest, to live on bread and milk, and to give up all entertainment. Nevertheless, he succeeded in passing his final examinations, and in August, 1843, was listed among the officers on active service, as an attaché of the engineering blueprint office.

One month earlier, on July 17, 1843, Balzac arrived in St. Petersburg to see Madame Hanska from whom he had been separated for seven years. The physical presence of a writer whom Dostoevsky had long considered his master increased his enthusiasm for the author of the *Human Comedy*. He resolved to translate *Eugénie Grandet* into Russian.

"I have translated Balzac's *Eugénie Grandet* into Russian," he wrote to his brother. "(O, marvel, marvel!) And my translation is wonderful. I will receive for it at least three hundred and fifty rubles in assignats. But in the name of the heavenly angels send me thirty-five rubles (the price of copying the manuscript). I swear to you by Olympus and the Jew Yankel (a character in a play I have completed) and by what else?—even by my mustache which I hope will end up by growing some day, that half of what I get for *Eugénie* will go to you. *Dixi.*"

Meanwhile Riesenkampf left St. Petersburg without having inculcated "the principles of German economy" into Dostoevsky. A marvelous piece of news comforted Dostoevsky for this departure: *Eugénie Grandet* was to be published in the *Repertory and Pantheon*. But the editor-in-chief cut the masterpiece by a third. Dostoevsky groaned, "That is treason!"

Actually he himself had betrayed Balzac in translating him. He had taken hold of *Eugénie* with a dangerous passion, and had been unable to confine himself to an honest adaptation. He inflated the emotions, exaggerated the epithets, and plunged that humble story of a provincial woman into an extravagant atmosphere. Under his pen Eugénie Grandet's "sufferings" became "profound and terrible torments." According to Balzac her face was "fringed with a light like that of an opened flower"; Dostoevsky crowned it with a "celestial aura." He thought it was better thus and was satisfied with his own efforts. As for his brother, he advised him to translate Schiller's *Don Carlos*. Mikhail obeyed.

"I have received *Don Carlos*," Feodor wrote him, "and I hasten to answer you. The translation is good, in spots even excellent, but several lines are less felicitous: this is because you worked in a hurry. I took the liberty of correcting certain expressions, and of improving the sonority of certain verses . . . I will take *Don Carlos* to those fools at the Repertory to make them gape with admiration, unless I give it to the *Annals of the Fatherland*. . . . But don't worry, I won't give it away just for a mouthful of bread."

An enormous project tormented him; he wanted to publish Schiller's complete works in three installments: "As for the publisher we shall see later, but it is a fact that it is better to publish oneself." He feverishly marshaled figures on sheets of paper: so much for the covers, so much for the printing, so much for the binding, so much for the paper. Everything was foreseen and calculated. Nevertheless, the plan failed. Dostoevsky blamed this failure on his occupation as a civil servant which bored him like "a dish of potatoes."

On September 30, 1844, he wrote to his brother Mikhail: "I am in a hellish fix. I have just resigned from the service . . . because, I swear to you, I could no longer go on with it. Life is a burden when the best of one's time is wasted on such stupid chores. Worse: they wanted to send me on a mission. But tell me, please, how could I have lived outside St. Petersburg?" Yet he was debt-ridden and did not know exactly how he could make a living. "I wrote a letter home

that I owed fifteen hundred rubles, because I know their
habit of sending me only one-third of what I ask. If these
Muscovite swine delay sending me the money, I am
lost."

"I received five hundred rubles from Moscow," Feodor
wrote a few months later. But this sum was inadequate to
cover his debts. At bay, he flung himself about like a madman
and conceived vague projects of translations or adaptations.
"You say that salvation lies in my play. But to stage it will
take time. And money!" He was willing to renounce his inheritance for the sum of five hundred rubles, to sell himself
to the devil for a few pennies. Once again he was reduced
to milk, bread, and tea, an icy apartment and solitude.

One day Feodor met his former schoolmate, Grigorovich,
in the street. The two friends fell into each other's arms.
Dostoevsky told him about his renunciation, his nebulous
plans and hopes. Grigorovich, on the contrary, could boast
of having realized his dreams—he wrote, published and was
paid. This handsome, elegant young man who seemed to
dance as he walked and spoke glibly dazzled Dostoevsky.
Grigorovich for his part was attracted by his comrade's
fierce exaltation. One was witty, light, talkative; the other,
taciturn, tormented, ardent. Yet they understood each other
from the very first words they exchanged. Grigorovich took
Dostoevsky to his home and read aloud *The Barrel-organ
Player* which he had just finished. Dostoevsky admired this
work and congratulated his friend. From that time on they
could no longer live without one another. They had an
apartment in common, but their funds were exhausted a few
days after the beginning of every month. Then they lived on
bread and barley water.

Dostoevsky was working day and night on a manuscript

about which he refused to say anything. Grigorovich saw the sheets pile up on the table, blackened with a tiny round handwriting, "fairly similar to that of Alexandre Dumas, father." Occasionally, Feodor Mikhailovich was exhausted and stopped writing, swallowed a glass of tea and opened a book—George Sand or Frederic Soulié's *Memoires du Diable*. Grigorovich begged him to take some exercise. Feodor would agree to go out for a walk, but fresh air, light and street noises seemed unbearable to him. He grew pale and dizzy, leaned on his friend's arm and had to be taken home in a cab.

One morning the two saw a funeral. A priest was carrying a cross behind a procession of holy banners. Behind him came the choir, and the bier, drawn by slow-moving horses. The coffin was open, showing the face of the dead man and it was the color of gray rubber. On his forehead there was a white paper crown ornamented with ritual inscriptions, and in his hands a little icon. Dostoevsky was seized with trembling, he turned away and tried to flee. But after a few steps he collapsed, the prey of a nervous fit. Some passers-by helped Grigorovich carry him into a near-by dairy. They had trouble reviving him.

During the days that followed, Dostoevsky was morose, dejected, remote; he said scarcely a word, ate little, and did not wish to write. Then he went back to work. Only his brother Mikhail knew the secret. Feodor Mikhailovich wrote in a letter to Reval: "I have one hope. I am about to complete a novel as long as *Eugénie Grandet*. It is quite original. I have begun to recopy it. . . ." On March 24, 1845, he wrote: "I am very well satisfied with my novel. It is an austere and neatly constructed work, although it has a few serious defects."

His desire for perfection made him postpone publication. "In February, I began to prune and polish my manuscript, to cut and to insert new passages. By the middle of March I was finished and satisfied. I swore that however difficult my situation might be I would never write to order. Writing to order crushes and annihilates everything. I want every one of my works to be sober and beautiful. Both Pushkin and Gogol wrote only a limited number of works and statues will be erected to both of them."

He reproached his brother for not approving this passion for making corrections: "The fate of first works is to be revised over and over again. Pushkin made innumerable corrections on the least of his poems. Gogol polished his stories for more than two years. . . ."

Once the book was completed, the problem of publishing it arose. Dostoevsky did not wish to give it to a periodical on the grounds that "in a review there is not one dictator, but twenty dictators. The way to get ahead is to publish oneself. . . ." However, he yielded to the opinion of experienced friends who dissuaded him from printing the book at his own expense. "Who will advertise the book to the public?" they pointed out. "The booksellers will do nothing for an unknown writer."

Finally Dostoevsky resigned himself to offering his book to the *Annals of the Fatherland*. But he was discouraged in advance; sure that the manuscript would be refused, that he would be crushed by criticisms, that he would not be understood—for how could anyone understand him?

"If I do not find a publisher for my novel," he wrote, "I will perhaps jump into the Neva. What can I do? I have thought of everything. I will not survive the death of my *idée fixe*."

This *idée fixe* unmentioned in his letters was his first novel, *Poor Folk.*

We know that at this period of his life Dostoevsky loved grandiloquent lyricism, the sonorous and the pathetic, "the beautiful and the great." How did he come to write the humble story of *Poor Folk?*

There was Schiller ("I feel moved the moment I hear the name Schiller pronounced!"), and Victor Hugo ("No one can be compared to him!"), and Corneille ("Only outraged angels can speak thus!"), and Racine ("He stole from Homer, but in what admirable fashion!"), and George Sand ("When I read her for the first time I had fever all night!"), and Walter Scott ("How could he, in a few weeks, write a work as magnificent as *Mannering?*"), Shakespeare, Pushkin, Lamartine and Byron, with their procession of noble loves, spectacular crimes and eloquent lamentations. There was also the poor copyist, Dievushkin, squeezed into his too tight and seedy uniform, living in an attic and warmed only by the tenderness of a little girl who lived in the same house. Here an orchestra of stormy passions, there the solitary flute of affection. What mysterious chemistry had changed these romantic and classical influences into the gentle grayish stuff of *Poor Folk?* How had the high-hearted brigands and lunar princesses shrunk into these minuscule slum dwellers? Why had the Venetian sets become obscure little streets, garrets and dens?

Of course, Dostoevsky also admired Balzac and Gogol, the masters of a new realism. But he seems to have considered them inferior to the "sublime gentlemen." He felt the need to magnify the story of *Eugénie Grandet* when he undertook to translate it, and his adaptation of Balzac ends with a solemn convocation in which the native of Saumur is compared to a statue of ancient Greece. Balzac's characters had seemed to him drab as compared to his own aspirations. Yet now he created even drabber ones. Why? Had he changed his artistic conceptions in a few months? Had he experienced the shock of a literary or sentimental revelation?

Let us imagine the adolescent brought up in the Engineers' Castle. He intoxicated himself on verses and romances; he was "Pericles or Marius or a Christian at the time of Nero or a paladin in a tournament or Edward in Walter Scott's *Monastery*." He declared himself the friend of the poet Shidlovsky, the man who said "Yes, I am a volcano, fire is my element." He shed tears over his brother's elegies. He knew nothing of life. The walls of the school, as formerly those of the Hospital of the Poor, confined him within a dream of grace and light. He could not even imagine that he would ever awaken from it. And then the doors opened.

They opened upon St. Petersburg, with its noisy streets, its too new palaces, its administration buildings crammed with copyists, and, as soon as one left the elegant district, its large barrackslike houses which sheltered a whole wretched world of petty functionaries, usurers, artisans, prostitutes and students, its dirty cook shops which stank of tobacco, singed rags and dishwater, its dead-end alleys lighted by lamps mounted on striped poles, its dirty stores where loud-mouthed hags waited for customers with a glass of tea in their hands.

The walls of this city built on marshes oozed with a sticky liquid. A milk-colored fog weighed on the roofs. Snow crunched under the heel. Passers-by hurried along, preoccupied and sullen, thinking of their positions, promotions and deals. Dostoevsky moved among them like a somnambulist. At first he still walked wrapped about in dreams, but gradu-

ally he opened his eyes and awakened to this new existence.
It was on the banks of the Neva, he relates in *St. Petersburg
Mirages in Prose and Verse*, that the revelation took place.

It was almost night and the temperature was thirty degrees
below zero. The nostrils of the cab horses smoked. The river
was covered with a white sheet that gleamed like sugar. On
his right the palace of the Admiralty thrust its arrow into a
frozen lavender and yellow sky. Lumps of hard snow stuck
to the pillars of the Senate and the Synod. "A strange
thought stirred within me. . . . It seemed to me at that
moment I understood something which I had sensed before
without ever having expressed it; it seemed to me I had just
awakened to a new world that was foreign to me, one which
I had known until then only through obscure tales and mysterious signs. I think my real existence began at that moment."

What was this world to which he had just awakened?
"They were strange, weird figures, quite prosaic, which had
nothing of Don Carlos and Posa, but were actually honorary
councilors, although honorary councilors of a fantastic
species."

Yes, perhaps all these *chinovniks*, these civil servants with
frozen noses, these young women with shabby muffs, had
emotions in no way inferior to those of princely heroes.
Petty bureaucrats, sick ragamuffins, maniacal old men and
drunkards, all of them lived fiercely their secrets, passions,
devotions or crimes. The oriental sets collapsed, the mighty
historical figures vanished forever. Only the poor folk, the
insulted and injured remained. "In some dark corner, there
is the heart of a pure and noble councilor, honorable and
loyal to his superior s, and with him, a little girl, wronged and
sad. Their story tore my heart."

"Honor and glory to the young poet whose muse loves the tenants of garrets and cellars and who says to the inhabitants of gilded palaces: 'They, too, are human beings, they are your brothers,' " Belinsky, the critic, wrote later.

"Come in, Grigorovich. I have finished copying my book and I want to read it to you."

Dostoevsky sat down on his couch. Before him, on a little table, a large notebook lay open: it was the manuscript of *Poor Folk*.

Grigorovich was eaten up with curiosity. He had always regretted that his comrade, so cultivated, so intelligent and so sensitive, had not yet produced anything except a few unpromising sketches of plays.

"How can it be," he wrote, "that I have already written and published some small works, that I already consider myself a man of letters, so to speak, while Dostoevsky has not yet given anything in this field?" (*Memoirs* of Grigorovich.)

In another passage, Grigorovich tells us of this first reading of *Poor Folk*. Doubtless he, too, had expected the new work to be along the lines of *Mary Stuart* and *Boris Godunov*. But he understood his error from the very first sentences. As Dostoevsky was to describe it in *The Insulted and Injured*, "it is a simple story, like everyday reality. And the hero is not a great man or a historical figure such as Roslavlav or Yury Matislavsky. He is a humble civil servant, a drudge, even something of simpleton, with several buttons missing on his uniform!"

Poor Folk is written in the form of an exchange of letters. Dievushkin, an obscure bureaucrat, elderly, illiterate, poverty-stricken, kind to the point of abnegation and sacrifice, lives in the room across the hall from Varenka and is distantly related to her. Because he fears gossip, he does not wish to receive her in his room or visit her in her own. So they reach each other by letters. He gives her a paternal, clumsy, but delicate and charming affection. She tries to bring to her aged friend the advantages of her culture and her superior education. She tells him about her life—her deprived childhood, her sudden love for a consumptive student, his death and her sad future.

For Dievushkin her letters are a delight. Now he is no longer alone, he can live for someone else, work and deprive himself for someone else. Trembling with joy, he accepts extra copying work at home and borrows money to buy candy and flowers for his young friend. But poverty always haunts him. His uniform is shabby, his shoes have no soles, and Varenka is sick. Moreover his neighbors are suspicious of his relations with his young cousin.

"Theirs is the union of the devil and a child," says the landlady. A quill pusher who lives in the same house treats him as a Lovelace. At the office the attendant is rude to him. "Do you know what is killing me, Varenka? Not the lack of money, but all the wretched worries of my life, all these whisperings, insinuating smiles and little pricking remarks. . . ." And how can anyone respect him since his shoes are worn through and the sleeves of his uniform are riddled with holes? "If one of my superiors noticed how unseemly my clothing is! It is a misfortune, Varenka, a misfortune, a real misfortune!"

One day "His Excellency" summons Dievushkin to scold him for an error in his copy. As the old man stands at attention before his chief a button of his tunic falls off and rolls at the general's feet. Surely his position is lost now! He will be reprimanded, dismissed on the spot. But "His Excellency" takes pity on the seedy copyist, questions him, shakes hands with him and gives him a hundred rubles to improve his wardrobe. "I swear to you that these hundred rubles have less value in my eyes than the handshake with which His Excellency wanted to honor me, me, an unworthy creature, a blade of straw, a drunkard . . ." For in the meantime, so that he could touch the bottom of his distress, he had taken to drink. At present he is rich, he can straighten his back. But his joy is short-lived. A fairly well-to-do gentleman and somewhat perverted asks Varenka to marry him. She accepts, exhausted by her illness and her privations. Now Dievushkin's real torture begins.

Varenka, usually so calm, so serious, is excited at the thought of all the purchases she must make for her trousseau. Her last letters are a froth of feverish insouciance. Heartlessly she commissions Dievushkin to buy these laces and jewels with the money of her future husband. "The monograms on the handkerchiefs must be tambour work, tambour, do you understand? Tamboured, not embroidered in flat stitch. . . . For heaven's sake, tell him to put a little braid on the mantle, and to trim the collar with lace or large furbelows." Dievushkin, crushed by despair, loses his head in this jungle of cloth buttons and braids, but with pitiful good will he rushes here and there, visiting modistes, jewelers and furriers.

"You mention furbelows in your letter. Well, she, too, spoke of furbelows. Only, little mother, I forgot what she told me about the furbelows. . . ."

Finally, the wedding day arrives. In his farewell message, Dievushkin who had refrained from complaining, cries out his despair. His sentences have no beginning, no end. He wants to explain quickly, quickly, how much he loves his dear Varenka and what a terrible void her departure will create. The book ends with this cry: "It cannot be that this letter is the last one we shall exchange. How can they stop thus all of a sudden! No, no, I will write to you and you will write to me, too. . . . Varenka, my style is shaping itself. Ah, my dearest, how can I speak of style! See, at this very moment I do not know what I am writing, I do not know at all, I know nothing, I am not rereading what I have written nor correcting my errors. I am thinking only of writing to you, of writing to you all that I can. . . . My beloved, my sweetheart, my little mother. . . ."

There is no doubt that *Poor Folk* was inspired by Gogol's *Overcoat*. This quaint bureaucrat brought up in the veneration of his superiors and the love for "copy," this gray citizen of St. Petersburg, ridiculed by his colleagues, stultified by his hardships, who accepts everything and resigns himself to everything with evangelical gentleness, is certainly the younger brother of Gogol's Akakyi Akakievich. But whereas Gogol's hero is only pitiable and grotesque, remarkable only for his absolute nullity, the charity and devotion and discretion of Dostoevsky's Makar Dievushkin have a rare moral quality. Ridicule does not destroy but exalt his qualities, for his mediocrity stops at the frontiers of feeling, and his suffering saves him from caricature.

Around Dievushkin vegetate his cronies, the most remarkable of whom is the father of Pokrovsky, the consumptive student. This abject old man, a drunkard and liar, has an apprehensive tenderness for his son whose education and independence he respects. His vices, too, are redeemed by affection and humility. "At first sight one might think that he felt ashamed of his person, he seemed to make such an effort to diminish himself. . . . The only vestige of noble emotions he preserved was his immense love for his son. . . ."

Gorchkov is another of these poor folk. He is involved in a lawsuit in which his honor, future and fortune are at stake. The court vindicates him. After the verdict he is beside himself with joy. He addresses the people around him in incoherent words: "My honor . . . honor . . . good name . . . my children. . . ." The same night he dies from excess of emotion.

Thus Dostoevsky's secondary themes appear in this first novel, also his whole flock of favorite supernumeraries. The derelict father whom his children treat with a mixture of pity and contempt later reappears as Marmeladov in *Crime and Punishment*, as the elder Karamazov in *The Brothers Karamazov*, as the "retired and unhappy" General Ivolgin in *The Idiot*. Worthy drunkards haunt all his books; indeed, at one time he planned to call *Crime and Punishment*, *"The Good Drunkards."* We recognize the old man whose happiness depends on the outcome of a court trial, and who is intoxicated with pride at the very depth of his debasement in Ikhmeniev of *The Insulted and Injured*. Perverted rich men on the lookout for young girls "wronged by life" are found again in Luzhin and Svidrigailov of *Crime and Punishment*. All, almost all of Dostoevsky's favorite characters are here, but they are only suggested, the author is trying them out, as the watercolor painter tries his paint at the bottom of his white sheet. Later, Dostoevsky's conceptions became more grandiose and he painted his figures life size. From the carefully prepared palette of *Poor Folk* there came the mighty pictures of his period of flowering; from these tentative chords was born the miraculous symphony of *The Brothers Karamazov*.

All this was to come later. Dievushkin and Varenka are limited, they lack a sky above their heads, and shadows around their feet. They suffer, but their sufferings are moral, social, material and earthly. They do not know metaphysical anguish. They live in a world where "two times two makes four." One character is absent from the cast: God. It took the ordeal of the gallows and Siberia to make Him loom enormous in the background of the Dostoevskian universe.

Grigorovich was stunned by *Poor Folk*. Many times he voiced his admiration, and rose to shake Feodor's hands. But Feodor, impassive, continued to read in a gloomy voice which pained the heart. After the last sentence of the book, Grigorovich, with his face bathed in tears, threw himself into his friend's arms and begged Feodor to allow him to show it to Nekrasov, the poet, who at that time was planning to publish a magazine. Grigorovich was sure that he would succeed in this enterprise.

Nekrasov was a strange young man. His father, a former army man, avaricious and hard, wanted him to enter the regiment of the nobility, but Nekrasov broke with him to attend free courses at the university. His family stopped his allowance, and the young man dragged out a miserable existence in St. Petersburg, stealing bread in restaurants and sleeping in flophouses. Nevertheless his ambition was boundless. Tenaciously he wrote articles, stories and poems for stingy newspaper editors.

One of his poems, *The Road*, aroused Belinsky's enthusiasm. This famous critic encouraged the beginner, gave him advice, and steered him through the literary shallows. Nekrasov's ascent was quick—the poet of the humble and downtrodden had a remarkably, well-developed practical sense.

"Nekrasov will go far," the old journalist said, "he is not like us. . . . He will pile up a little capital. . . ."

And true enough, the same Nekrasov who wrote:

> I was called to celebrate your suffering,
> People wonderfully resigned,
> And to cast the light of conscience
> On the road where God leads you.

the same Nekrasov who saw as his muse a serf girl lashed and bleeding, who was moved to pity at the sight of the Volga boatmen, shed tears over the muzhiks' red noses, and denounced the miseries of Russia, great and small, this same Nekrasov noisily elbowed his way to the best salons, became a friend of the writer Panaev, moved into his house, stole his wife, lived with her for fifteen years, and forced the deceived husband to finance a magazine of which they were codirectors. Proletarian lyricism and a good business sense complemented each other harmoniously in his soul. His enemies accused him of being a sensualist; his friends replied that he was perfectly natural.

When Grigorovich brought him *Poor Folk,* Nekrasov's reaction was skeptical. He was too busy to read the manuscript. Finally he condescended to listen to a dozen pages. "We'll see, then, what it's worth."

Grigorovich began to read. Ten pages, twenty, thirty pages rolled by without interruption. When he reacted the burial of the consumptive student, Nekrasov cursed with enthusiasm. When he came to the farewell letter, Grigorovich was unable to restrain his sobs. He sniffed, casting stealthy glances at Nekrasov. The poet's face was also bathed in tears—this unscrupulous careerist was still so young that he wept—wholeheartedly.

Grigorovich exulted. "Let us go to Dostoevsky and tell him the good news."

"But it's late," objected Nekrasov. "He must be asleep."

"Never mind, we'll wake him up. This will be better for him than sleep!"

Dostoevsky was not asleep. He had spent the whole evening at a comrade's house reading and discussing *Dead Souls* for the hundredth time. He had returned at four in the morning—it was one of those white St. Petersburg nights, clear and warm as a spring day. Once in his room he could not make up his mind to go to bed. He opened his window and sat facing that immense, pure, smooth sky which radiated a creamy light. The houses were asleep in the dim light, the passers-by few. Feodor Mikhailovich was not quite sure that he was in the real world. He felt that he was between two lives. As he waited for the sun to rise he was shaken by the sound of the bell ringing.

He opened the door. Grigorovich and a stranger stood before him. Vaguely frightened Dostoevsky turned pale, but the visitors pressed Feodor into their arms, exclaimed excitedly, shook his limp hands. "It is a work of genius!" they cried. "Of genius!"

Dostoevsky, stunned, radiant, answered half coherently. For half an hour they discussed poetry, politics, the theater. They quoted Gogol at every opportunity and invoked the authority of Belinsky.

"I will take your manuscript to him this very day," said Nekrasov, "and then you'll see! Ah, what a man, what a man! You must meet him! And now go to sleep, we must leave. Come to me tomorrow." Finally they left. But Dostoevsky did not even think of sleeping.

"As though I could sleep after such a visit," he says in *A Writer's Diary*. "What enthusiasm! What a triumph! And the thing that was particularly precious to me was their attention. I distinctly recall my thoughts at that moment: these people are successful, they are received everywhere with congratulations, welcomed warmly, flattered; but they came to me with tears in their eyes at four in the morning, because my book was more important than sleep! Ah, how beautiful it was!" Grigorovich on his sofa could hear Dostoevsky walking back and forth in the adjoining room until daybreak.

The next day Nekrasov, as he had promised, went to see Belinsky and declared solemnly: "A second Gogol has been born to us."

"Among your crowd," the critic answered severely, "Gogols grow like mushrooms!" He agreed, however, to keep the manuscript and promised to read it. This alone was an important concession, for at that time Belinsky was recognized as the greatest Russian critic, honest and feared.

This sickly man who lived in a humble apartment, who coughed and spat blood and knew he was doomed to die very soon, had outbursts of enthusiasm and anger that shook Russian public opinion. He applauded and deprecated alternately, in a sequence of rapid aboutfaces. Dostoevsky said he was "the most hurried man in Russia" and his contemporaries nicknamed him "Vissarion the Furious." He completed his education hastily, became infatuated with theories he had no time to assimilate, dropped them and picked them up again, all the time suffering with his whole soul. At the beginning of his career he took up idealism, art for art's sake, introspective contemplation and Olympian detachment from

the world, but gradually this rarefied atmosphere began to
weigh upon him. He could no longer be satisfied only with
literature and himself.

"Art suffocated me," he wrote to a friend. "Under this
regime, however, I could live within myself and I thought
that for a man no existence was possible save inner existence.
But at last I went out of myself (I was too crowded there,
although I was warm), I went out toward a new world of
suffering."

He resumed contact with reality, with the masses, and devoted himself to social problems. The fate of the Russian
people, he thought, was iniquitous, intolerable, and it was
the writer's duty to denounce the misery of the peasants. In
his eyes, a book had no value unless it contained a humanitarian message, and a talent was worthless unless it was useful. Around him huddled the Occidentalists opposed to the
Slavophiles. From then on he swore only by the French socialists and invoked only the advances of science. Even Pushkin, whom he had previously admired without reservations,
was now but a salon versifier to him. Had not this poet written: "Your pot is more precious to you because it serves to
cook your meals."

"Of course!" exclaimed Belinsky with flashing eyes, pacing from one end of the room to the other, "of course, it is
more precious to me! It is not only for myself but for my
family, for all the poor people, that I cook my food in it,
and before waxing ecstatic about the beauties of art, my
right and my duty is to feed my people and to feed myself
in defiance of all the aristocrats and whippersnappers!" (This
episode is reported by Turgenev in his *Memoirs*.)

Only his attachment to Gogol seemed unshakable. But
when Gogol published his *Correspondence*, Belinsky choked

with indignation. He had "worshiped" this author because his books revealed the disease of contemporary society; now he sensed that the novelist was really a reactionary mystic, a convinced Slavophile, a barbarian. On this score the critic wrote a lengthy and damning message, which later, by a curious detour, proved fatal to Dostoevsky. "Yes, I loved you," Belinsky wrote to Gogol, "as only a man bound to his country by his blood can love the hope of that country, its honor, its glory and one of the great leaders of its conscience, its development and its progress. I cannot give you the slightest idea of the indignation that your recent book aroused in me. You do not realize that Russia's salvation lies not in mysticism or pietism, but in the progress of civilization, in the maturation of that human dignity which for centuries has been dragged in mud and dung. . . . Look at your feet, they stand at the edge of an abyss. . . ."

In 1845, however, Gogol had not yet published his *Correspondence,* and Belinsky surrounded him with a jealous cult, a sort of maternal passion. A new Gogol, indeed! What a mockery! But the following day when the writer Annenkov came to visit Belinsky he looked up from the courtyard and saw the critic standing in front of the window with a large notebook in his hands. As soon as Belinsky caught sight of his visitor, he cried: "Come in, quickly. . . . I want to tell you a piece of good news. . . . Look at this manuscript, I cannot tear myself away from it. It is the work of a young talent. I don't even know what the author looks like or what his ideas are, but his novel opens such profound vistas of life and the character of the Russian people that no one has ever even dreamed of anything like it. It is the first attempt at a social novel in Russia, but something only an artist could write, that is to say, completely unconscious of its implica-

tions." And in an inflated, sonorous and excited voice Belinsky read a few pages of *Poor Folk*. That same evening
Nekrasov came to learn his reaction. Belinsky received him
with the words: "Bring him here . . . bring him at once."

Three days after he had read his manuscript to Grigorovich, Dostoevsky was introduced to the most enthusiastic
journalist in Russia. Turgenev described Belinsky as follows:
"I saw before me a man of medium size, stoutish, with an
irregular but unusual face and disheveled blond hair. His expression was restless as is often the case with timid and lonely
people. He began to speak to me, then was seized by a cough-
ing fit, asked us to sit down and sat down himself on the
sofa, glancing at the floor all the time, and rolling a cigarette
between his extremely delicate and graceful fingers."

To Dostoevsky, also, he must have appeared thus; somber,
grave and ill at ease. But Belinsky soon warmed up to his
visitors. "He kept repeating to me in the grandiloquent tone
which was his wont, 'can you understand what you have
written here?' He had the habit of raising his voice whenever
he was strongly moved. 'It is because you are an extremely
sensitive artist that you were able to write such a work; but
have you gauged the full extent of the terrible truth you
depicted? It is impossible that you can have understood it at
the age of twenty. After all, your unfortunate functionary
served with so much abnegation! He reached the point
where he did not dare have the slightest respect for himself,
because he was so abased, and in the end he considers every
complaint an impiety. He does not even grant himself the
right to be unhappy! The truth has been revealed to you, the
artist; you have received it as a gift; learn to appreciate this
gift, remain faithful to it and you will be a great writer.' "

Dostoevsky was stunned, intoxicated, dizzy. He wanted

to embrace and thank the first person he met, to swear eternal friendship to anyone and everyone. When he found himself in the street again he could hardly walk. He stopped at the curb and looked at "the sky, the bright day, the passersby," but he no longer had anything in common with them. He had suddenly been lifted up to another world, from which they looked like ants. "Is it really possible that I am so great? I said to myself seized by a timid exaltation. Oh, do not laugh: later I never imagined myself to be a great man; but then, was it possible to resist the idea? . . . Oh, I will deserve this praise. But what men, what men! . . . I will deserve their respect, I will try to become as excellent as they are, I will remain faithful. . . . We shall be victorious. Oh, to go with them, to be with them."

However, he was not to remain among them for long. While Belinsky was charmed by *Poor Folk*, he interpreted it in his own fashion, seeing it only as a good illustration of his social views. "It is a simple matter. Some worthy fools believe that love for mankind is the pleasure and the duty of every man. They do not understand what has happened when the wheel of existence with all the well-established privileges calmly crushes and pulverizes their flesh and bones. That is all. But what a tragedy! What characters!"

Actually he was unaware of the positive aspect of these characters. He was unmoved by their quiet resignation, their active kindness. He did not realize that Makar Dievushkin was more than a victim because he accepted his fate. In *Poor Folk* he saw an excuse for social rebellion, not a summons to human sympathy. He was indignant against the executioners, but he forgot to admire the martyrs. In any event, the critic and the author for the time being were intoxicated with each other. Belinsky communicated to everyone his recent discov-

ery. It became an obsession with him. Aksakov wrote testily:
"They have found a new star, a certain Dostoevsky, whom
they place almost above Gogol."

Poor Folk was not yet published, but thanks to Belinsky
the young author was now received with sympathetic curiosity in literary circles. Public readings of his book were held
and he was invited to the salons. Dostoevsky lost his head, he
ordered a slick hat for himself from Zimmermann, the fashionable hatter, was meticulous about his linen, believed himself to be a Rastignac, and found everybody charming. Belinsky was like a second father to him.

"It must be said," wrote Feodor to his brother, "that Belinsky explained to me two weeks ago how one can live by one's
pen. . . . I often visit Belinsky. He is as kind to me as one
can be, and seriously believes that I am the proof and justification of his own ideas concerning the public. . . . A good
half of St. Petersburg is already talking about *Poor Folk*.
. . . Grigorovich alone is worth the weight in gold. He himself says: '*Je suis votre claqueur-chauffeur.*' " This letter was
dated October 8, 1845.

By November 16 of the same year *Poor Folk* had not yet
seen the light of day, but Dostoevsky's intoxication almost
reached the point of insanity. "My brother, my glory will
never exceed the peak that it has reached now. Everywhere
I arouse incredible respect and extraordinary curiosity. I
have met dozens of members of the fashionable set. Prince
Odoevsky asked me to honor him with a visit, and Count
Sologub is tearing his hair on my account. Panaev told him
that there was a talented writer who would soon make all
the others return to mud. Sologub ran to everyone and in
the home of Kraevsky asked him: 'Who is this Dostoevsky?

Where can I find this Dostoevsky?' Kraevsky, who has no consideration for anyone and tells everyone the truth, told him that Dostoevsky would not honor him with a visit. And this is actually the case. This little aristocrat has climbed up on his high horse and imagines that he will dazzle me with the magnanimity of his condescension. Everybody considers me a marvel. I cannot open my mouth without people repeating in every corner: 'Dostoevsky said this. Dostoevsky wants to do that. . . .' In brief, little brother, I have not enough paper to tell you about all my literary successes. . . ."

Finally, greatest news of all, Dostoevsky met Turgenev. "Turgenev is in love with me. What a man, my brother! I myself almost fell in love with him. A talented poet, an aristocrat, handsome, intelligent, wealthy, twenty-five years of age. . . . I think nature has refused him nothing. Moreover, he is an extremely straightforward character, admirable, brought up in the best traditions. . . . I am crammed full of ideas, but I have only to mention them to someone, for example, Turgenev, and the following day all St. Petersburg will know that Dostoevsky is writing this and that. . . ."

He wallowed in his fame, he strutted before his mirror like a boy in his new Sunday best, he was unbearably happy and naïve and fatuous. And this was only natural considering his previous solitude and doubts. Only recently he had been unknown, writing in the mist, feeling that no one would ever appreciate his work. And here from one day to the next, strangers read, understood and admired him; more, they sought his company. No one is more conceited than a man who has for a long time denied himself the right to be conceited.

His boasting, however, was only in his letters. As soon as

he was alone before his paper, his original shyness regained its hold on him. He feared that he was unworthy of this glory. He had the feeling that "he was cheating clumsily and that everyone was aware of his maneuvers and was making fun of him."

When after reading *Poor Folk* Count Sologub came to see him, he found a pale morbid-looking young man.

"He wore a rather frayed dressing-gown," the count writes in his *Memoirs*, "with sleeves so short that it looked as if it had been cut for someone else. When I introduced myself and told him in a few carefully chosen words the profound surprise that the reading of his novel had caused me, he seemed to lose countenance and offered me the only chair in his room, an old shaky one. I stayed twenty minutes at his house and invited him to dinner. Dostoevsky was simply terrified by my invitation. It was only two months later that he suddenly decided to appear at my menagerie."

The term "terrified" is exact; for Dostoevsky was both exalted and terrified. All this was too good, too easy, to be true. He was dazzled, blinded. He embraced his enemies. He could not conceive that anyone should not love him, since he loved everybody. "These worthy people do not know any longer how to show their love for me; from the first to the last, they are all in love with me. . . ."

Nevertheless, at the musical salon of Count Veligorsky where he went with Belinsky, he had the distinct impression "of having been displayed as a spectacle." In the same salon, when Belinsky accidentally broke a glass, Feodor Mikhailovich heard Countess Sologub whisper behind him: "If they were only clumsy and savage! Alas, they are not even intelligent." And he learned that some of his colleagues reproached him for having asked that his novel be printed with a special ornamental border. Several years later, when Dostoevsky was in Siberia, Turgenev warned Leontiev against the excessive conceit of certain budding authors. "Take, for instance, that poor Dostoevsky. When he gave his novel to Belinsky to have it published, the unfortunate fellow lost his head, to such a point that he said to the critic: 'My text ought to be printed with an ornamental border.'" This allegation was never verified. In 1880, a year before his death, Dostoevsky protested with indignation against this story, in *The New Times*. Annenkov, however, claimed to have seen proofs of the novel with a border, and Grigorovich himself never dared to deny it. However, the book was published without any kind of border.

It is possible that Dostoevsky, intoxicated by flattery, actually did ask the critic to give his novel a special typographic presentation. At that time he was capable of any vanity. He was beside himself with excitement and no longer knew what he was doing or what he wanted to do.

"We have almost caused one of the little idols of the day to lose his mind," writes Panaev. "He actually began to rave. Soon we knocked him off his pedestal and forgot him completely. The poor fellow! We annihilated him. We made him a laughing stock."

At one reception Dostoevsky was introduced to a young society beauty. He found himself facing a pretty girl with a baby mouth, heavy blond curls, and calm cold eyes. She was about to make him a routine compliment on his work, when he grew pale, tottered and lost consciousness. He was taken to an adjoining room and sponged with eau de cologne. Some time later, Turgenev ("Turgenev is in love with me") and Nekrasov ("the delightful poet of the humble") wrote a satirical poem describing this incident:

O, Knight of the Sad Face,
Dostoevsky, gentle braggart,
On the nose of literature
You shine like a bright red pimple.

Soon the Sultan of Turkey
Will send his viziers to you;
But when at an elegant reception
Among an assembly of princes
—Oh, Myth and Problem of the Day—
You dropped like a falling star

And wrinkled your long nose
Before a blond beauty,
You stared at this charming object
With such tragic immobility
That you almost died on the spot
Cut off in the prime of life . . .

The two colleagues, helped by Annenkov, circulated infamous anecdotes about Dostoevsky. He may not have known anything about it, he may only have pretended that he did not know; he continued to see a great deal of them.

When he was invited to the Panaevs he smartened himself up and perfumed himself as though going to a tryst, and appeared in the great salon enlarged by mirrors and lights. Madame Panaev describes him as follows: "It was clear at once that Dostoevsky was an extremely nervous and impressionable young man. He was slight, thin, blondish, and his complexion was sickly looking. His little gray pupils darted restlessly from one thing to another, and his pale lips had brief twitches."

Thank God, he knew almost everybody there. But what

were they going to talk to him about? What would he say to them? Would he seem equal to his reputation, would he be able to distinguish sincere compliments from veiled jeers? He was self-conscious, stiff, haughty; he thought only of running away as soon as possible, of returning to his badly lighted little room, heavy with the smell of tobacco and encumbered with books and papers. To be alone, alone! Nevertheless, he returned to the Panaevs.

"Dostoevsky came to visit us frequently in the evening," writes Madame Panaev. "His embarrassment subsided; he even displayed a kind of teasing wit, started discussions with everyone, and contradicted his questioners out of sheer stubbornness."

The reactions described here are those of a shy young man. He attacked lest he be attacked. He gave himself airs, lest he be humiliated. He thought he was brilliant, when in reality he was unbearable; he thought he was witty, when in reality he was malicious and stupid. He thought he pirouetted with aristocratic grace but one could hear the tread of his heavy peasant boots.

The literati fell upon this easy prey like a swarm of wasps, worrying and harrying him with imperceptible pricks. According to Madame Panaev, "Turgenev was past master at this game. He had long discussions with Dostoevsky for the express purpose of driving him crazy." The unfortunate young man grew angry, took the matter to heart and exaggerated his opinions to the point of absurdity until everyone around him burst out laughing. The literary fashion of the day favored persiflage, ill-natured gossip, cabals, intrigues of little cliques. Dostoevsky was suffocating in this stuffy atmosphere. "Don't repeat it, but do you know what so and so says about you? Incidentally you shouldn't trust so and so." In Dostoevsky's opinion all this was very simple—everyone was jealous of him. Even Belinsky no longer loved him because instead of talking to him about *Poor Folk* he played cards.

"How can an intelligent man give even ten minutes of his time to a ridiculous amusement like cards?" wrote Feodor Mikhailovich. "Indeed, there is no difference between the society of the bureaucrats and that of the litterateurs: both of them indulge in the same stupid distractions." And Belinsky watched him out of the corner of his eye and whispered to Nekrasov, his partner in the game: "What is the matter with Dostoevsky? He is saying foolish things, and with what conviction!"

"When Belinsky was told that Dostoevsky considered himself a genius," writes Madame Panaev, "he shrugged his shoulders and said: 'What a misfortune! For Dostoevsky has an indisputable talent, and if, instead of working, he imagines that he is a genius, he will never get ahead. He should absolutely take care of himself. All this stems from his extreme nervous tension. . . .' One day Turgenev related in the presence of Dostoevsky that he had met in a provincial town a man who thought he was a genius, and he masterfully described the ridiculous character traits of this personage. Dostoevsky grew pale as a sheet, and ran away before the end of the story. I said to all those present: 'Why do you torment him like that?'"

Dostoevsky escaped from the large bright rooms. He ran along the sleepy streets, returned to his room and threw himself on his couch to brood over his spite and his fury. To be flouted by this scum of the salons, these dregs of the literary world! What a disgrace! Let them strike him honest blows, but let him be spared pricks and treacherous stabs! How ridiculous he had been that evening! Madame Panaev had laughed at him. The blood surged to his cheeks. He evoked Madame Panaev's comely face, her large black eyes, her satirical smile. The fact that this admirable creature should be Panaev's wife nauseated him. She deserved better than that. What, whom did she deserve? Himself? His mirror reflected the image of a little man with an earth-colored face and blondish hair. How unattractive, how sad he was! With the refinement of an expert he deepened his despair. He missed an unhappy passion to complete his misfortune, and he must have one—indeed, he had it already. He was at the bottom of human distress. "I was seriously in love with Madame P.," he wrote to his brother.

Everything in this woman was beautiful—her face, her soul, her life. She was the daughter of the actor Briansky and had risen by her own efforts. At the age of eighteen she had become infatuated with Panaev and married him secretly. Panaev's mother had at first opposed this marriage, but later changed her mind. According to Belinsky, "Panaev's mother threatened her son with her own death, nevertheless she is still alive, and it is very probable that she will bury both her son and her daughter-in-law."

The young Avdotia Panaev wrote in a charming light style. She had the grace and wit that Dostoevsky lacked. He considered declaring his love and writing poems to her, like one of her admirers, Suchkov, but he never dared. Disgusted with himself and all his acquaintances he tried to lose himself in dissipation. He railed at Belinsky, threatening to ruin himself, but the critic scolded him for the sake of appearances and advised him to be moderately chaste.

Dostoevsky was secretly pleased at the thought that he had caused his friend concern. He faced the world of the flesh with the spirit of someone setting out on an expedition.

"Ah, these Claras, Minnas and Mariannes," he wrote his brother, "how pretty they are. They cost me exorbitant sums of money." He posed as a professional sensualist, a Don Juan, but when he returned home he was probably horrified by what he had done and rinsed his mouth to chase away the odor of the perfumes that nauseated him.

"In my conversations with him" [from 1846 to 1849], writes Dr. Yanovsky, "I never heard him say that he was passionately infatuated with anyone nor even that he loved a woman." The one he loved he never discussed, because he admired her. As for the others, he never discussed them because he despised them. Every Friday he went to the Panaevs where he found the dreadful Annenkov who was invariably of the same opinion as his companion; the imposing Sologub with his monocle screwed into his eye socket; the execrable Turgenev who posed as an aristocrat; in short, the whole clique of his rivals, and the whole circle of the *Annals of the Fatherland;* all of "our own." And each time he suffered, was revolted, and "belched forth stupidities" which went from salon to salon.

One day Madame Panaev saw him running out of Nekrasov's office. "He was pale as a corpse and unable to put his arm into the sleeve of his overcoat that the lackey was holding for him. Finally he tore the overcoat from the man's hands and rushed to the staircase. I entered the office and found Nekrasov in a state of great irritation. 'Dostoevsky has gone mad,' Nekrasov told me in a voice trembling with emotion. 'Who told him this legend? He claims that I am reciting to everyone some infamous verses that I allegedly wrote against him!' " Actually, it was not a legend.

Another incident is reported by Pavlovsky. One night

Ogarev, Belinsky and Herzen met at Turgenev's to play cards. A *bon mot* of one of the players made the whole company burst out laughing. At that very moment the door opened and Dostoevsky came in. He stopped, stared at the players, grew pale, and withdrew. An hour later, Turgenev found him in the courtyard walking back and forth, livid, disheveled, his head bare in spite of the cold and the wind. "What is the matter with you, Dostoevsky?" asked Turgenev.

"My God! It is unbearable! Wherever I go I am jeered at. I saw how all of you burst out laughing as soon as you laid eyes on me!"

He was laughed at everywhere, and he did not know why. Should not talent impose respect? Ah, if *Poor Folk* could only be published soon! The praise of the press would soon shut the beaks of these evil birds. But publication was delayed because the board of censorship had not yet given the permission. Dostoevsky wrote to his brother: "This is a misfortune, the board of censorship does not give a sign of life. The novel is harmless, yet it must be dragged about from office to office, and I do not know what the end of all this will be."

On January 15, 1846, *Poor Folk* was published in Nekrasov's almanac, the *St. Petersburg Miscellany*. Belinsky praised the book in the *Annals of the Fatherland*. "To arouse the reader's laughter and to touch his heart, to compel him to smile through his tears—what skill, what talent this requires!" But Belinsky's views were not shared by his colleagues on the big newspapers. In a letter to his brother, Dostoevsky wrote: "*Poor Folk* appeared on the 15th. If you knew, my brother, with what horrible insults it was received everywhere! In the *Illustration* it was not a review that I read, but a series of imprecations. In the *Northern Bee* they published the devil knows what about me. But I remember Gogol's beginnings and we all know how Pushkin was received. Even the public is insane. Three-fourths of the readers drag my name in the mud, while one-fourth (or perhaps less) praise me extravagantly. Violent debates are going on about my book. I am insulted, insulted and insulted some more, yet I am read! Ah, I have given them a bone to gnaw. Let them gnaw it—they are building my fame, the fools! . . . But in compensation, what praise I hear sometimes, my brother! Can you believe that all of our circle, even Belinsky, think that I have by far surpassed Gogol. . . . He and the others consider me an original writer in that I proceed by analysis, rather than by synthesis, that is to say, I plunge into the depths and discover the whole by disintegrating the atoms. Gogol for his part takes the whole as it presents itself, and that is why he is less profound than I. . . ."

It was as simple as all that and Dostoevsky was again in high spirits! He was criticized, flattered, discussed. Now, he thought, his book would draw the boundary line between his true friends and his enemies—there would be two camps, devoted troops and an empty terrain where skirmishes would no longer be possible. Ah, what a glorious struggle!

Even before the publication of *Poor Folk* Dostoevsky had begun a new novel, *The Double*. His letters to his brother teemed with allusions to this new "masterpiece." "Iakov Petrovich Golyadkin [the hero of *The Double*]," he wrote, "is showing his character clearly and he is a real scoundrel. One does not know how to take him. He refuses to advance under the pretext that he is not ready. He refuses to end his career before November." (Letter of October 8, 1845.)

"Golyadkin is coming along splendidly. This will be my masterpiece." (November 16, 1845.)

"Golyadkin is ten times better than *Poor Folk*. Our boys say that nothing like it has been written in Russia since *Dead Souls*, that it is a work of genius, and a thousand other things. . . ." (February 1, 1846.)

Actually, the few chapters of the new novel that Dostoevsky read to his friends impressed them tremendously. "Belinsky," Grigorovich relates, "sat facing the author and jealously caught his every word; at times he was unable to conceal his admiration, and said over and over again that only Dostoevsky was capable of such psychological refinement." As late as 1877, Dostoevsky, while recognizing the weaknesses of his book, wrote: "Its conception was quite beautiful, and in the course of my whole career I have never developed a more serious one."

The story is that of Golyadkin, a civil servant, whose excessive shyness and self-effacement make him detestable. One day he meets his double. "Mr. Golyadkin recognized his nocturnal visitor. The visitor was himself, Mr. Golyadkin in person, another Mr. Golyadkin, but identical with the real one in every respect, in brief, what is called a double in the full meaning of this term."

The double is as unscrupulous, cynical, shrewd, calculating and evil as the real Golyadkin is unassuming, stupid and honest. This evil character soon usurps Mr. Golyadkin's identity, steals his friends, ruins his reputation in the eyes of his superiors, supplants him, destroys him and reduces him to the state of a dejected shadow. The two Golyadkins cannot exist one beside the other. The stronger one kills the weaker, the evil one kills the good one, and everything is again in order.

Dostoevsky called this long story a poem. Later he referred to it as a "confession." Actually it was a confession which his contemporaries were unable to discern under the Hoffmannesque anecdote. Golyadkin is the eternal intruder, the eternal stranger, the undesirable. "I am alone and they are all." This unfortunate who enters the salon of Andrey Philipovich where everyone is hostile toward him, who feels the jeering glances of all those present converging upon him, who tries to justify and impose himself, who loses countenance, falls into a panic, wants to leave, yet cannot make up his mind to leave—is this not a true picture of the author among his literary friends? And when Golyadkin, after committing all sorts of *faux pas*, flees from the brightly lighted house and runs along the waterfront "escaping from his enemies, from their persecutions, from the hail of quips directed against him"—does this not again evoke Dostoevsky on that November night, damp, foggy, rainy, snowy, full of head colds, agues, quinsies, fevers, in brief all the gifts of a St. Petersburg November?

Indeed all Golyadkin's crestfallen returns were his own, his relief upon regaining his dark little room after the splendors of the ball. Similarly Golyadkin's anguish before Clara Alsufievna, the young beauty, duplicates Dostoevsky's state of mind in the presence of Seniavana or Madame Panaev. "Mr. Golyadkin was pale and utterly bewildered. It was as though he had been suddenly stricken by exhaustion. He could hardly move."

And what about the other, the false Golyadkin, or the "usurper" as Dostoevsky calls him? He, too, is Dostoevsky—the successful worldly Dostoevsky who was eager to receive compliments, sought friendships and struggled against his own nature. We are dealing here with a split personality:

on the one hand, the real Feodor Mikhailovich, humble, sad
and resentful; on the other, the Feodor Mikhailovich who
was spoiled by success, who held his head high, strutted
about and attacked his fellow men. The real Feodor Mikhailovich despised his odious double and felt threatened by
him. He feared to be taken in by the charms of facile glory,
and to expose himself to people who would not forgive him
for being what he was. He was afraid of no longer being
himself. When the genuine Golyadkin vanishes, "he is
escorted by the shrill inhuman cries of his enemies," and
his hideous double triumphs.

This idea of the double haunted Dostoevsky all his life.
He conceived the punishment of the criminal first of all as
the splitting of his personality, as the appearance of a double
who is and is not himself, a double who is his frightful caricature, a distorting mirror in which his human face is swollen as with abscesses and displays all the signs of an accursed
inner life. Raskolnikov, the hero of *Crime and Punishment*,
recognizes himself in the infamous Svidrigailov: "Very well
then, didn't I tell you that we had something in common?"
In *The Adolescent*, Versilov is subjected to the same split
as Golyadkin: "You see, it seems to me that I am split in
two. . . . Yes, I am mentally split and I am afraid. It is
as though a double emerged beside me; you yourself are intelligent, sensible, while the other invariably wants to do
something absurd in your name." Stavrogin in *The Possessed* finds his double in Pyotr Stepanovich, the revolutionary agitator. "I laugh at my ape," he says to him. And
the other answers: "I am a buffoon, but I do not want you,
the better part of myself, to be one." And when Stavrogin
speaks of the devil, he is not less explicit: "I do not believe in
him. I do not believe in him yet. I know that he is myself in

different guise, that I split into two and speak with myself."
(This last passage was suppressed by Dostoevsky in the
definitive edition of the novel.)

Ivan Karamazov sees the devil in his delirium. And the
devil is himself, his shadow. "By injuring yourself you injure
me," said Ivan. "You are myself, but with a different face.
. . . Only you choose my silliest ideas to expand upon." Or:
"Everything that was stupid in me, that I had long since
digested and eliminated as dirt, you bring back to me as
something new. How could my soul produce a cad like
you?" The lackey Smerdyakov is also a parody of Ivan
Karamazov: "The clown Smerdyakov set himself up in his
soul."

"In every man," says Baudelaire, "there are two simul-
taneous aspirants—one for God and one for Satan." This
idea which is fully expressed in Dostoevsky's mature works
is inadequately treated in *The Double*, because the novelist
was as yet unable to overcome Gogol's influence. *The
Double* is not only inspired by Gogol's *Nose*, it is a parody
of Gogol, a school essay in which whole sentences taken
from Gogol can be found. Gogol's story tells of the adventures of a civil servant whose nose detaches itself from
his body to live an independent life. Dostoevsky's novel tells
the story of a civil servant whose soul is split into two parts
that acquire separate individualities. The second chapter of
the *Nose* begins as follows: "The assessor Kovalev awoke
very early and uttered a 'brr . . .' with his lips. . . . He
stretched himself and asked for a little mirror that was on his
table. He wanted to examine a pimple that had sprouted on
his nose the night before." And this is the beginning of
The Double: "It was nearly eight in the morning when the
councilor Iakov Petrovich Golyadkin awoke from a long

sleep, yawned, stretched himself and finally opened his eyes.
. . . Jumping from his bed he immediately ran to a little
round mirror that was on his bureau. How awful it would
be, he thought to himself, if a pimple had sprouted in the
very middle of my face!"

The parallel can be pursued throughout the entire book.
More, Dostoevsky's work teems with expressions such as:
"nose to nose," "take it on the nose," "stick one's nose into
something," "show the tip of one's nose," etc. When editing
the story for a second printing, Dostoevsky tried to cover up
his tracks, and eliminated as many references to "noses" as
possible, but he could not prevent *The Double* from being
but a medley of genius. In every chapter one meets Gogol's
characters, his jokes and his phrases. And Dostoevsky recognized his error immediately upon publication of the book.
On April 1, 1846, he wrote to his brother: "This is what
annoys and angers me: Our people, headed by Belinsky, are
dissatisfied with me because of Golyadkin. Their first reaction was unreserved admiration, shouts of praise, endless
discussions. Their second reaction was criticism. All of
them, that is our own people and the public, are unanimous
that Golyadkin is boring and flabby and that I have drawn
him out to the point of making him unreadable. . . . As for
myself I was dejected for a time. I have a terrible weakness
—boundless pride and conceit. The very thought that I have
disappointed the expectations of the public and botched a
work that could have been grandiose literally kills me. I am
disgusted with Golyadkin. I bungled quite a number of passages. All this makes my life hell, and I am ill from despair."

It is true that criticisms were severe. "I cannot understand," wrote Aksakov, "how this novel was even allowed to
be published. All Russia knows Gogol, knows him almost by

heart, and now Mr. Dostoevsky appropriates and repeats Gogal's very sentences. Having stolen a few shreds of that artist's admirable garment, Dostoevsky flaunts them boldly before the public." Even Belinsky mitigated his praise, hesitated, and dodged the issue.

"It is possible," he wrote, "that the author of *The Double* has not yet acquired the tact measure and harmony that are indispensable to maturity and that is why many people, not unjustifiably, reproach him with a certain slowness. . . ."

Feeling that he had alienated the sympathy of the public, Dostoevsky wanted to regain it as quickly as possible. For that purpose he had to write something, and at once. But what? He did a long story entitled *Mr. Prokharchin* about a fanatical and sordid miser. After the old man's death rolls of gold are discovered in his straw mattress, and there is a revolting scene—people rush upon the corpse and push it. "Suddenly and absolutely unexpectedly, he toppled over the foot of the bed, head down, showing only two thin blue legs rising in the air like branches of a charred tree."

The censor cut this harmless and meaningless story with surprising vigor. "Prokharchin is terribly disfigured in certain places. These gentlemen have forbidden the term 'civil servant,' God knows why. . . . Everything that was alive in it is gone. Only the skeleton remains," wrote Feodor to his brother.

Belinsky received this new work of his protégé with undisguised hostility: "A few sparks of talent gleam in this work, but amidst such darkness that their light does not permit us to distinguish anything. It is not inspiration, it is not the free work of an artist that produced this story, but something quite different . . . perhaps a certain affectation, a certain pretentiousness. . . ."

Nor did the *Novel in Nine Letters*, a sort of epistolary duel between two scoundrels, written in one night for the *Contemporary* find favor in the eyes of the critics.

"To my great surprise," Belinsky wrote to Turgenev, "I simply disliked the correspondence between these two cads. I could hardly finish reading it. And everybody is of my opinion."

Dostoevsky was thrown into a panic by these successive failures. He groped for a new path and lost his way in insignificant articles. He agreed to contribute to the humoristic review, *Zuboskal*, for which he himself wrote an anonymous prospectus.

"This prospectus made some noise. I was reminded of Lucien de Rubempre's first *feuilleton*," he wrote. The publisher Kraevsky advanced him some money and pressed him to deliver his stories. "I am paying all my debts through Kraevsky, and my only wish is to work enough for him this winter, so that I will not owe a kopek to anyone when summer comes." He buckled down to two stories: *The Shaved Sidewhiskers* and *The Abolished Chancelleries*. "Both are impregnated with vibrant tragedy, and I can tell you in advance that they will be extremely condensed," he wrote to his brother on April 1, 1846. But in October of the same year he informed Mikhail that neither of the two stories would be published. "I have dropped everything I was doing because all of it was only a repetition of what I had said before. At present new, more original, living and clear thoughts demand to be written down on paper. I am working on another story, and it is going very well." In another letter, written in 1847, he says: "You will soon read *Netochka Nezvanova*. It is a confession, as in the case of Golyadkin, but in a different tone, in a different form . . . I am writing

The Landlady, which is superior to *Poor Folk*, and incidentally is of the same genre. An inspiration which comes from my soul makes my pen run over the paper."

Netochka Nezvanova was published only in 1849. The heroine is a little girl brought up by a drunken stepfather, who believes himself to be a musical genius, and a sick mother, in a world "whose horizon is confined to the gray walls of a low-ceilinged room." At an age when other children squander their energy in play, Netochka is wrapped up in her impressions of the outer world. She feeds on dreams and is lost "in the fog of a disorderly life." She admires her stepfather because he is talented and because he "deserves to be pitied." "I am a cipher," the musician exclaims one day, and the next: "I am a genius." He represents a singular mixture of arrogance and humility. "He loved to feel persecuted."

Netochka hates her mother because she imagines that this ailing creature prevents her husband from devoting himself to art. Here is that hatred softened by pity, that love dampened with contempt, which Dostoevsky himself experienced as a child toward his own father. These same feelings, he always expressed, confessing them as he wrote. Netochka's mother dies under tragic circumstances and her stepfather becomes insane. The child is adopted by a megalomaniac prince who is the portrait of Count Veligorsky. The prince's daughter, Katia, is tyrannical, capricious and secretive, and "everyone in the house pampers and caresses her like a treasure." At first the young princess shows her contempt for the little intruder and tortures her, reminding her that she came as an orphan wearing a "nasty dress." Later, however, Katia becomes infatuated with Netochka and between the two little girls there develops a passionate and somewhat erotic affection which expresses itself in long chats in bed, embraces, vows and quarrels. "I noticed that you could live without me, and I thought: 'Wait, I'll torture her.' Or: 'I'll kiss her, I thought to myself, and pinch her till she dies of it.'"

In *The Landlady*, published long before *Netochka Nezvanova*, Dostoevsky also presents such a feminine character, ardent and unbalanced. The young student Ordynov who lives in seclusion, absorbed in religious meditations, rents a room in the house of an old man with the burning eyes and long beard of a philosopher. This old man lives with a beautiful woman and Ordynov falls in love with her. His passion for the mysterious Catherine appears through the trembling mist of delirium. He always has the feeling that he is either dreaming or awake in a hostile world, though he might be awake when he thinks he is dreaming. The reader oscillates between the dream world and the real world. Thus, Ordynov hears a fairy tale, then the voice which tells it dies out in a whisper, "but the tale continues somewhere. . . ." Suddenly the door opens, two burning lips touch his own, and a second later Catherine throws herself on her knees before the icons and accuses herself of murder. It is an insane woman for whom Murin, the old magician, and Ordynov are struggling. The story ends with the flight of the old man and the young girl.

There is no doubt that this story was inspired by Gogol's *Terrible Revenge* in which a magician who is secretly in love with his own daughter, Catherine, resorts to all his apparitions, potions and spells to detach her from her husband. Everything is there, including the storm on the Dnieper described by Gogol, which in Dostoevsky's story is transformed into a storm on the Volga. However, once again, this is not a simple literary imitation. Ordynov, the thinker, is Dostoevsky: his studies "make him a child with regard to everyday life," and "he bears the malice and rudeness of his comrades none of whom can forgive his strange and solitary character." The hero's passion for Catherine is that of Feodor for Madame Panaev who was separated from him by a barrier of conventions.

This imaginative art could only bewilder the contemporary critics infatuated with realism and social problems. Belinsky was beside himself. He wrote to Annenkov: "Did I tell you that Dostoevsky has published a novel, *The Land-lady*. It is the worst kind of nonsense. Each of his works is a new failure. We were grossly taken in by Dostoevsky's vaunted genius. . . . I, the first of the critics, was only a jackass in this respect. . . . I have just read Rousseau's *Confessions*, and I feel the greatest repugnance for that gentleman, so much is he like Dostoevsky who is persuaded that the whole human species envies and wishes to persecute him. . . ." And Belinsky's review of the book in the *Contemporary* was a scathing invective: "In this whole story there is not one word or one part of a phrase that is simple or living. Everything here is affected, far-fetched, stilted, artificial and false."

This savage attack probably crushed Dostoevsky. "This is the third year of my literary career," he wrote to Mikhail, "and I live as in a fog. I do not see life, I have no time to recover my senses. My art is being ruined for lack of time. I should like to stop. I have been given a dubious celebrity: I don't know how long this hell will last—poverty, bungled work. When shall I have peace?"

During this period of hasty and lusterless production, Dostoevsky's life was poisoned by small worries, petty betrayals and malicious tricks. He knew the commonplace misery of not having enough money to pay his rent, of being obliged to return advance payments and cultivate advantageous friendships—in brief, the horsemanship of little careerists.

The exceptional character of great misfortunes to some extent comforts the victim, but everyday worries erode, crush and destroy those who suffer them in silence. An average existence is without compensations, and this was true of Dostoevsky above all.

He lost his literary friends one by one. Belinsky could not forgive him the disappointments he caused the critic with each successive book. But the real reasons of the quarrel between the novelist and the critic went beyond art. "Vissarion the Furious" attacked the man more than the artist. It was a case of opposite conceptions of morals which soon proved incompatible. Belinsky placed science, social progress and the dignity of the individual in the foreground of his interests. He "refreshed his soul" in watching the construction of a railroad.

"From the beginning of our relationship," Dostoevsky writes in *A Writer's Diary* "he loved me with all his heart and rather naïvely conceived his task as that of converting me to his ideas. . . . I knew him as an ardent socialist, and first and foremost he wanted to win me over to atheism. . . . As a socialist he felt obliged to destroy the teachings of Christ. . . . All that remained was the luminous figure of Man the God, his moral elevation and supernatural beauty which could generate miracles. But in his impetuous zeal Belinsky did not stop before this insurmountable obstacle as was the case with Renan."

As late as 1871 Dostoevsky's indignation toward Belinsky had not yet subsided. He wrote to Strakhov: "This man in-

sulted Christ in my presence. . . . But when insulting Him,
did he ever ask himself, Whom shall we put in His place?
Ourselves? No, he never thought of that. And he was so
satisfied with himself! . . . Is not this the proof of his conceit and stupidity?" And elsewhere: "You say that he was
talented. Absolutely not. It was only very superficially, very
casually that he appraised Gogol's characters; he merely rejoiced over the fact that Gogol 'had denounced something.'
Four years ago I reread his critical writings. He demolished
Pushkin when that poet gave up his factitious genre and
published the *Belkin Stories* and *The Arab*. He dismissed the
end of *Eugene Onegin*. He was the first to label Pushkin
as a high society writer."

Going from one extreme to the other Dostoevsky no
longer attached the slightest value to the man whom he had
once called "a noble heart." He hated everything that Belinsky adored: utilitarian art and grandiloquent parlor hu-
manitarianism. And he adored everything that Belinsky
hated: the image of the Man-God and free art. He refused
to be judged by someone who could not understand him.
He refused to admit that a section of the public still listened
to this madman possessed by the desire "to trample everything that was, with volleys of spit, with grimaces of contempt. . . ." All those who gravitated around the critic were
Dostoevsky's enemies. First of all, Turgenev, that giant with
short thumbs, that effeminate and refined aristocrat who always tried to be witty just to keep in form. Ah! Belinsky had
surely won Turgenev over to his cause and stuffed the
novelist's head with his badly digested socialism, atheism and
occidentalism. "Personally I never liked that man," Dostoevsky wrote about Turgenev, forgetting that the day after
meeting this writer he had said: "I have almost fallen in love

with him." Turgenev, too, wrote: "He hated me even when both of us were young authors at the threshold of our literary careers, although I never did anything to deserve his hatred." Apparently Turgenev had forgotten the *Knight of the Sad Face,* and a thousand other little maneuvers designed to exasperate his rival.

Actually the hostility between Turgenev and Dostoevsky dated from the publication of *The Double.* Only a little while later Feodor Mikhailovich broke with Nekrasov.

"I must tell you," he wrote to his brother, "that I have just had the unpleasant experience of breaking for good with the *Contemporary* in the person of Nekrasov. He reproaches me for having given two stories to Kraevsky to whom I owe money and for not having told him that I had left the *Annals of the Fatherland.* Despairing of getting a story from me within the very near future, he spoke rudely to me and made the blunder of demanding the return of his advance. I took him at his word and promised to pay him before December 15. . . . It is a disagreeable business. . . . At present they are spreading the rumor that I am morbidly proud. . . . Nekrasov is preparing to criticize me very strongly. As for Belinsky, he is so weak that he changes his literary opinions as easily as his shirts. . . ."

Meanwhile new writers appeared on the horizon. Dostoevsky was no longer the young prodigy who had written *Poor Folk.* Since then he had produced several books that had surprised and disappointed the public. He was neither a beginner nor an established writer, and aroused neither sympathetic curiosity nor respect. He was marking time, and was annoyed to hear the steps of those who were climbing behind him. They were being widely discussed now, and their names were legion. Would he lose his head start, would he jeopardize his whole future? That would be too stupid! "A host of young writers have revealed themselves," he wrote to Mikhail. "Some are my rivals and among them the most noteworthy are Herzen and Goncharov. The first has already published something, the second not yet. They are enthusiastically praised. But I still have the advantage and shall hold it forever, I hope. . . ."

Forever! He wrote this to calm Mikhail, but in reality he was afraid. He had his doubts. He might have nothing more to say, perhaps Belinsky and his clique were right in denying his talent, perhaps it would be better if he disappeared. Yet if he had not yet given his measure it was because he worked under wretched material conditions. Poverty is not favorable to inspiration. He was short of money, and that was ruining him. He returned to this thought in every letter. "How terrible it is to have to work for a living! My work cannot bear constraint.". . . "Since our separation I have spent exactly four thousand and five hundred rubles, and have sold one thousand rubles' worth of my merchandise in advance." . . . "As for myself, it is always the same refrain—not a kopek and many debts. I write, but cannot see the end of my work in sight. Boredom, apathy and the feverish hope of something better torture me.". . . "The system of continuous debt advocated by Kraevsky is the sign of my slavery and of literary servitude in general." . . . "If there were no kind people in the world, I would be lost. . . . I live very miserably, and since I left you I have spent two hundred and fifty rubles in cash and three hundred rubles to pay my debts. . . . It was Nekrasov who played the filthiest trick on me by forcing me to pay him back one hundred and fifty rubles in cash. . . ."

Money, money, always money! Dostoevsky did not know

how to earn it, how to use it or how to keep it. He was in a hurry, and all his life he would be in a hurry. He was not at home in this world, and he needed a change of air.

First he changed apartments, once, twice, thrice, moving from one end of St. Petersburg to the other. He made new friends—Beketov, Maikov, Yanovsky—with whom he felt safe, because they loved him without envy or pity. In the literary salon of the Maikovs he watched young couples dancing and danced himself. However, even there he became involved in disputes and misunderstandings, as can be seen from his letter to Madame Maikov on May 14, 1848: "I feel that I left you yesterday on an angry impulse, that I seemed to you ill-mannered. . . . I fear that you judged me to be impulsive (and I recognize the fact that I am), brutal, and driven by some strange idea in the back of my mind. . . . Please understand me: constitutionally weak and nervous, I find it difficult to answer ambiguous questions. . . ."

Friendly gatherings, little dinners that he organized at the Hotel de France, the compliments he received from his intimates, all these were of no avail. He fell ill from exhaustion and nervousness. Dr. Yanovsky tried to treat him, and Dostoevsky visited him every morning. Soon the two men became good friends, and even pooled their funds. Dostoevsky's disease was a strange one. At nightfall he was seized by anguish and experienced "mystical horrors." "It is the most painful fear of something that I cannot define," he says in the *Insulted and Injured*, "of something that I cannot conceive, that does not exist as a fact but that can doubtless materialize at any moment. . . ." The minute details of everyday life acquired a favorable or terrible meaning in his eyes. He was lost in a forest of omens. He believed that he was either consumptive or mad, read medical books and

Gall's phrenology, and asked his doctor to study the bumps
on his skull.

One day in July, 1847, Yanovsky met Feodor Mikhailovich in the street, glassy-eyed, staggering, and leaning on the
arm of an army functionary. He had just had a violent
epileptic fit. Yanovsky took Feodor home in a carriage and
bled him. The blood spattered out, thick and black as ink.
Dostoevsky cried, "I am saved, I am saved." On another occasion, Yanovsky saw Dostoevsky in a public square walking
bareheaded, disheveled, and hilarious, arm in arm with a
soldier. When he saw his friend, Dostoevsky pointed at the
strange soldier, and exclaimed: "Here he is! . . . He will
save me!"

Dostoevsky visited his brother. He planned to go to Italy,
he longed for a shock that would release him from his past,
his present and himself. "I am wriggling about like a fish
under the ice." What if he fell under the wheels of a carriage? Or jumped into the water? Anything was better
than the boredom into which he was sinking further every
day. Why must he go on living? What was he to expect?

"Do you know what it means, not to know where one is
going?" says Marmeladov in *Crime and Punishment*.

Dostoevsky experienced the dreadful feeling of a life without purpose. His path was a blind alley, and he saw a wall
before him—a few steps more and he would be unable to
go on.

3. PRISON

THE CAMPAIGNS OF 1812–14 BROUGHT THE RUSSIAN SOL-
diers to the heart of Europe. Soon the officers of the
occupying armies became familiar with Western culture and
were "conquered by their own conquests." The European
nations, tired of Napoleon's military tyranny, awakened to
a new social life. Secret organizations, such as the Carbonari
and the Tugendbund, multiplied in France, Italy and Germany. When they returned to their native land, the Russians, too, formed societies such as the Northern Union, the
Southern Union and the Slav Union for the abolition of
serfdom and corporal punishment.

These movements were a reaction against the conservative
regime of Alexander I who, though he was not hostile to the

emancipation of the serfs, feared the consequences of sudden liberation. Upon the accession of Nicholas I, the opposition groups unleashed an insurrection that spread throughout the army and led to the bloody riots of December 14, 1825. The Imperial Guard defeated the Decembrists, as the rebels were called, and their leaders were hanged or exiled to Siberia. The revolt was crushed, but the agitation for social reform continued. The czar realized the urgency of the reforms demanded by the Decembrists, but he wanted to introduce them himself and to prevent the revolutionary section of the nobility from interfering in the government of Russia. He initiated a study of peasant problems and at the same time organized active police surveillance of the intellectuals.

Although the new sovereign had proclaimed his "Western modernism" and his solicitude for the welfare of the muzhiks, he remained in the eyes of the intelligentsia the symbol of arbitrary violence and reactionary absolutism. "There was no room to think," as the historian Kikin said. And people had never, at any period, wished more fiercely to think and think. They thought for those who did not think, and against those who prevented them from thinking. People thought alone, in groups, in their own rooms, in salons and on the street; they thought and at the same time decried abstract thinking. The men of the forties despised metaphysics, and focused all their attention on the immediate demands of the people.

"The spirit of our times is such," wrote Belinsky in 1842, "that even the greatest creative energy can cause only temporary surprise . . . if it imagines that the earth is unworthy of it, that its place is in the clouds and that the century-old sufferings and hopes of the people must not disturb its poetic visions and poetic contemplations."

The Occidentalists and the Slavophiles were equally suspect in the eyes of the powers to be. The Occidentalists held that Russia was a backward country, which could be regenerated only by a number of far-reaching reforms on the model of the great Western European nations. The Slavophiles, on the contrary, held that the regime inaugurated by Peter the Great was a clumsy imitation of European governments and that Russia should return to the spirit of the Muscovite era. They dreamed of a church independent of the state, of a Russia profoundly Russian, strictly Russian, self-contained, developing her institutions on the basis of her own traditions. The two opposite parties had only their dissatisfaction in common—and this was not a negligible factor.

Revolutionary books were circulated clandestinely. Students were infatuated with George Sand, Fourier, Louis Blanc. All the intellectuals went to the people without knowing anything about them, everybody dreamed of phalansteries of happy courteous men and women, and everybody's heart melted at the idea of sharing the wealth equally among all classes. Political economy took on a poetic hue and the revolution lost its charnel house odor. Scientific progress allied itself with the dogmas of the Orthodox church. To hitch conspiracies became almost a civic duty in the days of the young university students.

While the Decembrists were of the nobility, the revolutionary groups of the forties were composed of civil servants, students, journalists, writers, and merchants. The lower middle class was in a state of moral fermentation. Revolution was to be not *by* the people, but *for* the people.

One of these insurrectionist groups was founded by Petrashevsky, an ex-student who was an official at the Ministry for Foreign Affairs. Although he was a bureaucrat Petrashevsky wore a black beard and the wide-brimmed hat of a conspirator. Dostoevsky met him in May, 1846, but it was not until a year later that he began to attend the Friday meetings of the society. He went there for want of something better to do, moved chiefly by curiosity. The little frame house, its windows decorated with wood panels, charmed him. A shaky creaking staircase led to the second story, a single room furnished with a sofa covered in cretonne, a few old chairs and a table. A single candle illuminated this intentionally shabby interior—for in reality Petrashevsky was well-to-do, but extremely fond of theatrical effects. He refused to admit that it was possible to talk about the people in a comfortable bourgeois apartment. And who could conceive of a conspiracy hatched in broad daylight or in the bright light of chandeliers?

Actually, there was no question of a conspiracy—at least not yet. Petrashevsky's friends gathered at his home to discuss the latest political and literary news. They sprawled unceremoniously on the sofa and the chairs, unbuttoned their uniforms, drank tea and smoked pipes with long stems and tiny bowls. Among them were Saltykov-Shchedrin, Kaydanov, the Maikov brothers, Plesheyev, Miliutin, Durov, Deboux, Speshnev, and others.

"We did not form an organized society," writes Aksharumov in his *Notes*. "No specific program was studied at those meetings, but the regime was criticized and the existing situation deplored."

Kusmin, another "Petrashevets," says that "every injustice, abuse of power, constraint and arbitrary decree profoundly revolted our souls." And Bogoslov writes: "The only idea we had in common was a reaction against cards and parlor gossip."

All this was quite harmless, as Feodor Mikhailovich ascertained at his first visit. The guests struck him as young, ardent and appealing. The group had a library of forbidden books that Dostoevsky was anxious to read. Furthermore, he felt the need of belonging to a group to end his solitude, of acquiring a set of beliefs, good or bad, by which to live. He came often and took pleasure in these endless discussions. It was clear that society was going from bad to worse and that everything must be reformed. But how?

The "Petrashevsky" did not agree on the proper methods of carrying out the program of French socialism. Aksharumov wanted to leave the czar on his throne but thought that his power should be restricted by a constitution; Speshnev was a partisan of direct action; Petrashevsky floundered about among Fourier's theories, but could not formulate any definite ideas about the future. As for Dostoevsky, he remained skeptical. While recognizing the generous spirit that animated these humanitarian mirages, he doubted the possibility of realizing them in Russia. He thought that the Russians should turn to their own history to find a solution for their problems. Community of goods, and a communal spirit had long prevailed among the people, and the development of these traditions was preferable, in his eyes, to the dreams of Saint-Simon and his disciples. According to Miliukov, "he used to say that life in an Icarian community or phalanstery seemed to him more dreadful and repulsive than hard labor."

Some writers maintain that Dostoevsky was a revolutionary. He never was.

"I have never thought anything more absurd," he explained to the investigating magistrate, "than the idea of a revolutionary government in Russia. All those who know me, know my opinions on this question." He did not desire an upheaval, but an adjustment, not a social transformation, but a sensible evolution toward a more equable regime. "The Russian people will not march in the tracks of the European revolutionaries," he declared. And he would recite to his comrades Pushkin's *Isolation*:

> Will I see, my friend, the people liberated,
> And slavery abolished by a gesture of the czar. . . .

Indeed, the abolition of serfdom, the relaxation of the censorship, the suppression of corporal punishment, all these were eventually to come from the czar. He wrote later, "For the people, the czar is the embodiment of the nation, of its ideals, its faith and its hopes." He believed that the relationship between the czar and his subjects was not that of master and slave, but that of father and child. To kill this mutual love was to kill Russia, but to enlighten and guide it was to work for the universal welfare. One should wait and have faith in the czar and the people.

Meanwhile months went by, and the peasants remained bound to the soil while the police surveillance grew increasingly strict. In various regions the muzhiks rose against the landlords. In 1846, twelve landlords were killed by their serfs; in 1848, eighteen. As against twenty-seven rural insurrections in 1846, there were forty-five in 1848. Almost half the serfs in the Vitebsk government rebelled and marched on St. Petersburg but were stopped halfway by army units.

Echoes of the Revolution of 1848 in France shook the

little circle to its foundations. Dostoevsky began to lose confidence.

"What is to be done if it proves impossible to emancipate the peasants otherwise than by a rebellion?" someone asked.

"Well then, they would have to rebel!" exclaimed Feodor Mikhailovich.

He had become extremely impressionable, disarmed in the face of events by his literary failures and nervous exhaustion. On several occasions he took the floor to stigmatize the cruelty of the landlords or the rigor of military discipline.

"I can still hear him," writes Deboux, "when he told us how an officer of the Finland regiment was made to run the gantlet." And Semenov Tian-Shansky confirms the incident adding: "At such moments, Dostoevsky was capable of going into the street with a red flag."

Feodor Mikhailovich promised to write "indictments" and to read them at the meetings of the group. But he did not keep this promise. He confined himself at most to reciting pages from Derzhavin, Pushkin and Gogol. Meanwhile, his brother Mikhail had resigned from his post and come to St. Petersburg. He was introduced to the "chief conspirer." Mikhail agreed with Feodor that Petrashevsky was an eccentric braggart and a confused play actor unequal to his own ideas, a man who indulged in prophecies when action was needed. Characteristically enough, Petrashevsky tried to form a phalanstery in a woods on his estate, but the muzhiks, who were unfamiliar with the French socialists, burned the building that was the symbol of their own future happiness.

Durov, a mystic and poet, formed a separate group. In the eyes of this gentle and stubborn visionary, socialism was identical with Christianity. Later, Dostoevsky declared to the magistrate that "Durov was religious to the point of absurdity." Nevertheless he joined Durov's group, together with Palm and Plesheyev.

St. Petersburg society knew about these nocturnal meetings and considered them completely insignificant. Senator Lebedev in his *Notes* referred to these young men as "chatterers," "conspiring children," and described their activities as "schoolboy pranks." In 1845, a satirical play on Fourierism, entitled *The Two Egoisms*, represented Petrashevsky under the name of Petoushevsky, and Aksakov under that of Bykakov. Bakunin, the strategist of Nihilism, wrote to Herzen that these groups were "absolutely innocuous and absolutely without arms."

Among this host of timid and harmless young men the enigmatic figure of Speshnev slowly began to emerge. This revolutionist with the thin and beautiful feminine face, the full lips, large deep-ringed eyes and thick curly hair advocated direct action and accepted all its consequences. He thought that any means was justifiable to overthrow the government, including rebellion, skirmishes with the police, and political assassinations. When he was arrested, the following draft of a revolutionary oath was found among his papers: "I, the undersigned, undertake the following obligations: when the central committee decides that the time for insurrection has come, I pledge myself without reservations to take an open and total part in the uprisings and battles, having provided myself with firearms or other weapons. . . ."

This mysterious personage, whom Dostoevsky later called his Mephistopheles, exerted an evil influence on him. Dostoevsky detested Speshnev for his cold irony and unvarnished atheism, but was unable to resist him. Speshnev did not look quite alive. His satanic determination and arrogance discouraged sympathy—one could not love him, one could only

fight against him or submit to him. Dostoevsky submitted
with sorrow, disgust and fear. In a moment of cowardice, he
borrowed five hundred rubles from Speshnev, and then became melancholy, peevish and morose, at the thought of his
debts. When Dr. Yanovsky diagnosed his condition as a
temporary depression, Dostoevsky declared: "No, this frame
of mind will not leave me, but will continue to torment me
for a long, long time. I have borrowed money from Speshnev. . . . At present I am with him, I belong to him. I will
never be able to pay back this sum, moreover he will never
accept repayment in money, that is the way he is. Do you
understand now that I have a Mephistopheles at my side?"

One is led once more to evoke the devils and doubles that
people Dostoevsky's novels. In Speshnev, the revolutionary,
Dostoevsky doubtless saw the hideous end result of his own
liberalism. He himself wanted at most to improve the lot of
the peasants, to revise the censorship laws and draw the
czar's attention to the country's misery, but these ideas were
translated by Speshnev into calls to rebellions and fratricidal
massacre. What was barely suggested by the former was
pushed by the latter to monstrous and absurd dimensions.
And yet there was no break of continuity between them:
Dostoevsky began and led to Speshnev. Speshnev was Dostoevsky distorted, he was Dostoevsky's punishment. Dostoevsky "did not want that"; he would not have accepted the
Russian revolution. In the revolution his generous ideas
served as a label for a bloody and useless parody. Thus his
work, too, had its double.

"Everything that I long ago digested and eliminated as
dirt, you bring to me as something new. How could my soul
produce a clown like you?"

Dostoevsky struggled to withdraw from the circle and

break with this menacing creation but was caught in the toils
of the man. He felt the vertigo of the irretrievable plunge and
lost himself, all the time terribly aware of his responsibility.
It was he who proposed to Speshnev that they form a closed
society of not more than seven members. Speshnev agreed.
There was talk of purchasing an illegal printing press and
disseminating incendiary leaflets among the population.
Philipov drew up a blueprint of the apparatus, and various
parts of it were ordered from different St. Petersburg manu-
facturers. Later the machine was actually set up in the home
of one of the conspirers, where, by a miracle, it was not
discovered during the police investigation.

Dostoevsky not only advocated the formation of a secret
group around Speshnev, he also tried to recruit adherents.
In March, 1849, he went to see the poet Apollon Maikov,
stayed till very late and accepted his comrade's invitation to
spend the night on the little sofa opposite Maikov's bed. As
soon as the friends began to undress, Dostoevsky broached
the subject of revolutionary propaganda. He said, "Petrashevsky is a fool, a mountebank, a chatterer, he will never do
anything serious, but certain of more active friends have
organized a society of which Petrashevsky knows nothing,
and into which they have decided not to admit him."

Maikov refused to join the new group. He wrote in a
letter to Viskovatov: "I showed him the lightheadedness and
risks of this enterprise, and warned him that all of them were
bound to meet certain disaster. Moreover—and this was my
main argument—both of us, I told him, are poets, that is to
say, people devoid of any practical sense, we do not know
how to manage our own affairs, while political activity demands an exceptionally well-developed practical sense. . . .
And I can still see before my eyes Dostoevsky sitting like

dying Socrates before his disciples in his nightgown with his collar unbuttoned, using all his eloquence to explain to me the sacred goal of his ideas, how it was incumbent upon us to save our fatherland, and so on. . . ."

The next day Dostoevsky, upon leaving Maikov, adjured him to keep their conversation secret.

Since February 27, 1848, the officials of the Third Section, created by Nicholas I for the purpose of "seeing to it that the peace and rights of the citizens were not disturbed by a personal power," had been well aware that in the home of the "communist" Petrashevsky "high-school students, free-thinkers, and university students" gathered every Friday. General Count Orlov, chief of the gendarmes, ordered Liprandi, an official of the Ministry of the Interior, to follow up and investigate this affair. For almost a year Liprandi looked for an ideal spy who, to quote his own formula, "must be of an education equal to that of the circle into which he will penetrate . . . and be able to place himself above suspicion. . . ." He finally discovered this rare pearl in the person of Antonelli.

This Antonelli, the son of a painter of Italian origin, a blond man with a big nose, quick, clear eyes and obsequious manners, took courses at the University of St. Petersburg and had a civil service post. He accepted the mission only on condition that his name would not show up in the files. He came to a meeting for the first time on March 11, 1849, a little shy and embarrassed in his conspicuous scarlet waistcoat. He handed out cigars of foreign make, took part in the conversation, advanced liberal ideas and tried to provoke a speech against the government or the church.

"What is he doing here?" Kusmin asked Bogosoglo, who

answered: "Come, come, you know quite well that Mikhail Vasilievich [Petrashevsky] is ready to welcome and shower with kindness anyone who comes in. . . ."

From that day on Antonelli assiduously frequented Petrashevsky's circle and also went to meetings of other members of the group. When he returned home, he carefully recorded everything he had seen and heard in the course of the evening and transmitted his reports to the Ministry of the Interior where Liprandi studied them. The transgressions, however, of the "Petrashevsky" were minor ones—no more than abstract elucubrations and inconsistent criticisms. Antonelli was disappointed, he began to wonder whether the conspirators did not perhaps distrust him or whether they were really only harmless students.

One day Dostoevsky visited Durov, who handed him a copy of Belinsky's famous letter to Gogol, which has been mentioned above. Plesheyev had sent this copy from Moscow. Feodor Mikhailovich showed it to Palm, Mombelli and Ivanov, and promised Petrashevsky that he would read it aloud at one of the Friday meetings. This incident took place in March, 1849, and on April 15, Dostoevsky actually read the letter. Later he denied having given his approval to this message of hatred.

"Can the man who denounced me," he declared to the investigating official, "say to which of the two correspondents I was most attached? At present please take these facts into consideration: would I have read the article of a man with whom I had broken because of differences in our ideas (and this is not a secret, many people know it) presenting it as a breviary, as a formula everyone was bound to follow? As I read it, I strove not to give any indication that I favored one or the other of the correspondents. . . ."

Why did Dostoevsky agree to lend his voice and oratorical talents to read the credo of his enemy? There is no doubt that Belinsky's letter expressed a number of ideas to which Dostoevsky was hostile—attacks against mysticism, against the church, and against the emperor—but it also contained a vehement protest against serfdom and a glorification of the role of the writer which were in line with Dostoevsky's own opinions. Antonelli heard the following statements which condemned both Dostoevsky and his audience:

"The church presents itself as a hierarchy, that is to say, as a personification of inequality, a courtesan of established power, an enemy and a wrecker of brotherhood among men. . . . In most cases our clergy are distinguished only by their round paunches, their scholastic pedantry and their barbarous lack of courtesy. . . .."

"I shall not speak of your panegyric on the love of the Russian people for their sovereigns. I will only say this: your panegyric has not met with agreement from anyone. . . ."

All around Dostoevsky the young men uttered curses, burst out laughing and applauded. Their goose was cooked—Antonelli was already mentally touching up his report.

The following meetings were no less fertile for the secret agent. After a supper with Speshnev, for instance, Dostoevsky attended a reading of Grigoriev's *Tale of a Soldier,* "a subversive story directed against the army and the government." A few days earlier, a dinner had been organized in honor of Charles Fourier at the home of Evrapeus, one of the conspirators. Dostoevsky was unable to attend, but the affair was a success. Petrashevsky, in excellent form, concluded his speech with the following words: "We have condemned the society of our times to death; the problem now is to carry out the verdict." As for little Aksharumov, he demanded in scathing terms: the abolition of property, the family, the state, the laws, the army, the cities and the churches. Then he sat down well-satisfied with his contribution.

When the file was complete with all these disturbing details, General Count Orlov submitted it to Nicholas I. Reading these documents the emperor must have thought of the Decembrists whom he had to exterminate on the very day of his accession to the throne. He had hanged or deported the ringleaders of that rebellion, and now their descendants suddenly loomed before him. He must decidedly put an end to this poisonous infection of occidental ideas! Fearing a recurrence of the riots of 1825 he exaggerated the importance of the conspiracy and resolved to give the culprits an exemplary punishment. He wrote on the margin of the report, "I have read everything, this is a serious affair. Even if all of it were only chatter, it is nevertheless criminal and intolerable. They must be arrested, as you recommend. Go to it, in the name of God, and let His will be done."

Orlov acted accordingly. On April 22, 1849, Major Chudinov of the gendarmes received the order to "arrest at 4 A.M. Feodor Mikhailovich Dostoevsky, retired engineer and writer."

April 22 was a Friday. Feodor Mikhailovich had gone to see Petrashevsky where a plan for publishing a newspaper was discussed. He returned home at four in the morning, tired and drenched by the cold rain, undressed, went to bed and soon fell asleep. An hour later he was awakened by voices and the clank of sabers. Before his blurred eyes was a lighted lamp. The police superintendent of his district, a lieutenant-colonel with well-set epaulettes, stood over him, and a soldier.

"Get up. . . . By order. . . ."

Dostoevsky was bewildered: "But. . . ."

"Get dressed. . . . We are waiting for you. . . ."

The lieutenant-colonel had good manners and a suave voice. Dostoevsky was reassured—this could only be a misunderstanding, he would be questioned and released on the spot. He had committed no crime.

While Feodor Mikhailovich dressed, the intruders carefully thumbed through his books and papers and tied them together with a string. A policeman rummaged in the fireplace with Dostoevsky's pipe. The soldier climbed on a chair to reach the top of the stove, but slipped and fell on the floor. The superintendent noticed a bruised five-kopek coin on the table.

"Could it be counterfeit?" asked Dostoevsky.

"We'll find that out later," grumbled the superintendent, and added the coin to the other evidence. Dostoevsky had dressed in a hurry, and all of them left the disordered room. A carriage waited in front of the door. The landlady and the janitor shook their heads as they watched the police escort their tenant into the streets, deserted, cold and bleak in the first grim light of daybreak.

The coaches arrived at the courtyard of the Third Section where the various accused who had been picked up in every corner of St. Petersburg were identified and sent to several rooms guarded by armed soldiers. Among the glum and sleepy prisoners Dostoevsky recognized some of his friends and first of all his brother Andrey.

"What are you doing here?" They were separated.

An official with a list in his hand gathered the conspirators around him. At the top of the sheet Dostoevsky was able to read the following penciled words: "Agent: Antonelli."

On the same day, Mikhail went to see Miliukov. Mikhail was almost fainting.

"What's the matter with you?" asked Miliukov.

"What? You don't know yet?"

"What?"

"My brother Feodor has been arrested."

"Impossible! When?"

"Last night. . . . His place was searched, and he was taken away. . . . His doors were sealed."

"And the others?"

"Petrashevsky and Speshnev, too, were arrested. . . . I don't know whether there were any others. . . . As for myself I'll be taken tomorrow if not today. . . ."

"Why do you think so?"

"My brother Andrey was arrested. . . . He doesn't know anything. . . . He never went there. . . . He was taken instead of me, by mistake. . . ."

They decided to make the rounds of their friends' apartments. All of them had been arrested, and their doors were sealed. In the meantime, General Count Orlov wrote to Nicholas I: "I have the honor to inform Your Majesty that the arrests have been made and that thirty-four persons with their papers have been handed over to the Third Section."

On April 23, at 11 P.M., the prisoners were transferred to the Peter and Paul Fortress, the somber prison that Peter the Great built in 1718 and in which he imprisoned members of the conspiracy organized by his son, Alexei. In one of the bastions the guilty prince (he disapproved of his father's ideas) was questioned and tortured to death.

The little flock of the "Petrashevsky" were lodged in the vaults of the special prison within the fortress which Czarina Anna Ivanovna built and named the Alexei Ravelin—a strange tribute to the memory of Alexei Mikhailovich. Its first occupant was Princess Tarakanova, the alleged daughter of Empress Elizabeth Petrovna and pretender to the Russian throne. The Decembrists also had been guests of the Alexei Ravelin.

Not all the conspirators of 1849 were sent to the Ravelin. Only those who were considered the most important criminals, so Dostoevsky among them, entered the triangular prison washed by the gray waters of the Neva, passed through its little garden in which the prisoners took their walks and along the dark corridor with its nineteen doors, and the echo of steps recoiling from arch to arch.

The "Petrashevsky's" clothes were confiscated. In a prisoner's uniform—canvas shirts and trousers, and wrappers of coarse military cloth—Dostoevsky entered the dungeon. It was relatively spacious, six yards by three and a half, and furnished with a field bed, straw mattress and pillow, a little table, stool, water jug, and a suet candle attached to the window. The gable window, with its panes smeared with chalk, was heavily barred. A rag screened the tiny spy-hole door that the prisoners called the "eye." This door was opened five times a day: at seven o'clock for tea, at ten for inspection, at noon for lunch (a bowl of soup and a lump of meat), in the evening for dinner, and at nightfall when the guard came to light the candle.

The rest of the time the cell was filled with the enormous silence of stone and space. One could not hear the noises of the city, and even the steps of the sentries seemed to come from another world, another age. Humid air rose from moldy slabs, the flame of the candle grew lower, wavered, and died, and night fell suddenly like a collapsing wall-like death.

Dostoevsky would jump up, holding his head in his hands.

This was the end, he knew that he must sleep, sleep at any price, but his mind worked with feverish lucidity. Was he unhappy? Not at all. In his misfortune he experienced a relief that he would not have dared admit to anyone. For a long time he had realized the urgent need of a disaster, to change the course of his useless, wasted, futile life. His imprisonment had lifted him out of his monotonous existence; the gravity of his misfortune separated him from the rest of mankind; at last he was "exceptional," "irresponsible." Now he could rest, catch his breath. Destiny had played his hand for him. It no longer depended on Feodor Mikhailovich to be a great man or a cipher—he was in the hands of God. Thirty years later someone said to him: "What a sacrilege it was to deport you!" He replied: "Not at all, it was justice. The Russian people would have condemned us. And who knows, perhaps the Almighty on high wanted to send me to prison in order to teach me what is the most important thing of all, without which one cannot live?"

For two and a half months the prisoners were forbidden to write to their friends or to receive mail. Some of the group bore this period of preventive imprisonment very badly. Grigoriev suffered from pronounced neurasthenia; Katenev went insane and was transferred to the hospital where he died soon afterward; Yastzhembsky planned to commit suicide. He writes in his *Memoirs*: "I remained in the Ravelin from April 23 to December 23, and if I had stayed there any longer I would doubtless have lost my mind."

Petrashevsky, too, was deeply shaken. He addressed an incredible complaint to the investigating commission in which he claimed that he was prevented from sleeping by soft rapping on the wall that made him lose his memory, and that whispers came from every corner of his cell, killing in him all sense of personality as well as rational notions of time and space.

Aksharumov pulled a nail out of his bed and spent the greater part of his time sharpening it. "Now I would stand by the window, now walk back and forth in my cage. Often I knelt on the floor and, hiding my face in my hands, spoke aloud and wept; then I jumped to my feet and returned to the window."

Andrey Dostoevsky was released on May 6, 1849; Mikhail Dostoevsky, imprisoned in place of Andrey, was released on June 24. According to the report, "He not only did not commit any crime against the government, but even tried to prevent it."

July brought a great change in the life of the prisoners. They were given permission to read books, to write letters and to receive them.

"My dear brother," wrote Feodor Mikhailovich on July 18, 1849, "I was indescribably happy to receive your letter. I received it on July 11. At last you are free. I can imagine how happy you were to see your family again. You tell me not to lose courage. I have not lost courage. Of course, I am bored and disgusted, but what can I do? . . . As a rule, the time goes by unevenly, sometimes too fast, sometimes too slowly. At times I even feel that I have become accustomed to this life and that nothing matters to me. . . . At present, the days are beautiful and this cheers me a little. But under a rainy sky the casemate is lugubrious. I am not wasting my time: I have planned three stories and two novels. . . . There is a surprising vitality in human nature. Indeed, I would never have believed there is so much, but now I know it from experience."

This miraculous serenity is amazing, considering that

Dostoevsky knew nothing of his future and was unable to communicate with any of his companions. Solitude suited him. He was in better health than for many years. He listened to himself and knew that he was alive. His childhood memories and hope of a speedy release consoled him for his hard, narrow bed, his suet candle and the tread of the sentry in the resounding corridors of his prison.

It was during his captivity that Dostoevsky wrote *The Little Hero*, a story full of sentimental poetry and timidly sensuous. While awaiting the verdict the prisoner told the story of the awakening of the sexual instinct in a child. It was not published until 1857. Meanwhile weeks went by, and the letter Dostoevsky addressed to his brother on August 27 was less cheery than the first.

"As for myself," he wrote, "I cannot say anything for sure. I am still in the same ignorance regarding our case. My life is as monotonous as before, but I have again been granted permission to walk in the garden where there are seventeen trees. This is a piece of happiness for me. Another piece of happiness: I am allowed to have a candle at night. . . . Could you send me a few books of history? That would be fine. But a Bible (both testaments) would be even better. . . . I cannot say anything good regarding my health. For almost a month now I have been living on castor oil. . . . My hemorrhoids cause me even greater suffering, and I feel a pain in my chest, which I never had before. Especially at night my nervousness increases. Recently I have been having endless nightmares; I fancy that the floor is swaying under me as though I were in a ship's cabin. . . ."

On September 14, 1849, he wrote: "I am rather unwell; my stomach torments me, and my hemorrhoids, too. When will all this come to an end? Now the most painful autumn months are approaching and with them, my hypochondria. Clouds cover the horizon; the little corner of blue sky that I used to perceive from my cell insured my health and good humor."

In reality he was at the end of his tether. The total isolation in which he vegetated was slowly destroying him. For diversion he corresponded with Philipov, in the adjoining cell, by tapping on the wall. He had the impression of being in an air chamber, with the vacuum expanding above him, and he could not breathe. He no longer knew whether he was a human being like other human beings. He no longer could place himself in time or space, he did not know whether he was awake or dreaming. As a child he had often placed a little note on his night table saying: "It is possible that today I may fall into a lethargy; please do not bury me before so many days."

Now he was indeed in a lethargy. He was literally buried. He no longer existed.

The investigation dragged on. Interrogations followed one upon another. The prisoners were questioned separately. From time to time, an officer, accompanied by a gendarme, penetrated into the cell, ordered the prisoner to put on civilian clothes, and led him down long, dim corridors to the exit. Then they traversed a courtyard and entered the "White House," where the investigating committee held its sessions.

This committee was composed of five members: Prince Gagarin, Dubelt, chief of the gendarmes, Prince Dolgoruky, General Rostovtsev and General Nabokov, commander of the fortress, who acted as chairman.

Dostoevsky was accused of having taken part in meetings which criticized governmental decrees and the institutions

of censorship and serfdom, of having read to the assemblage
Belinsky's letter to Gogol, "which contained insults against
the Orthodox church and the supreme authorities," and of
having been present at the reading of Grigoriev's *Tale of a
Soldier*, "a revolting text." The members of the commission
tried to trap Feodor Mikhailovich by gentleness (as in the
struggle between Raskolnikov and the investigating magistrate Porphyr). "The emperor will forgive you if you tell
the whole story," Rostovtsev would say. Still Feodor
Mikhailovich kept silent. Then the general jumped from the
seat and left the room, crying: "I cannot look at Dostoevsky
any more."

The investigation went on. Dostoevsky did not deny the
facts, but added: "Who would not be guilty if everybody's
most intimate ideas were investigated, if everybody were
held accountable for what he said among a small group of
comrades. . . ." According to him, the reading of the *Tale
of a Soldier* "took place quite unexpectedly . . . and the
impression it produced was absolutely nil." As for Belinsky's
letter, Dostoevsky admitted that he had acted "lighthead-
edly," in giving it a publicity it did not deserve. He maintained that his "liberalism expressed itself only in his wish to
be useful to the fatherland." On another occasion he said:
"I have never been a socialist, although I always liked to read
and study works relating to social problems."

It was impossible to get from him the slightest accusation
against his companions in misfortune. Indeed, in order to
hasten the release of his brother, he accused himself: "I say
this because my brother met Petrashevsky through me, and
I alone am responsible for this relationship as well as for my
brother's and his family's misfortune. . . . This arrest is a
real blow to him and he is the least guilty of any of us."

The members of the investigating committee were embarrassed by the necessity of defining juridically a crime that had not been consummated. Was there a clearly revolutionary intention in the minds of these chatterboxes, and confused liberals? Where does evolution end and revolution begin?

The investigation lasted for five months; 232 persons, defendants and witnesses, were questioned orally and in writing. Despite Liprandi's repeated accusations, the commission ended by recognizing the innocence of the accused. In their resolution of August 31 they stated: "Neither the strict and sharp surveillance instituted by Liprandi during almost a year of Petrashevsky's activities, nor the numerous cross-examinations of the arrested persons . . . have disclosed the existence of an organized propaganda society."

The Ministry of the Interior demanded a new study of the case, and this time the investigating committee recognized the necessity of punishing the members of the conspiracy, stating that: "The commission holds that the facts which have been revealed deserve the attention of the government."

On September, 1849, the "Petrashevsky case" was placed before a military court. A special commission composed of six civilians and six generals studied the responsibility of twenty-eight young men guilty of crimes against the security of the state. On November 16, this commission sentenced seven prisoners to deportation and fifteen to be shot; the remaining six were released. But this did not end the affair. In violation of all the established judicial rules of procedure the emperor transferred the case to the Auditoriat General, which applied martial law. First, they extended the death sentence to all the accused, and then suggested to the emperor that he commute this sentence to hard labor. The final verdict stated: "Dostoevsky . . . for having harbored

criminal projects and having disseminated the letter of the
writer Belinsky, etc. . . . is sentenced to eight years of hard
labor in Siberia." Nicholas I noted in the margin of this
document: "For four years, the rest as a soldier." But he
demanded that his act of clemency remain secret.

On December 21, 1849, the prisoners still had no inkling
of the punishment that was in store for them. They were no
longer subjected to questioning, and the authorities refused
to make any specific statement concerning their case. They
thought they might soon be released.

On December 22, toward six in the morning, the young
men were awakened by the noise of steps in the corridor,
sharp commands, clicking heels, a sword sheath knocking
against a wall and finally the creak of opening locks. One by
one, the doors of their cells were thrown open; the prison
superintendent handed them their civilian clothes; the prisoners were led to the exit.

A blast of icy air struck Dostoevsky in the face. He
shivered with cold in the foggy light of the dawn. In the
courtyard stood a line of hired carriages about which the
gendarmes' horses pranced with a clatter of horseshoes and
jungling harnesses. Soldiers in blue uniforms darted to right
and left pushing the prisoners into the carriages.

"One in each cab!" someone commanded. Beside each
prisoner a gendarme took a seat. Then a brief command, and
the procession started, escorted by horsemen with drawn
sabers. The prisoners did not know where they were being
taken. Was it to hear the verdict? But then how could they
explain this endless trip, this strange detour?

"Where are we going?" Speshnev asked his escort.

"We are forbidden to tell you," he answered.

A film of hoarfrost covered the window panes of the cabs. The travelers guessed that they had crossed the Neva from the noise of the horseshoes on the floating wooden bridge, then that they were rolling down the cobblestone paved Litneynaya. Speshnev wanted to wipe the white dew from his window, but the gendarme stopped him.

"Don't do that," he said, "or I'll be beaten."

After three-quarters of an hour the cabs stopped, their doors were opened, and the prisoners found themselves on the immense drill field of the Semenovsky Regiment. Snow had fallen during the night, and above the fresh white roofs of the yellow barracks were gray wisps from the gently smoking chimneys. A dense crowd was massed on the edge of the field—bearded merchants with fur collars, women with handkerchiefs tied under their chins, students in military caps, officials with rosettes; altogether three or four thousand people.

In the center of the ground, within a fence, stood a platform of white wood, and in front a square formation of soldiers was drawn up before the scaffold. A little further there were three posts driven into the ground. Dostoevsky recognized Speshnev, serene and contemptuous as ever, Grigoriev, sick with fear, and Petrashevsky. He rushed to them and embraced them. An imperious voice cried, "Stand in a row!"

A black-clad priest holding a cross led the procession. The numbed prisoners stumbled in the soft snow.

"What are they going to do with us?" one of them asked in a low voice.

"They're going to read the verdict. . . . Everybody sentenced to hard labor. . . ."

"But why these posts?"

"They're going to tie us to them. . . . Perhaps they'll shoot us. . . ."

The twenty young men marched past the soldiers and climbed the narrow steps of the scaffold. An officer called the roll of the condemned, and placed nine of the prisoners to the right of the platform, eleven to the left. A gendarme stood behind each prisoner. At the foot of the scaffold a group of bemedaled generals with pompous faces strolled back and forth.

Dostoevsky stood next to Mombelli. He was not grieved, indeed he did not feel that he belonged to the world where this dramatic spectacle was taking place. Suddenly he had an impulse to tell his neighbor about the theme of a new story he had conceived in prison, but he was interrupted by the shouted command, "Attention! Bare your heads!"

No one stirred. The prisoners did not realize that they were the objects of this order. Among the generals another voice said, "Remove your hats! The verdict is about to be read."

Finally the "Petrashevskys" obeyed. They stood bare-headed in the cold that pressed upon their temples and brought tears to their eyes.

The sky was a limpid gray. The steps of the young men had left large soft holes in the thick snow. Crusts of ice gleamed on the tips of their shoes. They felt the hot breath of the gendarmes on their necks. The prosecutor stepped to the center of the platform and read the text of the verdict in a monotonous and rapid voice, enumerated the crimes of which each of the prisoners had been found guilty and ended the exposition with the simple words, "Sentenced to death."

Petrashevsky, Mombelli, Grigoriev, Aksharumov. . . .

The prosecutor had pronounced the sentence nine times. Now he added, "Dostoevsky . . . sentenced to death." Feodor Mikhailovich shuddered, as though awakening from a dream. "Death." At that moment, the sun pierced the fog and illumined the gilded dome of the Semenovsky church. "They won't shoot us!" exclaimed Dostoevsky. Mombelli silently pointed to a cart covered with a thick canvas, under which one could imagine the outlines of coffins. (Actually, the canvas covered a pile of clothes.)

Still Dostoevsky did not understand. He mechanically observed a wart on the cheek of a gendarme and a copper button shining in the sun. He watched—and all his life would remember—the prosecutor carefully folding his papers, sticking them in his pocket, pinching one ear with his fingertips, and slowly descending the steps of the scaffold.

This official was replaced at once by a priest. In a voice choked with emotion he delivered a sermon on the text of St. Paul: "the wages of sin is death." He explained to these unfortunates that nothing ends in this world, and that an eternity of bliss is in store for those who repent. Then he offered them the crucifix to kiss; only Shaposhnikov, a man of the people, asked permission to confess. At the moment no one noticed that the priest did not carry the usual instruments for administering the last sacraments.

Dostoevsky kissed the little silver cross, hard and icy. He straightened himself. Now he could not doubt. The presence of the priest dispelled his last hope—who would dare make a mockery of the church? But the punishment was out of all proportion to the crime. "I do not deserve this." No one deserved it. The injustice lent greatness to the wretches shivering on the wooden scaffolding, it raised them to the rank of martyrs. They realized this and experienced fully the voluptuousness of useless sacrifice. "The affair for which we were tried, the ideas and aspirations that were dear to our hearts, did not arouse in us any feeling of repentance; but it seemed to us that the penalty inflicted upon us would purify us, so to speak, and that our many sins would be forgiven for its sake," Dostoevsky wrote later in his *A Writer's Diary*. The cause which they had discussed in such a disorganized fashion, each pitting his dreams against those of his comrades, frivolous, boastful, deprecating and jeering, now seemed sacred because for it they were to die.

Meanwhile the priest had left the scaffolding. Two men in colored cloaks approached the condemned: the executioners. They had the large hairy hands of professional assassins. The trumpet sounded, the drums beat and their funeral roll echoed against the barrack walls. It grew lower, then began again, insistent, deafening, endless. . . . The conspirators were obliged to kneel. Above their heads the executioners broke swords as a sign of dishonor, then the young men were draped in white canvas robes with long sleeves and hoods. The first three, Petrashevsky, Mombelli and Grigoriev were tied to the posts, and the hangmen drew the hoods over their faces. At a brief command, three squads came forth from the ranks and drew up before the condemned.

Dostoevsky closed his eyes. He was the sixth man and would be in the next group of three. In five minutes he would be tied to the same post. In five minutes he would be dead. A horrible anguish seized him. He must not waste those five minutes! He must make the most of them, extract all their quintessence, all their secret joys, before sinking into eternal light. He divided those five minutes into three parts: two minutes to say farewell to his friends, two minutes for meditation, and one minute to cast a last glance upon the world.

But what could he meditate about, what could he look at? He was twenty-seven years old, fully conscious of his powers and his talent—and now, suddenly, he must die. He existed, he was living, and in three minutes he would be nothing—or something else or someone else. He looked again at the dome of the cathedral and could not detach his eyes from its surface, gleaming with sunlight and gold. It seemed to him that soon there would be nothing left except himself and that serene light, that they would merge, that he would become that light and that peace, that he would dissolve into the unknown. A convulsive fear seized him. "What if I did not die? What an eternity! . . . And all that would be mine! . . . Oh, then I would change every minute into a century, I would not lose a single one, I would keep track of all my instants and would not spend any of them lightly." (*The Idiot.*)

The soldiers loaded their guns and shouldered them. The silence was unbearable. One command: "Fire!" and those three bodies would founder to the ground, ridiculously limp. Then they would be taken away and replaced by three others . . . But why did they not fire?

With perfect self-possession Petrashevsky lifted a corner of his hood to see what was going on. An aide-de-camp waved a handkerchief. Retreat was sounded. The hangmen untied Petrashevsky, Mombelli and Grigoriev and led them back to the platform. The prosecutor stepped forth again and, stammering atrociously, read the commutation of the sentence: "The defendants, who deserved the death penalty in accordance with the law, are pardoned by the infinite clemency of His Majesty the Emperor. . . ."

So it was to be hard labor and exile. Joy descended on Dostoevsky like a huge, concrete mass. He was saved! Nothing else mattered. Twenty years later he said to his wife, "I cannot recall any day as happy as that one."

Some of his companions, however, were so exhausted by their emotions and so disgusted by this farce that they longed for the death they had escaped. Grigoriev was livid and trembling. His teeth chattered. In those few moments he had gone insane.

At first it was doubted that this odious comedy had been approved by the czar. We know now that he organized it down to the last details. For two days a lively correspondence had gone on among the various government offices involved—how many cloaks were needed? How many posts? Was it necessary to dig graves? Were the condemned to be tied and blindfolded? Nicholas I wanted to teach the young "hotheads" a salutary lesson, but he overstepped the bounds and killed their repentance instead of arousing it.

The memory of this false execution remained alive in Dostoevsky's works. He wrote in *The Idiot*, "there are men to whom the death sentence was read, who were allowed to suffer horribly and who then were told: 'Go away, you are forgiven!'" In the same novel Prince Myshkin relates a scene analogous in every detail to the one which took place on the Semenovsky training grounds. And in *A Writer's Diary* Feodor Mikhailovich wrote: "Do you know what a death sentence means? He who has not grazed death cannot understand it."

No, he would not forget, he would never forget. The hangmen now proceeded to remove the hooded shrouds from the condemned. They were given sheepskins, felt boots and fur hats. Iron smiths mounted the scaffold and approached

Petrashevsky. He was to be sent to Siberia at once. Someone threw up a bundle of chains that clanked on the platform. The smiths fixed them to Petrashevsky's ankles, and he calmly helped them in their work. Then he embraced his companions in misfortune, and supported by two gendarmes descended the staircase, dragging his chained feet. He was hoisted into a carriage. The whip cracked, and the carriage split the crowd which closed ranks again as soon as it passed.

The condemned were shivering with cold. Someone said, "Rub your nose"; another, "Rub your cheek, it is frost-bitten." Kashkin and Palm fell to their knees and prayed.

"The good monarch. . . . Long live the Emperor!" murmured Palm. Then the hired carriages brought the condemned back to the fortress.

Upon their arrival a physician examined them to find out whether their faculties had been affected by the shock. Once again, alone in his cell, Dostoevsky wrote the following letter to his brother:

"My brother, my dear friend:

"Everything is decided. I am sentenced to four years at hard labor (I think at Orenburg) and then to serve as a soldier. . . . I have just been told that we will be sent away today or tomorrow. I asked to be allowed to see you, but was told it was impossible. . . . My brother, I am not dejected, I have not lost courage. Life is life everywhere, life is in us and not in the world that surrounds us. There will be people near me, and to be a man among men, and to remain one forever, under whatever circumstances, not to weaken, not to fall, that is what life is, that is the real meaning of life. I have realized this, and this idea has entered into my flesh, my blood. . . .

"Perhaps we shall see each other again, my brother. Take

care of yourself, try to live, for God's sake, until our next meeting. Perhaps one day we shall be able to embrace each other and recall our beautiful past existence, our youth, and our hopes that I must now uproot from my bleeding heart, to bury them. . . . Will I ever take up writing again? I think I will be able to, in four years. If I were forbidden to write, I would die. Fifteen years in prison would be preferable if one could have a pen in one's hand. . . .

"If anyone has retained a bad memory of me, if I quarreled with anyone, if I made an unfavorable impression upon anyone, tell them when you meet them to forget their grievance. There is no wickedness, no hatred in my heart. I should like so much to love and embrace my companions at this moment. When I look at the past, when I think of all the time I wasted, of all the time I lost in errors, mistakes, futilities, because of my ignorance of life, blood surges to my heart. I will change for the better. That is my entire hope, my entire solace.

"Ah, when will I see you, when will I see you? Farewell, I am tearing myself away from everything, from everything that was lovable. It is hard to leave all that. It is hard to break oneself in twain, to tear one's heart in twain. Farewell, farewell! But I will see you again, I am sure of it, I hope it.

"Don't change, love me, remember me, and the thought of your affection will be the greatest joy of my love. Farewell! Once again, farewell! Farewell, to everybody!"

On December 24, on Christmas Eve, Dostoevsky was to be sent to Siberia. His brother Mikhail and the writer Miliukov obtained permission from the governor of the fortress to see him before his departure. The meeting took pace in a large bare room, on the ground floor of the governor's house at dusk with only one lamp to light the room.

Mikhail and his companion had been waiting for half an hour when Feodor Mikhailovich and Durov were led in. The two convicts were calm, relieved and smiling. Miliukov writes, "Witnessing the farewells exchanged between the Dostoevsky brothers, I should say that the one who remained in St. Petersburg suffered more than the one who was scheduled soon to leave for hard labor in Siberia. The elder brother's eyes were dimmed by tears, his lips twitched nervously, while Feodor Mikhailovich was calm and tried to comfort him. 'Please stop this, my brother,' he said, 'you know me, I am not descending into my grave, and this is not my funeral. Those whom I will find in the penal colony are not beasts, but human beings, perhaps better than myself, perhaps superior to me. . . . And after I leave the penitentiary I will resume writing. I have experienced a great deal in these last months; I will see and experience much more out there. I will have something to write about. . . .' "

This man who only a few months before, when he was free, imagined that he was afflicted with all sorts of illnesses, suffered from nocturnal fears, was constantly offended and hurt, always quarreling and panic-stricken for no reason at all, now accepted with serene courage the ordeal of the gallows and separation from his loved ones. That this physical and moral invalid did not fear four years of cold, hardship and severe labor is not surprising. For Dostoevsky was a man of unbalanced emotions who felt at ease only in exceptional circumstances, and breathed well only in a storm. Later in *Notes from the Underground*, he wrote, "As for myself, in my life I pushed to the extreme what you yourselves only half-dared. . . . Thus I am perhaps more alive than you."

Half an hour later the officer on duty led the prisoners back to their casemates, and exactly at midnight the guard fixed ten-pound chains to Dostoevsky's ankles. Then Feodor, together with Durov and Yastzhembsky, was taken out to the courtyard where open sleighs, troikas, were waiting for them. The cortege was headed by the closed coach of the ministerial courier who was to escort them as far as Tobolsk. In the clear, cold night the horses breathed gray steam.

Mikhail Dostoevsky and Miliukov stood at the gate of the prison.

"Farewell," they shouted to the prisoners.

"Good-by," answered the condemned men.

The troikas glided along the quiet streets beneath the lighted windows. Behind the panes pine trees glowed with candles and silver toys. Shadows danced behind the curtains. Dostoevsky loved Christmas; people were happy, they laughed, ate, drank and played with their children. None of them suspected that at that very moment three men huddled in hired troikas, frozen, exhausted and lost, were leaving St. Petersburg for the Siberian penitentiaries.

In 1854, Dostoevsky wrote to his brother: "I began to look with curiosity at St. Petersburg as we traversed it. . . . We passed your house. Kraevsky's house was brightly illumined, and it was at that point that I became mortally sad. You yourself had told me about the Christmas tree there and that Emilia Feodorovna was supposed to bring the children to see it; and it seemed to me that I was saying farewell to them. How I longed to see them, and how many times afterwards, for several years, did I evoke them with tears in my eyes!"

It was a difficult trip. The troikas were open, and the convicts' short sheepskins were inadequate as a protection against the cold. After a few stops at postal relays, the cortege came to a halt before an inn at Schliesselburg. It was daybreak. Dragging their chains and blowing upon their numb fingers, the young men sat down in the inn to drink a few glasses of tea. "I was cheerful," writes Dostoevsky. "Durov talked incessantly. As for Yastzhembsky, he saw the future in black colors."

The ministerial courier, "a worthy and experienced old man," agreed to procure covered sleighs for his prisoners. He also promised to stop for a longer time at each relay, and to pay half the cost of the comforts they demanded. The cortege set out again in full daylight. In honor of Christmas Day the drivers put on their coats of gray German cloth with scarlet belts. The villages were deserted, the roofs bent under the weight of the snow. Against the blue-green sky, the branches of the trees were motionless, as though caught in ice. The ten-hour stages exhausted both the horses and the travelers. The cold was becoming unendurable—in the Perm region it reached forty below zero.

The crossing of the Urals was hideous. Blinded by a raging blizzard, the horses tottered and the sleighs sank in the snow. The travelers were forced to get out in the night to disentangle the runners, calm the beasts and smooth out the road before them. The snow lashed their faces and hands. The dim light of the lantern flickered, ready to die out at any moment. Dostoevsky writes, "Around us, snow, a blizzard; before us, Siberia and our unknown future; behind us, all our past. It was sad, I wept."

On January 11, 1850, after eighteen days of traveling, the deportees arrived in Tobolsk, which at that time was the redistribution center for all prisoners sentenced to hard labor. As soon as they got off their sleighs, the three young men were led to the office of the prison administration. In this

somber and filthy building they saw copyists wearing the
convict's garb and branded with infamous letters on their
foreheads. Their nostrils were cut, their cheeks marked with
scars, and they scratched away at the registers with the intent
air of high-school boys.

"Are these men chained?" asked the prison superintendent.
"Yes."
"Then, search them."

The prisoners' pocket money and a bottle of rum that they
had bought on the way were confiscated, then they were led
to the prisoners' hall, "a dark, narrow, cold, dirty room,"
furnished with field cots covered by straw bags. A smell of
decayed meat and frozen filth hung in the air that was riddled with shouts, curses and laughter. When these noises
abated one could hear the steps of the sentry behind the door.

Durov's hands and feet were numbed by the cold; Yastzhembsky's nose was frostbitten; Dostoevsky was suffering
from scrofulous abscesses in his mouth. In a feverish activity,
the convicts who occupied the room were preparing for the
last stage of their journey. Their chains were adjusted, their
heads were shaven and ignominious marks were branded on
their forearms and shoulder blades. These marks had various
and mysterious meanings. "KAT" designated those condemned to hard labor; "SK," the deportees, and "SB," those
who had attempted to escape. For each attempt the prisoner
received an additional mark starting from the elbow. This
job was done by the convicts themselves, who performed it
with a serious, frowning face.

This was more than the young conspirators could bear.
Yastzhembsky began to lament in a loud voice. He spoke of
suicide. "I thought of what my sister would have said if she
had seen me there." Dostoevsky comforted him. Soon they

obtained permission to drink some tea and smoke the cigars that Feodor Mikhailovich had managed to conceal from the prison superintendent.

Dostoevsky and his companions stayed in Tobolsk for ten days. In this city there were several Decembrists, released from the penitentiary but made to stay in exile in Siberia; among them Frantsev and Fonvizin. Their wives belonged to charitable societies which did everything they could to ease the misery of the prisoners who were detained for a short period in the municipal prison. When the revolutionaries of 1825 learned of the arrival of others who like themselves had had faith in the "cause of freedom," and had fallen victim to a summary justice, they were deeply moved and tried to encourage the new prisoners. Their wives brought food and wine to the young men and asked the superintendent to arrange a meeting with them in his house.

In *A Writer's Diary*, Dostoevsky wrote, "We saw those great martyrs who had voluntarily followed their husbands to Siberia. Innocent of any fault, they endured the same tortures as their husbands for twenty-five years." The interview lasted an hour. Before leaving the wives of the Decembrists gave the convicts their blessings and handed to each of them a copy of the Gospel, the only book allowed in the penal colony. Dostoevsky kept this souvenir for the rest of his life. When the visitors had departed, he examined the volume in his hands. Its binding was split and inside it there were ten rubles in assignats.

On January 16, Dostoevsky and Durov left Tobolsk for Omsk. "Treat them without favor," the governor of Western Siberia wrote in his accompanying order. Seven versts from Tobolsk the sleigh stopped in an open field. Madame

Fonvizin and Madame Frantsev had bribed the guards and gained permission to say farewell to their protégés. They were there waiting, little black figures lost in the snow. The meeting was short—just a handshake and a few words of comfort, "We have written to Omsk; you will be taken care of, some friends of ours will try to lighten your woe."

The guards who stood only a few paces away were becoming impatient. The two women made the sign of the cross over the heads of the prisoners. "May Christ be with you." Dostoevsky and Durov climbed into the sleigh. The driver clicked his teeth, and the cortege drove off amidst the tinkling of bells, over the long white road to *The House of the Dead.*

4. EXILE

ON JANUARY 23, 1850, AFTER THREE DAYS OF TRAVELING
through snow and wind, Dostoevsky and Durov
reached their destination, the fortress of Omsk, a desolate
pile of buildings surrounded by an embankment with fifteen
hundred oaken posts. Near the entrance stood the Administration Building, the Engineering Office and Military Head-
quarters, beyond them, ancient barracks built of badly
sawed-off logs, and still farther, the kitchen, the garage and
the barn. In the center of the courtyard a large empty space
served as an assembly ground for the convicts.

The commandant of the garrison was a brute called Major
Kryvtsov, but the convicts nicknamed him "Vaska Eight

Eyes," because nothing could escape his sharp gaze. Stupid, conceited and cruel, he was madly intoxicated with power as well as alcohol. When he entered the prisoners' barracks with blazing eyes and foaming mouth, even the most hardened criminals were seized by panic as though they were little boys. He did not mind getting up in the middle of the night to inspect his lamentable cattle. Taking an unsteady stance in the middle of the dormitory, this disheveled drunkard would scold the convicts for *their* drunkenness. Dostoevsky wrote to his brother, "Sometimes he abused a convict for not sleeping on his right side or for crying or raving during his sleep." And the punishment was always lashes.

Kryvtsov studied and judged the prisoners' complaints, and each month he wrote a report on the behavior of his charges. This creature was empowered to lighten a prisoner's lot or to kill him by obliging him to do work that was beyond his strength. Once he had ordered one hundred blows with a stick for a fifty-year-old Pole, a former university professor, solely because this unfortunate had declared upon his arrival, "We are not bandits, we are political prisoners."

When Dostoevsky and Durov were introduced to Kryvtsov on the day of their arrival, they saw before them a swollen fellow with bleary eyes, a mottled nose and heavy purple cheeks.

"What is your name?"

"Durov."

"And yours?"

"Dostoevsky."

"Sergeant. . . . Take them to the prison at once and have them shaved at the guardhouse, civilian style, that is to say, half their heads. Their chains will be changed tomorrow. . . . Take off their clothes. Leave them only their linen if it is white. All the rest to be sold at auction. A convict has nothing that is his own. And look out, both of you, behave yourselves! Don't let me catch you in any offense or else . . . corporal punishment. . . . For the slightest transgression, lashes!"

That afternoon the prison barber carried out the major's orders. Dostoevsky's skull was shaven on half its surface, he was shorn of half his mustache and the whole of his beard. This operation which was repeated each week was a real torture, for the barber's razor was no sharper than a piece of tin. The blade did not cut but grated the skin till it bled, roughly tearing loose the hair. The men writhed on the stool, roared with pain and threatened to rebel. Later, a convict who had his own instruments shaved Dostoevsky for the price of one kopek.

The convicts' garb consisted of gray trousers, a coat half black and half gray with a yellow patch on the back, a short sheepskin and a cap without a visor. Let the reader imagine for a moment Dostoevsky, "the writer of the future," the intimate of the Maikovs, the young man who had been in love with Avdotia Panaev, dressed in this clownish fashion with his skull naked and bluish on one side and covered with bloody hair on the other, with a half mustache on his face and chains on his feet, amidst a horde of laughing, cursing brutes.

"No one here could surprise anyone," he wrote in *The House of the Dead.*

Among these living dead the diversity of crimes was matched only by the diversity of races: Cherkassians, Jews, Mongols, Ukrainians, Poles, Muscovites, thieves, counterfeiters, murderers, parricides, political prisoners. . . . There

was one Mikhailo who had killed his master with an ax—for
the *barin* had kidnaped the unfortunate's young bride only
a few hours after the wedding. This same Mikhailo had dis-
emboweled a guard as a result of a "misunderstanding." He
was quite young and peaceful, and gentle as a girl. Another,
Aristov, condemned for blackmail, spied on his companions
in misery and sold them vodka and cards. A young moun-
taineer had helped his brother rob an Armenian merchant,
and a striped murderer had killed a five-year-old child after
luring him with toys.

Some were unconcerned about their crimes and never discussed them; others were tormented by remorse and burned
with the desire to confide in someone. But among them all
there prevailed a strict rule: "It is forbidden to tell *that.*"
They displayed a kind of coquetry in their denial of curiosity. The newly arrived prisoners soon realized that their
adventures could not surprise anyone here. These people
were blasé, hardened. They considered the status of a convict
honorable, everyone was supposed to have earned it and to
be proud of it. They did not consider obedience to the orders
of the penitentiary guards humiliating—they looked upon it
as part of the bargain the convict had made with public
authorities.

"The penitentiary and hard labor do not improve the
criminal," wrote Dostoevsky, "they simply punish him and
guarantee society against possible further crimes on his part."
Among this hideous fauna of thieves, informers and murderers, Dostoevsky was to spend the four most fruitful years of
his life.

As soon as night fell guards locked the door of the barracks, a huge frame building, dilapidated and icy. The rotten

floor was covered with a thick and shiny layer of filth. The small casement windows were green with mud in summer, and clouded with hoarfrost and snow in winter. The ceiling oozed dampness. Sudden drafts penetrated the loose boards of the walls.

"We were squeezed in like herring in a barrel," Dostoevsky wrote to his brother. "In vain did we put ten logs in the stove, there was no heat (ice could hardly melt in the room), only unbearable smoke. The convicts washed their clothes in the rooms, and there were puddles of water everywhere, one did not know where to set one's foot down. From nightfall till day it was forbidden to go out for any excuse whatsoever, and at the entrance a bucket was placed for the purpose you may guess; all night long the stench was suffocating. The convicts stank like pigs. 'Since we are living beings,' they said, 'how can we help being piggish?' Two bare boards served us as beds. For blankets we had only our short coats that left our feet uncovered; all night long we shivered from cold. The bedbugs, lice, and other insects could be counted by the bushel. . . ."

As soon as the steps of the guards died out in the night, the convicts organized parties—drinking bouts, card games, quarrels. Certain convicts, nicknamed "innkeepers," specialized in the sale of vodka which helpers got from the "outside" in the course of their work and brought it into the penitentiary, wrapped around their bodies in oxen's bowels. This alcohol was then diluted by various processes. One had to drink a considerable quantity of it in order to get drunk, but it somehow flattered the vanity of the prisoners.

Card games were forbidden in the prison, but certain convicts agreed to keep watch in the entrance hall and warn the others of the major's approach; they answered with their

backs for the slightest oversight. Quarrels were frequent,
noisy and of epic violence. Some of the prisoners were
famous for their vocabulary of curses. Various groups of
convicts whistled and shouted to spur on their favorite
champions in contests of obscene eloquence. Dostoevsky
writes, "Later I learned that this kind of spectacle—perfectly
innocent—took place only for the purpose of general entertainment."

Sometimes brawls broke out, brutal and stupid. Then at
last the convicts fell asleep, and while the flickering light of
the candles gradually died out, the vast room was quiet
except for the noise of snoring and the rattling of chains.
Amidst this animal odor, intense cold and ignoble din, Dostoevsky tried to sleep and forget. His mate's hand was hang-
ing from the upper bunk and would doubtless rummage in
Feodor's pockets the moment he was asleep. To the right
someone groaned in a dream, another coughed and sniffled
and spat with horrible hiccups, a third got up like a somnambulist and went to the bucket. Feodor Mikhailovich,
drowning in this mass of tortured flesh and dulled thought,
touched the Gospel of the Decembrists' wives and kept it
under his coat.

At daybreak a drum sounded the reveille. An officer
opened the door of the barracks, and a blast of sharp air
rushed into the room, struggling with the stench of unclean
bodies and raising a whirlwind of milky dew from the floor.
The prisoners sat up on their cots, numb with cold and
grumbling with fatigue. Some made the sign of the cross,
others abused each other. The scene was illumined by a suet
candle.

Later, amidst the slow tinkling of chains, the prisoners
flocked around pails of water. Each in turn grabbed the cup,

poured some water into his mouth, rolled it from one cheek to another, spat it out on his hands and washed his face with it. Dostoevsky stood in line, stamping his feet and blowing on his cold hands.

The food was execrable—bread and cabbage soup with rare bits of meat. On holidays the convicts received a bowl of grits; during Lent, sauerkraut with water. Dostoevsky writes, "No more than ourselves could the ordinary convicts satisfy themselves with this diet, all of them engage in trade inside the barracks to earn a few kopeks. As for myself, I drank tea and sometimes was able to buy a piece of meat. That was what saved me. Moreover it would have been impossible to do without smoking in that suffocating atmosphere. But one had to hide to do it."

Dostoevsky and Durov were received by their prison companions with suspicion. The new convicts were educated people, nobles, and therefore regarded as enemies. Moreover, their crime seemed incomprehensible. Whom had they killed or robbed? "They would have eaten us," writes Dostoevsky, "if they had been given the opportunity. And what protection could we hope for, when we had to live, eat, drink, and sleep with these people for several years? We had not even time to complain of all their offenses, they were so numerous. 'You are nobles with sharp claws, you used to belabor us. Formerly you were gentlemen, you made the people suffer, and now you are less than the least among us,' such was the theme of their reproaches for four years."

Feodor Mikhailovich who wanted to win the sympathy of his comrades suffered from their hostility and malice more than the others. With patient good will he tried to be like them, to accept their ideas, quarrels and demands. But the convicts felt that he was overstepping the bounds, that since he craved their friendship he must be unworthy of it.

One day the convicts, dissatisfied with their food, decided to submit their grievances to Major Kryvtsov. Dostoevsky joined the group, but they shouted at him, "What are you doing here?" . . . "He, too, has come out of his hole." . . . "Look at that killer of flies!" . . . "Don't you eat your own stuff in the kitchen?"

"But among you too," argued Dostoevsky, "there are some who eat separately and who nevertheless are protesting. . . . We should all of us be together, in a comradely spirit. . . ."

"Ugh, how could you be our comrade?"

Dostoevsky was forced to withdraw. He wrote that "two hours after his arrival in prison, every new convict is considered the equal of the others. But this is not the case with an educated man. However just, kind and intelligent he may be, he will be hated and despised for years on end. . . ."

It is true that there were among the convicts a few intellectuals of Polish origin, sentenced to hard labor for their part in the insurrection. They were Professor Jadowski, nicknamed "the saint" by the convicts because he prayed frequently, Boguslawski, "the sick man," and Tokarzewski and Mirecki who had been lashed with sticks before being deported to Siberia. But they did not really like or understand Dostoevsky. Inflamed by a nationalism that fed on hatred of Russia and the Russians, they made it a point to proclaim this hatred on every occasion. They refused to recognize in Feodor Mikhailovich a socialist, a democrat, or even merely a pioneer of freedom, and considered him a weakling, lacking in pride. They refused to admit that a man who had been sentenced for endangering the safety of the state, who by the emperor's expressed will was being subjected to hard labor, exile, cold, misery and the odious promiscuity of convicts, should forbid himself the slightest complaint against the central authorities and proclaim the Messianic role of a monarch and a people who had unjustly disavowed him. Such submissiveness in the face of injury, such placid acceptance of the worst human suffering, such humility and delight in humility seemed to them an irritating and absurd pose.

And yet Dostoevsky was sincere when he claimed that he felt no resentment against those who had ruined his life. He believed that there are blows so hard that any riposte is ridiculous; that there are mysterious signs which a man must obey because they bring him back to his true and wretched dimensions. He is agitated, he writes, he chatters, and then suddenly an enormous hand swoops down upon him, a powerful voice drowns out his cries, and he is nothing, and happy to be nothing, to belong to himself no longer, to let someone else play the hand for him, win and lose for him, prepare for him a future either of joy or of sorrow. What foolish vanity it is always to demand the leading role! What impudence, always to try to defeat fate! Sometimes the presence of God is so obvious, so terrible and so sweet, that it cuts one off from his own life. This feeling can last a few moments, a few hours or a few days, then it is as though the leash slackened and one is again responsible. Man's real tragedy begins when he must act and be self-reliant.

Such sudden fits of sleep in the midst of events, followed by painful awakenings, are familiar to all of Dostoevsky's characters because he knew them himself. Raskolnikov after killing the old usurer feels paralyzed, constrained, *excused*, as though someone had ordered him and he could make no

resistance, "as though he were being led out to be executed
. . . as though one end of his coat were caught in the toils
of a machine, and he were being dragged away along with
it . . ." But after the deed is done the teeth of the machine
relax their grip, the individual regains a foothold on everyday existence, stirs his limbs and at last is free. Free and condemned—for he now depends only upon himself—and flees,
although no one is pursuing him.

Dostoevsky was able to pass victoriously through the ordeal of the penitentiary because he had accepted it from the
beginning. He could become himself once more because he
had renounced being himself for a time. He could conquer
because he had accepted the alternative of losing.

Dostoevsky was in the second section of convicts, composed of serfs and subject to the military authorities. It was
considered worse than the first, assigned to mining, and the
third, assigned to road building, because it was organized
like a disciplinary battalion. "Always in chains, always under
escort, always under lock and key."

Every day the convicts were sent to do hard labor, to carry
rocks, turn milestones or cut alabaster. Dostoevsky wrote to
his brother, "The work was hard. Sometimes I worked, exhausted before I began, in bad weather, in rain, in mud or
in the unbearable cold of winter. One day I had to do an
extra job for four hours; the mercury in the thermometer
was frozen; the temperature was forty below zero; I had a
frostbitten foot."

His favorite task was transporting bricks from the banks
of the Irtysh River to the barracks. "I liked this exercise, although the rope that held the bricks constantly cut into my
shoulders. It was pleasant to think that I was thus increasing

the strength of my muscles." In the beginning he could lift only six bricks weighing twelve pounds, then ten and finally a good dozen.

Before the convicts the river flowed, powerful and calm. Above the steppe that extended as far as one could see, the air was fresh. From the other side of the river came the sound of Kirghiz songs. In the distance one could see a skin tent from which smoke rose gently, and a Kirghiz woman tending her sheep. Everything suggested freedom, flight and the simple easy life. There were flowers in the cracks of the rocky bank, and the men's hearts were heavy at the thought of everything they had lost.

Feodor Mikhailovich also liked to clear the snow from the yards of the municipal buildings. The shovel plunged into the soft mass and vanished as far as the wooden handle. A slow pressure and a lump of white powder left the ground on the wet, old sheet of iron. Then again, the shovel entered the gleaming mass. It was impossible to think about anything, he could forget the chain that bound his chafed ankles. For an instant he could imagine himself free. But soon a command resounded, and the convict was compelled to join the ranks and return to the barracks. Sometimes a passer-by, seized by compassion, handed a couple of kopeks to one of the prisoners as they marched to their quarters.

Except for Major Kryvtsov, the local authorities favored Dostoevsky. Because of his precarious health, and doubtless also as a result of the intervention of his friends in St. Petersburg and Tobolsk, he was one day summoned to work at the Administration office where he experienced three months of relaxation and animal comfort. But Colonel Martens decided that a political prisoner could not properly be employed at clerical work, so Dostoevsky rejoined the horde of his comrades.

The noncoms of the prison guard were former Baltic sailors degraded to the ranks and sent to Siberia because they had mutinied at the Navy School. A year later they were promoted to the ranks of noncoms and assigned to supervise prisoners who did light jobs inside the prison. Sometimes the "little sailors," as they were nicknamed, selected the convicts for these light jobs, and as often as they could they chose Dostoevsky. The Administration closed its eyes to such innocent infractions to the regulations.

One day Dostoevsky stayed in the barracks to work in the guardhouse. Suddenly Major Kryvtsov entered the room and found Feodor Mikhailovich lying on his cot. He began to shout: "What does this mean? Why is he not at work?"

"He is sick," said the sailor on duty.

"Nonsense! I know you always protect him! To the guardhouse! Give him lashes!"

While preparations were being made for carrying out this order, the sailor succeeded in warning the commandant of the fortress. General De Grave came to the prison and publicly forbade Major Kryvtsov to subject sick prisoners to corporal punishment. Kryvtsov listened to the reprimand standing at attention and purple with rage.

Troitsky, the chief physician of the prison hospital, also was kind toward Dostoevsky. He often received Feodor in the hospital after a summary examination and allowed him to rest there for several days. Dostoevsky would put on a gown filthy with pus and dried mucus, a dirty cotton cap, and worn slippers. Everywhere on the walls and on the sheets were suspicious stains of crushed bedbugs and vomit.

A fetid smell pervaded the place. At night a bucket was placed in the room, although there was a toilet in the corridor, two steps from the door.

A night lamp cast its dim light on the tormented bodies that yearned for sleep. The lashed convicts moaned in childish voices. Sometimes the noncom on duty sent for a smith to unchain a dead patient.

Troitsky's wife sent tea, sometimes even wine, and the French newspaper *Le Nord* to Feodor Mikhailovich. This was discovered by one of Troitsky's colleagues who reported this indulgence to St. Petersburg. A court councilor was sent from Tobolsk to Omsk to investigate, but he was unable to obtain any formal proof, and the case was forgotten. To the councilor's question, "Have you written anything while in prison or during your stay at the hospital?" Dostoevsky answered, "I have not written anything, but I am gathering material which I will use later."

"Where is this material?" asked the councilor.

"In my head," answered Dostoevsky.

Actually his papers were concealed under the pillow of the medical assistant on duty.

One day a gang of convicts were busy demolishing an old ship at the river bank. Rozhnovsky, one of the gang, dropped his ax in the water. The guard ordered him to go after it. Grumbling, Rozhnovsky undressed, tied his chains and plunged into the water. Dostoevsky and one of his companions held him with a rope. But the major, drunk as usual, appeared on the scene and shouted, "Let no one stop working! Drop the rope, he must manage by himself!"

Neither Dostoevsky nor his comrade obeyed. Kryvtsov

turned purple with rage. His fat cheeks trembled. He ordered, "Take them to the guardhouse immediately after work!"

That night Dostoevsky returned to the barracks pale, haggard and with his mouth strangely distorted. Later, in the middle of the night, the convicts were awakened by a barking cry, as of a wild beast. Dostoevsky was rolling on the floor shaken by an epileptic fit and knocking his head against the wall. He had to be tied with a rope.

Opinions differ as to whether Dostoevsky was really flogged by order of Kryvtsov or whether the whole episode is only a legend. The flogging of a nobleman was an unusual event. When the Polish noble Jadowsky was forced to run the gantlet, the whole town of Omsk heard about it and condemned the major's absurd cruelty. But there is no specific information about the alleged whipping of Dostoevsky. Dr. Yanovsky writes, "I have never heard anything of the kind, either from Feodor Mikhailovich or from his brother Mikhail with whom I often discussed the matter quite openly. . . ." (Letter to Maikov, March 12, 1881.)

Baron Wrangel writes no less emphatically. "I can affirm on Feodor Mikhailovich's own authority that neither at the penitentiary nor during his service as a soldier, was there a commander or a convict or a soldier who raised his hand against him."

Dostoevsky's daughter also declared in a letter to the editor of *The New Times*, "I do not know the origin of the absurd and baseless literary legend concerning the corporal punishment inflicted upon my father at the penitentiary."

It is beyond doubt, however, that the ordeal of hard labor developed Dostoevsky's propensity to epilepsy. While his first attacks date from the period of his father's death, and while he was shaken by more or less violent fits during his first years in St. Petersburg, it was at the penitentiary that his epilepsy assumed its true proportions. Miliukov notes, "Before his return from Siberia I did not suspect anything of the kind; but after he came back to St. Petersburg, his disease was no longer a secret to anyone."

In March, 1852, the commanding general of the Omsk fortress requested the authorization of his superiors to change the classification of Dostoevsky and Durov and to release them from their chains. This request passed through the whole penal hierarchy before reaching the emperor who refused to grant it. And life went on, weary and monotonous, each day like the preceding one, "as one drop of water is like another drop of water."

Before holidays the convicts were led to the bathhouse, a tiny, overheated room filled with white vapor. In it a hundred convicts floundered in the mud, climbed on the steps, splashed themselves with dirty water and smacked themselves with birch besoms. They were naked and deformed, and on their backs, softened by the steam, the scars from their lashings stood out, violet and swollen. They yapped, shook their chains and demanded additional buckets of water.

"In the vapor," writes Dostoevsky, "appeared scarred backs, shaven heads and abbreviations of crooked hands and legs. . . . It occurred to me that if we were all to meet again in hell, it would remind us of the place where we were now." The Lenten season in the penitentiary awakened in Dostoevsky many poignant recollections. He saw himself as a child entering an illumined church, which seemed to be enlarged

by the oceanic rumble of the choirs, and it was as though his
soul and body were renewed by this solemn music, this
solemn invocation of voices and rising incense. At that time
he looked with compassion at the common people massed
before the entrance. "It seemed to me then that before the
gate the people did not pray as we did in our seats, that they
prayed with humility, fervor, deep genuflections, in full consciousness of their abasement. And now it was my turn to
occupy this place, and under even worse conditions. We
were chained, branded with the seal of infamy; the faithful
shied away from us, seemed to fear us; they gave us alms and
I recall that this fact was excessively and strangely pleasing
to me. . . ."

On the important religious feasts, the prisoners dressed in
clean blouses and made it a point of honor to display particular kindness to the prison personnel. The main meal was
copious and served on a white tablecloth. But the same night
the convicts were again drunk as beasts, debased and
wounded from brawling. The Circassians who were teetotal-
ers sat on the threshold and watched with disgusted curiosity
the antics of the drunkards who yelled, sang, strummed
balalaikas, vomited and played interminable card games.
"Gradually the atmosphere of my barracks room grew suffocating, nauseating. There was no lack of clownish spec-
tacles, but I felt so sad, I pitied those wretches so much that
I was choked."

For the third day of the holidays the convicts organized a
play. The theater was in the barracks of the military section.
A few benches were reserved for the noncoms and a few
chairs for the officers whose attendance was hoped for. Behind, stood the convicts, bareheaded, with scarred faces and
shaven skulls. "Each wanted to show himself at his best to

gentlemen and visitors." Then the canvas curtain was lifted, revealing a makeshift setting. The convicts who played the parts of lords or society women dragged their chains on the floor like the others. "It was a great pleasure for the spectators," writes Dostoevsky, "to see, for instance, Vanka or Netsvetaev or Baklushin in costumes quite different from those they had worn every day for years. They were convicts, nothing but convicts, with clanking chains, and here they entered upon the stage dressed in a frock coat, with a round hat and cloak like gentlemen."

After the holidays life was resumed as before. Days and days went by, months and months in monotonous horror. Feodor Mikhailovich had no one to confide in and nothing to read except a few copies of French newspapers and the Gospel. This solitude was the worst of tortures. If only he could keep in touch with his family! But the convicts were forbidden to correspond with private persons, except in a few severely restricted and exceptional instances.

Mikhail himself did not send letters to Siberia, for fear of reprisals. He was a married man, the father of a family, had suffered unjust imprisonment, and wanted to avoid compromising himself and Feodor by writing him. After his release Dostoevsky sent a moving message to his brother in which he wrote, ". . . First of all, let me ask you for God's sake, why have you not written me a single line? I would never have believed that! I sent you a letter through our general staff, which surely reached you; I waited for your answer and received nothing. Is it possible that you are forbidden to correspond with me? But correspondence is authorized, and all the political prisoners here received several letters a year. Durov received quite a few. . . . I think I understand the real reason for your silence. Out of sheer laziness, you failed to inquire of the police, or if you did go, you took as final the first refusal you met with on the part of someone probably uninformed."

Later, Mikhail justified his attitude in a letter insufficiently known and dated April 8, 1856: "Three months after our separation I tried to obtain permission to write to you. God and my conscience can bear witness to my diligence and persistence, but I could achieve nothing. I was told on the basis of legal texts, that it would be impossible to write while you were at hard labor. . . . As for secret letters, I was warned repeatedly not to risk them. That is why I resolved to help you at every opportunity, but without exposing you or myself to reprisals for the slightest line written by my hand. My brother, my friend, I have six children, I was and am still perhaps under police surveillance; do you not think that such a decision was excusable on my part?"

It must be noted, however, that after Feodor Mikhailovich's liberation, Mikhail's letters did not become much more frequent.

The last year at the penitentiary was less painful for Dostoevsky than the previous ones. He had succeeded in winning the friendship of a few convicts, he found some acquaintances in town, and obtained permission to read certain books. "It would be difficult for me to describe the strange impression made on me by the first volume, a copy of a magazine. . . . I clung to the words, tried to read between the lines, to discover the secret thoughts, the allusions to the past; I sought the traces of what formerly, in my time, had disturbed and agitated men's minds. And what sadness seized me when I was forced to admit that I was a stranger to contemporary life!"

At last the leaves of the trees grew yellow, the grass dried in the steppes, the first snow fell, light and whirling. The hour of liberation was close at hand. Dostoevsky was very calm. A convict in the courtyard congratulated him.

"Soon it will be your turn, too," he answered.

"Oh, me? Not so soon. I've still seven years to serve," answered the convict, and he contemplated the sky with an absent-minded look.

On the eve of the last day, at nightfall, Dostoevsky walked as usual around the fence. With a feeling of grave melancholy he took leave of those blackened posts, those dilapidated stakes. In this enclosure he had killed his youth and his hopes. He was about to leave the penitentiary tired, aged and disillusioned, and once again he would have to struggle, suffer and live. . . . For what? For whom?

At daybreak before the hour of departure for the day's tasks, Dostoevsky visited the barrack rooms to say farewell to his companions. "Many hard, calloused hands were stretched out to me. But those who shook my hands as comrades were not numerous. The others understood that I would soon become another man. Some turned their backs to me and obstinately refused to answer my greeting. Some cast hateful glances at me."

After the departure of the labor contingent, Dostoevsky went to the engineering workshop, where convict-smiths removed his chains. When they fell to the ground, Dostoevsky picked them up and looked at them for a long while.

"Go along. . . . We must trust in God! We must trust in God!" the convicts repeated. But Feodor Mikhailovich did not stir. He was choked by a desire to weep, to sob.

Free, at last free—staggering he left the smithy and looked up at the sky.

Dostoevsky left the penitentiary on February 15, 1854. But he was not transferred to Semipalatinsk before March. For almost two weeks he stayed at Omsk with his friends, the Ivanovs.

Madame Ivanov, the daughter of the Decembrist Annenkov, had met Dostoevsky when she went to Tobolsk. Throughout the captivity of the writer she and her husband had taxed their ingenuity to relieve his hardships, to send him a little money and food. "K. I. Ivanov was a real brother to me. He did everything he could for me. I owe him twenty-five rubles in silver."

Dostoevsky was sent to Semipalatinsk to become a simple soldier in the 7th Battalion of Siberian Infantry. The former convicts walked on foot along the bad roads. On the way a cart loaded with cables caught up with them. Dostoevsky and his companions climbed on top of the rolls of rope. The cart rolled along slowly. The air was sharp. In the sky the clouds scattered in a silent debacle. Feodor Mikhailovich was happy, wistful and mysteriously grateful.

5. DISCOVERY OF THE PEOPLE

EKRASOV TELLS THE STORY OF DOSTOEVSKY'S STAY AT THE penitentiary in a poem called *The Unfortunates*. A political prisoner with a gentle voice and "white hands" is at first jeered by his companions in chains, until, one night, he summons them to the bedside of a dying man, asks them to honor the last moments of their comrade, commands their attention, wins respect, and becomes their teacher.

When Dostoevsky returned to St. Petersburg, Nekrasov showed him the poem. "On the contrary, it was I who was the disciple of the convicts," said Dostoevsky. Indeed, he was their disciple, and the lessons he learned in the penitentiary stayed with him for the rest of his life. These four years were like a secret source that fed his genius. They came in

the middle of his life, dividing it into equal parts, the Dostoevsky of before *The House of the Dead* and the Dostoevsky
of after *The House of the Dead*. To be sure, the two personalities are not fundamentally different, but the second is
richer than the first and fulfills all the promise of the first.

Feodor Mikhailovich both cursed and blessed this "Siberian period." In the letters he wrote after his release, complaints alternate strangely with expressions of gratitude and
Christian humility.

"Never alone! And that for four years, four years! My
word, to say that we were badly off is to put it mildly!"

"The constant meditation into which I escaped from bitter
reality will not have been useless: I now have wishes and
hopes that formerly I did not even dream of. . . ."

"There were moments when I hated everybody whether
innocent or guilty, and looked upon every inmate as a thief
who was robbing me shamelessly of my life. . . ."

"I am waiting for I don't know what. . . . It seems to me
that soon, very soon, a decisive event will take place, that I
am approaching a real crisis, that I am ripe for a mysterious
future, and that something very sweet and very radiant or
perhaps very terrible is in preparation, something that certainly cannot be avoided. . . ."

"The penitentiary killed many things in me and made
others blossom."

"This is my cross and I deserved it."

"As for the four years, I regard them as a period when I
was buried alive and locked in a coffin. What a terrible
period it was! . . . I have not the strength to recount it to

you, my friend. . . . During those four years, there was not a moment during which I did not feel that I was in the penitentiary."

In *The House of the Dead* Dostoevsky tells us what the ordeal of the Siberian penitentiary meant to him. It is true that he masquerades under the name of Alexander Petrovich Gorianchikov "sentenced to hard labor for having murdered his wife." But actually it is his own experiences that he relates here with agonizing exactitude.

When he published this book, life in the Russian prisons was no longer as he had known it. Alexander II's reforms had eliminated the barbarous practices advocated by Nicholas I. The prison personnel was supervised more carefully and corporal punishment was forbidden. Thus, Dostoevsky's book criticized a state of affairs condemned by the czar himself. The board of censors authorized its publication on condition that "certain indecent expressions be eliminated." In addition, Dostoevsky took care to explain his statements by author's notes such as: "What I say about corporal punishment refers to my own time. I have been told that all this has been changed or is now in process of being changed." Or: "In my day, not only the major, but many of his subordinates, especially those who had come up from the ranks, used this expression."

It must not be assumed that in *The House of the Dead* Dostoevsky drew up a balance and presented the sum total of his prison experiences. This magnificent work, full of human truth and cruel honesty, is the first fruit of four years of suffering and meditation. Dostoevsky had seen a whole world and he described it masterfully. But in this book he presented only the small change of his vast treasure, he dropped it as one drops ballast. Having done this, he could

rise to the heights, detach himself from the Siberian landscape, forget the shaven skulls, deformed faces and obscene
utterances, and devote himself to the spiritual lessons of the
penitentiary. He told what he had observed; now it was his
task to tell what he had learned. And his whole life was not
long enough to accomplish this.

Discovery of the people, discovery of Russia, discovery
of the Gospel—this triple miracle took place in a fetid barracks in the heart of Siberia, at the very time when Dostoevsky's intimates thought he was lost for ever.

The Russian intellectual elite developed quickly toward
the middle of the nineteenth century, in an immense empire
which was not ready to receive it. It was an artificial product
that lacked tradition and the mystery of truly living things.
In the beginning the group found itself between two poles of
equal power. Above it was the czar whose authority was
sanctioned by the church, who represented the supreme
power concentrated in one being and the highest expression
of national life. Below were the people, grayish, incomprehensible, ever-changing. The intellectuals could no more
merge with the people than they could usurp the imperial
power. The czar and the people were two eternal entities
which drew strength from their permanence. The czar and
the people could not be explained: they existed, they had
the mystery of living creatures, and it was possible to believe
in them because they were literally *different*.

This irresistible appeal of the masses is a phenomenon unknown to the West; it can exist only in a country where
social classes are clearly opposed. On the one hand, the intelligentsia; on the other, the people; here refined European
culture, there utter barbarian ignorance; and no perceptible

transition between the two worlds. The elite were few, the people innumerable. This handful of cultivated men were hypnotized by the crowd, and afraid of being absorbed. They wanted to understand it, to "learn" it, in order to dominate it. And the less they understood it, the less they "learned," the more they admired it.

Even as a child, Feodor Mikhailovich had been attracted by the muzhiks of Darovoe and the patients of the Hospital of the Poor. Later, in St. Petersburg, he became interested in the people, but from a purely "materialistic" point of view; thus he demanded the abolition of serfdom, the suppression of corporal punishment, and the extension of learning to the villages. But as soon as he entered the penitentiary, another tendency manifested itself in him. Here he was at last before the people, among the people. But this people into which he ardently wished to be incorporated rejected him. He was a gentleman—he could not be a muzhik. He could not become a muzhik after being a gentleman.

He reacted to this rejection with grief, but not with resentment. For the space of four years he lived isolated among these men who were not of his race. For four years he was haunted by a forbidden world, leaning over an abyss which refused to engulf him. Little by little he discovered that the stupid, ugly and wicked brutes who surrounded him had a soul.

"In the penitentiary," he wrote to his brother, "I ended up by discovering men, real men, profound, powerful and beautiful characters. Gold under filth."

This revelation seduced and obsessed him. The people were not intelligent or educated. The people were all those who worked with their hands, who did not think, who contented themselves with feeling. The people were the expres-

sion of the organic Russian life. A muzhik was first of all a
child, who preserved the candor and truth of childhood in
all their freshness. He was cut off from civilization, social
conventions and scientific lies. He was close to God. Without knowing it, he had the secret of life in accord with God.
To go toward the muzhik was to go toward God.

Dostoevsky developed this idea several times in his novels
and his diary. The peasant, Marey, for instance, and the incident with the wolf. "What an extraordinary people," Dostoevsky wrote on February 22, 1854. "I have not wasted my
time. If I have not studied Russia, at least I know by heart the
Russian people; very few know it as well as I do. . . ."

Soon he would attribute a Messianic role to this people.
For the time being he contented himself with loving it and
humiliating himself before it. A few years later, Perts tells
us, Dostoevsky, while visiting the Suslovs, was reproached
by a young physician for his mystical ideas on Russia's future.

"Who has given you the right to speak thus in the name
of the Russian people?" the doctor exclaimed.

Dostoevsky, with a brusque gesture, raised the bottom of
his trousers and showed his ankles on which the mark left
by his chains was still visible. He answered, "This gave me
the right."

This idealization of the people, this contempt for civilization, were all the more thoroughgoing because Dostoevsky
was cut off from the intellectual world. He did not receive
any letters and did not read books. The Gospel was his only
intellectual nourishment, and the Gospel represents the
triumph of the heart over the mind. His meditations on the
Bible were of major importance; all his works and his whole
life from then on bore the imprint of the doctrine of the

Gospel. What are the novels of his second period but contemporary histories of apostles, touched by grace, precipitated into doubt, forgotten, redeemed and driven toward ineffable certainty? The study of the Scriptures changed the perspective of Dostoevsky's world. The joys and sorrows of his creatures were no longer entirely earthly. His novels now had two levels—on the first, the events of everyday life, with its worries and jealousies, its problems of self-preservation, money, and precedence; on the second, the real human drama, the search for God, for a new existence. A student murders an aged usurer, a son hates his father to the point of desiring his death, a brute laments before the bolted door of his wife's room, but all this is secondary in the development of the action; the real tragedy is purely moral and takes place on the highest levels of the soul. The only joys and sorrows that count are not of this world. These disembodied heroes do not desire wealth, comfort, social status or peaceful marital union. They do not want anything of this world, they want the infinite, certainty, God.

"God has tortured me all my life," exclaims Kirilov in *The Possessed*. This divine torture was Dostoevsky's own.

He never knew the calm faith and smooth-flowing love that he constantly calls for in his books. He wanted to have faith, but a demonic lucidity kept him at the edge of grace. He questioned himself and the sacred texts, and discussed, instead of accepting, the dogma.

"I will tell you of myself," he wrote to Madame Fonvizin after his release, "I am a child of the century, a child of disbelief and doubt; I have been thus so far and I know I will continue until I go to my grave. What terrible tortures I now suffer because of this thirst for faith which is all the stronger in my soul that the arguments against it are more numerous. And yet sometimes God gives me moments of complete serenity. In such moments I compose for myself a profession of faith in which everything is clear and sacred. This profession of faith is simple. Here it is: believe that there is nothing more beautiful, more profound, more appealing, more reasonable, more courageous, more perfect than Christ. Not only is there nothing, but—I say to myself with jealous love—there can be nothing. More: if anyone proved to me that Christ is outside the truth, and if it were really established that truth is outside Christ, I would prefer to be with Christ than with the truth."

Dostoevsky accepted this solution without knowing Kierkegaard or Overbeck. In his eyes, faith was never definitively acquired; it always had to be defended against the enemy, oneself.

His was divine ecstasy lashed by doubt, metaphysical despair shaken by fanaticism. The threat gave its price to the threatened object. Faith was a risk. The church with its well-established rules, its confessions and absolutions, decreased this risk. The church was faith made accessible to everyone, it was security in faith. But Dostoevsky hated anything that was comfortable. He wanted to struggle alone and find his path by himself.

"My song of praise," he writes, "has traversed the furnace of doubt."

In reality Dostoevsky's whole work was this song of praise. Or more accurately, his real work began only with the first notes of this song.

Semipalatinsk was a way station for camel caravans, an Asiatic village of one-story log houses with inner court-yards, so that the passers-by could not watch the Moslem women at work in their apartments, and low doorways where the family chieftains could more easily cut off the heads of intruders. Long wooden fences followed the edge of the roads which were not lighted at night. There were no paved streets, no trees, no bushes; only sand, dry and burning, up to the ankles, and with every gust of wind rising in a whirl to sting the traveler's face. When the first rain came, it changed into thick grayish mud and hardened quickly.

Seven mosques and a stone church and the infantry barracks, a pharmacy, an elementary school and a general store which sold nails, perfume and even food; that was all. There were very few books, irregular postal deliveries and only an occasional newspaper passed from hand to hand. Here was solitude, the total oblivion of the desert. The little town had five to six thousand inhabitants—Tartar merchants, soldiers and officials. Beyond the Cossack suburb, Kirghiz shepherds dwelled in skin tents.

The town was more than a hundred years old. The fortress, surely half as old, had been razed time and again by hordes of Kara-Kirghiz bandits. On these occasions the troops were alerted, and repelled with more or less success the attacks of the insurgent khans.

Immediately upon his arrival in Semipalatinsk, Dostoevsky was put in the First Section of the 7th Battalion of Siberian Infantry. Service in this army was arduous: marches, rifle practice, reviews, parades. At night the soldiers were sent on watches near the edge of the steppe. These exercises and bivouacs exhausted Feodor Mikhailovich.

"I came here in March," he wrote to his brother, "knowing almost nothing about military training, yet by July I did as well as the others at the review. . . . To learn one must toil hard. I do not complain: this is my cross and I deserve it."

The battalion was composed of illiterate serfs, professional soldiers and deportees. The intellectual level of the garrison was no higher than that of the penitentiary. Once again Dostoevsky found himself in foul-smelling barracks, once again he knew quarrels, public sleeping quarters and reveille at daybreak. Feodor Mikhailovich conceived a friendship for a seventeen-year-old "army child," named Kats who slept in the next bed, won the boy's confidence and proposed to him that they keep their money in common. They took turns going to town for purchases or to the kitchen for cabbage and *kasha*, brushed each other's uniforms and polished each other's belts. Kats bought a samovar with his savings, and Dostoevsky often replaced the execrable meals served in the refectory with a few cups of tea. The food in the battalion was very bad. Officially, four kopeks a day were supposed to be spent for each soldier's subsistence, but the company commander, the quartermaster and the sergeant usually kept one and a half of these four. This petty embezzlement netted the officers the sum of seven hundred and forty-four rubles a year. Everyone in Semipalatinsk knew this but no one was indignant about it.

With infinite patience Dostoevsky strove to win the affection of his comrades, helping them in their chores, sharing with them the food he purchased in town, even lending them money. His superiors were satisfied with him and, thanks to the intervention of his friends in Omsk, he was given permission to live in town. He rented a room near the barracks in the house of a soldier's widow, a dilapidated *izba* that sagged in the sand but had a meager little garden with a well and an archaic well-sweep. Dostoevsky occupied a dark, low-ceilinged room, whose clay walls were decorated with woodcuts. It was furnished with a semicircular bench, a bed, a table, a chair, a chest and a big Russian stove. A length of cloth separated this den from the rest of the house. Dostoevsky paid five rubles a month for rent, board and laundry, but the widow earned more money through her two daughters for whom she acted as a procuress. "Ah, *barin*," she used to say, "they would have ended by sleeping with a battalion clerk or a sergeant anyhow, for two loaves of gingerbread, maybe, or a pound of nuts. But with you gentlemen, it's good business for them and a great honor for me. . . ."

On November 20, 1854, young Baron Wrangel arrived in Semipalatinsk to assume the duties of public prosecutor. When this handsome, twenty-two-year-old officer arrived in his beautifully tailored uniform, ordered from a St. Petersburg tailor, he stroked his black sideburns in honor of this provincial hole, several thousand versts from the capital. What would become of him, condemned to remain for two years in this remote village lost in the sands, among these illiterates, without any diversion except hunting and fishing?

Before leaving St. Petersburg he had received a visit from Mikhail Dostoevsky who gave him a package of books for Feodor. Baron Wrangel knew Dostoevsky only from his works, but he happened to have been present at the sham execution of the "Petrashevsky" on Semenovsky Square.

Having paid his formal visit to the governor, Baron Wrangel sent his lackey to summon Dostoevsky. The latter received the serving-man with suspicion. Who was this Baron Wrangel? What did he want of him? His title of public prosecutor had a disturbing ring in Feodor Mikhailovich's ears. Nevertheless, he accepted an invitation to tea.

At the appointed hour a soldier dressed in a gray over-coat with a red collar entered Baron Wrangel's room. This man had a rather stooped posture and his arms hung down; his pale face with its blunt nose was freckled. His steel gray eyes looked straight ahead with a sad and painful expression. The stranger who seemed annoyed and worried stood waiting for an explanation of the baron's summons. When Wrangel told him that he had met Mikhail in St. Petersburg and handed Feodor his brother's letter and package of books, Dostoevsky's face brightened in childish gratitude. He relaxed, unbent and asked permission to read his letter on the spot. As he read, tears came to his eyes.

Wrangel, who also had just received a number of letters from St. Petersburg, cut a few envelopes and glanced at several sheets. The recollection of his old happy life smote his heart. Suddenly he felt very lonely with this stranger. There they were, both of them, in the depths of Siberia, far from everything they loved and all those who could understand them, alone, forgotten, lost. Forgetting his dignity, Baron Wrangel, His Majesty's public prosecutor, burst out sobbing and threw himself into the arms of the soldier Dostoevsky. This was the beginning of a deep and enduring friendship.

"Fate has brought me face to face with an amazing man," wrote Wrangel to his parents, "amazing both in the qualities of his heart and of his mind: he is our young and unfortunate writer, Dostoevsky. I am indebted to him for many joys, and his words, advice, and ideas have strengthened me for the rest of my life. For heaven's sake, dear father, try to find out whether he will not be amnestied." And: "Is it possible that this admirable man is doomed to die here as a simple soldier? That would be horrible. I love him like a brother, and respect him like a father."

He did more than love and respect him, he did everything in his power to cheer his existence. The society of high Semipalatinsk officials had welcomed with open arms this nobleman whose face was as pure as a medallion, whose gestures were elegant and whose clothes were impeccable. On the day of his arrival it became known that he had a lackey, that he had reserved a large apartment and rented a coach, and that his salary enabled him to live on an ample scale. The men declared gravely that he was of aristocratic lineage and that he was destined for a brilliant career. The ladies were charmed with him, and the young girls dreamed that their future bridegrooms would look like him.

Wrangel tried to introduce Dostoevsky to his new acquaintances. This was a ticklish undertaking. Everyone knew that Dostoevsky had been a convict; moreover, he wore a shabby gray uniform which marred even the most unpretentious gathering. The baron was told that it was never advisable to be seen in the company of a former convict and that a public prosecutor should be more careful in choosing his friends. But Wrangel persisted and as a result of his efforts General Spiridonov, the military governor, agreed to receive Dostoevsky in his own house.

"All right, bring him," he said. "But let him come without ceremony, in his undress uniform."

Spiridonov was a worthy man, cordial, generous and hospitable. He soon recognized Feodor Mikhailovich's great merits and asked him to come "as often as he liked." Following the example of the highest-ranking official, all the salons opened their doors to the former convict. Belikhov, the battalion commander, who until recently had been wont to send for Dostoevsky to read the newspapers to him, now often invited him to dinner. Lieutenant Stepanov's wife recited her poems to the writer and asked him to edit them. Colonel Messarosh, an inveterate gambler and the leader of the Semipalatinsk military band, could no longer do without Dostoevsky. The writer's gray tunic and the prosecutor's brilliant uniform were seen together at every society gathering.

It was only with reluctance, however, that Dostoevsky accepted the invitation of the Semipalatinsk military and civilian notables. He was bored in these provincial salons and preferred to spend his evenings conversing with his new friend. As soon as he had completed the day's service he would go to the baron's apartment, make himself comfortable in an easy chair, unbutton the collar of his uniform and light a pipe. At that time he was planning *The Uncle's Dream, The Village of Stepanchikovo* and *The House of the Dead.* He was cheerful, hummed airs from operettas, related scenes from his forthcoming books, and uttered joyous exclamations when Adam, the "lackey-tailor-cook," brought in a pot of fish chowder.

This Adam was a filthy and morose drunkard, with a huge swollen head and crooked fingers. He often sat near the window bellowing tunes so wretched and interminable that the two friends, after several fruitless remonstrances, were obliged to pour a pail of water on his head.

When the table was cleared, Feodor and the baron discussed literary subjects. Dostoevsky recited Pushkin's *Egyptian Nights* or pages from *Dead Souls,* begged Wrangel to drop his "academic books," and turn to poetry, or talked

about himself, his childhood, his friendship for his brother
Mikhail and his literary debut. But he avoided any mention
of the trial of the "Petrashevsky."

Late at night Feodor Mikhailovich returned to his own
smoke-filled *izba*, lighted a suet candle, and wrote. Part of
The House of the Dead was written in this wooden shack
by the feeble light of a candle. Outside, the night was still
except for the occasional barking of a dog. On the other side
of the curtain the widow turned over on her pallet and
groaned in a dream. After a while, Feodor Mikhailovich
pushed aside his sheets of paper, and put down his pen. He
could not work.

"I could do nothing," he later wrote to Maikov. "A certain
circumstance, a certain long-expected event, had at last come
to pass, had at last shaken me and absorbed me completely.
I was happy, I was unable to work."

What was this "circumstance," this "long-expected event?"
Dostoevsky had met the Isaev family even before Wrangel's
arrival in Semipalatinsk. Isaev was the local schoolmaster
who, although he was neither stupid nor wicked, had been
dismissed from one position after another because he loved to
drink beyond all measure. Even in Semipalatinsk he lost his
position. Maria, his young wife, was the daughter of a French
émigré, M. de Constant, the director of a leper colony in
Astrakhan. She and her two sisters had been educated in a
genteel school and had attended the balls of the local aristocracy. Proud of her social success—she could dance the
shawl dance with charming grace—Maria had dreamed of
a glittering social life far from the sandy beaches of the

Caspian. Isaev had seemed an excellent choice for a husband, but now Maria found herself in her late twenties stranded in Semipalatinsk.

This small blonde with thick lips, a dry skin and delicate features that flooded with a rush of blood at the slightest emotion, was a nervous young woman undermined by consumption and given to moods of exaltation. Deprived of a dependable income, with a drunken husband who had no hope of improving his lot and drowned in alcohol his sorrow over his wasted life, she proudly tried to conceal from outsiders the pitiable state of her marriage. All day long she darned, washed clothes and cleaned her house. With the provincial gentry, hungry for scandal, she played the role of the dignified matron, well-pleased with her conjugal happiness, while her husband, idle, disheveled and loquacious, dragged himself about the town from morning till night.

Isaev met Dostoevsky at Belikhov's, and a mysterious sympathy developed between the two men. Perhaps Feodor Mikhailovich pitied Isaev, or, more likely, sensed in the wretched schoolmaster a magnificent subject for his novels. This tearful drunkard who could discourse for hours on man's fate, the teachings of Christ, good and evil, culture and barbarism, later provided Dostoevsky with material for Marmeladov in *Crime and Punishment*, the dismissed official with a consumptive wife and a prostitute daughter, who drinks to achieve the extreme limit of sorrow. "So you imagine, you profiteer, that your half-pint has brought me relief? . . . It is sadness, sadness, that I sought at the bottom of this glass, sadness and tears. . . ."

Just as Marmeladov brought the student Raskolnikov to his home, so Isaev introduced Dostoevsky to his wife. But the latter meeting was more cordial than the one in the novel.

Madame Isaev was enchanted at this opportunity to become acquainted with a man of breeding with whom she could discuss literature, politics, soirées and the shawl dance. She befriended the soldier, pitied his misfortunes and assured him of her affection. However, according to Wrangel, she was not really in love with him.

"She knew," the baron writes in his *Memoirs*, "that he was an epileptic and that he was poor; and she herself used to say that he had no future." How could this soldier of the line, with a heavy-set face, a bilious complexion and close-cropped hair, seduce a woman who dreamed only of splendor and gallantry in the French manner?

Dostoevsky, however, was completely conquered by Maria Dmitrievna. This was the first time in his life that a woman listened to him with an air of vaguely sensual tenderness, that a woman answered him in a sweet, hesitating tone, full of complicity. Both of them were beings ill-treated by fate, lost to the world; for both of them the dreams of their youth had faded into joyless reality, and the future was a void. Dostoevsky interpreted Madame Isaev's compassion as budding love. He did not dare declare himself to his friend's wife, but multiplied his visits, attentions and hints. Soon a troubled and desperate friendship developed between them. His own voluntary renunciation exasperated the writer's desire to such a degree that he could hardly sleep and was unable to work. Every day Baron Wrangel was subjected to the amorous confidences of his companion. Dostoevsky implored the Baron to visit the Isaevs with him.

"But I disliked this milieu," writes Wrangel, "because of the husband."

Madame Isaev had an eight-year-old son, Pavel, familiarly called Pasha. He was a swarthy little fellow, as lively as a

monkey. Dostoevsky agreed to tutor him, which was another
pretext for seeing his mother. Ah, if only he were free! If
only she were free! He alternately intoxicated himself with
absurd projects and was dejected with grief; he refused to
listen to Wrangel's wise counsels and maintained that never
again in his life would he be so deeply in love. Gradually,
Maria Dmitrievna was infected by the ardor of her wooer
with the red collar. She was flattered by his shy, but boundless homage and, feeling again some of the exaltation she
had experienced at the balls of her youth, she was consumed with feverish impatience. The two lovers exhausted
their energies in waiting, they were thrilled by their own
noble attitude, and lived a kind of morbid and silent romance
with no possible fulfillment in sight.

On March 12, 1855, the military aide-de-camp Akhmatov
came to Semipalatinsk bearing a sensational message: Emperor Nicholas I had died on the preceding February 18.
The Moslem population of Semipalatinsk received this news
with indifference, but the "intellectual officials," most of
whom had suffered from the severity of the regime, became
excited. They talked at length of the enlightened tolerance
and humane spirit of the new emperor, and discussed the
significance of the imminent reforms. Feodor Mikhailovich
was filled with new hope. With Wrangel he attended the
funeral mass celebrated in honor of the man who had sent
him to Siberia. In the church, all around Dostoevsky, the
faces of the people were serious but, according to Wrangel,
no one wept.

From the first days of summer the heat in Semipalatinsk
became unbearable with temperatures as high as one hundred

and five degrees. The sand burned Feodor's feet through the soles of his shoes. Baron Wrangel rented a country house—the only country house in the region—called the "Cossack Garden," a large frame building with a leaky roof and a rotten floor, surrounded by an immense park refreshed by living springs and ponds. Behind it a meadow sloped gently to the banks of the Irtysh River.

Dostoevsky and Wrangel planted flowers along the walks. Wrangel notes, "I clearly recall Feodor Mikhailovich as he helped me to water the young shoots. He was sweating; he had removed his soldier's tunic and wore only a pink blouse faded from many launderings. Around his neck swung a coarse little chain of blue glass beads which originated I know not where. From it was suspended a silver watch in the form of a crescent."

The two friends led a peaceful life in the Cossack Garden. They bathed, smoked, read old newspapers and rode horseback, but Dostoevsky's horsemanship was poor and he himself made fun of his clumsiness. They also tried to tame the grass snakes under the terrace by feeding them milk and accustoming them to the presence of men. One day some ladies from Semipalatinsk paid a visit to the country squires and found them surrounded by snakes. The ladies fled in terror, and after that no one ventured to disturb the two friends.

Meanwhile Dostoevsky's passion for Maria Dmitrievna grew ever stronger. He often visited the Isaevs and each time, Wrangel tells us, "he returned in a kind of ecstasy." Maria, like Madame Panaev, had for him the attraction of the unobtainable. Both were married women, both received him in their homes, and he loved them both in the certain knowledge that he could never become their lover.

We know nothing about Dostoevsky's sexual life before his return to Russia. Was he frigid or passionate? Questioned on this subject by Madame Kashina-Evreinova, Chukovsky declared: "In my opinion it is absolutely certain that Nekrasov and Dostoevsky could not do without women even for one week." But Dr. Yanovsky maintains, "I never heard him say that he was passionately attracted by anyone, not even that he merely loved a woman." And Riesenkamp writes in his memoirs, "He was indifferent toward women, he almost had an antipathy for them."

Actually Dostoevsky does not seem to have had a single liaison before his marriage. His sexual instinct developed quite late. This sickly, high-strung and imaginative man admired women from a distance, feared them obscurely, perhaps desired them, but reproached himself for desiring them. The heroines of his first novels, except for Netochka, are the pale and literary, bloodless creations of a man who had never really loved. This strange repression, this pleasure in confused situations, in attachments without a future, in sensual denial, characterizes Dostoevsky's whole youth. Impatient by nature, he deliberately sought the torments of waiting, chaste, he delighted in grazing the adorable danger of sin. Like his heroes, he was willing to live for the impossible.

But the strange idyl between Feodor Mikhailovich and Maria Dmitrievna reached its denouement earlier than he had expected. Friends obtained for Isaev the position of assistant at the court of Kuznetsk, a town situated some seven hundred versts from Semipalatinsk. This news, which made a separation inevitable, broke Dostoevsky's heart.

"And she accepted, she did not protest, that is what revolts me!" he groaned. Despairing, furious, he walked around his room like a somnambulist. From time to time he stopped to tell Baron Wrangel that his life had been wasted and that he longed only for death; then he resumed his gloomy pacing. Wrangel tried to comfort him, paid the Isaevs' debts, and arranged their departure. Wrangel and Dostoevsky were to escort the travelers for a stretch in their conveyance. The Isaevs, who did not have enough money to hire a decent carriage, had hired an open cart.

On the appointed day, Wrangel invited the schoolmaster and his wife to drink champagne with him for a farewell celebration and took this opportunity to make the unfortunate Isaev completely drunk. Then he invited the husband to share his cab while Feodor Mikhailovich sat on the cart between Maria Dmitrievna and Pasha. This arrangement was satisfactory to everyone concerned.

The two vehicles traveled slowly. Isaev fell asleep on Wrangel's shoulder, and Feodor Mikhailovich and Maria Dmitrievna talked together in a low voice. A limpid, fragrant May night descended lightly on the tops of the pine trees, and a new moon illumined the road. The serene beauty of the landscape increased the sadness of the lovers. Finally the cortege stopped, the hour of separation was upon them.

The drunkard was snoring in a corner. Little Pavel murmured in his sleep. Maria Dmitrievna and Dostoevsky fell into each other's arms. They wept, made the sign of the cross on each other, swore never to forget and to write to each other. . . . Baron Wrangel dragged the husband from the cab to the cart. Maria Dmitrievna and Pasha installed themselves beside the drunkard who remained asleep. The driver lashed his horses, and the cart left in a cloud of dust. It was over, but Dostoevsky stood motionless in the middle of the road with bent head while tears rolled down his gray

cheeks. Wrangel took his friend by the hand and without
a word led him to the cab.

The two companions returned to Semipalatinsk at dawn.
Dostoevsky locked himself in his room and paced back and
forth till morning call, then he went to the summer camp for
training. Upon his return he went to bed without eating or
drinking, and began to smoke pipe after pipe, staring at the
ceiling.

On June 4, he wrote to Madame Isaev as follows: "If you
knew how lonely I feel here. In truth, I am reminded of the
time when I was arrested in 1849 and was buried alive in a
cell, torn away from everything that was lovable and joyful.
I have become so accustomed to you. I never considered our
friendship an ordinary one, but now, when I am deprived
of you, I understand many things from my own experience.
I have lived outside society for five years, alone, with literally
no one to whom I could open my heart, but you received
me as one of your own. How much I made you suffer because of my bitterness, and yet both of you loved me. I
understand all that, I feel it, I am not heartless. You are an
amazing woman, you have an exceptional soul, the kindness
of a child. You have been a sister to me. The very fact that
you, a woman, stretched out your hand to me marks a date
in my life. At night, in the dark, when I used to confide in
you, I am so sad that if I wept easily, tears would pour from
my eyes, yet you will not think me ridiculous. At present I
live entirely alone. I no longer know where to turn. Everything bores me here. What a vacuum!"

And actually Dostoevsky lost all his ardor for work, his
gaiety, and even his common sense. He became morose, irritable and superstitious. Because Wrangel was in love with a
thirty-four-year-old woman, the mother of six children, who

lived four hundred versts from Semipalatinsk, he compared
his friend's fate to his own, lamenting over their double misfortune and interpreting their most insignificant dreams
symbolically. He felt sudden fears and joys with no reason,
tried to find talismans, and ended by frequenting a fortune
teller who read the future in beans.

The news from Kuznetsk was bad. Maria Dmitrievna
complained of her solitude, her poverty, her husband's inveterate drunkenness and the gossip that was the curse of the
small towns. Her only pleasure was to chat with a new friend
of Isaev's, a charming young schoolmaster, serious and kind.
Dostoevsky was devoured by absurd jealousy. Who was this
young schoolmaster? Did she really love this stranger? Had
she forgotten the past? His letters grew to the size of volumes. He now lived only to receive her mail. He lost his appetite, grew thin and suffered from nervous fits.

Baron Wrangel decided to help Dostoevsky and arrange
for him to meet Madame Isaev at Zmiev, a little town halfway
between Semipalatinsk and Kuznetsk. Maria Dmitrievna
was informed by letter of the date and place of the meeting.
But the military authorities did not allow soldiers to undertake such long trips. Baron Wrangel resorted to a subterfuge, he told everyone that Dostoevsky had had an epileptic
fit, and that he must remain in his room for a day. Lamotte,
the physician of the regiment, was part of the plot and confirmed the young man's story. Adam received the order to
close the shutters and to forbid anyone admittance to the
house. At ten in the evening when all the lights of Semipalatinsk went out, Wrangel's cab took the two friends to
Zmiev.

"We did not drive, we flew like a hurricane," writes
Wrangel, "but my poor Feodor Mikhailovich did not realize

this. He maintained that we were traveling at a snail's pace and constantly urged the driver." Alas, instead of Madame Isaev, they found only a letter from her at Zmiev. She apologized for not being able to come but her husband was ill and she could not leave him. The return trip was sinister. They had traveled three hundred versts in twenty-eight hours, Dostoevsky was in danger of being declared a deserter, and all for nothing. Fortunately no one had noticed the absence of the two friends.

Baron Wrangel did not lose courage. Some time after this trip he got permission to take Dostoevsky with him for a few days to Zmiev with "friends, engineers." Wrangel's lackey made an elegant frock coat for Dostoevsky—this was the first time in years that the former convict had worn civilian clothes. The two friends set out with the feeling that on this occasion they would surely be rewarded for their trouble.

Once again they drove in a clear night, along a flat road without ruts or cobbles. The troika dashed on across a dreamlike landscape. Suddenly, at five versts from the town, they saw a bloody glow against the sky. The peasants were burning weeds; the fire surged in luminous waves, spitting sparks and burning stars that dropped far away and lit other fires. The horses took fright and galloped past the flames. Finally they approached the silver mines of Zmiev, a factory surrounded by small workers' houses. Further on, stood the villas of the engineers and higher officials, and beyond, flowed the river.

Immediately upon his arrival, Dostoevsky wrote to Maria Dmitrievna, imploring her to join him as soon as possible. But five days went by, and she failed to appear. He returned to Semipalatinsk and resumed his monotonous life in the barracks. He must wait, always wait. Feodor Mikhailovich was at the end of his tether.

Finally, on August 14, 1855, he received a letter from Kuznetsk informing him that Madame Isaev's husband had died after a long illness. Maria Dmitrievna described his agony and miserable funeral. Having no more money, she had been compelled to borrow from acquaintances in order to pay the hearse. A stranger had sent her three rubles, and she had accepted this charity.

Dostoevsky was grief-stricken—he had conceived a real liking for the drunkard—nevertheless, a strange relief, a filthy little joy stirred in him. The last obstacle had vanished —Maria Dmitrievna was free, and he would be able to marry her. He had no sooner articulated this thought than he was seized by indignation. He recalled that he had often jeered at the unfortunate husband and cursed his presence in the home of his beloved. Perhaps he had even secretly wished for the man's death. Now death had come and, as in the case of his father, long ago—he was once again responsible, guilty beyond all ordinary laws.

Wrangel was away on a mission at Biesk. Dostoevsky wrote him a disturbed letter asking him to send some money to Madame Isaev: "Of course I will give it back to you, although not very soon. . . . Only I do not wish her to be grateful to me when I do not deserve her gratitude, because I have taken the sum from the pocket of another, true, with the intention of paying it back, but at an indeterminate date." He also implored his friend to add a few words that would spare the widow's suffering pride. "One must be very tactful with a person who owes one something: she is touchy. She always feels she is being treated in an offhand manner, that she must pay for the services rendered her by permitting a kind of familiarity."

"I answered her that the twenty-five rubles came from you and not from me," he later wrote to Wrangel. "Ah, my God, what a woman! . . . It is a pity that you know her so little. . . ."

The hope for a quick and happy consummation further exasperated his love. He confided it to his brother Mikhail: "Listen to me, my friend. It is a long time now that I have been in love with this woman, and I know she loves me. I cannot live without her, and as soon as my situation improves, I shall marry her. I know she will not refuse me." And a few months later: "From a distance we have exchanged vows and oaths. She loves me and has proved it to me."

Actually the unfortunate woman had never been more undecided than at the moment when she promised him her hand. Without anyone to lean on, without resources, she was touched by Dostoevsky's active compassion, but she did not love him. He was poor and ill. Kind souls in Semipalatinsk informed Feodor Mikhailovich that she planned to marry someone else, and, true enough, he had noticed a certain reserve which frightened him, in his "fiancée's" latest letters.

"What should I do," she wrote to him, "if there appeared a man of settled years with a good character and an assured position who asked me to marry him? What should I answer him?" She asked his advice as a friend. This subtle stratagem disarmed him. He could not advise Maria Dmitrievna to break with this honorable and well-to-do man in order to marry him, Dostoevsky, a soldier, a former convict and a physical wreck, without being accused of selfishness. But he could not admit that she should marry another man, when she loved him, she still loved him.

He decided that she could not of her own will have envisaged the possibility of union with a stranger. Her provincial cronies must have forced her hand, taking advantage of his own absence and Maria Dmitrievna's weakness. And he could defend his chances only by a few lines jotted down on paper. Now every minute, every second, threatened his love and here he was, friendless, powerless, without money, alone among people who did not understand him. Yet he knew well that he would not survive a final break.

Meanwhile Wrangel had left Siberia for St. Petersburg. Dostoevsky wrote to him, "I will die if I lose my angel, I will go mad, or jump into the Irtysh. I have rights on her, do you understand, rights! For God's sake, write her a letter to Kuznetsk, explain to her clearly, in detail, all my hopes. Especially learn if anything has been decided concerning my future. Tell her all the details of my case, and she will soon pass from despair to confidence. . . . But perhaps you do not know how to write to her? It is very easy. This is how: 'Feodor Mikhailovich sent me your regards. . . . Since I know that you are greatly interested in everything that concerns Feodor Mikhailovich, I hasten to gladden your heart, for there is such good news, such high hope for him. . . .' "

Ah, if only he could be promoted in the army. He implored Wrangel to intervene in his favor. While waiting, he sent Madame Isaev a mad letter in which threats alternate with humble reproaches and protestations of love. After two years of silent passion and ten months of separation, he could no longer do without her. He assured her that he would obtain a pardon, that he would leave Siberia, that he would write for publication. "I can even publish incognito." He could earn money, a great deal of money. He would lift them out of their poverty, her and her son.

Madame Isaev's answer calmed him a little. She had only wanted to "test" his love, because she was jealous. He exulted, he was overwhelmed by tenderness, he accused himself of brutality, and hoped again. But the respite was short-lived. In her following letters, Maria Dmitrievna spoke about the young schoolmaster whom her husband had introduced to her, praising his character and intelligence. As for herself, she said, "she could not make a man happy." She and Feodor were "two unfortunates," and, "it would be better for both of them . . ." At this point Dostoevsky in his exasperation risked everything. He pretended sickness to escape from Semipalatinsk, but was forced to turn back. Then he obtained a regular leave, and the longed-for meeting at last took place.

Maria Dmitrievna wrung her hands, sobbed, called upon Jesus, but ended up by confessing that she was in love with the young schoolmaster, Vergunov. She was twenty-nine years old, he was twenty-four. She was a distinguished woman, educated, mellow. He was a Siberian boy, a school-teacher, barely literate, underpaid, unsophisticated, and conceited as a peacock. Thus Dostoevsky deprecated his rival to improve his own position. Was this boy a fit husband for her? Would he understand her? Would he be strong enough to protect her? Youth was the one advantage of this puppy. But later? But later? Would not Maria Dmitrievna suffer from his coarseness? Would she not regret the affection of the man who now stood before her, imploring her for the last time to reconsider her decision?

Maria Dmitrievna could not answer. This passionate plea softened her, almost seduced her. She whispered: "Do not weep, do not be sad, everything is not yet decided. You and no one else . . ."

Dostoevsky regained courage. He went to see the new lover. Vergunov turned out to be unequal to the situation. Upon Dostoevsky's first words, he burst into tears.

"To weep, that is all he knows how to do," said Dostoevsky. Two days later, having convinced the young couple, he returned to Semipalatinsk. From there he sent them a moving letter, restating his point of view. Meanwhile the lovers had collected themselves; Dostoevsky received an indignant message from Maria Dmitrievna and a letter of abuse from Vergunov. "The same thing happened to me that happened to Gil Blas when he told the truth to the Archbishop of Granada," wrote Dostoevsky.

So everything was lost. He accepted his defeat with a kind of lugubrious pleasure. Once again he touched the bottom of misfortune, once again he was hurled into the night. Then he conceived the idea of total sacrifice. If he could not become this woman's husband, he could still contribute to her happiness. He was exalted at the thought of this chivalrous attitude and imagined for himself a sacred mission as his beloved's guardian angel. He was rejected—very well, then, he would astonish the world by the generosity and delicacy of his heart; from now on he would be the sincere friend of the couple who had hurt him. He took steps to place Madame Isaev's son in the cadet corps of Siberia, got in touch with his friends in Omsk and St. Petersburg, begged them to send subsidies to the young widow, and addressed a fantastic letter of supplication to Baron Wrangel, "imploring" him "on his knees," to procure a better post, with a higher salary, for Maria Dmitrievna's future husband. "All this is for her, for her alone! . . . So

she will not be obliged to live in poverty! Since she is marrying him let them at least have money! . . . At present I love
him more than a brother; it is not a sin to ask anything for
him, he deserves it."

This affection of the betrayed lover for his rival is the
main theme of Dostoevsky's *Insulted and Injured.* "I betrayed you, but you forgave me everything and think only
of my happiness," says the heroine of this book. Likewise,
Prince Myshkin of *The Idiot,* although in love with Nastasia
Philipovna, lets her elope with Rogozhin and maintains
friendly relations with his rival. The incident was virtually
closed. But then a sudden turn of events made everything
uncertain again. On October 20, 1856, Dostoevsky was
promoted to the rank of second lieutenant. This ensured for
him an honorable position, a decent salary, and, most important, the possibility of a total pardon and eventual return to
Russia. He regained hope and renewed his offer of marriage.

On November 24, he obtained permission to travel to
Kuznetsk and arrived shaken by joy, certain of success,
magnificent. He pleaded his cause, cited figures and dates.
Maria Dmitrievna was infected by his enthusiasm. They
were made for one another, they must be married. But where
would they find the money, six hundred rubles at least?
Dostoevsky made a plan. No sooner was he back in Semipalatinsk than he wrote to Wrangel: "If I am not prevented
by one *circumstance,* I will be married before carnival. You
know to whom. She loves me. She has said yes. . . . She
quickly lost her illusions about her recent infatuation. I
guessed that already in the summer, from her letters. . . .
Oh, if you knew what a woman she is! . . . I am penniless.
According to the closest and most rigorous calculations, I
need altogether six hundred rubles in silver. I intend to bor-

row them from K . . . [Kovrygin]. But by the next mail
I will write to my uncle in Moscow who is wealthy and
who more than once has helped my family to ask him for
six hundred rubles in silver. If he gives them to me, I will at
once pay K."

To be sure of obtaining the six hundred rubles from his
uncle, Dostoevsky asked his sister Varvara to intercede for
him. "My friend, my dear sister, do not argue with me, do not
grieve for me, I cannot do anything better. She is absolutely
the woman for me. We have equal education and we understand each other. . . . I am thirty-five, she is twenty-nine. . . .
I know that your first question, as a good sister who loves
her brother and is worried about his future, will be: 'What
will you live on?' for my pay will doubtless be insufficient
for two persons. But I will manage. I know a kind and
wealthy man who is my friend, and I will ask him for a
loan. . . . But I must return this money. That is why I
intend to turn to my uncle, to tell him everything, without concealing anything, and to ask him for six hundred
rubles. . . . I will send my letter to him by mail, I implore
you, hand him this letter personally *when he is in a good
mood* and explain everything to him. . . ."

On January 23, 1857, Captain Kovrygin who was employed at the Loktevsk factory, sent Dostoevsky six hundred
rubles. On January 27, Feodor obtained a furlough of two
weeks to prepare for marriage. He wrote to his brother
Mikhail asking him to send a certain number of indispensable
things: a dress, a hat, a velvet cloak, half a dozen handkerchiefs of fine linen, and two bonnets, if possible with blue
ribbons. He knew well that his brothers, sisters, aunts and
uncles would all unanimously disapprove of this union, but
he did not care. Before the ceremony he was examined by a

physician who completely reassured him as to his health. Finally, on February 6, 1857, in the Russian Orthodox Church of Kuznetsk, Second Lieutenant Dostoevsky was wed to Maria Dmitrievna Isaev. The couple immediately set out for Semipalatinsk where Dostoevsky was to resume his duties.

The nervous tension of these last days proved too much for Feodor. Exhausted by the sudden alternations between hope and despair, the petty worries and hasty preparations, at a halt in Barnaul, he was shaken by a violent epileptic fit. He writhed and pawed the air with his hands like a demented creature, his twisted mouth slobbered yellow foam. A sudden convulsion choked him. He was near death. And Maria Dmitrievna was there, before him, witnessing this degrading spectacle, frozen with fright and disgust. How could she love this mysterious man who suddenly became a beast, who was nothing but a beast? Her first marriage had nailed her to a drunkard who came home hatless, perspiring, staggering, stinking of wine, and who vomited stealthily; her second marriage bound her to this sick man who rolled on the ground, roaring and choking like a madman. Once again her honeymoon had ended in an ugly farce.

A doctor urgently summoned stated bluntly that this was an epileptic fit and prescribed a long rest. The couple spent four days in Barnaul, in the house of a friend. Dostoevsky was crushed by his new misfortune. Without knowing it, he had betrayed his wife. Hoping to save her from a miserable existence he imposed on her one still more miserable; he had killed every chance of love between them, yet they must live side by side, protect each other, lie and feign affection. Maria Dmitrievna was too proud to acknowledge her mistake before others. She wrote to her sister, "Not only am I loved and spoiled by my husband who is so kind, so intelligent and so much in love with me, but I am also respected by my friends."

On February 20, 1857, Dostoevsky and his wife returned to Semipalatinsk. He immediately began to look for an apartment, procure himself some money, and organize their new life. Maria Dmitrievna fell sick from exhaustion, and to crown his misfortunes, a review of the troops by a general was announced. The whole town was in a turmoil. But gradually things returned to normal. Maria Dmitrievna decorated Dostoevsky's apartment, created a semblance of comfort around this man who had known every misery, charmed the little society of Semipalatinsk, and finally created a sort of literary salon, where a few people actually spoke French. At the end of May, Dostoevsky obtained a furlough on account of his health and set up housekeeping near Semipalatinsk. In the meantime his stepson, Pavel, was admitted to the cadet corps at Omsk. The couple lived modestly. The orderly Vasily combined the duties of driver, lackey and cook. Dostoevsky rested, took on a little weight and thought only of his future works.

6. THE SOLDIER WRITER

DURING HIS FIRST YEAR OF MILITARY SERVICE, DOSTOEVSKY had no time to work; and after that, he was occupied with his love for Maria Dmitrievna. "My friend," he declared in one of his letters, "I have been so upset during this last year, so sad and so tormented, that work has been impossible for me." This declaration seems exaggerated, for he continued to make notes for *The House of the Dead* and sketched the plan of a comic novel. "I am writing a comic novel, but so far I have composed only a few separate incidents. . . ."

In 1855, Dostoevsky laboriously put together an ode on the death of Nicholas I, who had sentenced him to hard labor. This poem was dedicated to Empress Alexandria Feodorovna:

All is over. . . . He is no longer. I venerate him so deeply
That I dare not pronounce his name with my sinful lips.
The monuments to his reign are his immortal works.
Like an orphaned land, Russia burst into sobs;
Seized by fear and horror, she was petrified, like a block of ice.
But you, you yourself, lost more than all the others. . . .

There are about a hundred lines in the same tone. This
high-flown elegy was followed in 1856 by another poetic
effort in honor of the coronation of Alexander II:

Toward you, source of all mercy,
Source of sacred humility,
Rise the prayers of the Russian people. . . .

Later on, we shall see the fate of these disguised pleas for
forgiveness.

Meanwhile, Dostoevsky spent himself on various projects.
He wanted to write an article on art to be dedicated to Princess Maria Nikolaevna, president of the Art Academy. Her
distinguished patronage would doubtless have sufficed to
break down the rigid barriers of the censorship. "I will ask
permission to dedicate my essay to her and to publish it
anonymously." But he soon dropped this idea for *Provincial
Letters*, a criticism of contemporary writers, and hastily fa-
miliarized himself with the most recently published works.

"I like Turgenev best of all," he wrote Maikov, "but it is
a pity that such a great talent should be marred by so much
carelessness. I like L. Tolstoy, too, but it seems to me that
he will not write a great deal; however, I may be mistaken. . . . Our women writers write like women writers,
that is to say, intelligently and pleasantly, but they are in
a terrible hurry to tell what is in their hearts. Can you explain
why a woman writer is never a serious artist?"

Dostoevsky was forced to drop his projected *Provincial Letters* because he was short of material. He had no books or newspapers. He wrote to his brother, "Thus everything is dying in me, my literary ideas, my literary career. . . ."

He also thought of publishing a magazine and of writing a novel on life in Siberia. But in the meantime Mikhail had remembered a short story that Feodor Mikhailovich had written eight years earlier, in the Alexis Ravelin, called *The Little Hero*. Dostoevsky was dissatisfied with this work, and in his first letter to his brother after his release from the penitentiary asked him not to show the manuscript to anyone. Mikhail disregarded this, and submitted the text of *The Little Hero* to the editor of the *Annals of the Fatherland*. He immediately wrote Feodor Mikhailovich that he had taken this step and was awaiting his brother's reproaches. But at the very mention of the word "publication," Dostoevsky lost all critical sense. Could it be that after eight years of silence he was to read his words in print, return to the world of letters, resume his ties with the past? An avalanche of questions crashed down on his brother and Baron Wrangel.

"Why hasn't my children's story been published yet? Was permission refused? Tell me, please, I beg of you, do they really intend to print it? And if they intended to, have they tried? And if they have not tried, why don't they? . . . You must admit that the fate of this little piece is important to me for several reasons."

He was impatient, he rediscovered in himself the exhilaration of the beginner. His whole career was at stake: the publication of *The Little Hero*, he thought, would reopen the path that had so long been closed to him. Once recognized as a writer, he would write. He had so many things to say;

the rest of his life would not suffice to spend the rich treasury of his meditations.

Finally, in August, 1857, *The Little Hero* was printed in the *Annals of the Fatherland*. The story was signed with the initials M.Y.

Mikhail urged his brother to send the new novel he had mentioned in his letters, so that it might be submitted to *Russian Word*, a periodical then in process of foundation. He had asked the editors for five hundred rubles as an advance payment to Feodor Mikhailovich and had undertaken to deliver the manuscript before the end of 1858. But in the meantime Feodor had got in touch with Plesheyev, one of the members of the conspiracy who had escaped the ordeal of the penitentiary, and had been condemned only to deportation and military service in the Orenburg garrison. As early as 1856, this Plesheyev had agreed to write for the *Russian Messenger*, a periodical published by Katkov. The same year Dostoevsky, urged on by his former comrade, promised Katkov a novel and received five hundred rubles as an advance.

These two offers from the *Russian Messenger* and the *Russian Word* considerably embarrassed Dostoevsky. He had wanted to make his second debut with a novel of which he himself would be proud; and the book he had been planning for years could not be written in haste.

"As for my novel," he wrote to his brother, "a very unpleasant adventure has happened to it and to me. I have resolved, I have sworn, that from now on I would not publish anything that had not been properly meditated upon and ripened, and that I would not agree to write anything by a given date (as I used to) solely for the reason that I had been paid in advance. . . . That is why, seeing that my novel was assuming gigantic proportions, that it was developing admirably, and that on the other hand it was necessary, absolutely necessary (because of money), to complete it very quickly, I was seized by doubt. I saw myself obliged to spoil a subject on which I had been meditating for three years, for which I had gathered a host of documents (I cannot even arrange them myself, they are so numerous) which I partly utilized, for I wrote down a number of scenes and various chapters. More than half of the work was completed in rough draft. But I clearly realized that I could not finish that final draft even of the first half by the date when I would need money. . . . That is why the whole novel and all my notes for it are at present lying in a drawer. . . ."

Having given up the project for the novel, Dostoevsky set to work on two lesser stories: *The Uncle's Dream* and *The Village of Stepanchikovo*, but he was dissatisfied with his results. Of *The Uncle's Dream*, he wrote to his brother, "I don't like it, and I am saddened at the thought that I must reappear before the public under such unfavorable conditions. There is no way of writing what I want to write; I must write what I would never have thought of writing had I not needed money. I must invent stories for money. And that is, alas, so difficult!"

The Uncle's Dream was published in 1859 in the *Russian Word*. *The Village of Stepanchikovo*, because of a misunderstanding with the *Russian Messenger*, was published in the *Annals of the Fatherland* and did not achieve the success it deserved. Dostoevsky had been forgotten by the public and the reviewers. He was of another age, another world. He could not simply resume his interrupted career, he had to retrace his steps, start from scratch again, and reconquer one by one the readers and friends he had lost. And despite his debts, his need to execute rush orders and his uncertainty about the future, he took up the struggle with amazing courage.

First of all he had to obtain his release from the Siberian army. The stages of this march to freedom are as moving in their sobriety as a ship's log. As early as 1855 Dostoevsky wrote the poem which we mentioned above, dedicated to the empress. General Gastfort saw it and requested the rank of noncom for its author "in order to encourage his good behavior and zeal, and in view of the fact that he sincerely regrets the gross errors of his youth." This first stripe was granted to Dostoevsky in November, 1855.

In 1856, he handed the poem he had written in honor of Alexander II to General Gastfort who was going to the capital to attend the coronation ceremonies. In addition he sent a copy to Baron Wrangel, asking him to submit it to the august personage to whom it was addressed. "Take note of it"— was the decision of General Sukhozanets to whom General Gastfort presented Dostoevsky's supplication. Without waiting for this meager result, Feodor Mikhailovich, in March, 1856, attempted to approach Totleben, the commanding general of the Engineering Corps. The brother of Totleben had distinguished himself at the siege of Sebastopol, won the emperor's favor and received the title of count. About him Dostoevsky wrote to Wrangel, "I once knew this man quite well. His brother was my childhood friend. Only a few days before my arrest I met him and we cordially shook hands. Perhaps he has not forgotten me!"

He addressed a long letter to Totleben, which is a masterpiece of flexibility and humility. "I fear that when you cast a glance at my signature, at my name that you have doubtless forgotten—even though a long time ago I had the honor of being known to you—I fear, I say, that you will be annoyed by me and my insolence, and that you will push this letter aside without reading it. . . . You would insult me if you thought that I fail to realize the enormous distance that separates me from you. I have had too many unhappy experiences in my life to fail to understand this difference."

He told the story of his arrest, exile and life in the penitentiary. Then he went on: "I know that I was sentenced for ideas, for theories. But ideas and beliefs change and man himself changes with time. Why must I suffer now for something that no longer exists, that has changed in me, suffer for my old errors of which I have fully realized the gratuitousness? . . . I wish to be useful. It is hard, when one has a certain strength of soul and a head on one's shoulders, to be tortured by inactivity. . . . My only wish is to leave the army and to take whatever civilian employment presents itself, anywhere in Russia, or even here. I wish to have the right to publish my works. I am sure that only thus can I be useful. . . . I know that by writing this letter I have violated the regulations. But you are indulgent and I commend myself to your indulgence."

Totleben was more than indulgent, he was energetic in behalf of his old acquaintance. Very quickly he persuaded Grand Duke Nicholas himself to plead Dostoevsky's cause before the Minister of War. On October 1, 1856, Dostoevsky was made a second lieutenant. Six months later his rights as a nobleman were restored. This meant that he was fully pardoned.

Finally, on January 16, 1858, Dostoevsky asked for permission to retire for reasons of health. The case dragged on for almost a year. On March 18, 1859, an imperial edict granted him the right to leave the army and return to Russia. But he was forbidden to live in St. Petersburg or Moscow, and was confined to the little city of Tver. In spite of all that had happened, a letter dated May 7, 1859, ordered the governor of Tver to have the secret police watch the former convict.

The great news did not reach Dostoevsky until four months after the imperial edict had been signed. In the meantime he was devoured by impatience and floundered in innumerable projects. He planned to publish a collection of his stories in two volumes and to write a great novel.

"You keep telling me," he wrote to his brother, "that Goncharov, for instance, got seven thousand rubles for his novel, and that Turgenev, for his *Nest of Noblemen* (at last I have read it, it is excellent) received four thousand rubles, that is, four hundred rubles per sheet of thirty-two pages from Katkov (of whom I asked one hundred rubles per sheet). My friend, I know very well that I do not write as well as Turgenev, but, after all, there is not that much difference, and eventually I hope to write as well as he does. Why then, despite my poverty, must I accept one hundred rubles, while Turgenev, who owns two thousand serfs, gets four hundred? My destitute condition compels me to hurry, to write for money, and as a result, invariably I must spoil my work."

Dostoevsky needed money more than ever, and was less able than ever to procure it. The expenses of his impending journey would be considerable, and he did not know what he would live on in Tver. He asked for an advance from the publisher Kushelev, who sent him one thousand rubles. These, to quote Dostoevsky, "soon melted away like wax." Having paid his debts, he was left with hardly enough money to pay for his trip as far as Kazan so he implored Mikhail to send him two hundred rubles to that city: "Save me once more."

Finally, on June 30, Dostoevsky obtained a provisional ticket, No. 2030, authorizing him to leave Semipalatinsk. He wrote to his brother that he would leave on the morrow at five o'clock, said farewell to his friends and gave his former commander his pictures, books and dishes, some chairs and a little table, his uniform, his saber, and his epaulets. Thus rid of these burdens, on July 2, 1859, he left Semipalatinsk where he had lived for more than five years.

The way back was long and hard. The Dostoevskys stopped at Omsk to take with them Maria Dmitrievna's son, a student in the cadet corps. During their three- or four-days' stay in this city Feodor Mikhailovich saw the friends who had helped him when he was a convict. He even visited the prison, and meditated gravely as he stood before the fence and the huge closed gate.

After a second halt of two days at Tiumen, the travelers reached the forests of the Ural. It was hot, the road was bad, and the horses advanced slowly, surrounded by swarms of flies. The *tarantas* creaked at every step. Suddenly, at a turn of the road, Dostoevsky caught sight of a guidepost surmounted by the two-headed eagle—the frontier between Europe and Asia. The driver stopped his horses, and everyone got down from the carriage.

Dostoevsky stood before the very line he had crossed ten years before, sick, in chains, bound for the prison and the penitentiary. Throughout his captivity he had lived only for the moment when he would again set foot on Russian soil. Now his dream was realized. He removed his hat, made the sign of the cross, and said, "The Lord has at last permitted me to see once more this promised land."

Near the guidepost stood the shack of a frontier guard, a disabled veteran of the Turkish war. Dostoevsky called him, took a bottle of spirits and some glasses out of the baggage, and those who were going from one world to another clinked glasses with him who must stay at this post. Then Dostoevsky, his wife and his stepson went to pick strawberries in the woods.

When the Dostoevskys arrived in Kazan their entire fortune consisted of one hundred and twenty rubles in cash. The two hundred rubles that Mikhail had promised to send to this city had not yet arrived, and Feodor Mikhailovich did not receive them until ten days later. On August 10, more than six weeks after they had left Semipalatinsk, the Dostoevskys reached Tver. But in this gray, ugly and extremely provincial city Feodor Mikhailovich did not find rest. "I am suffocated in Tver," he wrote to Wrangel, "I am worse off here than in Semipalatinsk. It is dark and cold; the buildings are of stone; there is not the slightest life; not even a library. It's a real prison."

Dostoevsky rented a small furnished apartment in a house where Pushkin had lived. His older brother came to spend a few days with him and cheered him up for a little while, but after Mikhail's departure, he again sank into impatient melancholy. "You have gone, and I realize that we did not renew our acquaintance as we should have, that we did not entirely open our hearts to each other, that we did not reveal ourselves. . . ." He was lonely and bored, and he felt that he was wasting precious time.

The governor of the city, Count Baranov, invited Dostoevsky to his home where the writer met the governor's wife,
Prince Sologub's cousin, whom he had known in the St.
Petersburg literary salons. This reminder of the past only
exasperated his impatience. He could no longer live far from
St. Petersburg, and his frequent letters to Baron Wrangel
were all devoted to this subject. He kept asking for advice as
to whom he should approach—Prince Dolgoruky, Count
Totleben, Count Baranov, Timashev—in order to obtain the
czar's permission for his return to the capital. In September,
Wrangel paid a visit to Feodor Mikhailovich, but said he
could do nothing to help.

In October, Count Baranov suggested that Dostoevsky
present his request to the emperor and undertook to transmit
the letter to the monarch through Count Adlerberg. Dostoevsky hesitated for a while and then sent two entreaties, one
to Totleben, and the other to Alexander II. On October 4,
he wrote to Totleben: "I have been here for a month and a
half, and I do not know how and when my difficulties will
end. It is impossible for me to live far from St. Petersburg. I
am suffering from epilepsy. I must be treated, seriously, radi-
cally. I have a stepson whom I must bring up and I must also
take care of my wife's needs. . . . Save me once again. . . .
If you speak to Prince Dolgoruky about me, perhaps you
can persuade him to hasten the final disposition of my case.
All my hope is in you."

On October 19, Count Baranov sent the following letter
written by Dostoevsky to the emperor: "Your Majesty, it is
only upon you that my fate, health and life depend. Permit
me to go to St. Petersburg to consult the doctors. Make me
free and by restoring my health give me the opportunity of

being useful to my family, and, in one way or another, to my native land. . . .

"Most Gracious Sovereign, may Your Majesty also forgive me for making a second request, and condescend to grant me a special favor by ordering that my stepson, Pavel Isaev, be admitted on a government scholarship to a Gymnasium in St. Petersburg. . . . Thus you will ensure the happiness of his mother who every day teaches her child to pray for the prosperity of Your Imperial Majesty and Your Illustrious Family.

"Sire, you are like the sun which shines alike upon the good and the evil. You have already made millions of your subjects happy; be also the providence of a poor orphan, of his mother and of an unfortunate and sick man whose sentence of excommunication has not yet been lifted, and who is ready at any moment to sacrifice his life for the Emperor, the benefactor of the people. . . .

"With my heart full of profound reverence and ardent and infinite devotion, I venture to assert that I am the most faithful and most grateful of Your Imperial Majesty's subjects.

"(signed) F. M. Dostoevsky."

This letter which may seem odiously servile from the Western point of view, was, in Dostoevsky's eyes, only the natural expression of his confidence in the czar. To the sovereign he was like a child, and complained to him as an unfortunate son complains to his father. Any Russian would have understood and approved. In May, 1849, when the revolutionary Bakunin was arrested and imprisoned in the Peter and Paul Fortress, Emperor Nicholas I dispatched Count Orlov to him with the following message: "The em-

peror has sent me to you. He ordered me to tell you this:
'Let him write to me as a son would write to his spiritual
father.' "

And Bakunin, the professional nihilist, the negator of all
traditions, the apostle of universal destruction, bowed to the
sovereign's will and wrote his confession in which we read:
"Yes, Sire, I will confess to you as to a spiritual father, of
whom man expects his absolution not here, but in another
world. I pray to God that He inspire me with simple and
sincere words, without malice and without flattery, worthy
of finding their way to Your Majesty's heart." Thus, shame
had no place in the relations between the czar and his subjects.

On the original of Dostoevsky's request, Prince Dolgoruky wrote the following sentence in his own hand: "The
emperor's order is: concerning Pavel Isaev, put him in touch
with the proper authorities. As for Dostoevsky, his request
has been granted."

But not until November 25, 1859, was the governor of
Tver officially advised of the emperor's resolution. What a
long delay! It is more terrible to mark time at the threshold
of paradise than to be thrown into hell.

"We shall speak about the past," Dostoevsky wrote to
Wrangel, "about the period when it was so good to be alive,
about Siberia, which has become so dear to me now that I
have left it."

To endure this distance from, or rather this proximity to,
happiness, Feodor Mikhailovich would have needed to find
some comfort in his wife. But Maria Dmitrievna was ill, and
her illness only emphasized her acrid, capricious and jealous
disposition. She had never loved Dostoevsky, she had married him in a moment of romantic exaltation and she could

not forgive herself for having been mistaken. He was poor, ugly, sickly and absurd; even his kindness was strangely unbearable. And was it not also unbearable that "highly placed people" should conceive an affection for him, invite him to their homes and shower attentions upon him? There was between the couple a continual exchange of petty recriminations.

Is it true, as Lubov Dostoevsky, the writer's daughter asserts, that his wife had confessed having betrayed him with Vergunov, after her marriage? The story is plausible, but unsupported by any documentary evidence. Dostoevsky was extremely discreet about the intimate details of his life. There is only a vague reference to his marriage in his letter to Wrangel dated September 22, "What shall I tell you about myself? I have taken upon me the burden of a family, and it is dragging me down." In 1865, he also wrote, "We were not happy together." Nor did his work give him interludes of much sought tranquillity. "I cannot work peacefully because of the continual visits."

The epileptic fits became increasingly frequent, and Dostoevsky's hemorrhoids caused him severe pain. Nevertheless, with a courage born of exasperation he corrected the proofs of *The Village of Stepanchikovo* and put into shape his notes for *The House of the Dead*. He also planned to revise his early works for a new edition.

"At last they will see what *The Double* is. When will I revise it if not now? Why should I lose a magnificent idea, a character that is superior to most other literary creations because of its social importance, and one which I was the first to discover and present to the public?" About *The House of the Dead*, he wrote, "They are not completely stupid, they realize how much curiosity such an article can

arouse in the first issues of a magazine. . . . Do not imagine
that I am strutting. But I am well aware of the interest and
significance of my work, and I want to get what is due to
me." The fact that Dostoevsky refers to his work as an "article" shows that he at first conceived it in modest dimensions,
and that only as he wrote it did he develop it to its eventual
proportions. "I will begin to write *The House of the Dead*
after October 15. My eyes hurt; I am absolutely unable to
work by candlelight."

In 1850, Mikhail had founded a cigarette factory and sold
his cigarettes in pretty boxes with surprise souvenirs. At
first the success was tremendous, but its novelty soon wore
off, and the former engineer-poet planned to liquidate his
business with heavy losses (actually he kept it going until
1861). His business experience qualified him to manage his
brother's affairs, but Feodor was unreasonably impatient, and
Mikhail's letters to him are full of remonstrances.

"I don't understand, my friend, why you worry and are
so excited. You have done your work, you have written a
novel, you have sent it to me; very well, then, perfect: be
calm and wait for the result, if you trust me." (October 2,
1859.) "Today, my dear friend, I have again received a
bombshell from you." (October 3, 1859.)

Finally, on November 2, Dostoevsky received a letter
from Totleben, which reassured him completely; it stated
that Prince Dolgoruky was not opposed to his return to the
capital. On November 25, 1859, a paper with the letterhead
of the Third Section reached the governor of Tver. It read,
"The emperor has graciously consented to the request mentioned above, but solely on condition that the secret surveillance of Dostoevsky be continued in St. Petersburg."

Dostoevsky's friends found for him an apartment in the great city, furnished it and hired a cook. When his train pulled into the station his brothers Mikhail and Nicolai, the writer Miliukov and other friends were waiting on the platform and waved joyously when they caught sight of him. The train stopped. Dostoevsky jumped from the footboard.

"There he is!" There were shouts, laughter, embraces. "Ten years! After ten years!"

"He had not changed physically," writes Miliukov, "his eyes had an even more fearless look than before, and he did not seem to have lost any of his energy."

7 · "THE HOUSE OF THE DEAD"

ST. PETERSBURG WAS A NEW WORLD. THE RUSSIA OF ALEXAN-
der II had little in common with the Russia of Nicholas I.
The new emperor had declared to a deputation of the Moscow nobility, "It is better to suppress serfdom from above
than to wait for its spontaneous disintegration from below."
In 1860, the emancipation of the serfs was only a question of
months. A so-called Central Committee under the chairman-
ship of the czar in person envisaged a method of emancipation that did not involve the payment of indemnities to the
landowners and enabled the peasants to acquire the lands
they had cultivated.

Other great liberal reforms were being studied. The press
was relatively free, and censorship was relaxed. The abolition

of corporal punishment and the complete publicity of court proceedings were openly debated.

These sudden transformations, coming after centuries of social stagnation, had stirred public opinion. The nobility, whose privileges were threatened, was naturally hostile to the governmental projects for reforms. Nor did the progressive circles support Alexander II's courageous initiatives; the unexpected realization of their own program only half satisfied them; these reforms granted in small doses fanned their impatience.

Having aroused the appetite for humanitarian progress, the czar was unable to satisfy it without renouncing some of his own prerogatives. The central authorities were outraged by demands of the radicals; and the radicals had concluded that they might as well demolish at one blow the ancient structure they were attacking.

Every citizen felt called upon to supply his answers to questions of domestic policy. Prompt and reliable information was the most urgent need, and there was no time for reflection, for any news was swallowed whole, and people were starved for news. In this sultry atmosphere, the press held a privileged position; it was now a vehicle of information, which determined the mood of the people. The progressive newspapers denounced the abuses of the old regime and demanded a complete political change. Thus, far from appeasing popular resentment against the monarchy and the church, Alexander II's concessions intensified this feeling.

Dostoevsky, with his great love for the czar and for Russia, was suddenly thrust into this bewildering milieu. He came from another world, another era, but he hailed the latest social reforms with joy, and was confident in his country's future. He was happy, but he soon discovered that no one shared his feeling, and then threw himself into the fray. Faced with a new situation, he reasserted his ideas of the forties. The prison had not changed him: he was not a conservative, he was a Russian conservative; he was not a liberal, he was a Russian liberal. This Russian conservative liberalism endorsed a number of reforms that did not imitate those of the West but conformed to the old Russian tradition. According to Dostoevsky, the Slav peoples had a way of life that must be preserved. The reactionary Slavophiles were more Muscovite than Russian, and the progressive liberals were more European than Russian. Between these two extremes there was a middle course, the only right one, and Dostoevsky wanted to follow it.

But he was not understood, for no one wanted to understand him. In the eyes of the students he was an ex-convict, a martyr for freedom. When he was asked at literary gatherings to read passages from *The House of the Dead*, it was not the author whom they applauded, but the partisan. The fame they bestowed upon him was based on a misconception. He was not one of them, and he suffered from being acclaimed for ideas that he had never had, for an ideal he had never defended. Later he told Strakhov how reluctant he was to read aloud certain passages from his book, "As if I were complaining in public! As if I were always complaining! That is not right!"

This false situation was unbearable. Dostoevsky felt that he must clarify his stand. He and Mikhail resolved to publish a journal. The idea of founding a journal actually dated back to 1858; and its program had been submitted to the board of censorship on October 31, 1858, but only in 1860 did the two brothers carry out their project.

The journal, a monthly, was called *Time*. The nominal

editor-in-chief was Mikhail Dostoevsky who took charge of
the administration. Feodor was the literary and political editor. It was he who wrote the initial statement of policy, a
detailed defense of Russian liberalism.

"At last we have come to understand that we too are a
nation with a clearly defined and highly original character,
and that our task is to create a new form of life, developed
from our own earth, drawing its resources from our own soul
and our own popular tradition." The editor took care to
specify that his magazine must not be confused with the publications of the Occidentalists nor with those of the Slavophiles.

"The public understands at last," he wrote, "that the Occidentalists stubbornly want us to wear a cast-off garment that
does not fit and bursts at the seams, and that the Slavophiles
dream poetically of resurrecting Russia with ideals and customs of the past." As a result of this courageous statement,
Time became the target of both Slavophiles and Occidentalists.

Nevertheless, readers flocked to it, and the circulation
increased at a satisfying tempo. Dostoevsky obtained contri-
butions from Turgenev, Ostrovsky, Nekrasov, Apollon
Grigoriev, the critic, and Strakhov, the young philosopher.
To attract the public, Dostoevsky did not hesitate to publish
The Crimes of Lacenaire and passages from the *Memoirs of
Casanova*. He himself did a considerable amount of work,
writing fantastic stories, critical articles, and planning and
revising serials.

He worked almost exclusively at night, before a samovar
in his silent house, all the while drinking cold tea that was as
thick and strong as syrup. At five o'clock he would lie down
and sleep until two in the afternoon.

This routine proved too much for Dostoevsky's strength. Three months after the publication of the first issue of *Time* he fell ill. Although he recovered quickly, his epileptic fits became even more frequent, one or two a week. He could always somehow feel them coming. Then it was as though all his doubts and agitation were resolved in a transcendent harmony; he was serene, cleansed of all cares, and prepared for the dazzling joys of the beyond.

"But these radiant moments," he writes in *The Idiot*, "were but the prelude to the second phase, which was followed by the seizure. This second phase is assuredly indescribable. . . . What does it matter that it is a disease, if at such moments I had an unprecedented undreamt-of sensation of fullness and peace, of participating in the highest synthesis of life with a passionate prayer."

"For the space of several minutes," Dostoevsky explained to his friends, "I know a happiness that cannot be conceived in normal moments, that other people cannot even imagine. I have a feeling of complete harmony within myself and with the world, and this feeling is so strong, so sweet, that for a few seconds of this joy one would willingly give ten years of one's life, perhaps even all of one's life."

It was when he reached the peak of this mystic ecstasy that the spasm seized him, flung him down to the ground, shrieking and foaming at the mouth, Strakhov who was present once, describes it as follows: "He stood still an instant, as though searching for words to express his thought and was about to open his mouth. I watched him intently; I was certain that he was going to say something extraordinary. But suddenly he emitted a strange, drawn-out cry, collapsed and fell unconscious in the middle of the room."

Sometimes Dostoevsky hurt himself in these falls; covered

his face with bruises. When he recovered consciousness, his
muscles were sore from spasms, his head felt light. He says
that he felt, according to his own account, he had committed
some terrible crime which nothing could redeem. Was it the
death of his father, was it the death of the drunkard Isaev
that tortured him? A need for self-punishment dominated all
of Dostoevsky's inner life.

After an epileptic seizure Feodor Mikhailovich would
often lose his memory for several days; he would be ill-
tempered and could write only with difficulty. His notebook
for the years 1862 and 1863 contains the following appalling
entries:

> Epileptic attacks:
> April 1—violent.
> August 1—weak.
> November 7—medium.
> January 7—violent.
> March 2—moderate.

It was under these conditions that Dostoevsky wrote his
first great novel after his return from Siberia, *The Insulted
and Injured* and completed *The House of the Dead*. The
first installment of the former was published in January,
1861, in the first issue of *Time*.

The reviewers were severe with *The Insulted and Injured*.

"Mr. Dostoevsky will forgive me if I say that his novel is,
so to speak, beneath criticism," wrote Dobroliubov.

"Implausibility can never be the result of art," wrote
Kushelev-Bezborodko. "All this is artificial beyond measure.
The greatest flaw of this novel is the author's failure to de-
pict or illumine even one living character, one real type."

"Worst of all," wrote Zarin, "is the fact that one cannot

find in it anything solid to lay one's hands on. One hears someone moaning about something. But who is moaning? And about what?"

Apollon Grigoriev, the critic of *Time*, Dostoevsky's own magazine, declared that the characters of *The Insulted and Injured* were just automatons, "walking books." Dostoevsky accepted this verdict.

"The new magazine whose success was dearer to me than anything else needed a novel," he writes, "and so I decided upon a work in four parts. I assured my brother that I had a plot ready, which was untrue. . . . I am fully aware that the characters of my novel are puppets, not living people—'walking books,' not figures animated by art. (To achieve this I would have needed time for my ideas to ripen in my mind and heart.) . . . Thus I produced a barbarous work, which, however, contains some fifty pages that I am proud of."

The astounding success of *The House of the Dead* soon redeemed the failure of *The Insulted and Injured*. This time the critics were unanimous in recognizing the author's tremendous gifts. Miliukov wrote, "It is a long time since a work as gripping as *The House of the Dead* has appeared in our literature." Some critics compared Dostoevsky to Dante. They praised his description of the bathhouse and the spectacle of naked, deformed, scarred bodies struggling in a nauseous steam. They quoted the scene in which the chained convicts give a performance for their comrades, and the scenes of the hospital, of the whippings, and of the departure.

The censor had at first thought it advisable to demand certain alterations in the text. "Will not uninformed readers interpret the highly humanitarian measures of the government in relation to the penitentiaries as a softening of the penalties for very serious crimes?" wrote the anonymous bureaucrat. Dostoevsky had even prepared an additional text to explain that loss of freedom took away the prisoners' appetite for rye bread so justly reputed in Russia. But on November 12, 1860, the Ministry of the Interior, overriding the objections of the board of censorship, authorized the publication of *The House of the Dead*, provided that certain "indecent expressions" be eliminated.

The publication of *The Insulted and Injured* and *The House of the Dead* in *Time* brought new readers to the magazine. In 1861, it had 2,300 subscribers; in 1862, their number increased to 4,302. Mikhail liquidated his cigarette business to give all his time to the magazine. He and Feodor determined the editorial policy and advised the contributors. The young writers and critics of this group had courage and faith, and were convinced that they were working for Russia and the world.

Meanwhile important political events followed one another with increasing rapidity. On February 19, 1861, an edict of Alexander II emancipated the serfs of the empire. But the reform had been too long in coming; it had been too much discussed to satisfy public opinion. In the words of Chelgunov, "When all that remained to be done was to write the statutes of February 19, society had had time to think of other things." The radicals were eager for action. In London, Herzen, the revolutionary exile, wrote in his journal, *The Bell*, "When the generals and functionaries began to apply the new law, the people realized that they were receiving freedom only in words, not deeds. . . . A new form of serfdom has been created." (July 1, 1861.) A few months later he wrote, "Listen! From all the corners of our immense country, from the Don to the Urals, from the Volga to the Dnieper, the grumbling is increasing, the revolt is rising. It is the first booming of a tidal wave that heralds many storms after a depressing lull."

Herzen's journal was banned in Russia but it was imported clandestinely and circulated from hand to hand. The university students were in a ferment. They wanted a new order. They did not quite know what this new order was to be like, but that mattered little. Suddenly, in November, 1861, the so-called Student Affair exploded. Liberal ideas had inflamed the university youth. They had been reading revolutionary publications, holding meetings, assembling libraries of forbidden books, raising funds for the needy, publishing liberal tracts, and they had even created a secret tribunal to try their peers. All this inconsequential activity on the margin of official politics distracted them from their studies. The classrooms were transformed into meeting halls. Academic authorities appealed to the emperor to issue a decree forbidding meetings and deputations. The students protested at this "bullying." The police were compelled to round up groups of rebels in the streets; were to arrest demonstrators and release them two or three times a day. Finally the ringleaders were imprisoned in the Peter and Paul Fortress, delighted with this sudden notoriety. The whole community admired their courage, and at visiting hours, large crowds gathered in the prison. Mikhail Dostoevsky, in the name of *Time,* sent the young men a large roast, a bottle of cognac, and a bottle of wine. Those condemned to deportation were escorted as far as the suburbs by an admiring throng.

Later the university was closed "for purposes of reorganization." But the professors obtained permission to lecture in the Duma. The students took charge of organizing the lec-

tures and maintaining order. But on March 3, 1862, this new
municipal university was also outlawed. At a literary and
musical soiree on the previous day Professor Pavlov had read
a paper that, like the rest of the program, had been passed by
the censor. But he read in a tone that entirely changed the
meaning of his speech. At the sentence: "At the moment of
his accession to the throne, the emperor who at present reigns
so felicitously over us found the cup overflowing," he was
interrupted by a wild ovation and was unable to explain that
Alexander had spilled out of the cup the few drops of bitterness that remained because serfdom still existed.

The professor was deported from St. Petersburg, and
when his colleagues manifested their indignation by suspend-
ing their lectures, the government forbade all public lectures.

Dostoevsky, who was one of the speakers at the meeting of
March 2, later revived the scene in *The Possessed.* "The
clamor of the crowd prevented the last words from being
heard. . . . The audience shouted and clapped, and some of
the ladies even cried: 'Enough, enough, better not say it!' "

Despite the closing of the municipal university the revolutionary agitators continued their work relentlessly. Secret
societies sprang up everywhere. Chernyshevsky and Utin,
who wrote for the *Contemporary*, together with Colonel
Lavrov founded the group, *Land and Freedom*, whose task
was defined as that of "fighting against the imperial government, which is the people's worst enemy." Under the doors
of private citizens were slipped revolutionary tracts that bore
such slogans as: "Long live the Russian social and democratic
republic!", or "We shall have only one cry: To the axes!",
and declarations like the following: "We shall put to death
the members of the imperial party, and we shall be just as
sorry for them as they are now for us. Strike them down in

the public squares if these villains dare to show themselves there, strike them down in their houses, in the narrow streets of the little towns, in the wide streets of the big cities; strike them down in the villages and in the hamlets." Another proclamation read: "One hundred thousand persons in Russia are opposed to public warfare; let their blood redden the streets, let us not leave a stone unturned!"

Dostoevsky found one of these appeals "to young Russia" tied to his door knob. He was beside himself with indignation. "And I," he later wrote in *A Writer's Diary*, "had not been in agreement, intellectually or emotionally, with this kind of people, and with the spirit of their movement. I was suddenly grieved, and almost ashamed of their blunders. . . . These facts revealed a crushing truth: the horrible decline in the level of education and intelligence, of which these proclamations gave evidence." He paid a visit to Chernyshevsky and asked him to beg the authors of the manifestoes to listen to reason.

"My intervention would probably be of no avail," Chernyshevsky answered him with indifference. "And anyhow, such phenomena are inevitable sideshows."

On May 16, mysterious fires broke out in St. Petersburg; entire city quarters remained ablaze for two weeks despite the efforts of the police and the firemen. "I recall," writes Strakhov, "that Feodor Mikhailovich and I went for a sail out of the city to take our minds off things. From the deck of the boat one could see great clouds of smoke rising from three or four different parts of the city. We disembarked at a garden where an orchestra was playing and gypsies were singing."

The government was unable to discover the arsonists, but suspicion pointed to the nihilists of the *Land and Freedom* group. The *Contemporary* was suspended for eight months, and shortly afterward, the revolutionary, Chernyshevsky, was imprisoned in the Peter and Paul Fortress.

Dostoevsky, for his part, was upset by the political events and so exhausted by his editorial work that he resolved to go to France. His doctors had been urging him for some time to take a long rest outside of Russia. The trip was so expensive that he could not afford to take his wife along; moreover, Maria Dmitrievna did not wish to leave her son who was preparing for admission to the Gymnasium. In June, 1862, Dostoevsky left Russia for his first trip abroad.

Dostoevsky arrived in Paris toward the middle of June. He knew no one there, and no one knew him. He did not meet Victor Hugo, who at that time had published *Les Misérables*, nor Flaubert, who had published *Salambô*, nor Théophile Gautier, who had just published *Capitaine Fracasse*, nor Renan, nor Sainte-Beuve, nor Taine. He led a secluded life and regretted having left Russia. Homesickness led to ill humor.

"Paris is a terribly sad city," he wrote to Strakhov. "If it were not for a number of admirable monuments here, I would have died of boredom." He stayed only ten days in France, and came to the conclusion that "the Frenchman is calm, honest, polite, but false, and loves only money."

He left France for England. In London, he met Herzen, the nihilist, and although his political views were in direct opposition to Herzen's, the two writers got on well together.

"Dostoevsky came to see me yesterday," Herzen wrote to Ogarev. "He is naïve, a little confused, but very amiable. He has an enthusiastic faith in the Russian people."

Dostoevsky for his part was "quite gentle" toward Herzen

during this visit, but several years later reproached the nihilist for having betrayed Russia. Feodor Mikhailovich wrote in
A Writer's Diary, "Herzen did not emigrate, he was born
an *émigré*. Because he separated himself from the people, he naturally lost his God. It goes without saying that
Herzen was bound to be a socialist, motivated solely by the
logic of his ideas and total lack of any feeling for his native
land. . . . He denied the family, yet he seems to have been
a good father and husband. He denied property, but managed his affairs quite well, and had the pleasure of not feeling
the pinch of poverty in a foreign land. He organized the revolution and urged others to action; at the same time, he loved
peace and comfort in his own home."

Because Herzen showed him around, Dostoevsky found
London more attractive than Paris. "The streets are lighted
by gas jets, such as are unknown in Russia. At every step,
there are cafés with mirrors and gilt ornaments. People
gather together there and find shelter." On July 8 he returned to Paris. During his first stay in Paris, Dostoevsky had
written to Strakhov, suggesting that they go to Switzerland
and Italy together. Strakhov agreed, and Geneva was chosen
as their meeting place. Dostoevsky returned to Paris on
July 8 and proceeded to Geneva by way of Cologne, Düs-
seldorf, Fayence and Basel, joining Strakhov on July 22.

The two friends found Switzerland "dull and gloomy";
nevertheless, they went to Lucerne and thence to Turin and
Genoa. From Genoa they took a boat to Leghorn; and from
there they went to Florence by rail. But Dostoevsky was not
a good traveler. He walked about like a somnambulist, and
came out of his trance only to catch a glimpse of the silhou-
ette of a fat bourgeois seated in a café or of a landlady blowing her nose, pulling it like a bell cord. In a flash he evoked

the wretched personal dramas, the anemic joys, the carefully
nurtured remorse of the people he saw. He turned their living flesh inside out like a rabbit skin, but their background
receded into the fog: Dostoevsky never saw beyond human
beings, his vision was confined to man. Scenery did not interest him. If he noticed the flat, straight streets of Turin, it
was only to compare them with those of St. Petersburg, and
the Arno reminded him of the Fontanka. "Neither nature
nor the monuments nor the works of art interested him,"
wrote Strakhov. "All his attention was centered on people."
Finally, after spending a week in Florence, Strakhov made
up his mind to go to Paris, and Dostoevsky to return to
Russia.

Immediately upon his arrival in St. Petersburg Dostoevsky
wrote for *Time* his *Winter Notes on Summer Impressions*,
in which he ridiculed with ferocious irony the countries he
had visited.

"One can never take away from a Frenchman—that is to
say, a Parisian, because at bottom all Frenchmen are Parisians
—the idea that he is not the first man in the world. With the
exception of Paris, however, he knows very little of the
world, and he does not insist at all on knowing it." So much
for French patriotism.

"Every year, at an opportune moment, the Chamber of
Deputies has a debate on the most important political problems, and the Parisian is touched with sweet emotion. He
knows there will be a flood of eloquence and rejoices in that
fact." So much for French eloquence.

"The bourgeois of Paris has another legitimate need—like
eloquence—that of lying on the grass." So much for appreciation of nature.

And what about love? "When the bourgeois wants to in-

dulge in sentiment or to deceive his wife, he always calls her
ma biche, 'my little doe.' Conversely, the loving wife, in a
mood of playful teasing, calls her dear bourgeois *Bribri.* . . .
In the eyes of the Parisian, a good simulation of love is for
the most part equivalent to real love."

All this, Dostoevsky perceived during his first brief visit
to Paris. From London he brought back the image of an immense, noisy, bustling city: "The railroad, which runs above
the houses (and soon will run underneath), the spirit of bold
initiative, the apparent disorder, which is in reality the bourgeois order at its height, the polluted Thames, the air impregnated with coal, the splendid squares and parks, the sinister
quarters, such as Whitechapel, with its half-naked, fierce,
hungry population, the city with its millions and its far-flung
trade." He felt that he was in the temple of Baal. All Europe,
all the West seemed to him ruined by progress. These countries without God, he thought, these countries of man-made
God, of money, calculation, science, were being gradually
smothered under the weight of their artifacts, and salvation
was to be sought elsewhere—in a new people, the Russian
people among whom the simple faith of childhood still prevailed, and who waited at the gate of history for its hour to
strike. It was Russia, Dostoevsky concluded, that would save
Europe.

In the beginning of 1863, however, all Europe rose against
Russia in a storm of criticism. This was the climax of a long
development that began with the czar's visit to Warsaw in
1856, when he promised his Polish subjects that the past
would be completely forgiven and forgotten.

"But do not indulge in illusions," he said. "It is my conviction that you can be happy only if Poland is, like Finland,

part of the great family that constitutes the Russian empire."

In 1861, an imperial decree granted Poland a Council of State composed of Poles, to hold authority over the local elective councils. Moreover, special Polish commissions were now to take charge of the courts, schools, and church affairs. Marquess Wielopolski, a Pole, was appointed head of the administrative machine, and Grand Duke Constantin Nicolaevich, a partisan of liberal reform, was named viceroy of Poland.

Wielopolski was a moderate, and the tempering of the regime had the same effect in Poland as in Russia—it exasperated instead of appeasing the passions of the malcontents. The emperor's concessions were interpreted as a sign of weakness. Finally, on January 13, 1863, after an attempt on the life of Grand Duke Constantin, open rebellion broke out; groups of insurgents attacked Russian troops in various points of Poland and Lithuania.

The Russians repressed the insurrection mercilessly. In Lithuania, Governor Muraviev, nicknamed "the hangman," ordered his troops not to take prisoners; in Poland, General Berg gained notoriety from the massacre of Fishau. France, England, and Austria were aroused by these cruelties, but Russia turned a deaf ear to their warnings and threats.

In London, the revolutionary Herzen took the side of the Poles. His stand was, "You cannot support a government that by force of arms brings misfortune on the Poles and yourselves, without deliberately committing a crime or degrading yourselves to unconsciously playing the part of hangman. At the point where discipline calls for murder, it is no longer a duty."

In adopting this line with regard to the Polish problem, *The Bell* committed a serious blunder. Polish independence presupposed the dismemberment of the Russian empire, and if the liberals followed Herzen, they must betray Russia. Most of them were not sufficiently enlightened to place the general interests of mankind above national interest. Russia was under attack, Russians were fighting, Russian blood was flowing in Poland, and foreign powers were attempting to intervene in order to impose their arbitration on the imperial government. Patriotic pride was suddenly awakened, and the liberals and Slavophiles found themselves in the same camp. The circulation of *The Bell* began to decline rapidly, and Herzen was compelled to cease his propaganda.

It was in this feverish atmosphere that Strakhov wrote his great article on Poland entitled "The Fatal Problem." This somewhat abstract and confused philippic condemned the Poles on the ground that they were part of Western civilization. Their ardent Catholicism, their pride, their contempt for their neighbors, were severely criticized. In order to stress the absurdity of the Polish claims, Strakhov resorted to the device of speaking in the name of the Poles. This subtlety led the public astray. The Slavophiles thought that the author of the article had gone over to the enemy, and *The Moscow Gazette* violently attacked *Time*, for what it assailed as the latter's partiality to Poland. Even the Poles and their supporters considered Strakhov one of them. In France, the *Revue des Deux Mondes*, which was hostile to Russia, printed a translation of Strakhov's article, with an editorial comment to the effect that it expressed the views of the civilized world.

On May 24, 1863, the Russian Minister of the Interior suspended the publication of *Time*, on the ground that it was pursuing a policy "contrary to the intentions of the government and to Russia's interest." Mikhail and his friends protested and tried to prove their innocence of disloyal motives, but to no avail. Strakhov was aghast, and Dostoevsky, driven to despair by this absurd contretemps on the very threshold of success, resolved to go abroad in order to get away from it all. He borrowed fifteen hundred rubles from the Literary Fund, giving as security the income from his works, promising to pay back the loan before February, 1864. This time, however, Dostoevsky did not intend to travel alone.

Since his return to St. Petersburg, Dostoevsky had led a feverish intellectual life. His work as a novelist, the administration of the periodical, the writing of editorials, all kept him in a state of constant nervous tension. Overworked and worried, he would have liked to find in his wife a refuge from his literary tribulations, but Maria Dmitrievna was ill, her eyes were hollow, her cheeks sunken, her whole face was like a death mask. Moreover, she did not love him; she had told him so, she had screamed it in his face. She seized every opportunity to renew the old quarrel.

"I should not have married you," she said to him, "I would have been happier without you, and you would have been happier without me. I am a burden to you, I see that clearly." And each of these accusations and reproaches touched Feodor Mikhailovich to the quick.

"I am married, I am sick, I edit a magazine," he wrote sadly to Belinsky's wife. He needed to escape from the stuffy room where a withered woman continually talked of her past, cursed and sobbed. He yearned for a young, pure love, dreamed of coquettish laughter, light flirtation, tender words.

In 1860, he became infatuated with Madame Shubert, a frivolous and gay young actress, but never went beyond the status of helpful cavalier, a role that he accepted naturally because he was accustomed to it. With morbid pleasure he mediated between her and her husband. He loved without declaring his love, and spent himself on this woman who never made him happy. As with Madame Panaev and with Maria Dmitrievna, he experienced the gratifying ordeal of a platonic passion. He said that if he possessed the slightest talent he would have composed vaudeville sketches for the young woman. On June 12, 1860, he wrote to her, "I love you very deeply, very ardently, and I told you that I did not love you only because I wanted you to trust me, but, God, how sad I was when it seemed to me that you no longer counted on me. . . . Your letter settled all that, however, and heaven send you every kind of joy. I am so happy to be sure that I do not love you. This enables me to be even more devoted to you without fearing to be carried away by my feelings. Good-by, my little dove, it is with respect and reverence that I kiss your teasing little paw and press it with all my heart between my two hands."

It is not known for how long Dostoevsky remained involved in this confused and mild flirtation, but one day he was given another chance to be happy. At a party organized for the benefit of poor students, where he had been invited to read excerpts from his works, he met pretty Polina Suslova, a pale girl with a hard, proud face and deliberate gestures. Rozanov, who later became her husband, wrote of her, "She was like Catherine de' Medici. She would not have hesitated to commit a crime, even murder. Wholeheartedly on the night of St. Bartholomew, she would have fired on the Huguenots from her window. Most of the time she had a majestic appearance. I know people who were completely seduced and dominated by her."

Polina's father was an illiterate muzhik who by dint of shrewdness and tenacity had risen to the position of steward on the estate of his landlord, had enriched himself by honest means, and had in the end founded a factory of his own. Nadezhda, one of his daughters, became the first woman physician in Russia. As for Polina, her ambition was limited to remaining an "eternal student."

Polina typified the volatile girl who registers for one course after another but goes to only one lecture in ten, takes notes that she never rereads, prepares for examinations that she never takes, but assiduously attends all the conclaves of the student body. She was infatuated with politics, she fed on hollow ideas and inflated emotions and was all for total revolution, for deputations, representations, manifestations, proclamations, and agitation of every description. A fanatical feminist, she extolled free love and equality before the law. She did not believe in God. A report of the director of the Vladimir School described her as follows: "Suslova is a person in whom one can have no confidence. First, she wears blue glasses; second, her hair is cut short. Moreover, it appears that she is very independent in her opinions, and that she never goes to church."

The growing reputation of Dostoevsky had made a large impression on the young nihilist who felt that only one who had suffered and loved as he had, and who had such deep knowledge of the human heart would be capable of understanding her and appeasing all her doubts. Beside him, she thought, all her feminine anxieties would be easily controlled; he would advise her, give a new meaning to her disordered life, make her a useful woman. She needed him.

With uninhibited abandon, Polina wrote Dostoevsky a frenzied letter imploring him to receive her, brought to the meeting the manuscript of a short story, and requested the honor of becoming a contributor to *Time*. Although he printed the story in the issue of September, 1861, Dostoevsky fought against the love of this young woman until December, 1862. He was older than she, and doubted the attractiveness of his round face, ruddy mustache, wide forehead, and eyes clear and hard as glass, while she was beautiful, robust, and proud. He was a married man, jaded with life, overburdened with cares and debts, while she was single, carefree, inexperienced, and full of life and ardor. He realized that such a union could only be unhappy, but he was anxious to escape from his sick, dispirited, nagging wife who coughed and spat, who was always on the point of dying, and still smarted from the mischievous coquetry of Madame Shubert. He wanted to be loved tempestuously, he wanted to begin life anew with Polina, and so he yielded to the temptation of her fair body and her ardent mind, feeling that he was committing a crime. Actually, the crime was not against her but against himself.

From the very beginning of this liaison, Polina Suslova felt a hatred for her quadragenarian seducer. She had naïvely hoped that he would set her soul at rest, make her one of the few who could lay claim to a high destiny; but he flagged and descended to her level instead of raising her to his. She had hoped that he would dominate her with his mind, actually it was she who dominated him sensually. He revealed to her a happiness that she could no longer do without: but the very fact disgusted her strangely. She felt humiliated and defiled. She hated to see his freckled face, his mustache and imploring eyes, and yet she lived only for the presence of this man. She pitied him, despised and detested him. He was her indispensable enemy. Later she wrote in her diary, "At night I would awake and recall with horror the events of the day, and I would run around the room, sobbing." But when Feodor Mikhailovich decided to leave Russia after the suppression of *Time*, she consented at once to accompany him.

The liquidation of the periodical, however, proved to be more difficult than had been anticipated and Dostoevsky was compelled to postpone his trip. He hoped Polina would wait for the end of the negotiations, and that they would start off together at the beginning of August, but Polina seized this opportunity to escape, to travel alone, and to live in a big city where no one knew her. She wanted to make a last attempt to break the abominable hold he had on her. She packed her bags, left her lover to his difficulties, and went to Paris where he promised to join her.

Several months later, on August 19, 1863, Polina received a letter from Dostoevsky announcing his coming. He was on his way, he wrote, and would be in Paris in a few days. But despite his impatience to join Polina, he could not resist the temptation to try his luck at roulette, in Wiesbaden. He went straight from the railroad station to the casino. In the immense room with its great, heavy chandeliers and its faded mirrors, the green cloth of the table seemed to cast an absinthe glow. Around it was a ring of ravaged, petrified faces that looked moldy in the dim light of the chandeliers. Their eyes stared at the whirling roulette bowl; they hoped, prayed, cursed and calculated feverishly.

Dostoevsky wagered a modest sum and won. He played again, and again he won. Then he staked all he had, and again the croupier's scoop pushed a heap of chips and gold pieces toward him—ten thousand and four hundred francs. He was a rich man! He rushed from the casino, bought a ticket at the railroad station, and went back to his hotel looking like a madman. But he had hardly shut his valise when the impulse to try the "grand slam," to win one hundred thousand francs, overpowered him. Returning to the casino, he lost all his stakes, one after the other. At the end of the day he still had five thousand francs. Happy and exhausted, he decided to leave Wiesbaden for Paris.

"Do not tell anyone of this, dear Varvara Dmitrievna," he wrote to his sister-in-law. "It is Pasha [Pavel Isaev, his stepson] that I have in mind. He is still so naïve that he might imagine one could easily earn one's living by gambling. . . . It is not necessary to tell him that his father goes to gambling establishments." He declared that he now knew the secret of gambling. "Nothing is simpler and more stupid. You need only to keep your self-control, and no matter what sudden turns fortune may take, avoid becoming excited."

Later, Dostoevsky wrote in *The Gambler*, "Yesterday, as soon as I approached the gambling table and began to gather up the piles of bills, my love receded to the background. . . . Is it possible that I am a gambler?"

On August 26 Dostoevsky finally arrived in Paris and wrote to Polina asking for a rendezvous. On August 27 she made the following entry in her diary: "I have just received a letter from Feodor Mikhailovich, sent this time from Paris. How happy he is that he is going to see me soon. I sent him a very short note that I had prepared before his arrival. I am very sorry for him."

The same night he saw her, in the little pension in Rue Soufflot where she was staying. She came toward him, very pale, her eyes dry. The scene that followed is described in her diary:

" 'Good evening,' she said in an uncertain voice. And as he

embraced her awkwardly, she murmured: 'I thought you
would not come, I wrote you a letter.'

" 'What letter?'

" 'To tell you not to come.'

" 'Why?'

" 'Because it is too late.' "

He recoiled, bowing his head. She could see only his hair,
and his enormous forehead contracted with pain. Suddenly
he cried in a hoarse voice, "Hear me, Polina, I must know
everything. Let us go somewhere else. You must tell me
everything or I shall die."

With utmost composure Polina proposed going to his
room.

"We went the whole way in silence," she writes in her
diary. "I did not look at him. From time to time he called to
the cab driver in an impatient, desperate voice: 'Hurry,
hurry!' The driver would turn around and look at us with
surprise. Every now and then Feodor Mikhailovich seized
my hand in a nervous grip. 'Calm yourself, I am with you,'
I said."

They finally arrived at Dostoevsky's hotel and entered his
room. He slammed the door shut and fell at Polina's feet.

"Clasping my knees and sobbing aloud, he exclaimed: 'I
have lost you, I knew it!' "

She had never seemed as desirable as at this moment when
she was breaking away from him. She stood before him,
straight, motionless, protected by the silk of her billowing
dress. With his mind he saw her body whose full warmth
he knew so well. He moaned, "He may be young, handsome,
eloquent, but you will never find a heart like mine."

Polina soothed him with gentle detachment. When at last
he had regained control of himself, she told him calmly of

her new liaison. During these months of freedom in Paris she had become infatuated with a handsome Spaniard named Salvador, who had an arrogant face and a red, sensual mouth. "Fine down" covered his upper lip, his gestures exuded self-assurance, and when he looked at her she almost fainted with joy. She had unthinkingly given herself to him to escape from Dostoevsky. Salvador's passion was a relief to her after the intellectual complications and refined tortures that Dostoevsky delighted in. She, the eternal student, needed a young animal, not a writer of genius. She talked and talked, and Dostoevsky listened, with a stricken face.

"Are you happy?" he asked at last.

"No."

"You mean to say that you are in love with him and that you are unhappy? Is such a thing possible?"

"He does not love me."

"He does not love you!" Dostoevsky exclaimed, clasping his head in despair. "Then you love him like a slave? Tell me, I must know: You would follow him to the end of the earth, wouldn't you?"

"No . . . I . . . I will bury myself in a remote village," she whispered between sobs. For she was weeping at last, and Dostoevsky beheld her tears with rapture. If she could still cry before him, all was not lost; it meant that he could still comfort her, that he could still be something to her. He was filled with infinite tenderness and he took her in his arms as one would a child.

"Oh, Polina, why are you so unhappy?" he said. "I clearly foresaw that you would end up by loving another—I knew it, it was by mistake that you loved me."

He told her that he would now be her friend, since he could no longer be her lover. He would protect her from others. With morbid relish, he resumed his role of intimate confidant and enthusiastic helper. As with Madame Panaev, Maria Dmitrievna, and Madame Shubert, he would be the hungry man before the groaning board, the bystander, the third member of the triangle. He said, "Let us go to Italy. I will be a brother to you."

"I promised to see him the next day," we read in Polina's diary. "I felt calmer after talking with him. He understands me."

But she was still reluctant to accompany him. Then she received a letter from a friend of Salvador, informing her that her lover was ill with typhoid fever and asking her to refrain from visiting him. She was frantic, and Dostoevsky comforted her. He told her, "The Paris specialists are excellent physicians, the climate is good here, and Salvador will recover quickly." He recovered even sooner than Dostoevsky had predicted, for on the street the following day Polina met her lover, bright-eyed and glowing with health. She decided to break with the handsome Spaniard and accompany Feodor Mikhailovich to Italy.

"I am happy," he said to her. "But who will ever understand you?"

Thus began the strange escapade of this cold amazon and her lascivious chaperon. They stopped at Baden-Baden.

"Feodor Mikhailovich is very happy, and gambles incessantly at roulette," Suslova wrote in her diary. They drank tea in her room, then Polina lay on her bed and held Feodor Mikhailovich's hand, and he, the good companion, told her that "he had not lost hope." Suddenly he drew back and wiped his forehead with his hand.

" 'Do you know what has just happened to me?' he exclaimed with a strange expression.

" 'What?' I looked at his face which showed extreme agitation.

" 'I felt an impulse to kiss your foot.'

" 'But why,' I said very much troubled, even frightened a little. I withdrew my feet and covered them.

" 'I had an impulse and I decided to obey it.' "

At last he ceased insisting, but began to pace up and down in the little hotel room, bumping into the furniture. Polina begged him to leave.

"Go back to your own room, I want to sleep."

He left, but soon came back, under the pretext that he wanted to shut the window. He approached her and told her in a low voice to undress. She saw his face, tense with desire, his starved eyes and dilated nostrils.

"I will undress later," she said. "Go away."

He went like a beaten dog. He returned to his room and lay on his bed. He dreamed of the warm body only a few steps away.

Feodor Mikhailovich was exasperated to the point of madness by the sensual atmosphere in which he lived, crushed under the burden of the emasculated love life that he had imposed upon himself. He sought release in gambling in which he found a substitute for the sexual act that was denied him. In the excitement of roulette he recaptured the emotional ecstasies that he had experienced with Polina, also the experience of tasting a vile joy, of committing a crime against someone, of destroying something beautiful within himself that had until then remained unpolluted. He would return from the casino to his hotel, exhausted as after a night of love, and the next day he was again calm and friendly.

At Baden-Baden Dostoevsky lost three thousand francs.

"How can one gamble while traveling with a woman one loves?" Mikhail, who knew of his brother's liaison, wrote to him.

"Here one can win ten thousand francs without any effort," Feodor Mikhailovich answered his brother. "I have made this trip to save you and myself from poverty. Moreover, I have faith in my lucky star."

In Geneva Dostoevsky pawned his watch and Polina's ring in order to continue the journey, but the money he obtained was just sufficient to enable the couple to reach Turin, where funds from St. Petersburg awaited them. By the time they reached Rome, the relation between the two lovers had begun to deteriorate; Feodor Mikhailovich was irritated by this woman who shared his life but refused to give herself to him. He said one day to Polina, "One cannot torture a man as you are torturing me. He will end up by no longer desiring you."

In *The Gambler*, which describes Dostoevsky's liaison with Polina, we read "There were moments when I could have given half my life to be able to strangle her. I swear it, if I could slowly have plunged a knife into her breast, I think I should have done it with delight. And yet, if on the Schlangenberg she had said to me: 'Throw yourself over the precipice,' I would have done so with joy." A little later, there is this important statement, "Yes, on many occasions she did not look upon me as a man."

To realize that he was no longer a man to her made him suffer more than everything else. She no longer feared him since she had agreed to travel with him.

"Feodor Mikhailovich told me," Polina wrote, "that he felt humiliated to leave me thus (it was one o'clock in the morning, I was lying on my bed, undressed), humiliated because Russians never retreat."

Time, reflection, habit gradually wore out Dostoevsky's infatuation. He was weary, he longed to return to Russia and resume writing, all the more so because Maria Dmitrievna's condition had suddenly become worse. For Feodor Mikhailovich had not forgotten his wife in the course of this harrowing trip. He often referred to her in his letters.

"I think often of Maria Dmitrievna; how I long to receive some good news of her. How is she?" (Letter to his brother Nicolai, August 28, 1863.) "When you hear something about your mother, write to me." (Letter to Pavel Isaev, August 28, 1863.) "Write me something about Maria Dmitrievna." (Letter to V. D. Constant, September 20, 1863.)

From Rome, Dostoevsky and Suslova went to Naples, and from Naples back to Turin. Finally, in the middle of October, the lovers separated. Polina went to Paris, and Dostoevsky to Russia.

On the way he stopped at Hamburg and lost in gambling all the money that remained for his trip. Panic-stricken, he wrote to Polina, who, although in dire straits herself, pawned her watch and chain, and borrowed a small sum from her friends, and thus was able to send a little money to her former lover. Later she wrote: "When I recall what I was two years ago, I feel a great hatred for Dostoevsky. He was the first to kill faith in my heart."

By a curious coincidence it was Vasily Rozanov, the great commentator on Dostoevsky, whom Polina married in 1880. At that time she was forty and Rozanov only twenty-four years of age. He worshiped her, and she laughed at him. After six years of hellish life together, she left him and he remained inconsolable. He implored her to come back to him but she answered, "Thousands of husbands are in your predicament and do not howl. Men are not dogs."

Rozanov in despair complained to Polina's father who called her "an enemy of the human race." Later, the unfortunate husband appealed to his friends and even to the police, but the person who received his most pitiful confidences was none other than Anna Grigorievna, the widow of Dostoevsky.

This liaison with Polina provided Dostoevsky with one of his great themes. For this woman, alternately ardent and frigid, served as the model for Dunia, Raskolnikov's sister, in *Crime and Punishment*, for Aglays in *The Idiot*, for Lisa in *The Possessed*, for Catherine Ivanovna in *The Brothers Karamazov*, and especially for Polina Alexandrovna in *The Gambler*.

The Gambler was actually planned during the trip with Polina. On September 30, 1865, Dostoevsky wrote to Strakhov, "At this time I have nothing ready but I have conceived the plot of a novel that I think will be very good. I describe a man skilled in many respects . . . but incomplete in everything. He is both in revolt against authority and afraid of it. His need of taking risks, however, redeems him in his own eyes. The story will deal only with the three years of his life during which he gambles at roulette."

On his return to Russia, however, Dostoevsky had no time to write this novel because Maria Dmitrievna's condition was critical. She had to be hurriedly transported to Moscow, where the climate was more salutary than in St. Petersburg. Pavel Isaev accompanied his parents, but he was sent back to St. Petersburg as Maria Dmitrievna had become so irritable that she could not endure even the presence of her son. Soon Dostoevsky too was compelled to leave for that city where Mikhail was planning to publish *The Epoch*, a new magazine to replace *Time*.

There was no money to finance the magazine: paper was obtained on credit, the printing was done on credit, the binding was done on credit, and the authors were not paid at all. After countless difficulties had been surmounted, the board of censorship sanctioned the publication on the condition that "the editors pledge themselves to follow the declared policies of the magazine."

Dostoevsky now divided his time between his magazine and his dying wife. This lugubrious shuttling between St. Petersburg, where the magazine was struggling for life, and Moscow, where Maria Dmitrievna, half-crazed, was slowly dying in a furnished room, went on for months.

"There are devils, there are devils in this room!" the sick woman sometimes screamed, and to calm her, someone would have to open the windows and pretend to chase the apparitions by wildly brandishing a napkin.

Beside the waxen, emaciated form of his wife, Dostoevsky was seized with frantic remorse for his elopement with Polina, for that great sin locked within himself. At the deathbed of Maria Dmitrievna, he wrote a confession that is one of his highest literary performances—*Notes from the Underground*.

8. "NOTES FROM THE UNDERGROUND"

THE "UNDERGROUND MAN" WHOSE CONFESSION DOSTOEV-
sky relates is perhaps as much like Dostoevsky as Golyadkin's double is like Golyadkin. This underground man
lives in a dark, disgusting hole which is his "shell." He lives
alone, he has no friends. He says, "I am sick, wicked, utterly
unattractive," but he secretly enjoys his wickedness. He
wallows in remorse, malice, grandiose frights; he loves to
withdraw into his den "on certain infamous St. Petersburg
nights," and to brood over all the mean things he has done
and all the humiliations he has endured during the day; he
experiences a queer pleasure in persuading himself that he has

reached the lowest rung of degradation, that he will never be as other men are, that he is something quite special, quite extraordinary, that he is outside the crowd, on the margin of creation—"I am alone whilst they are all together."

In his solitude he observes the man of action, the "direct men" with strong nerves who have no power of reflection; and who, if they are to be active, must have empty heads. He who thinks must remain motionless, for thought, like an acid, erodes the artificial frame in which action is encased. The very essence of action is the defeat of the spiritual. Action presupposes governing laws and is possible only in a carefully ordered universe. The positive sciences have catalogued experiences, set up axioms, and built stone walls that limit the horizon; and people bow with respect to these stone walls.

"Here is a strong wall," they say. "Here is a wall that one can lean against—here is a self-evident truth." The herd of fools confined within these walls does not realize that science has transformed a boundless domain into a prison. They think only of their little momentary security, of their jobs thus protected; they gleefully rub their hands because they are comfortable and warm. And if some philosopher—some underground man—dares to scorn the wall, they exclaim: "We beg your pardon, it is impossible to rebel. Two times two makes four. Nature does not ask for your advice, she does not consider your wishes, or care whether her laws find favor in your eyes or not. You must accept her as she is, and therefore you must also accept all the consequences. The wall is a wall, etc."

To this, the underground man (or rather, Dostoevsky) gives an admirable answer. He says, "My God, what do I care for the laws of nature and arithmetic, if I dislike them for one reason or another? Of course I cannot break this wall by batting my head against it but if I am not strong enough to demolish it, I will not be reconciled to it just because it is a stone wall—as if it were a comfort, a small measure of tranquillity solely because it is built on the axiom that twice two makes four."

"Are there mathematical absurdities and madmen who think that twice two makes three?" writes Baudelaire.

The underground man, the contemplator, negates all artificial constructions, upsets all self-evident truths, disregards all prohibitions deriving from scientific laws. He thinks in terms that go beyond the limitations of numbers and matter. He dwells in the impossible. Moreover God demands the impossible of His creature. What a miserable idol God would have been if He approved of this padded cell by which man has shut himself in, if He approved of man's falling asleep in his comfortable surroundings, of his diminishing himself and forgetting the divine spark of thought in order to become an automaton!

"The whole purpose of man," writes Dostoevsky, "surely consists in proving to himself that he is a man and not a cog in a machine." This applies to the moral world as well as to the physical world. Moral principles can imprison human beings just as physical principles do. To go beyond the range of such lifeless principles is to attain superior truth.

Once the moral frame is broken, there is no longer good or evil. Likewise, if the scientific laws were nullified, there would be only chaos. And it is to this chaos that the underground man invites us. In it he experiences the sensation of total freedom which he prefers to well-being. He says, "Man has need only of free will, no matter what he has to pay for it, no matter where it leads him. . . . I am convinced that man will never renounce real suffering, that is to say, ruin and chaos." It is by virtue of suffering that man comes close to the inconceivable, the inaccessible, the miraculous; by virtue of suffering that he rises above himself.

The path of suffering, the path of freedom, leads either to the discovery of God or to the deification of man, God-man and man-God. Nietzsche wanted man to become super-man, or man-God. In the eyes of Nietzsche, the emergence of superman will eliminate everything that is human in man. Superman is not merely man at a higher stage of evolution—he is an idol, a god without a vestige of his earthly origin. In contrast to this, Dostoevsky harmonizes human essence with divine essence. God does not swallow up His creature, man is not engulfed in God. Both God and man exist. They are protected one from the other by an adorable mediator, Christ. Man's freedom is perhaps a suffering, but at the end of the ordeal, however abject and wounded he may be, he reaches the ineffable light of Christ.

During his epileptic fits, Dostoevsky had perhaps the privilege of reaching the top of the wall and beholding the forbidden expanse. He would fall back dazed, blinded, longing for the miraculous vision. But he had seen, he had seen! And he was one of the few. This fact he admits in *Notes from the Underground*, which thus can be regarded as the key to all his writings. For in all his works, Dostoevsky was torn between the natural and the supernatural conception of the world. He was suspended between earth and heaven. He did not choose between the universe of causality and the universe of twice two equals three, but more or less successfully balanced the two structures, striving clumsily to incorporate extravagant fantasies into the compact mass of reality. Around a nightmare he would accumulate realistic details worthy of Flaubert, as though trying to justify himself, as though saying, "You see, I don't lose my head. All this is possible, all this is true."

Nevertheless, the heterogeneous structures of Dostoevsky's novels crack at every joint. Everything rings false in the carefully staged drama: events succeed one another in an unreal sequence; the characters are swept off their feet by an irresistible force; they make speeches a hundred pages long and read their confessions in public. When do they sleep or eat? The author himself does not know. Nothing depends on anything, no one can count on anyone, the good and the evil are merged. There are tremendous gaps in the "wall," and the actors with a perfunctory make-up on their faces play their parts amidst a mass of stone, in the icy, dead, supernatural light of the Day of Judgment.

Their drama is not possible according to scientific laws; it is conceivable only outside of these laws. Dostoevsky's men and women are not true in the ordinary sense of this term, but they are true in a more profound sense. They are what we would have been if we were not subject to social rules and held in check by physical limitations and habits. They are beings like you and me, seen independently of their words and actions. What they do is perhaps what we might do *if*. . . . What they say is what we might have said *if*. . . . Dostoevsky has eliminated the *if*, he has negated the conditional. He makes his heroes speak and act as one speaks and acts only in the world of ideas. His characters are ideas that evolve in a framework of matter. The underground man, Raskolnikov, Stavrogin, Kirilov, Shatov, Verkhovensky, Ivan Karamazov, are all consumed by an idea. Comfort, money, social position mean nothing to them. They do not concern themselves with the ground they walk on, the things they handle, the food they eat, the landscape they see. They are unaware of the boundaries between reality and dream. They go from one to the other, thus extending the area of the world.

Therefore it is absurd to claim, as some did, that Dostoevsky's characters are essentially Russian, that they would be inconceivable in any country outside Russia. It would be naïve to imagine that nineteenth-century Russia was populated by neurotics, epileptics and consumptives, and that the Russian public recognized themselves in Dostoevsky's novels. On the contrary, both readers and critics declared, "Such people are not Russian." For instance, Count Kuchelev-Bezborodko, referring to a character in *The Insulted and Injured*, wrote, "He would be more plausible abroad, in France, England or Belgium, than he is in Russia."

To be sure, love for great ideas, intellectual exaltation, sudden changes of mood, all these are well recognized traits of the Slav character, and among the Slavs the deeper truths are perhaps closer to the surface than amongst the Latins or Anglo-Saxons. But this is a difference of degree, not of nature. Dostoevsky's creatures are not exclusively Russian just because they are dominated by universal problems. The ideas they embody go beyond the domain of national literature. They express the anguish of the world, not solely the anguish of Russia. Dostoevsky's underground transcends national frontiers and unites all countries in a secret catacomb.

However that may be, when *Notes from the Underground* was published in *The Epoch*, the official critics failed to recognize it. But one, Apollon Grigoriev, said to Dostoevsky, "Hereafter you should write only in this vein." And Dostoevsky never forgot these simple words.

The magazine was published irregularly; subscribers asked

to have their money refunded; the sales decreased rapidly. Mikhail, who had no practical sense and who for some time had been drinking too much, allowed the business to fall to pieces. Feodor Mikhailovich was forced to stay in Moscow. Maria Dmitrievna's condition grew steadily worse, but she still refused to see her son. "She says that she will summon him to give him her blessing when she feels that she is going to die." (Letter to Mikhail, March 26, 1864.) "Each day we expect her to die. Her sufferings are terrible, and I have to bear the brunt of them." (Letter to Mikhail, April 2, 1864.) "Your mother's condition is growing worse and worse. The doctor has given up hope. Pray to God, Pasha." (Letter to Pavel Isaev, April 10, 1864.)

On April 15, Maria Dmitrievna had a violent attack, she vomited quantities of blood and almost choked to death. Dostoevsky wired to his brother: "Send Pasha here at once. Perhaps he has a black coat. You will have to buy him trousers."

Maria Dmitrievna, worn out but conscious, said farewell to those about her, and with great courage prepared herself for death. She was shaken by nervous tremors, her breathing was raucous, labored. A little later "her yellow parchment-like face fell back, her mouth opened, and her limbs stiffened convulsively. She sighed deeply." Thus Dostoevsky describes the death throes of Catherina Ivanovna, the consumptive in *Crime and Punishment*.

"Tonight at seven o'clock," Dostoevsky wrote to Mikhail, "Maria Dmitrievna died, after wishing a long life to all of you. Do not forget her in your prayers. She has suffered so much that I wonder who could refuse to forgive her." And the same night, before his wife's dead body, Dostoevsky wrote this strange sentence in his notebook: "Masha [Maria] is lying on the table. Will I see Masha again some day?"

Dostoevsky could not bear the idea of being separated from this woman who had betrayed and tortured him, and whose life had been only a useless burden to him. She was a part of his past. She was his youth. It was his entire youth that lay there on the table, with heavy eyelids and tightly closed lips. All at once alone, helpless, frightened, he realized the inestimable value of this woman whom he had lost after many years of common life.

On March 31, 1865, he wrote to Wrangel, "Oh, my friend, she loved me infinitely, and I loved her immeasurably, but we were not happy together. . . . Although we were an absolutely wretched couple because of her strange, suspicious, morbid character, we never ceased to love each other. The unhappier we were, the more we were attracted to each other. She was the most noble, the most loyal, the most generous of all the women I have known in my life. . . . I could never have imagined how painful and empty my existence would be after she was buried."

After the funeral services Feodor Mikhailovich went to St. Petersburg to look after his magazine. He tried to overcome his grief with hard work but three months later he was struck by another blow. On July 9, Pavel Isaev received the following letter, "My dear Pasha, send me some linen. My brother is dying. Say nothing of this to anyone. I have written to Nicolai. Perhaps I shall come to Moscow for a moment. Do not mention this. Yours, F. Dostoevsky."

On July 10, at seven o'clock in the morning, Mikhail died after months of suffering from an abscess in the liver. Dostoevsky was disconsolate. It seemed to him that fate was determined not to let him catch his breath. He was alone, more alone than in prison, than in Siberia. He did not know what he was living for.

"I was alone and frightened," he wrote later. "My life was broken in two. The first half, now finished, contained everything that I had lived for, and in the second half, still new, everything was strange, without a heart capable of replacing for me the two hearts that had ceased to beat. . . . Was I to create new ties for myself, to invent a new existence? The very thought of this was repulsive to me. I understood for the first time that no one could ever replace them, that I had not loved anyone else in the world, and that a new love would be not only impossible but also sacrilegious. Around me I felt a frost and a vacuum."

Mikhail left only three hundred rubles, just enough to pay for his funeral. His debts amounted to twenty-five thousand rubles, of which fifteen thousand represented unpaid draft notes. The magazine had been kept in existence only on the strength of its director's personal credit, and when he died the debacle was complete. There was no cash in hand, and six more issues had been promised to the subscribers. Just the printing of these issues would have required eighteen thousand rubles. Thus the total deficit of the magazine was thirty-three thousand rubles.

Dostoevsky was not bound legally to pay his brother's promissory notes. He could also suspend the publication of the magazine, and let the creditors recover what they could from a public auction of the assets but this would have dishonored his dead brother's name. He therefore rejected this course of action, and assumed full responsibility for the debts, whatever their nature. He did even more than that: he generously undertook to support his brother's widow and children.

Having made up his mind to do this, Dostoevsky went to Moscow, borrowed ten thousand rubles from his old aunt, Kumanina, and returned to St. Petersburg with the firm intention of continuing the publication of *The Epoch*. But the business was in an extremely bad shape. Moreover, a new approval was needed from the board of censorship, and the issue of January 31 was published only on March 22. Feodor Mikhailovich was forbidden to sign his articles, either as editor or as publisher. The subscribers, disgruntled at the delays, protested loudly.

Dostoevsky was working himself to death at his task. The magazine was printed in three different printing shops, and then assembled. Feodor Mikhailovich, the only editor, read proofs, received the authors, discussed matters with the censors, revised the articles, and solicited money all over the city. He worked regularly until six o'clock in the morning and slept only five hours a day.

"Ah, my friend," he wrote to Wrangel, "I would willingly return to prison for a term as long as my previous one if I could thereby pay my debts and feel myself free again. Of all my store of strength and energy, there remains only a feeling of uneasiness and anxiety akin to despair. . . . Anguish, bitterness, restlessness without passion—all this is a most abnormal state for me. And I am alone. . . . Yet I have constantly the impression that I am just preparing to live. It's funny, isn't it? I have as much vitality as a cat!"

His need of diversion, warm affection, devotion, was so great that he strove gradually to renew his contacts with his relatives and to form new friendships. He recovered slowly. He made the acquaintance of the Korvin-Krukovsky family, whose oldest daughter, Anna, had sent two likable stories to *The Epoch*. This tall, slender woman with fine features, long, straw-colored hair, and eyes "as green as a mermaid's," was intelligent, independent and proud. She was resolved to play a great role by the side of some exceptional man.

Dostoevsky felt a strange embarrassment in the presence of the beautiful Anna and her parents. According to an eyewitness, "he always seemed to be in a bad humor, he nervously fingered his blond goatee and bit his mustache while his whole face twitched."

One day, to the justifiable indignation of the parents, he felt impelled to tell Anna and her young sister the story of what was later to be the confession of Stavrogin in *The Possessed*. The girls were overcome by his tale, and Anna felt proud that a man of such great mind was interested in her, but she criticized his contemptuous attitude toward the youth of the *avant-garde* and their new ideas.

"All youth today is stupid and ignorant," he said. "To all of them a pair of boots is worth more than Pushkin."

"It is true that Pushkin is a little old-fashioned for our generation," answered Anna.

Dostoevsky became angry, shouted, threatened to leave, and finally left, but returned the next day with a contrite face.

One night, while Sonia, the younger sister, played Beethoven's *Sonate pathétique*, which she had learned for Dostoevsky, he had a final discussion with the elder sister in the little parlor.

"Please, understand me," Dostoevsky whispered. "I have loved you since the first time I saw you—and it is not friendship that I feel for you, but a passion that fills my whole being."

Anna Krukovskaya feared to tie herself to this sick man of genius and refused to give him her hand. While they talked in low voices, little Sonia stopped playing and listened. This fourteen-year-old child was madly in love with Dostoevsky and disapproved of her sister's trivial maneuvers. But he who so skillfully penetrated the souls of Netochka and little Nelly was unable to discern anything in this tender child whose eyes followed him until he reached the door, stooping, limp in body and mind, defeated, thrust back into solitude.

Later Sonia became a famous mathematician under the name of Sofia Kovalevskaya. As for Anna, she realized her dream of great phrases and high gestures when she married Jacquelart, a French conspirator, who was under sentence of death and imprisoned in a fortress near the German border. He escaped by the aid of the young woman's father who bribed a sentry with twenty thousand francs.

Once again Dostoevsky had been humiliated by a woman. He returned to work with increased energy, but the magazine declined from day to day. The number of subscribers fell to thirteen hundred. The creditors whose notes he had endorsed harried him with letters and visits.

At the end of the summer he received a summons to pay up or face bankruptcy and imprisonment. The most pressing debts amounted to three thousand rubles. Dostoevsky tried to argue with the creditors, but the miserable state of the magazine made them ruthless. On June 9, *The Voice* announced the suspension of *The Epoch*, whereupon Stellovsky, a publisher, came to see Dostoevsky and offered him three thousand rubles for the right to publish all of his writings in three volumes. In addition he wanted Dostoevsky to give him a new novel before November, 1866. If it was not ready by that date, Dostoevsky was to pay a fine, and if the manuscript was not delivered by November 1, he was to lose all his rights in his existing and also in his future works, which would automatically become the exclusive property of the publisher. Stellovsky hoped that Dostoevsky would be late and that he himself would thus be empowered to publish all of his debtor's works without remuneration.

Stellovsky was known as a shark operating in literary and artistic circles. He had exploited Pisemsky, Krestovsky, and Glinka. Scheming and petty, he wallowed in the misfortunes of writers, and a visit from him was almost the equivalent of a death sentence. But Dostoevsky was in a tight corner. By a curious coincidence, the twelve-day period that Stellovsky had allowed him to make up his mind synchronized with the term of reprieve granted him by his creditors. He accepted Stellovsky's terms, but he received only a small part of the sum that he had been promised, because Stellovsky had acquired at a low price a certain number of the notes endorsed by Dostoevsky, and what he gave the writer in the form of advance payments he took back as a creditor.

Soon Dostoevsky had only one hundred and seventy-five rubles left. Nevertheless, he decided to go abroad, for three reasons: he wanted to see Polina whom he still loved ("I still love her, I still love her deeply, but I wish I did not love her. She does not deserve such love," he wrote to Suslova's sister); he wanted to try his luck at roulette; and finally, he wanted to work in peace on the books that he had promised to write.

He arrived in Wiesbaden at the end of July. Suslova was to join him early in August, and in the meantime he returned to the gambling establishment. Once again he saw the green cloth piled up with louis d'or, ducats, florins, the same tense, rapacious faces, and the same nervous hands clutching the edge of the table as though it were the railing at the edge of a precipice. Once again he heard the magic words: "Thirty-one, red, odd, even, four, black, pair. . . ."

"I was feverish," he writes in *The Gambler*. "I placed my pile of gold on red, and suddenly I came to. It was only for an instant—the only time in the course of that evening. A cold shiver passed through me, my hands and knees trembled with anguish, and in the light of that single flash of lucidity I realized with horror what a loss would mean to me at that moment."

In five days Dostoevsky lost his one hundred and seventy-five rubles. He pawned his watch, did not pay his hotel bill, and swallowing his pride, sent a distressed appeal for help to Turgenev, although he held an old grudge against the writer.

"I am sorry and ashamed to have to bother you," he wrote, "but you are the only person to whom I can turn at present. And then you are more intelligent than anyone else. This makes it easier for me to write to you. I can speak to you as man to man: I am asking you for one hundred taler. . . . What can one do when all is lost?"

Turgenev sent him fifty taler.

"Thank you for the fifty taler, my good Ivan Sergyeevich," Dostoevsky wrote to him. "They did not completely pull me out of the water, but they helped a little."

Humiliated, disgusted, he waited for Polina, hoping that she would have some money. But Polina arrived at Wiesbaden without even enough to pay for her hotel room. Very soon Dostoevsky wanted her to leave. He had imagined that this elopement would be a joyful reunion; it turned out to be only a brief stay in a shabby hotel with the proprietor cold-shouldering him while the servants snickered. At the end of August, Polina left Wiesbaden for Paris. After her de-

parture the manager of the hotel refused to serve meals to
Feodor Mikhailovich. He said, "You don't need to eat because you don't know how to earn a living. We'll give you
tea, that's all."

"Thus, since yesterday," Dostoevsky wrote to Suslova, "I
have not eaten, and have fed only on tea; and it is frightful
tea, without anything to nibble on. They do not clean my
shoes or clothes. They do not answer my rings, and the em-
ployees treat me with an indescribable and typically German
contempt. In the eyes of a German, there is no greater crime
than to be poor and fail to pay on the appointed date."

To preserve his dignity, Dostoevsky would leave the hotel
before mealtime and return only at nightfall, but this daily
exercise only sharpened his appetite, so he resigned himself
to staying in his room. He read books and wrote a considerable number of letters asking for money although he could
not afford to buy stamps.

"For three days now," he wrote, "I have had only tea
mornings and nights, and strangely enough I am not too
hungry. What is annoying is that they find fault with me at
every turn, and occasionally I am unable to get a candle for
the night."

He implored Polina, Baron Wrangel at Copenhagen, Herzen in Geneva, Miliukov and the publisher Katkov in Russia. But Wrangel was away on leave, Herzen was on a mountain trip, and Miliukov, whom Dostoevsky asked to sell
one of his future books for three hundred rubles, met with
refusal at the *Reading Library*, the *Contemporary*, and the
Annals of the Fatherland. Katkov, to whom he offered a
novel of five or six sheets for the *Russian Messenger*, gave no
sign of life.

Nonetheless, Dostoevsky was captivated by the plot of his

new book. "The action takes place in our time," he wrote to Katkov. "A young student of middle-class origin, who has been expelled from the university and who lives in extreme poverty, decides by one stroke to escape from his painful predicament. His light-hearted action is the result of the instability of his ideas and of the influence of certain embryonic thoughts in the air. He decides to kill an old woman, a pawnbroker. This woman is stupid, deaf, sick, stingy, wicked; she exacts exorbitant rates of interest from her victims and ill treats her young sister whom she employs as her maid. 'She is completely useless, she does no one any good, why should she live?' Such are the questions that torment the young man's mind. He decides to kill her, to rob her, and to use her money for the benefit of his mother who lives in a little town, and of his sister, whom he wants to protect from the amorous advances of a landowner in whose house she is employed as a governess. He also needs money to continue his studies.

"But the divine truth and the earthly laws are operating, and in the end he is self-constrained to give himself up, even though he may have to die in a penitentiary, because this is his only hope of again being able to associate with people. For the feeling of exclusion and isolation which followed the crime was the greatest of tortures. The laws of truth and human nature are victorious, and the criminal resolves to accept suffering in order to redeem his action."

Such is the essential outline of *Crime and Punishment*. In this room, dark and narrow as a closet, while deprived of food, light, and fresh linen, and begging his acquaintances for funds to return to Russia, then at the lowest rung of misery and solitude Dostoevsky prepared the book which made him famous.

"Perhaps," he wrote, "what I am writing at present will be superior to anything I have written so far."

In the meantime Wrangel had returned to Copenhagen and found Dostoevsky's two desperate letters. He at once sent the money necessary for the return trip to Russia and invited Dostoevsky to spend a few days with him, and Feodor Mikhailovich gladly accepted.

He arrived in Copenhagen on October 1 and on October 10 left for St. Petersburg. Upon his return to the Russian capital he suffered three consecutive epileptic seizures. "Nevertheless I am up and working," he wrote to Wrangel.

The three hundred rubles that he had asked of Katkov finally reached him after having been sent to Wiesbaden, but now the money was insufficient.

"I am writing for your magazine, and consequently I cannot accept other offers that would enable me to subsist in one way or another. Now I am penniless, and I have pawned my clothes. Therefore I beg you to send me an advance of one thousand rubles."

Mikhail's family was in dire straits, and Dostoevsky himself was being persecuted by a few remaining creditors with whom he had not yet settled.

"Some of them are sensible and have accepted my offer to pay my debts by installments over a period of five years, but others will not listen. This puts me on edge and upsets me for long periods. Then I have to sit down and write. It is sometimes impossible."

Epileptic fits also delayed his work, and to complete his bad luck, a hemorrhoidal difficulty kept him bedridden for two weeks. Notwithstanding all this, and by dint of frantic labor, the greater part of his novel was written by November. But he was dissatisfied with it and burned his manuscript.

He began again. "A new form and a new plan have seduced me."

Working night and day he merged into one structure a story that he had mentioned to Kraevsky—it was entitled "The Poor Drunkards" (the episode of Marmeladov)—and the story of the student murderer that he had summarized for Katkov. He discarded the idea of a diary as a vehicle for the story of Raskolnikov and adopted the novel form. Keeping one jump ahead of the printer he wrote each month the chapters scheduled for publication the following month, that is, the equivalent of ninety-six printed pages in four weeks.

On February 18, 1866, Dostoevsky wrote to Wrangel, "Two weeks ago the first part of my novel was published in the *Russian Messenger*. It is called "Crime and Punishment." I have already heard much praise of this book. It contains much that is courageous and new."

The problem of Raskolnikov, the hero of *Crime and Punishment*, is as that of the underground man—the problem of total freedom. A poor yet proud student seeks a way out of his poverty. He knows an old pawnbroker. What value has the life of this wicked character in comparison to his own? If he killed her and stole her money, he could come to the aid of his mother and his sister, pay his tuition, become a man of means, do good to those about him. "For one life, thousands of lives would be saved from stagnation, from disintegration. What does she weigh in the scales of life, that wicked witch?" His plan is horribly logical, dangerously alluring. "He returned home feeling as though he had been sentenced to death. He no longer reasoned, and would have been unable to reason about anything, but with his whole being he felt suddenly that he no longer had freedom of will or judgment, that everything had been settled forever."

Events seem to favor his scheme. He is driven by a tremendous force, "as though one end of his coat were caught in the wheels of a machine, and he were being dragged along with it." He can no longer resist; he strikes, he kills, he steals, and as a result of a strange coincidence, he leaves no external clue that would point to his guilt. But then the drama of inner punishment begins. "If everything was done deliberately, if you had a clearly defined goal, why have you not yet looked into the purse, why do you not know what you have earned by this deed which brought all these sufferings upon you?" Raskolnikov wonders.

Little by little, he succeeds in discovering the real motive for his crime.

"I did not kill to be able to help my mother," he confesses to Sonia, "nor to become a benefactor of mankind after acquiring the means to be one. No, I just killed, I killed for myself alone, and I did not care at the moment whether I would become a benefactor of mankind or whether I would spend my life like a spider catching victims in my web and sucking the life out of them. And it was not the money I wanted when I did it; I needed money less than something else. . . . I wanted to find out something else, it was something else that led me on. I wanted to know, as quickly as possible, whether I was a worm like everybody else or a man. Could I jump over the barrier or could I not? I wondered, would I have the courage to bend and pick up power or would I not? Am I a trembling creature or have I the right?"

Thus Raskolnikov, like the underground man, is stifled within the wall of official morality. He feels that he has the power to rise above the anonymous herd around him. He feels different from the others, summoned to a special destiny, designated for the fearsome experience of spiritual independence. Men such as he have the right to disregard all the rules. For them there is a superior morality or rather no morality at all, but complete freedom. For them, a crime has not the significance of a crime, and punishment is a word devoid of meaning. Probably Napoleon thus justified himself in his own eyes, if he ever felt the need to justify himself at all.

"A real master, to whom everything is permissible," Raskolnikov thinks to himself, "bombards Toulon, organizes a massacre in Paris, *forgets* his army in Egypt, *spends* half a million men in Russia, and in Vilna, when questioned about it, dismisses it all with a pun. And it is to this man that they erect statues after his death. Thus everything is permissible."

Everything is permissible to some people—to those who want to permit themselves everything, because this very wish is a sign of being exceptional.

In the eyes of Raskolnikov, the old woman is the primary obstacle, the wall of flesh that has to be breached, surmounted, forgotten, before he can reach the path of freedom.

"It is not a human being that I have killed, but a principle." He believes that after killing this principle he will find his vocation of superman, of God, that he will relax and find independence.

In reality he has never been less independent than since his flight from the human condition. An *idée fixe* gnaws his very sense of freedom. He wanted to escape from all moral constraint, but he only imposed a new constraint upon himself. Day and night the heinous crime of which he wanted to be proud is re-enacted and tried in his mind. Night and day, he is harassed by the same arguments and the same answers.

At once a lawyer to himself and to his victim, he is no longer an individual but a battleground.

Murder cannot be justified before the higher tribunal of conscience, and the murderer's personality disintegrates and vanishes like the victim's corpse. No lofty purpose, no ideal, no religious principle, can justify crime. Whosoever draws his sword against his brother, draws it against God and against himself. When Raskolnikov brought down his ax on his victim's head, it was not the avaricious old woman that he killed, but himself, or rather the divine spark dwelling in him.

"After all, Sonia, I killed only a louse, a dirty louse, a useless and wicked creature," he exclaims.

"But this louse was a human being," says Sonia.

Any human life has more value than the abstract idea of an individual. No human desire is worth the death of a man because this man, whatever he may be, is made in the image of God. Yes, the "useless and wicked louse" that was the pawnbroker; Marmeladov, the cowardly drunkard; or Sonia, the wise prostitute—they are all loved by God and made in the image of God. This fact is tremendous, inconceivable, but in the eyes of God, they are all equal to Raskolnikov.

Thus beyond the wall Raskolnikov totters at his very first step. He is not at home in this vast expanse. The strength, which was enough to sustain him within the wall, suddenly fails him here. He wanted to be a superman, and here he trembles and cries like a child in a dark room. Far away from everyone, stranger to everyone and to himself, he is not himself. The people around him think that he is a madman; so he flees from all those who no longer have anything in common with him and turns toward the unfortunate. He loves Marmeladov, the drunkard, Catherina Ivanovna, the consumptive widow, and Sonia who prostitutes herself to support her brothers and sisters. But even they are different from him. His crime isolates him in the middle of the human stream, confines him to himself. Only complete confession and harsh punishment can reinstate him in the crowd, but he fears discovery, arrest, and trial. He consorts with policemen and discusses the murder with them. Porfiry, the judge who has suspected him from the beginning, toys with him, tries his patience to the breaking point, reassures him, and then frightens him again with diabolical cold-bloodedness.

"If you leave you will come back," the judge says to him. "You cannot get along without us. . . . I am even convinced that you will come to the point of wanting to accept suffering."

The ordeal of freedom is too hard for Raskolnikov. After countless inner conflicts, he, the superman, prostrates himself at the feet of Sonia, the prostitute, and confesses his crime to her. She advises him to give himself up.

"Then you want me to go to prison, Sonia?" he says.

"What you must do is to accept suffering and thus redeem yourself," she answers.

He heeds her words. He goes to a crossroads and kisses the earth "that he has defiled," then he reports to a police station. "Gently, with pauses and hesitations, but distinctly, he says, 'It is I who killed with an ax the old pawnbroker and her sister and who robbed them.' "

Raskolnikov is sentenced to hard labor, and Sonia accompanies him to Siberia.

"But," writes Dostoevsky, "he did not repent of his crime. . . . Why does my deed seem so heinous to them, he wondered. Because it is a crime? What is the meaning of the word crime? My conscience is clear. To be sure I committed a murder. . . . Very well then, to respect the letter of the law, take my life, and let us not talk about it any more."

He thinks that many benefactors of mankind have been justified by posterity only because they stubbornly held to their course. What condemns him is the fact that he lacks greatness. His flesh is weak. "Thus, what he considered to be his fault, was the fact that he had been unable to hold out, that he had given himself up."

It is from this untruth, from these doubts, that suddenly Raskolnikov's faith is born—yes, suddenly, just as a spark sets a haystack ablaze. Sonia had once read to him the story of the resurrection of Lazarus: "I am the Resurrection, and the Life: he that believeth in Me, though he were dead, yet shall he live: And whosoever liveth and believeth in Me shall never die." At the time he did not understand these words, and it is only at present, in Siberia, that the word resurrection comes to his lips. "How did this come to pass? Raskolnikov himself did not realize it, but suddenly something gripped him and flung him at Sonia's feet. . . . They wanted to speak but could not. Their eyes filled with tears. Both were pale and trembling, but on their worn faces there shone the dawn of a new future—of a complete resurrection of life."

Thus, thanks to Sonia, the prostitute, Raskolnikov discovers real freedom at last. Man is not God. The strongest man exists only if God exists. To deny God is to deny oneself. To want to become God is to want to die as man, to merge with the cosmos, to be and not to be at the same time.

Within the walls of official morality there is freedom to choose the right path. This lesser freedom presupposes the possibility of sinning. Man can choose the wrong path but he refrains from doing so because "it is forbidden," because he thus runs the risk of "punishment," "prison," or "hell." Those who despise such rules as stupid, those who are nauseated by such spiritual prescriptions, the thinkers, the strong, jump over the wall and find themselves in the domain of superior or ultimate freedom. There they no longer do the right thing in order to abide by a rule that they learned in their childhood, they no longer fear evil because of earthly or heavenly reprisals; they choose the good or evil according to their own will, following their instincts. Some imagine themselves to be supermen and break their necks at the outset; others discover the joy of doing good for its own sake. Such freedom, such good deeds born of pure love, lead them imperceptibly in the train of God and save them.

Raskolnikov achieved divine serenity by the detour of crime. He did wrong, he sinned through pride and wasted the freedom that had been granted to him. He wanted to destroy what was human in him. He thought that the instinct of goodness would be the first to vanish from his heart after he climbed the wall, but it is this very instinct for the good that most firmly withstood the ordeal, that tortured him and bent him to the ground for his own salvation. His repentance redeemed his sin and in the end gave him freedom. In his recovered humility, Raskolnikov understood himself and God and understood himself in God and in the world. He found his place and his life. "He that findeth his life shall lose it: and he that loseth his life for My sake shall find it." Thus Dostoevsky's conclusion brings us back to the very words of the Gospel.

Around Raskolnikov, the central figure, the living heart of the book, there gravitates the destinies of other sinners who, like him, have transgressed the laws of the common morality and who, like him, are forgiven. In a house of ill repute Raskolnikov meets Marmeladov, the drunkard, husband of Catherina Ivanovna and father of Sonia. Marmeladov is a coward, a braggart, who has lost his job and drinks away everything he owns. He pawns his wife's clothes and allows his oldest daughter to prostitute herself to earn money because he has not the guts to earn it himself. With morbid pleasure he plumbs the depths of his degradation and realizes the impossibility of rising again.

"But He will take pity on us," he says. "He who pities everyone, who has understood everything . . . will judge them all. And when He has finished with all of them, He will summon us too. 'Come closer, you others, come, you drunkards, come you lewd ones!' And we shall all come forward without any shame. . . . He will say to us: 'Pigs that you are, your image is that of the beast and you bear its seal, but approach anyhow.' And then the wise men and the reasonable men will exclaim: 'Lord, how can you admit them, too?' And he will answer them: 'If I receive them, you the wise ones, and you, reasonable ones, it is because not one of them thought that he deserved heaven.' "

Thus humility offers a chance of salvation to anyone who experiences it. And Sonia, the prostitute, is the humblest of them all.

"You too have transgressed the law," Raskolnikov says to her. "You were able to transgress it. You did harm to yourself, you ruined your life. . . . Consequently it is fitting that we should go together, follow the same path."

But while Raskolnikov is boundlessly proud of having widened the human horizon, little Sonia realizes her degradation and accepts it as an inevitable disease. She becomes deeply attached to the only man who has not despised her. In the words of Dostoevsky, she feels for Raskolnikov an "insatiable compassion." And before this purity preserved in the very heart of sin, he kneels gravely. "It is not before you that I have prostrated myself," he says, "but before all human suffering." Or, "It is not because of your dishonor and your sin that I have said this, but because of your great suffering.

" 'But tell me now,' he articulates the words in a kind of paroxysm, 'how can such vileness and baseness cohabit in you with the most sacred and noble feelings.' "

When Raskolnikov confesses his crime to Sonia, she says to him, "What have you done, what have you done against yourself? No, no, now there is no one in the world unhappier than you."

Later she follows him to Siberia and helps him on toward resurrection.

The figure of this fragile sinner, this woman condemned by earthly laws but vindicated in the eyes of heaven, is one of Dostoevsky's most charming creations. Her self-effacement and gentleness are deeply moving, and the reader feels mysteriously responsible for her distress. It is as though she had assumed the burden of all human sin, as though by losing herself she had saved us. But in reality no one who thinks he is lost will be lost, because no one is guilty unless all are.

Dunia, Raskolnikov's sister, the tender, resigned Dunia also shares the experience of sublime sin. She, too, while she sells herself to the cold scoundrel, Luzhin, is a sinner and a saint—sinner because she is ready to give herself to a man whom she does not love; a saint because she does this only to save her brother.

"This marriage is wretched," Raskolnikov says to her. "I

am willing to be wretched myself, but I don't want you to be, not you."

Another great sinner is Svidrigailov in whose household Raskolnikov's sister is employed as a governess. This cynic who pursues the young woman with his advances is a total unbeliever, afraid of nothing. According to him, the future life is nothing but "a little room, something like a bathroom in the country, stuffy, with spiders in the corners; there is the whole of eternity for you." He takes his pleasures wherever he finds them and is unconcerned over the possible consequences of his whims.

"Imagine, I gave her only two blows with my riding crop," he says, referring to his dead wife. Before that, he had raped a little deaf-mute of fourteen, who hanged herself in a barn when he left.

Svidrigailov follows Dunia to St. Petersburg and tries to seduce her. He lures her into a room and promises to save her brother, whose confession he has overheard, on the condition that she give herself to him. Dunia seizes a gun but, as she is about to kill her seducer, throws down the weapon in disgust. And he, seeing that she does not love him enough to kill him, sadly lets her go. Her dignified refusal overwhelms him. He, who never loved or hated anyone, is now aroused to passion.

"That night until ten o'clock he spent visiting pothouses and brothels."

After giving Sonia a large sum of money he stops at the house of his fiancée, a sickly girl whose unfortunate parents have sold her to him, and makes a present of fifteen thousand rubles to the family. Finally he rents a room in a dingy hotel and bravely tries to sleep, but successive nightmares wear him out. In a dream he sees a child lying in a coffin, and he recognizes the girl who killed herself for him. He also dreams that he finds a five-year-old girl deserted in a corridor and takes her to his room. She turns her face to him and opens her arms. He cries, "Ah, accursed one," raising his hand against her. But at that moment he wakes up. Then, in a fit of fever and disgust, he goes out into the street and commits suicide.

Marmeladov, Sonia, Dunia, Svidrigailov, Luzhin, all the scoundrels, cynics and unfortunates who surround the towering figure of Raskolnikov, bear their justification in themselves. They realize their degradation. And in the eyes of Dostoevsky, only the judges deserve to be judged. The vilest thing on earth is a man without desire, a dry mind, the proud intellectual. There is no crime that deprives its author of the right to be forgiven. Love and humility can save everyone, and human love must be humble.

Dostoevsky has been accused of describing only monsters and neurotics, and called "the hospital muse," and "a cruel talent." Doctor Chizh, the great expert on Dostoevsky, thinks that one-quarter of Dostoevsky's characters are neurotics: he counts six of them in *Crime and Punishment*, two in *The Brothers Karamazov*, six in *The Possessed*, four in *The Idiot*, and four in *The Adolescent*.

True enough, Raskolnikov is continually "trembling with fever" or "seized with delirium," Svidrigailov has voluptuous and terrifying hallucinations, Marmeladov is on the threshold of delirium tremens, Catherina Ivanovna is in the last stage of consumption, and more generally, as Svidrigailov has it, all St. Petersburg "is a city of half-mad people."

At first glance we seem to have nothing in common with these disconcerting characters, yet they attract us like the

depths of an abyss. We have never met them, but they are
mysteriously familiar to us. We understand and love them,
and finally we recognize ourselves in them. This is because
they are no more abnormal than we are. In fact, they are
what we do not dare to be, they do and say what we do not
dare to do and say, and they bring to the light of day that
which we keep buried in the darkness of the unconscious.

But what about their illnesses, their insane actions? The
truth is that these are only trappings. Dostoevsky was obliged
to make his characters insane, consumptive, epileptic or
hysterical in order to give them plausibility in the eyes of
his readers. He burdened his characters in order to unburden
us. He compromised with us by sticking a pathological label
on their backs, by providing them with medical certificates.

"What I am telling you," he seems to say, "is perfectly
plausible, since I am dealing with a sick man."

The official reviewers were deceived by this subterfuge.
They read Dostoevsky's books as though they were dealing
with textbooks of psychopathology. It did not occur to
them to remove the mask, to look at the true faces of the
alleged monsters, their human faces—our own faces. "Once
again the reader will wonder whether literature has the right
to concentrate on morbid exceptions," wrote De Voguë.
But actually Dostoevsky's characters are neither exceptional
nor morbid. To be morbid one must have a body, but
Dostoevsky's characters have no bodies, they are but the
vehicles of our own thoughts. They are nothing but our
thoughts, and the world in which they live seems to be like
ours only as a result of the author's clever trickery. Even so,
these icy rooms, sordid gambling dens, foggy alleys, the street
lamps growing crookedly out of the mud, the soiled linen

at the windows—all these are more like the setting of a
dream. It is a picture, not of reality, but of a nightmare. And
even the details that the author lights up in this dark and
vermin-infested labyrinth strike one as symbols of a supernatural sadism. The "pictures representing German *Fräu-
leins*" at the pawnbroker's, the "rings of cucumber, charred
biscuits, and sliced fish" in the alehouse, the "sofa covered
with printed cotton" at Marmeladov's, or the "dog caked
with mud, his tail between his legs," which catches up with
Svidrigailov in the street when he is about to kill himself—
each of these has a mysterious import, each gives us a shock
like that of an electric current. But this does not awaken us;
such details serve only to help us appreciate the distance
from reality to dreamland. They are units of measurement
Dostoevsky charitably tosses at us from time to time. And
then he forces us to continue our sleepwalking.

To have his book published in the form in which he had
written it, Dostoevsky was forced to struggle with his publisher, who demanded certain alterations. Katkov and Leontiev, his assistant, thought that the chapter containing the
scene of the reading of the Gospels might be misinterpreted,
and that "traces of nihilism" might be discovered in it.
Dostoevsky tried to argue with them, but to no avail. He
wrote in a letter, "I undertook the revision. To transform this
long chapter entailed as much work as the writing of three
new chapters."

Nevertheless, the modification did not prevent the critics
from branding Raskolnikov as a nihilist. Strakhov wrote,
"Here, for the first time, we have before our eyes a nihilist
who suffers, a nihilist tormented by profoundly human

suffering." Parallels were pointed out between Raskolnikov
and Bazarov, the revolutionary portrayed by Turgenev. In
reality, there is a considerable difference between these two
characters. Bazarov is a modern man, a hero of his time, and
exclusively of his time—a nihilist. Raskolnikov is of all time.
It is not a social but a metaphysical problem that torments
him, he reflects not an intellectual fashion but an abiding
human trait. Bazarov is conceivable only in a nineteenth-
century setting, Raskolnikov could have lived in the Middle
Ages or in our own day. Bazarov is a man, Raskolnikov is
a man.

The Russian students agreed with the critics and saw in
Raskolnikov only a summary indictment against the university youth. By a strange coincidence, a murder was committed by a student in Moscow shortly after the publication
of the book, and this incident served to confirm their point
of view. Their infatuation with Dostoevsky declined rapidly.

The public at large acclaimed *Crime and Punishment* with
naïve enthusiasm. This book was a detective novel, a love
story and a philosophical treatise all in one, and it satisfied
everybody. It was not always understood but it was admired
without reservation. The author's name was on everyone's
lips; Dostoevsky was ranked with Turgenev and Tolstoy.
This was fame.

This sudden renown did not rescue Feodor Mikhailovich
from his financial difficulties. November 1 was drawing near.
On that date he was to deliver an unpublished novel to
Stellovsky, and he had not written a line of it. On October 1
Miliukov paid a visit to Dostoevsky.

"Dostoevsky was walking up and down the room in great
strides, smoking a cigarette; he looked very much upset.

" 'What is the matter with you?' I asked.

" 'It is frightful, I am lost,' he answered, and kept on walking.

" 'Why? What is it?'

" 'Do you know by what contract I am bound to Stellovsky?'

" 'You once mentioned this contract to me, but I do not know its clauses.'

" 'Well, then, have a look.'

"He went to his desk, handed me a paper, and resumed his pacing.

"I was horrified. Not only did Dostoevsky receive a laughable sum for his previous works, but he was bound to deliver for November, that is to say, five months after the signing of the contract, 'a new novel, unpublished, containing at least one hundred and sixty printed pages of large size,' failing which, Stellovsky acquired the right to publish Dostoevsky's future works without remuneration.

" 'Is this novel well advanced?' I asked him.

" 'Not a line is written.' " (From Miliukov's *Recollections.*)

Miliukov suggested gathering together several friends, dividing the task among them, and writing the work in common.

"I will never agree to sign other people's work," said Dostoevsky.

Then Miliukov suggested dictating the novel to a stenographer. Feodor Mikhailovich hesitated; he feared that he would be unable to adapt himself to this new method of working. And where would he find an able secretary?

"I will take care of that," said Miliukov.

The next day, October 2, Miliukov went to Olshin who directed courses in shorthand for women, and explained his problem. On October 3, at six o'clock in the evening, Olshin approached one of his pupils and said to her: "Anna Grigorievna, would you accept a little job? I have been asked to find someone, and I thought of you."

On October 4, 1866, Anna Grigorievna Snitkin left her mother's house early in the morning, bought some pencils and a notebook in a stationery store, and walked along Stolarnaya Street on her way to Dostoevsky. She was a young girl of twenty, with a pale face and beautiful, gray, candid eyes. She came of a good family and had graduated from the Maria Gymnasium with a gold medal. Her mother had agreed that she should become Dostoevsky's secretary only because her father, who was dead, had been a fervent admirer of the novelist.

Anna Grigorievna wondered what Dostoevsky would be like. Was he an obese and bald gentleman, or very thin, very tall, and very severe? She was overcome at the thought of "collaborating" with an author as famous as Dostoevsky. Would he not find her too stupid? Would she know how to talk to him of his books? She could not recall the names of certain characters in *Poor Folk*. What should she do if he questioned her on this subject—acknowledge her forgetfulness or pretend to be absent-minded?

At eleven o'clock she stopped in front of the Alonkin House, a large building full of countless little lodgings like the house of Raskolnikov in *Crime and Punishment*.

"Where is apartment thirteen?" she asked the janitor.

"Under the arch, on the second floor," he said.

The study into which a servant of uncertain age ushered her was a large room modestly furnished with a sofa, a few chairs, and a desk. She had hardly sat down when the door opened and Dostoevsky entered, apologizing for having kept her waiting.

"He was of medium height," she writes in her *Recollections*. "His light brown, perhaps even reddish, hair was heavily pomaded and carefully smoothed. But it was his eyes that struck me most. Dostoevsky wore a fairly worn blue coat, but the collar and cuffs of his shirt were snow-white."

He came toward her looking tired and dejected. On the day before he had had a violent epileptic fit and he had not quite recovered from it. In a gloomy voice he asked Anna Grigorievna to sit down and he dictated to her a passage from the *Russian Messenger*. He read very fast, and she protested, "No one speaks as fast as that!"

Later when she was transposing her notes into longhand, he walked back and forth in the room and exclaimed impatiently, "How slow! What a long time it takes!"

On examining the work he discovered that the secretary had forgotten a punctuation mark and had not indicated an accent clearly enough.

"That is inadmissible, absolutely inadmissible! But anyhow, I am unable to dictate today. Come back tomorrow," he said to her.

"Ah, Mother, don't speak to me of that Dostoevsky," said Anna Grigorievna on coming home.

She went back the next day, and this time everything went well. Feodor Mikhailovich was in a good mood and dictated the first chapters of *The Gambler*. From time to time he interrupted himself to tell the young girl some incident of his past. He spoke of his childhood, his imprisonment,

the episode of the gallows, Siberia. Enraptured, moved, she
listened to this man who had suffered so much and thought
so deeply and who was also interested in her.

"How many pages have we done? Will we be ready on
time?" he asked.

The novel progressed, and Feodor Mikhailovich gradually
regained confidence. He experienced a strange pleasure in
working beside this young girl, who was so fresh and kind.
The very fact that he was dictating a love story to her introduced an element of delightful embarrassment into the situation. With timid enjoyment he evoked the proud figure of
Polina Suslova before this industrious young girl. He even
gave the first name of his former mistress to the heroine of
his novel.

In *The Gambler*, Alexei Ivanovich, the tutor who tells
the story, is desperately in love with Polina Alexandrovna,
General Zagoriansky's stepdaughter. Polina is aware of the
young man's love and allows him to express it, but treats
him with contempt.

"I must admit," Alexei says to her, "that I delight in being
your slave. There is a pleasure in tasting extreme humiliation
and degradation. . . . Take advantage of my enslavement!
Do you know that some day or other I shall kill you?"

When Polina tells him that she needs money, he goes to
the casino and stakes at roulette the seven hundred florins she
has given him. He is seized with a sudden fever—"I felt an
impulse to challenge fate, to thumb my nose at it, to stick out
my tongue at it"—he loses everything and leaves the casino
in a daze. But Polina sends him back, and this time luck
favors him. "My temples were moist, my hands trembled.
Some Poles offered to help me, but I listened to no one. My
luck was unbroken. Suddenly I heard shouts and laughter.

Everyone cried 'Bravo, bravo!' Some even clapped their hands. I swept up thirty thousand florins, and the bank closed until the next day."

He hastens to his hotel and enters his room where Polina is waiting for him.

"I will not take this money without giving something in return," she says.

She caresses him, embraces him, and gives herself to him.

"You are sweet, sweet," she repeats. "Very well then, will you give me fifty thousand francs?"

When he hands her the money, she throws it in his face and runs out of the room.

After Polina's departure, Alexei Ivanovich goes to Paris where he spends his money with an adventuress. Later he turns again to gambling to make his living. "There is really something peculiar in the feeling you have when you stake your last florins, your very last, although you are alone in a strange land, far from home and your friends, without knowing whether you will have enough money to buy food that day."

The novel ends on this melancholy note: "Tomorrow, tomorrow, all will be over."

In addition to the central figures of Alexei and Polina, there is a remarkable farcical character—the general's rich old aunt whose death the whole family is awaiting with impatience. One fine day she arrives in the gambling town, with a retinue of servants. On her order, they wheel the chair into the casino, and she begins to gamble like one possessed.

"The grandmother could scarcely sit still in her seat. With feverish eyes she followed the little ball dancing on the spokes of the turning wheel. She even thumped on the table with her fist when the croupier announced 'thirty-six' instead of the zero that she had hoped for." She wins a considerable sum of money, which is immediately swallowed up in heavy losses, and, completely ruined, leaves the town.

This swift novel, dictated in haste, as can be inferred from its style, supplies us with clear information regarding Dostoevsky's two passions: gambling, and Polina.

The Gambler often strikes the reader as almost an exact replica of Polina Suslova's diary. The two texts reflect the same atmosphere of unsatisfied love, the same sudden changes of mood, the same sharp turns of passion.

"In your presence I lose all pride," says Alexei to his beloved, and Dostoevsky must often have said the same words to Polina Suslova.

"I took her in my arms, I kissed her hands, I fell on my knees before her," writes Dostoevsky in *The Gambler*. "He fell at my feet, embracing me, clasping my knees, and sobbing aloud he cried: 'I have lost you, I knew it,'" wrote Suslova in her diary. Such comparisons could be multiplied.

As for his passion for roulette, Dostoevsky explains it in this striking formula: "I felt an impulse to challenge fate, to thumb my nose at it, to stick out my tongue at it." Roulette enabled him to toy with fate as fate toyed with him. Thanks to roulette he could jump over the "wall," reach the domain of the illogical, of total possibility, of chance. "Twice two makes four" no longer had any meaning. The shrewdest systems could be nullified by a caprice of chance. In gambling, and only in gambling, things depended on nothing. Gambling was the first experience of freedom in the physical world.

On October 30, 1866, after twenty-five days of successful work, *The Gambler* was ready for the printer. On November 1, Dostoevsky went to Stellovsky to deliver his manuscript. But the publisher had forestalled him and left town; his servants did not know the date of his return, and at his office the editor-in-chief refused to accept the novel saying he had been instructed to do so. Dostoevsky went to the nearest police station and deposited his book with the head officer who gave him an official receipt duly signed and dated. Thus Stellovsky's plot was foiled; the work was delivered on time. But Dostoevsky was not completely satisfied; he had become accustomed to the girl who came every day to his house, and who discussed his characters with youthful enthusiasm. With her to assist him, work was easy and amusing. It was good to think, talk, and live by her side.

The idea that he would now be separated from her saddened him. He paid a visit to Anna Grigorievna's mother and asked the girl to "collaborate" with him in the writing of the final chapters of *Crime and Punishment*. She accepted at once, and on November 8 she came to Dostoevsky ready to work.

He received her in a state of extreme agitation. Very pale and nervous he helped her take off her hooded cape and led her to an armchair. He looked at her face, simple and unafraid. How young she was, how ignorant of life, and how he loved her! But what right had he to declare his love to her —he who was more than double her age, who was sick, poor, and debt-ridden. He had felt the same scruples when he faced Anna Korvin-Krukovskaya. He feared that he would be rejected—he was certain of it.

"Listen," he said to her, "I have thought of a new novel. But I am worried about its conclusion. I have the problem of a young girl's psychology. If I were in Moscow I would consult my niece, Sonia; today I am turning to you."

And he proceeded to tell her the story of a painter, "a man no longer young, that is a man of my age." This painter has a wretched life, has lost his father, his wife, his favorite sister. He is alone, disillusioned, miserable, and yearns for new happiness. At this decisive moment he meets an intelligent and sensitive young girl.

"Do you think that she could love him sincerely?" asked Dostoevsky. "Put yourself in her place for a moment. Imagine that the painter is myself, that I tell you of my love, that I ask you to be my wife—tell me, what would be your answer?"

He stopped, embarrassed by his own boldness. Had he spoiled a tender friendship by speaking in this manner? Was he frightening this young girl, who could not previously have suspected anything? But Anna Grigorievna looked at him with serene and joyful eyes, and she said simply, "I would answer that I love you, that I will love you all my life."

Mikhail's family, and Pavel Isaev, his stepson, saw their interests threatened by the writer's new marriage. They tried to prove to him that it was absurd and even wicked for an "old man" to wed such a young girl. These reproaches greatly tormented Feodor Mikhailovich because they duplicated his own secret doubts.

"My youth obviously worried him," Anna Grigorievna wrote in her diary. And later Dostoevsky wrote to Suslova, "I noticed that my stenographer loved me very sincerely, although she had never said anything to me; and for my part I liked her more and more. Since my brother's death life is a burden to me and I am lonely so I asked her to be my wife. She has accepted. . . . The difference in our ages is enormous (twenty and forty-four), but I am convinced that she will be happy for she has a heart and knows how to love."

This letter to his "eternal friend" shows obvious embarrassment and shame. Bourgeois happiness, contentment, the tender age of his fiancée—he was worried by all this as if he were committing a wicked deed. Perhaps he also wondered whether, once anchored in port, he would not regret the storms of the open sea. And all these people around him who did not conceal their astonishment, and who behind his back were doubtless making fun of him and calling him an "old fool" and a "sadist," must have given him food for thought. But he dismissed all these considerations, and on February 15, 1867, at seven o'clock in the evening, Feodor Mikhailovich Dostoevsky married Anna Grigorievna Snitkin at the Cathedral of the Holy Trinity in St. Petersburg.

"You are everything to me, for all time to come," Dostoevsky wrote to his wife in the first letter he addressed to her —it was on the occasion of her birthday. "You are my hope, my faith, my happiness, everything." The young bride was both moved and worried by this declaration. Would she be equal to her task? Would she be worthy of this responsibility suddenly thrust upon her?

She was as devoted and as dull as could be desired. From the age of fifteen she had admired her future husband, and she continued to admire him all her life without quite understanding him. She simply tried to make him happy. She had evolved a convenient and comforting idea of her husband. A petty bourgeois herself, she saw him as a petty bourgeois too; a retarded ingénue, she depicted him as a worthy paterfamilias, without any defects, innocent of all low instincts, loving, likable, and distinguished by great kindness in the

midst of all the complicated and wicked people about him.
She turned a Rembrandt full of depth and shadows into a
flat, pretty picture postcard, a violent and mysterious genius
into a sentimental hero.

She was far from intelligent, and she was not very learned
either, despite her gold medal, but she had an infallible practical sense. She was a born secretary. One of her friends said
of her, "If she had not married Dostoevsky she would have
opened a foreign exchange shop on the Nevsky." She did not
bring into Dostoevsky's life any of those fertile despairs,
those great spectacular passions or supernatural ecstasies to
which women had accustomed him, she did not provide him
with material for his novels, she did not enrich the treasure
of his notes, but she kept this treasure in order with the care
of a model housekeeper. Meticulous, economical, virtuous,
she loved her ledger, recorded in her diary the price of a cup
of coffee or a cake, studied her husband's contracts, kept his
creditors at bay, copied, classified, catalogued his works and
attended to all the material details of his life. She was the type
of woman who tidies everything.

She dusted, so to speak, Dostoevsky's life. She was not the
muse of this genius but his nurse. And the fact is that Dostoevsky had much greater need of a nurse than of a muse.

Anna Grigorievna's debut in married life was difficult.
Dostoevsky's sister-in-law, brothers, nephews, Pavel Isaev,
his good-for-nothing stepson, felt that they had been
wronged by his marriage, and treated his wife as an intruder.
Pavel Isaev, who lived in Dostoevsky's house, forbade the
servants to take orders from the new mistress of the house,
stole the sugar, stealthily drank the cream put aside for his
stepfather's coffee, and declared, shrugging his shoulders,

"You see, Father, when I ran the house nothing was amiss."

He complained to Dostoevsky of imaginary offenses that the young woman inflicted upon him, the "son." Dostoevsky gently scolded his wife, "Anna, stop fighting with Pavel, do not offend him, he is a good boy."

As family scenes became increasingly frequent, Dostoevsky's health was affected. He had epileptic fits of exceptional violence. Anna Grigorievna writes, "I seized Feodor Mikhailovich by his shoulders, and forced him with all my strength to sit on the sofa. But imagine my surprise when I saw his unconscious body slide to the floor at the very moment I no longer had the strength to hold him. I pushed back a table with a lighted lamp on it, and gave the sick man space to lie on the floor. Then I sat beside him the whole time that the convulsions lasted, holding his head on my knees. . . . Alas, to my great sorrow he soon had another seizure, much more violent than the first, and it was only two hours later that he came to, crying with pain. It was a frightening sight."

And Feodor Mikhailovich wrote to Maikov, "There is nothing more unbearable than to experience this shock to one's nerves and brain. I am really beginning to lose my mind."

The doctors advised Dostoevsky to go abroad, and Anna Grigorievna approved this means of escape. As his creditors harassed him constantly, Feodor Mikhailovich asked for nothing better, but when he announced his intention to leave to the family, they protested unanimously. He had promised them, they claimed, to rent a summerhouse in which all of the little tribe could rest during the summer. If he had changed his mind, they argued, he must compensate his relatives and leave them enough money to support them during his absence. Each translated his demands into cash, and the total amounted to eleven hundred rubles. Dostoevsky had exactly one thousand rubles.

"You see, my dear Anna," he said, "fate is against us. If we go abroad in the spring, we shall need two thousand rubles, and we have barely one-half of this amount. If we stay in Russia, we shall be able to live comfortably for two months."

In the meantime the creditors renewed their attacks and threatened Dostoevsky with imprisonment. He wrote, "To go to the debtors' prison might have been useful to me from a certain point of view. I would have gathered material for another *House of the Dead*, which would have meant a profit of from four to five thousand rubles. But I had just got married, and I was not sure at all whether I could endure the intense summer heat in the Tarasov House [the debtors' prison]."

Anna Grigorievna, advised by her mother, suggested to her husband that they pawn the furniture which was in her own name. She would rather lose her possessions than remain exposed to the smoldering hostility of the family. Moreover, there seemed to be no other way out, for Feodor Mikhailovich was liable to being sent to prison any day by his creditors. Reluctantly Dostoevsky accepted his young wife's first sacrifice.

On April 12, the appraisers came to look at Anna Grigorievna's humble furniture. On April 14, at five in the afternoon, the couple left St. Petersburg, to which they were not to return for four years.

9. "THE GAMBLER"

"**I** WAS POOR AND ALONE WITH A YOUNG WOMAN WHO welcomed the idea of wandering over the earth as my companion with naïve joy; but I also realized that this naïve joy indicated a certain overexcitement and inexperience, and that worried and tormented me. I was afraid that I would bore Anna Grigorievna."

From St. Petersburg the couple went to Berlin by way of Vilna. But Berlin seemed to Feodor Mikhailovich so cold, empty, and boring that they stayed only forty-eight hours and left for Dresden—"The sullen Germans got on my nerves to the point of exasperation." In Dresden Dostoevsky rented an apartment of three rooms and hastened to buy for his wife a Leghorn straw hat trimmed with black ribbons

that were called *suivez-moi*. To Anna Grigorievna's great
surprise her husband did not mind attending to these purchases.

Almost at once Dostoevsky began to follow a regular routine. Feodor Mikhailovich worked at night and got up at
eleven o'clock for breakfast. At two o'clock he met his wife
at the art gallery, where he would explain to her Raphael's
"Madonna," Titian's "The Tribute Money," or a hunting
scene by Ruysdael. At three o'clock they dined in a restaurant, after which they walked in the large park, listening to
the public orchestra.

"Feodor Mikhailovich had musical culture," wrote Anna
Grigorievna. "He liked Beethoven, Mendelssohn, Rossini,
but couldn't stand Mozart."

At nine o'clock they went home and drank tea. Dostoevsky would read a little before starting to work, and Anna
Grigorievna would open her notebook in which she recorded
her daily impressions in shorthand.

There is a little of everything in this childish and charming
young girl's diary—the menus of the meals, the prices of eggs
and of yeast, delightful accounts of dear Fedya's gossiping
and fits of temper and sketches of the people in the restaurants. One is dumfounded to discover that at the time when
Dostoevsky was preparing *The Idiot*, his wife, friend, and
confidante, wrote in her little daybook, "I arose early and
began to wash myself, which awoke Fedya. But he was not
cross at me"; or, "Yesterday, lending me his comb, he begged
me to take good care of it, but my hair being tangled caused
me to forget all his admonitions, and I broke three teeth of
the comb in trying to do my hair. I burst into tears and decided to leave the house, taking the comb with me, and to
walk until nightfall." There is no reference to *The Idiot*.

Anna Grigorievna lived outside her husband's intellectual laboratory. She loved the man without understanding the artist. If she had married a grocer, she would not have written differently.

"My dear Anna, I would give much to know what you are writing there with those loops and hooks," Dostoevsky would say to her. If he had but known, poor man!

Toward midnight Feodor Mikhailovich would come to kiss his wife before returning to his work. He would sit on her bed. And these nocturnal visits were the young woman's reward. She wrote in her diary, "There were always long confidences, little tender words, laughs, kisses." When at last he went from this gentle and ignorant child, he would go to his desk, on which were piled the notes for his next novel.

Dostoevsky had left Russia to work, yet his work did not progress. Once again, the experience of voluntary exile was tormenting him. He wrote to Maikov, "Russia is indispensable to me, indispensable on account of my literary work. . . . Like a fish out of water, I am losing all my strength, all my ability."

Why had he come to Dresden? Where would he find the money to return to St. Petersburg? He had only one hope—roulette. He did not yet dare mention it to his wife. But he became ill-tempered, resentful. He vented his feelings in carping at marriage, the Germans, the landscape.

"He criticizes everything. Why are the alleys straight? Why is there a pond in that place? Why this? Why that?" wrote Anna Grigorievna.

Finally Feodor Mikhailovich made up his mind to tell her about his plan, and she approved of it. She approved because she dreaded a scene, an attack. She approved against her better judgment, against her intuition. Dostoevsky was so obsessed with the idea of gambling that he did not hesitate to go to Hamburg and leave his young wife alone in an unfamiliar city.

"Fedya says that if he wins he will come and get me and that we will stay in Hamburg. How wonderful that would be! But perhaps it would be better if he did not go at all."

On May 16, at three in the afternoon, he left. His wife, who was in tears, accompanied him to the station. On May 17, on his arrival in Hamburg, he wrote to her, "Why did I leave you, my dear Anna? I realize that I do not deserve an angel as gentle, as good, as pure as you are, who moreover has faith in me. Where am I going? Why? God gave you to me so that through you I could redeem my great sins by giving you back to him developed, preserved, and saved from everything that is unworthy and kills the soul. And I, I trouble you with things as stupid as my trip here!"

On May 18 he wrote another letter, "I began to play in the morning, and by noon I had lost sixteen ducats. . . . After lunch I returned with the intention of being as sensible as possible, and thanks be to God, I regained all that I had lost and won a hundred florins in addition. I might have won three hundred because I had them in my hands, but I risked them and lost. Now, this is my conclusion, Anna: If one is reasonable, with a heart of stone, cold and superhumanly cautious, one can beyond the shadow of a doubt win as much as one wants to. In brief, I will try, with exceptional energy, to be prudent."

But his energy must have betrayed him, for the next day he confesses to his dear Anna, "Yesterday was altogether disastrous. I lost more than I could afford. My angel, with my nerves one cannot gamble. I played for about ten hours, and

I ended by losing. Tomorrow I want to make a last attempt
with what is left—a drop in the bucket. . . . Our situation
has really something strange about it. Would any of our
friends in St. Petersburg dream that we are separated at this
moment, and why?"

For emotional relief he walked in parks, visited the *Kursaal*,
and listened to the music "which is much superior to that of
Dresden." He was sick with remorse. He tried to persuade
himself that he was gambling to save his dear Anna and all
his family in St. Petersburg from misery. But very soon he
could no longer fool himself. It was only the gambling that
interested him. He loved gambling for its own sake. He lived
only for that moment of intense anxiety when all eyes were
focused on the spinning ball in its vertiginous course—red,
black, even, odd. Win or lose. All existence hinged on the
turning of the wheel. Pleasure and pain were always extremely intense and brief. He was bathed in sweat, he trembled, he no longer thought of anything.

"Everywhere and all my life," writes the underground
man, "I went beyond all limits."

To go beyond the limit, to graze danger, to risk everything
for everything—was this not the only way to live? But far
away in Dresden a young woman was worried, and she wept
and wrote in her diary, "New losses—what will come of it?"

Dostoevsky, as though sensing his wife's thoughts, regretted his indifference. He decided to return as soon as he
had some winnings. Alas! "I am always at the same point,"
he wrote on May 20. "I go round in circles, I have achieved
nothing, so that I cannot yet leave. What will tomorrow
bring me?"

The next day brought nothing good. "My dear angel, yesterday I experienced terrible suffering. As soon as I had fin-

ished my letter to you, I went to the post office, and they told me that there were no letters for me. I tottered on my legs, I could not believe it. I thought you were sick, dying. For about an hour I walked in the garden, trembling all over. Then I went to the roulette and lost everything. . . . I went back to my room, and then went out again to pawn my watch. Hear me, the gambling is finished, I will return as quickly as possible. Send me therefore immediately, as soon as you get this letter, twenty ducats."

Having sent this supplication, Dostoevsky went back to the roulette and risked ten gulden of the twenty he still had. Chance favored him for a moment, and he won three hundred gulden. But instead of going home, he risked all he had won, and lost. "I realize that I can do nothing if you cannot endure my absence and if you are so worried about me. Just think a little, my darling! My own worry about our separation prevented me from finishing this accursed gambling profitably and returning to you, because my mind was not at rest. . . . Twenty times on approaching the gambling table I told myself that if one plays calmly, with composure and reflection, there is no possibility of losing."

Anna Grigorievna sent the twenty ducats, and on May 25 went to the station to welcome her prodigal husband. But Fedya was not on the train. The young woman was in a panic. When she returned home, she was handed a letter dated May 24.

"Anna, my friend, my wife," Dostoevsky wrote to her, "forgive me and do not call me a scoundrel. I have committed a crime, I have lost everything that you sent me, everything, down to the last penny. I received the money yesterday, and yesterday I lost it. Anna, how can I face you? What will you think of me? The only thing that frightens me is what you will say, what you must think of me. O my friend, do not condemn me without appeal. I hate gambling, and not only today but yesterday and the day before I cursed it. As soon as you have received my letter, send me ten ducats."

On May 27, Dostoevsky finally returned to Dresden. His wife was waiting for him on the platform. He was pale, his eyes were sunken. He had lost weight. She threw herself in his arms and as soon as he saw her he understood that she had really forgiven him.

The same day Anna handed Dostoevsky a letter that had arrived during his absence. She had opened it because she had recognized Suslova's handwriting, but she had cleverly re-sealed the envelope.

"It was a stupid and vulgar letter, which was evidence of the poor intelligence of this creature," she noted in her diary.

Dostoevsky read the letter and was embarrassed. Anna Grigorievna, although devoured by jealousy, made a great effort not to show she had noticed anything.

"Anna Grigorievna revealed herself to be more profound and better than I believed possible," Dostoevsky wrote to Maikov.

Worries, regrets, boredom were undermining Feodor Mikhailovich's good humor. He thought of the money that was lost. He accused himself of having played badly, and explained his failure as due to his haste and his anxieties. Moreover, he argued, he had gone to play roulette for no more than two or three days, with only a negligible sum of money. Ah, if he could only spend two weeks in a gambling town, he would know how to attack chance with the cool-ness of an automaton. To go to Switzerland and stop at Baden-Baden—that would be the wisest course, to his way of thinking. He expounded his plan to his wife, and she agreed, convinced or weary.

The prospect of a stay in Baden-Baden then calmed him down, and he resumed his work. He wrote an article on Belinsky. "I sweated in writing it. This work has exhausted me. I could have written ten pages of a novel more easily than one page of this article." In reality Dostoevsky was not yet sure of his opinion of the critic whom he had admired and detested with equal vigor. He wanted to express his gratitude to the man who had encouraged him as a beginner, but a certain rancor checked his enthusiasm. He rewrote his article five times.

Upon his return to Dresden, Dostoevsky had sent a letter to Katkov asking for an advance of five hundred rubles, which he needed to go to Switzerland and Italy. But it was only on July 3 that the couple were able to leave Dresden for Baden-Baden.

At Baden-Baden, Dostoevsky dragged his wife to the gambling halls and explained roulette to her. They played, won, and then lost what they had won.

The next day Feodor Mikhailovich took ten ducats and left his wife alone in the hotel room. Three hours later, at seven o'clock, he had not yet returned. Anna Grigorievna lay on the bed, sick, anguished; all around her the shadows deepened slowly. At eleven o'clock her husband finally appeared, pale, haggard, disheveled, with his tie awry. He had lost. He explained that his old pocketbook had brought him bad luck, and decided to throw it away.

On the next day, the program was the same. He left for the casino with five ducats, and Anna waited for him. On his return she asked: "Did you lose?"

"Yes," he answered, greatly troubled.

At the end of six days Dostoevsky had squandered all their resources. Then the couple entered upon a crazy, hopeless existence that lasted for almost a month. Fedya pawned his wedding ring, played, lost, won, redeemed his wedding ring, pawned it again. One day he came back so pale and dejected that Anna thought that he had lost everything; actually he had won, and he had brought back forty-six gold pieces. With feverish joy he described to the young woman the phases of his play: "I had unbelievable luck. I played 'red' and won. Everyone marveled at me."

She listened to him and admired him. "What joy! Now our life is assured for a little while," she wrote in her diary. But the same night she found her husband collapsed on a bench in the park. He told her that some gamblers had jostled him at the roulette; that had made him angry, and as a result he had lost.

Another time an Englishman, his neighbor at the gambling table, was too perfumed, and as a result Dostoevsky was unable to control his nerves and miscalculated his plays. But the moment his luck was good, Feodor Mikhailovich was again hopeful, and bought fruit, flowers and bonbons for his wife. On July 15 he had four thousand francs. But on July 18, the wallet he reserved for gambling funds contained only twenty-four gold pieces.

In a few hours Dostoevsky did away with this modest sum. He begged his wife to give him some object to pawn. She removed her earrings, contemplated them for a minute, burst into tears, and put them into his outstretched hand. "Fedya threw himself on his knees before me, kissed my hands, and told me that he had never known anyone better and dearer than I." He left her, and she crumpled into an armchair cry-

ing and sniffling like a little girl. Her husband's heart was
filled with agonizing remorse. He was a scoundrel, a thief, a
coward, and he knew it. His awareness of his infamy was
mysteriously agreeable to him. He hurried to the pawnbroker's, and then to the gambling establishment. He trembled like a criminal. The more desperate his situation was, the
more the green table attracted him. It was at such moments
that gambling became a real hand-to-hand fight with fate.
Win, and you will be forgiven; lose, and you are a murderer.
Raskolnikov before going to prison reasoned in the same
terms.

"Fedya returned two hours later having lost the earring
money. He threw himself into a chair and wanted to take me
on his knee. But I slid to his feet and tried to calm him. He
swore that he had that day gambled for the last time and that
he was renouncing it forever. He hid his face in his hands
and cried, yes, he cried. 'I took, I stole your last jewels,' he
said, 'and I have lost them.'"

This forty-six-year-old man, now a famous writer, sobbed
before his young wife like a boy caught in mischief. Nevertheless, the next day he begged her for twenty francs, and
pawned his wedding ring and his wife's lace shawl and wedding ring. On the night of July 19 he won enough money to
redeem the two wedding rings. On July 20 he lost everything and pawned the wedding rings again.

At about that time Anna Grigorievna received a letter
from her mother who wrote, "Unless we sent to K. the
money to redeem our furniture, he will keep it. That would
be terrible. My parents acquired this furniture at the price of
heavy sacrifices, and the thought of losing it now is unbearable." Anna had hardly finished reading this letter when
Dostoevsky entered the room, livid, tense, his eyes red. "It

was the end. . . . He had lost everything. His grief was so great that I feared he would have a seizure."

They wrote to Katkov, to Madame Snitkin; they borrowed three gold pieces from Goncharov, the novelist, who was taking his vacation in Baden-Baden; they got hold of a pawnbroker who took their furs, and they summoned "a little Jew" who gave seven florins for Fedya's overcoat, six florins for a dress of Anna's and two for an old suit. They were forced to remove some of these articles stealthily in order not to be detected by their landlord. "I made the package as small as possible, and Fedya stuffed it under his coat."

Again he gambled, lost, occasionally won ridiculously small sums. "Poor Fedya came back dejected; he said that he would go insane or shoot himself."

The rent was unpaid, they no longer had anything to eat, and there was no tea to drink. The room was suffocatingly hot. Children bawled in houses near by. There was a smithy beneath their windows, and they could hear the hammer of the forge thumping down upon the anvil at regular intervals. The noise, the heat, the moldy wallpaper with flies sticking to it—everything conspired to drive Anna to despair. Dirty linen was piled up in a corner. She would get up and begin to launder with a heavy heart.

Several days later Fedya won enough to recover the articles they had pawned and Anna received one hundred and fifty rubles from her mother. After dinner Fedya went out to retrieve the wedding rings, the brooch, and the earrings. "At eight o'clock Fedya returned. He flung himself toward me in tears and with gestures of despair, and confessed that he had lost everything, all that I had given him to redeem the jewels. . . . He asked me for money to get the things, but

as I could not trust him, I accompanied him to Weissman.
. . . On the way Fedya kissed my hands and implored me
to forgive him, as though he had really been a great criminal."

"Anna Grigorievna has pawned everything she had," Dostoevsky wrote to Maikov. "What an angel! What a solace
she was, and how bored she was in that accursed town of
Baden-Baden, in those two tiny rooms that we rented above
a smithy!"

Besides Goncharov, the only Russian whom Dostoevsky
saw at Baden-Baden was Turgenev. Long ago, Feodor Mikhailovich had borrowed fifty taler from Turgenev—"And
I have not yet paid them back to him!" Anna Grigorievna
advised her husband to pay a visit to his creditor, to prove to
him that the debt was not forgotten.

Dostoevsky did this reluctantly, for he disliked Turgenev's
languishing, haughty demeanor and he disapproved of his
latest novel *Smoke*. One sentence particularly displeased
him: "If Russia should disappear from the face of the earth,
it would be no loss, mankind would in no way be affected."
Their interview soon degenerated into a heated argument.

"He told me," writes Dostoevsky, "that he was a complete
atheist. But, my God, deism has given us Christ, that is to
say, such a lofty representation of man that one is forced to
venerate him, and one cannot doubt that he is the eternal
ideal of mankind. And what can all these Turgenevs, Her-
zens, Utins, and Chernyshevskys give us? They are so dis-
gracefully irritable, so stupidly conceited, that sometimes I
think they are just an awful dream. What can they hope for,
who will follow them?"

Worst of all, Turgenev despised Russia while claiming to

love her. "Among other things, he told me that we should
make obeisance to the Germans, that there could be only
one common path for mankind, that of civilization, and that
all independent, specifically Russian attempts were crude and
stupid. He told me that he was writing a long essay on the
Slavophiles. I advised him to order a telescope from Paris for
greater convenience. He asked me why. 'Because you have
placed yourself very far away,' I told him. 'Turn your telescope on Russia and examine us, otherwise it will be difficult
for you to see us.' "

At these words, Turgenev became red in the face and bit
his lips. But Dostoevsky, recalling that *Smoke* had received
unfavorable reviews, went on with perfidious candor, "I did
not think that the failure of *Smoke* and all those wretched
reviews would exasperate you to such an extent. I assure you
it is not worth your attention—think nothing of it."

"What is the matter with you?" cried Turgenev. "I am not
in the least exasperated."

When Dostoevsky changed the subject and began to criticize the Germans, Turgenev answered him in a voice choking with rage. "In speaking thus you offend me personally.
I want you to know that I have settled here for good, that I
consider myself a German, not a Russian, and that I am
proud of it."

Dostoevsky went home enchanted at having infuriated this
uprooted aristocrat.

At the beginning of August, the Dostoevskys were able to
leave for Geneva thanks to a remittance from Katkov, whom
Feodor Mikhailovich had again asked for an advance of five
hundred rubles. But after paying their debts they had only
one hundred and forty francs left. The trip would cost one

hundred francs. Fedya paid a brief visit to the roulette, and all that remained was one hundred francs. Anna Grigorievna writes, "Upon hearing this, I was seized with anger. How can one be as careless as that? I wanted to scold him, but he knelt down and asked forgiveness."

The earrings were pawned for the last time, for one hundred and twenty francs, and the wedding rings redeemed for twenty francs. "Then Fedya went to play roulette. I begged him not to stay long. . . . He came back twenty minutes later and told me that he had exchanged the twenty-franc gold piece for taler and had lost them all. I told him not to worry about it and to help me pack the trunk."

When the Dostoevskys arrived in Geneva, they had only thirty francs left. They rented a furnished room from two spinsters at the corner of William Tell and Barthelier streets. Four days later they had only eighteen francs. All they had to wait for was a remittance of fifty rubles that Anna Grigorievna's mother had promised them. Feodor Mikhailovich wrote to his friend Maikov, "I know, my dear Apollon Nicolaevich, that you yourself have no money to give away. I would not have addressed myself to you, but for the fact that I am drowning, literally drowning." Maikov immediately sent him one hundred and twenty-five rubles, which were soon spent.

In Geneva, Dostoevsky resumed work at once. He completed his article on Belinsky, which, however, remained unpublished, read Russian newspapers, Balzac, George Sand, attended the congress of the League for Peace and Freedom, and saw Garibaldi drive by in the flag-decked Rue du Mont Blanc. The Italian hero was standing in a barouche and waved a funny little hat in response to the ovations that greeted him. Later, in the congress hall, Feodor Mikhailovich was exasperated by the torrent of speeches.

"It is difficult to imagine," he wrote, "what falsehoods these honorable socialists and revolutionaries—whom I beheld for the first time in the flesh and not in books—could recite on their lofty platform to their five thousand listeners. The absurdity, weakness, and incoherence, of all this were beyond human conception. And these blackguards are arousing the working population! It is sad. They began by telling us that to establish peace on earth, one must do away with Christianity, destroy the great nations, and replace them with the little ones, and abolish capital, so that everything will be commonly owned—and all that without a single proof to support it."

Meanwhile winter was drawing near, the sky was gray, the wind blew cold. People hurried in the streets. Dostoevsky who suffered from this "rotten" climate was again subject to epileptic fits, and his old hatred of foreign lands was stirred up.

"Everything here," he wrote, "is hideous, putrid, and the prices are exorbitant. Even in London I did not see as many violent, brawling drunkards. And the people here describe the smallest block of stone as 'elegant and majestic.'

" 'Where is such and such street?' you ask.

" 'You see, Monsieur,' you are told, 'go straight ahead, and when you reach that majestic and elegant fountain over there, turn to your right.'

"This majestic and elegant fountain is a filthy thing in rococo style, tottering at its base and in bad taste, but your informant cannot help being puffed up about it, even if he only shows you the way."

According to Dostoevsky, the *Jardin Anglais* was far inferior to the shabby Moscow squares, and Geneva was in general "a temple of boredom."

Confronted with this rising bad humor, Anna Grigorievna advised her husband to go to Saxon-les-Bains, a watering town forty miles from Geneva, with a world famous gambling casino. She knew that her Fedya's disastrous ventures at roulette always soothed him in a mysterious way, and that when he had suffered disastrous losses he would regain confidence and be eager to redeem his failure by hard work. When his wife suggested that he try his luck again, he agreed with joy.

He arrived at Saxon-les-Bains on October 5, intending to return the following day after a round of roulette. But on October 6 he wrote to his wife: "Anna, my dear, I am nothing but a brute. Yesterday at ten in the evening I had a clean gain of thirteen hundred francs. Today I have not a penny left, I have lost everything, everything. And all this because that scoundrel of a flunkey did not awaken me as I had ordered him to do, in time for the eleven o'clock train to Geneva. I slept until eleven-thirty. There was nothing to do about it, the next train would not leave until five o'clock. At two o'clock I went to the roulette and lost everything, everything."

Anna Grigorievna's scheme turned out successfully: immediately upon his return Dostoevsky took up his work with redoubled vigor. He wanted to write "a simple story with no moral theme . . . based exclusively on events, and the characters will act of their own accord, unmotivated by any general idea." He thought of making use of the Umetsky trial about which he had read in *The Voice*. It involved a young girl, ill-treated by her parents, who four times set fire to the buildings on the family estate. But that could be only a starting point, and Dostoevsky was annoyed because he was unable to elaborate the incident.

On November 17, exhausted by his work and his illness, he went once more to Saxon-les-Bains. The next day he wrote, "Ah, my dearest, you should not have let me go to the roulette. As soon as I come near it, my heart stops beating, my hands and my feet tremble and turn cold. I arrived here at a quarter to four and found that the gambling establishment was open until five. . . . There was just an hour left, and I ran to the casino. On my first play I lost fifty francs. Then suddenly I began to win. I don't know how much, I didn't count it. Then I lost terribly, almost everything. Then unexpectedly, on the last play, I rewon my hundred and twenty-five francs and an additional one hundred and ten francs, so in all I have two hundred and thirty-five francs. I wonder whether I should not send you the hundred francs. But it is not enough, there should be at least two hundred francs. However, I have promised myself that to-night from eight to eleven I shall be a real Jew, I will gamble in the most reasonable manner. I swear it. . . . Until Tuesday, without fail."

On Monday the tone changed. "Anna, my dear one, my incomparable one, I have lost everything, everything. Oh, my angel, do not be sad, do not worry. Believe me the time will come when I shall be worthy of you, when I shall no longer strip you, like a vile and miserable thief. Now the novel, the novel alone can save us." He went on to say that he had pawned his wedding ring and winter coat, that he needed fifty francs to return to Geneva, and that for the future he would manage somehow—he would appeal to Katkov and to Ogarev, the poet whom he had met in Geneva, and he would pawn the jewels if necessary. "I will salvage and restore everything. The last time I came back dejected, but now there is hope in my heart." He added a postscript: "Do not think, for the love of Christ, that I will gamble with your fifty francs."

This time his return was followed not by intense work, but by the destruction of the first chapters of his novel—all that he had written. He had reread his manuscript, found it execrable, and burned it. Yet he wrote to Katkov asking him for an advance of one hundred rubles a month, and for two hundred rubles for December. And Katkov proved himself to be "a charming man," as Dostoevsky once said, and granted the request on condition that Feodor Mikhailovich deliver the first part of his novel by January 1, 1869.

At the end of December nothing was ready. But in the interval Dostoevsky had conceived an astounding idea—"the idea of depicting a man who is admirable from every point of view." As he wrote to Maikov, "There cannot be anything more difficult than that in our era. You will doubtless readily grant this. Once before I was obsessed by this idea, but in a limited form, and it was necessary to give it full artistic breadth. My distress alone drove me to exploit this subject when it was still unripe. I took a risk as at roulette hoping that it would develop under my pen. It was unforgivable."

As the book gradually took shape, there emerged a heroine and other characters almost as attractive as the hero. "I think the first part is weak, but nothing is lost as yet. . . . For the time being the first part is nothing but an introduction. The novel is entitled *The Idiot*."

In another letter Dostoevsky dwelt on the difficulties that he was encountering in writing this story. "There is in the world but one indisputably admirable figure—Christ. Among the most admirable characters in the literature of Christianity, Don Quixote is the most successful. Even he is admirable only because he is at the same time comical. Dickens' Pickwick, a conception much inferior to that of Don Quixote, but nevertheless remarkable, is also comical, and holds the interest of the reader only by this aspect of his character. Jean Valjean is another courageous attempt, but he arouses sympathy by his terrible misfortune and society's injustice to him. In my novel there is nothing like that, absolutely nothing, hence I am terribly afraid that it will be a complete failure. Some details will perhaps be passably good. But I fear that the whole will seem boring."

Exile, poverty, sickness—all the scourges of the earth seemed to pursue Dostoevsky ruthlessly and gave him the inner courage to bring his undertaking to a successful end. He was cold, there was only a wretched little fireplace in his room, and there were no double windows as in Russia. Although he used a large part of his income in the purchase of wood, he could not bring the temperature of his room above forty degrees, so he sat writing in his heavy winter coat. Katkov's remittances were spent in the first days of the month, and once again Dostoevsky was forced to pawn his belongings. It was in this condition of physical and moral distress that he learned great news: Anna Grigorievna was pregnant.

He was intoxicated with pride at the thought of having a child. He wrote, "We already love the little one who is to be born." They decided that if the child was a girl they would name her Sonia in memory of Sonia Marmeladov, and if it was a boy, Mikhail in memory of Feodor Mikhailovich's brother. By cutting down his daily expenses Dostoevsky was able to engage a midwife and a nurse. A few days before the birth of the baby was expected he was seized by a real panic and had a violent epileptic attack during the night. After the attack he fell asleep until his wife, who was suffering terribly, awakened him.

"How sorry I am for you, my dear one," he answered, then his head sank back on his pillow, and he fell asleep again.

The next morning he ran to get the midwife. She was not up yet. He rang, stormed, threatened, and finally got her to come to Anna's bedside.

"It will be seven or eight hours yet," said the midwife after seeing Anna. "I will come back."

She did not return. Feodor Mikhailovich went again in search of her, and found her having dinner with some friends. He brought her back.

"You cannot expect anything before the night," she said.

Toward nine in the evening he again disturbed the woman who was playing lotto.

"Ah, these Russians, these Russians," she exclaimed.

She followed him nevertheless, but forbade him to come into the room where Anna Grigorievna was undergoing the last agonies of her travail. Feodor Mikhailovich shut himself in the next room, fell on his knees, and prayed. Suddenly, amidst the increasing groans of pain, he heard a shrill cry, the wailing of an infant. He hurled himself against the door, smashed it open with a thrust of his shoulders, fell at the foot of the bed, and kissed the limp hands of the young mother.

"It is a boy, isn't it?" he asked.

"It is a girl, an adorable little girl," said the nurse.

He seized the bundle that was held out to him, embraced it, and cried out, "Anna, look, how beautiful she is!"

"Ah, these Russians, these Russians," the midwife repeated, exasperated at this flood of joy.

Later Dostoevsky used these impressions when describing the labor of Shatov's wife in *The Possessed*: "In his exaltation, Shatov stammered incoherent words: 'There were two human beings, now suddenly there is a third . . . a new soul, whole, finished, such as a human hand could never have wrought . . . a new thought and a new love . . . it is frightening . . . there is nothing greater in the world.' "

From the very beginning Dostoevsky worshiped his daughter to the point of foolishness. He declared that she recognized him, that she smiled at him, and that she understood him. He helped with the infant's bath, he dressed her and fastened the safety pins. He carried and rocked her in his arms. Whenever she uttered a cry, he stopped his work at once and ran to her alarmed. He wrote to Maikov: "This little, three-months-old thing, insignificant like a crumb, already had a face, a character. . . . She did not cry or frown when I kissed her, and would stop crying when I bent over her."

As the money sent by Katkov was quickly spent in paying the nurse, the midwife, and the landlord, Dostoevsky decided to return to Saxon-les-Bains and try his luck for the last time. The result was not long in coming.

"Anna, my dear angel," he wrote on April 16, "I have lost everything! And within half an hour after I arrived. Well, what can I say to you now, to you, my angel, to whom I bring so much suffering? Forgive me, Anna, I have poisoned your life. And yet there is Sonia! I have pawned the ring. Send me as much money as you possibly can. Not for gambling—I would give you my word, but I do not dare, I have lied to you too often. Send me one hundred francs. You will have twenty left, and perhaps even less. If so pawn something. But I want to return to you as quickly as possible."

While waiting for this money he risked and lost the sum that he had obtained by pawning his wedding ring. He had fifty centimes left. "My friend, this is to be the last lesson, the final and terrible lesson," he wrote to his wife the same night. But he added: "You should know, my angel, that without this bad and vulgar adventure, without this needless wasting of two hundred and twenty francs, I might not have had a wonderful idea that will contribute to our immediate and general salvation. Yes, my loved one, I believe that God in His infinite mercy has perhaps done this for me, a miserable little gambler, to inspire me and to save me from gambling, and to save you and Sonia, and all of us, for the future.".

He was referring to his project of writing a letter to Katkov to apologize for the delay in delivering *The Idiot* and to propose offering his publisher the rights to the second printing of his novel as a guarantee for the advances he would request. He wanted an immediate remittance of three hundred rubles. This money, Dostoevsky thought, would enable him to settle at Vevey, where the climate was better than in Geneva, and at Vevey he would write great things. As soon as the novel was finished, he would leave with his family for Italy.

He returned, proud of his new project. But several days later little Sonia was taken out for an airing, caught cold, and began to cough. The physician declared that there was no cause for alarm, but Dostoevsky was not convinced. He no longer wrote, he did not leave the cradle. His premonitions came true. The little girl died on May 24.

Feodor Mikhailovich's grief was an agony. He sobbed and wailed before the little corpse; he bent over the little face and tiny hands and covered them with kisses. He helped his wife to clothe Sonia in a white satin dress, put the body into a little coffin lined with white satin, and arrange for the burial. And when the first shovelfuls of earth sounded on the wooden lid, it was though he was being stabbed in the heart, killed, and buried.

He had put all his hope, all his pride in this child. He had imagined the future of all three of them, the evenings at home, the books that they would read together—all kinds of little joys that were now suddenly swept away. There had been few joys in his life, but this one had been so great, so pure, that he felt it had made him a better man. And now even this joy had been taken away from him. It was all over, irretrievably lost—never again would he see that little, still unformed face, never again would he anticipate the least frown of those little brows, or fondle with his fingers that warm little neck. He could not pass a child in the street without at once evoking the image of his baby. This memory shattered him, tore him to pieces. For the first time he was tempted to revolt against destiny.

"Ah, Apollon Nicolaevich," he wrote to Maikov, "what does it matter that my love for my first child was ridiculous. What of it if I spoke of her in a foolish manner in my numerous answers to the people who congratulated me. I only seemed ridiculous to them. But to you, to you I no longer fear to write. They try to comfort me by telling me that I will have other children. But where is Sonia? Where is this little being for whom I would have accepted crucifixion if I could thus have saved her life? But let us have no more of this subject. My wife is here and she is weeping. The day after tomorrow we shall at last leave our little grave and we will go no matter where."

Toward the end of May the Dostoevskys left Geneva where everything reminded them of little Sonia and crossed the lake to settle at Vevey. But even at Vevey they were inconsolable. Their existence seemed useless. "All our thoughts, all our words, turned around Sonia and the happy days spent by her cradle when she brightened our life," wrote Anna Grigorievna.

"I will never forget her and never cease to suffer," wrote Feodor Mikhailovich. "Even if I have another child, I do not know how I can love it. Where will I find the love? I need Sonia. I cannot admit that she is no longer and that I will never see her again."

At night Anna Grigorievna had fearful dreams and sobbed. Her mother, who had come from St. Petersburg, tried in vain to comfort her. Vevey was a dull little town. The beautiful lake, blue and transparent, like vapor, the milky white mountains against the radiant sky, all this serene beauty in the end only nauseated Feodor Mikhailovich. He fell ill, and so did Anna. He felt that he would only recover when he had completed his novel. "I detest my novel to the point of disgust. By a great effort I have forced myself to work, but without result. If I retrieve my novel, I will retrieve myself. If not, I am lost."

In the meantime the police of St. Petersburg intercepted his letters and kept close watch over him. The Russian priest of Geneva was a secret agent. One day Feodor Mikhailovich was informed by an anonymous letter that he would be searched when crossing the Russian border. At about the same time he received a proscribed pamphlet, *The Secrets of the Czar's Palace*, in which he and his first wife were represented as exiled revolutionary heroes. The author also alleged that Feodor Mikhailovich was dead and that his wife had become a nun. This absurd pamphlet exasperated Dostoevsky. In a frantic denial which he did not send—the draft of it has been preserved, however—he wrote, "Any slander, however absurd, attains its purpose."

At the beginning of September, the Dostoevskys left Vevey for Italy. They stopped first at Milan, but this city bored Feodor Mikhailovich. It rained all the time, and he could find no Russian books. "Nothing Russian. I have not had one Russian book, one Russian newspaper, for six months. *The Idiot* is a complete failure."

He begged his friend Maikov to keep him abreast with everything that was happening in Russia. Maikov told him of the launching of a new periodical, *Dawn*. Strakhov who had contributed to *Time* and *The Epoch* was editor-in-chief. Dostoevsky was proud and wrote to Strakhov, "Thus our work in common was not in vain."

From Milan the Dostoevskys went to Florence where they rented quarters near the Pitti Palace. The change of scene helped to distract Feodor Mikhailovich and his wife. They visited the churches and the museums. Dostoevsky went to see the paintings of Raphael, his favorite artist, and he also discovered a library that subscribed to two Russian newspapers. Every day he spent the afternoon in the reading room.

Katkov's remittances came regularly. The novel progressed. Dostoevsky decided to rush it through. "If there are readers who are following *The Idiot*," he wrote, "they will perhaps be a little surprised by this unexpected conclusion. But upon reflection, they will understand that no other end would have been possible."

The *Russian Messenger* began the publication of *The Idiot* in January, 1868. Dostoevsky, in speaking of this novel, said that he had never had a richer subject, but that he had not succeeded in expressing one-tenth of his ideas. Nevertheless *The Idiot* ranks as one of his major works, along with *The Possessed* and *The Brothers Karamazov*.

In the story, Prince Myshkin, an epileptic, returns from a clinic in Switzerland, where a professor has treated him out of charity. He is an orphan and knows nothing of life. All that he has in the world is a meager bundle of clothes.

"I am perfectly convinced," the professor says to him, "that you are an absolute child, that is to say, a child in the true sense of the word, and the only adult thing about you is your size and face. In development of character, of soul, perhaps even of intelligence, you are not a grown man, and you will remain as you are even if you should live to be sixty years of age."

This child of twenty-six is deferential without being obsequious, he is timid, good and naïve. He has not lived, or at least he has not lived actively. He has spent his life in inward contemplation, living outside of the social wall, outside of the world of "twice two makes four." He is untainted by contact with people, and when he finds himself among his fellow men, in a great city filled with knaves, libertines, clowns, and drunkards, he behaves like an intruder.

On his arrival in St. Petersburg he pays a visit to General Epanchin who is vaguely related to him and from whom he expects to receive advice about his personal affairs. Fresh from his seclusion, Myshkin displays his awkwardness. He makes long speeches to the footman, he blunders before the general's secretary, and later in the course of an inspired tirade, breaks a Chinese vase. This vase is a symbol of the materialistic world with which he clashes and which he jolts when he is carried away by his convictions.

Yet this sympathetic breaker of vases, this candid and blundering talker, does not anger those around him. Even those who are hostile to him are disarmed by his simplicity and frankness. To be sure, they make fun of him, but they forgive his violations of convention just as one forgives a foreigner his errors of speech because they feel that he is of another world. It seems absurd to expect him to speak or behave in a way unknown in his world. But this traveler, this passer-by, who seems at first glance devoid of all orientation, is endowed with a particular kind of knowledge that the "walled-up ones" cannot possibly conceive of. He has what Dostoevsky calls primary intelligence. "Primary intelligence is more developed in you than in anyone else," the general's daughter says to him. "You possess it to a degree that they have never glimpsed, even in a dream. For there are two kinds of intelligence, primary and secondary intelligence. Isn't that so?"

The main theme of this novel can actually be defined as that of the incursion of primary intelligence into the domain of secondary intelligence. The former, which is intelligence outside of the laws of causality and contradiction, beyond the rules of morality, creates disturbances in the new milieu where it is transplanted. Myshkin's appearance in this stuffy atmosphere is like a breath of fresh air. At first he is laughed at: he is grotesque, backward, he is an idiot—his own mother used to call him an idiot when he was a child. But little by little this idiot, this moron, casts doubt upon the most solidly established principles of those around him. This being, so poor in spirit, gives wise men food for thought. This intruder becomes indispensable, this weakling tames the strong.

All this unwittingly he does—convinced that everyone about him is generous and that everyone loves him. By treating the most corrupt and evil creatures as if they were the gentlest and the most godly, he makes them his allies.

People become good because he wishes them to be good and believes that they are. He is in the center of a magnetic field of attraction; he radiates mysterious rays. Thanks to him the proud know the blessedness of humility, the egoists open their souls to repentance, the embittered rediscover childish candor. Shame and hatred vanish in his presence. For those about him life acquires an unearthly meaning. In the eyes of all he is the proof that there is another life and that another world is possible. No one is unchanged after knowing him.

Those who are most affected by the charm of the idiot are people given to violence and evil, the lost souls, those who have gone beyond the limits. The first man to understand him is Rogozhin, the brutish merchant who, at the end of the story, murders his mistress. Nastasia Philipovna, the prostitute, also understands him. Why? Because they have freed themselves from the principles of current morality. They have jumped over the wall. To be sure, they have lost their way, now that they are outside the wall that formerly surrounded them. But those who attempt to conquer freedom, who suffer, who have sinned, are closer to the truth and deserve to know more than those who have not tried to learn. Passion justifies everything. Any passion, even criminal passion, is worth more than quiescence.

Among Myshkin's friends, besides those who escaped from the prison of the world, are those who have not yet entered it—the children. Children have malleable minds that have not experienced constraint. They have not had time to form a petrified vision of the world. Everything is movement, everything is chance for them. Things have no bond to reality. Anything can beget anything. These new creatures, these "birds," are by instinct what adults endeavor to become through terrible ordeals. They live close to nature and to God. Later they will believe in human rules and will be lost to freedom. Their parents and their teachers will make the little ones old people before their time, strong in scientific knowledge, icy reasoners, bourgeois careful of their comforts—in other words, monsters. But for the time being they are unpolluted and vulnerable. And because they are unpolluted and vulnerable, they are the friends of Myshkin who, like them, is a child lost in the world of adults.

"Grown people do not know," he says, "that even in the most difficult affair, a child can give extremely important advice. O God, when such a pretty little bird looks at one with so much confidence and happiness, one would be ashamed to deceive him. I call them little birds because little birds are the best thing in the world . . . as for Thibaut [the schoolmaster], his hatred was nothing but jealousy. At first he wagged his head and was astonished when he saw that the children understood at once everything that I said to them, whereas he could not succeed in making himself understood. Then he jeered at me when I told him that we do not teach them anything, neither he nor I, but that it is they who teach us."

Ignoring divine revelation, the intellectuals build a wall of human truth that deprives them of the light of heaven. Their own pride stands between them and the truth of God. "He has hidden from the wise and the learned that which he has revealed to children."

All these simple spirits, all these unruly saints, are united in a mysterious brotherhood. Infinitely absorbed in their

emotions, they communicate with each other by telepathic
currents. They have the gift of prophecy. Nothing surprises
or disappoints these ecstatic visionaries. Thus, when the idiot
is asked whether he believes that the marriage between
Nastasia Philipovna and Rogozhin is possible, he answers
simply, "Yes, I think he will marry her, and not later than
tomorrow—but in a week he will murder her."

"I am afraid, I don't understand why, but I am afraid,"
says another character in the book. "It is as though there
were something in the air, some evil that flies about like a bat.
I am afraid, afraid."

Nastasia Philipovna accurately foresees her death. She
writes about Rogozhin, "I would gladly kill him, I am so
afraid of him. But he will kill me first."

Prince Myshkin, when he sees a knife on Rogozhin's table,
guesses that it is the weapon which later will be used by the
criminal.

"Do you use this for cutting pages?" he asks.

"Yes, for cutting pages," answers Rogozhin.

"But it is brand-new," says the prince.

On leaving his host he wonders whether it has been written that Rogozhin will commit murder. Later he pays a visit
to Rogozhin without being invited, simply because he has
an intuition that a calamity has taken place. And Rogozhin
waits for him in front of his house simply because he "feels"
that Myshkin will visit him. "Leon Nicolaevich, follow me,
my friend, it is necessary," he says.

These people who have such a clairvoyant awareness of
their fate do not, however, escape the dangers that lie in wait
for them. They cannot, they do not want to, they do not
know how to avoid the abyss toward which they are being
driven. They are the slaves of their own prevision. They do

not control their lives, they only feel. They are starved for
strong impressions, they desire neither happiness nor despair,
they desire only to have the awareness of existing. And any
suffering is a good medium for experiencing the limits of
existence. I suffer, therefore I am. I surmount pain, therefore
I shall be. He who accepts everything drifts toward God.
Whoever resists the current, drifts away from God. "He
who seeks to save his life will lose it, and he who will lose his
life for My sake will gain it."

The novel is nothing but a succession of disasters, each of
them foreseen by the sensitive characters, and none is deliberately rejected. Dostoevsky's heroes strive only for that
which will destroy them. Prince Myshkin, the "absolutely
good man," has just arrived at General Epanchin's. He has
hardly been introduced to the family when he meddles in all
the intrigues. He interferes in what does not concern him,
although by doing so he exposes himself to unpleasantness
and danger. When he sees Nastasia Philipovna's melancholy
face in a photograph, he decides to marry this great sinner.
Yet he realizes that this desire is absurd. He fights the brutal
and sinister Rogozhin for possession of the young woman,
and when he gives her up, he knows very well that he is
sending her to her death. Nastasia Philipovna marries Rogozhin because it is the greatest error she can commit, and
Rogozhin kills her because he knows that he will regret this
deed all his life. The murderer and the absolutely good man
are reconciled by the side of the dead woman because they
feel that they have at last accomplished the inevitable.

"Rogozhin was uttering some incoherent words. . . .
Then the prince held out a trembling hand to him, gently
touched his head, and caressed his hair and cheeks. That was
all he could do."

The Idiot seems to be Dostoevsky's first great novel of love. Yet love, and the loves that constitute the plot of this book, have no real significance. They are obstacles to be overcome, not havens of the heart's desire. They are the stages of a journey to truth, they are not the truth. In the eyes of Dostoevsky love is never a relaxation for the body or a rest for the soul. Desire is never satisfied, and the carnal act is never truly consummated. Woman exists for him only as an agent. Placed between man and God, her function is to awaken man to suffering, to torture, to cast him down, to raise him up again, to lure him beyond the moral law, and to precipitate him breathless, dazed, completely renewed, into the ineffable world of freedom. She represents the temptation that precedes final appeasement.

It would be vain to search in Dostoevsky's novels of the second manner for a woman who is the central motif of the work, a counterpart of Tolstoy's Anna Karenina or of Pushkin's Natasha, or of Madame Bovary or Eugénie Grandet. Dostoevsky's great novels are male novels. His anthropology, to use Berdyaev's term, is a male anthropology. Women have no value of their own in his world; they are a means, not an end. And usually one woman serves two men simultaneously. Each of these men is attracted to the woman for different reasons; likewise, each man can love two women at the same time. Woman initiates the splitting of male personality. Love can be pity, and love can be sensuality. Myshkin loves both Nastasia Philipovna and the pretty Aglaya, General Epanchin's daughter. He is attracted and seduced by Aglaya's beauty, but he feels infinite compassion for Nastasia's tormented face. "I cannot stand her face, I am afraid of her face. I do not love her with love, but with pity."

Challenged to choose between Nastasia and Aglaya, he turns to the former. "He saw before him only the mad woman, the desperate one, who had made upon him a lasting, heart-rending impression."

Nastasia Philipovna for her part hesitates between the sick prince, who is chaste and good to the point of stupidity, and the cruel and sensual Rogozhin. She awakens pity in Myshkin and violent desire in Rogozhin. Her body and her heart play separate roles in the fate of the two men who are chained to her: one will be destroyed because of her body, the other because of her heart. Yet when she lies dead, the two reconciled lovers discover that they have advanced together toward the same deliverance.

Thus in the eyes of Dostoevsky a love dedicated to an earthly creature takes nothing away from God. Earthly love, because it is imperfect, ephemeral, painful, and ridiculous, stirs the soul and prepares it for the only love that will not fail it.

One notes, however, that altruistic love is the only help Dostoevsky's characters can demand of each other. Myshkin, the saint, cannot act, he can only love. When he tries to act, he makes mistakes; he not only does not succeed in helping anyone, but he compromises the happiest situations. The coming of this absolutely good man results in murder and three or four family tragedies. And he himself goes insane. He is unable to survive in an alien climate, to adapt himself to the human condition, to become a man. However, his ruin saves those around him. His presence has enriched certain lives and brought people to the awareness of fundamental problems.

"And I say to you verily, if the grain of wheat planted

in the earth does not die in the earth, it will remain solitary, and if it dies it will bring forth many fruits." This verse of the Gospel seems to be the hidden conclusion of *The Idiot*.

The character of the idiot is perhaps the least human of all those conceived by Dostoevsky. Aliosha Karamazov is a good man but he is not unaware of evil; he knows passion, the temptations of the flesh and the spirit, and dominates them. He is a complete being. But Prince Myshkin is not of this world. He is free of all sensuality. "I cannot marry any woman," he says, "because I am sick."

It was necessary to link this supernatural being with the everyday world, to endow this pure idea with a body, a face, a voice, and a history. To give substance to this hero who has neither weight nor size, Dostoevsky was forced to draw upon his own personality. Thus, Myshkin is an epileptic. Like Dostoevsky, he experiences great joy before a seizure. Like him, he awaits and anticipates the precious moment in which the supreme harmony of the world is revealed to him in a flash. "In this moment it seems to me that I understand the extraordinary phrase of the apostle, 'There will no longer be any time.' " The disease keeps him in a sort of perpetual, luminous trance. The world is transparent for him; he sees beyond people, he dwells mysteriously in the future.

The prince's memories are borrowed from Dostoevsky's own memories. For instance, the prince tells the story of a political criminal to whom the death sentence was read. "Twenty minutes later, his sentence was commuted. But between the reading of the death sentence and that of the decree of commutation twenty minutes elapsed . . . during which the wretched man was sure that he would die in a few minutes." There follows an accurate description of the execution of the "Petrashevsky."

Another illustration of Dostoevsky's utilization of personal detail is Myshkin's aversion to a picture owned by Rogozhin, a copy of Holbein's *Descent from the Cross*. "On seeing this picture, a man could lose his faith!" exclaims the prince. Now, Anna Grigorievna in her memoirs relates the following incident: "On our way to Geneva we stopped one day at Basel to visit a museum in which there was a picture that had been mentioned to my husband. It is a canvas of Holbein that shows Christ just after his inhuman martyrdom, already taken down from the cross and abandoned to decay. Too much affected to look at it for any length of time, I went into another room. When I returned, my husband was still there, spellbound, glued to the same spot. He wore the expression of fright that I had often noticed at the beginning of his epileptic attacks." And he said to her: "Such a painting as this one could make one lose one's faith."

Likewise, the prince's attitude toward Rogozhin, his rival, is reminiscent of Dostoevsky's attitude toward Vergunov, his rival in Siberia. The prince says, "I am not your enemy. I do not wish to cross you in anything. If it is true that you have made up your quarrel, I will not show myself before her eyes, and I will not visit you any more."

Throughout the book the reader feels that Dostoevsky is striving to pile up material details and personal observations in order to give plausibility to his story of another world. He projects characters conceived under the sign of "twice two makes three" into the world of "twice two makes four." He tries to reconcile the irreconcilable. And yet there is not one character in this novel whose feet are really on the ground.

Rogozhin, Nastasia Philipovna, Hippolyte, Lebedev, Aglaya, Ivolgin, all are illumined by a nightmarish glow.

"Is Rogozhin incapable of enduring light?" the prince wonders. He would like to understand the soul of his rival. He wonders whether this man has only blind passions, whether he is incapable of suffering or compassion.

"Rogozhin is uncommunicative," says Nastasia. "He observes a fearsome silence, only his eyes speak." It seems that this man does not belong to himself. From the beginning of the book one feels him entangled, caught in the vise of his crime, driven to it. He kills the girl whom he has so desired at the very moment when she gives herself to him, and he does this because he has hoped to understand her in the embrace of their bodies, and because this embrace completely separates them from each other. Her flesh conceals a being that no caress can reveal. Rogozhin is confined in his own solitude, and Nastasia is enclosed in hers. Human gestures are not sufficient to bring them together. Bending over her face and feeling her breath, Rogozhin suffers because he realizes that the woman whom he holds close is in reality far away from him. She is not wholly his; she will never be wholly his; sooner or later she will leave him again. Death alone can keep her for him. He stabs her in the heart, and goes out to wait for Myshkin.

"A white cloth covered the sleeping figure, but the body was vaguely outlined. . . . The room was in disorder; garments were strewn everywhere, on the bed, on the armchair, on the floor. . . . The tip of a bare foot was visible under a ruffle of lace that made a white spot in the darkness. This foot seemed to belong to a marble statue. Its immobility was frightening. The longer the prince looked, the more sinister the silence of the room became. Suddenly a fly awoke, flew buzzing above the bed and lighted on the bolster. The prince shivered."

Myshkin is not surprised by Rogozhin's confession, and when the latter says to him, "We must not let her be taken away," he answers:

"No, no, not for anything in the world! No, no!"

Little by little both of them sink into unconsciousness. When the police come to arrest Rogozhin, they find him howling at the foot of the bed while the prince gently strokes his face and hair.

Nastasia Philipovna had foreseen her death from the outset. She says, "I am pale as a corpse," and smiles, before leaving for the church.

Actually, death is the only way out for this anguished and simple soul. She is attracted to Rogozhin just as one animal is attracted to another by his smell. She loves him yet she recognizes that this boor is unworthy of her. Only Myshkin can understand her, and only Myshkin's love can save her from degradation. But his love is too much like compassion to satisfy her; she is proud, and she does not accept the alms of pity. Thus she comes to cherish the dishonor that prevents her from being loved as she wishes to be.

"You can love only your disgrace," Aglaya said to her, "your obsession that you are ruined and that someone has made you a lost woman. If you were less defiled, or if you were not defiled at all, you would be even more unhappy."

Nastasia's thirst for humility is coupled with a boundless conceit: she wants to humiliate herself but she does not want to be humiliated. And this holds for all of Dostoevsky's characters.

Around these three main characters swarms a picturesque

crowd of parasites, cynics, and degenerates. Lebedev is a
servile hireling, a greasy procurer, a usurer, a perjurer, but
he excels in explaining the Revelation of St. John, and laments
in rounded phrases the fate of Madame Du Barry.

"If you whip me," he says to Rogozhin, "that will be proof
that you do not reject me. Whip me! By your blows you are
taking possession of me."

There is General Ivolgin, "resigned and unhappy," who
lies for the pleasure of lying, and who in the end is no longer
able to distinguish falsehood from truth. There is General
Epanchin, the pompous and faint-hearted lover of Nastasia
Philipovna. There is Gania, who wants to marry her only
because he hopes thus to attain a profitable career. He says,
"Yes or no? Is seventy-five thousand rubles worth undergoing such a torture?"

There is pretty Aglaya, who laughs at the prince and
adores him. Finally, there is the interesting figure of Hippolyte, the young consumptive, whose days are numbered
and who feels the need of reading his confession in public.
With this dying man, Dostoevsky tackles the problem of
the ultimate meaning of life. Hippolyte, like the author himself, is torn by the conflict between thought and matter. Is
there something beyond the walls? Is there a force that can
transcend the laws of nature? Are miracles possible, or is
everything regulated according to "twice two makes four?"
Hippolyte turns to Christ as the embodiment of thought
triumphant. He thinks of the picture in Rogozhin's waiting
room. "The face of Christ is atrociously disfigured by the
blows He has received, He is covered with bleeding wounds,
His eyes are wide open. They stare and shine with a glare
of death. But strangely enough, the corpse of this man who
has suffered so much suggests a curious question. If such was

the body (and it must have been exactly like this), how could the disciples, the apostles, the women who followed Him and who waited at the foot of the cross, all those who believed in Him and adored Him—how could they think when they saw these remains that the martyr would resurrect? If death is so horrible, one says in spite of himself, if the laws of nature are so powerful, how can one triumph over them, how can they be surmounted, if He Who when He was alive made nature obey Him, Who cried *Talitha cumi,* Who brought to life a young girl and resurrected Lazarus—if even He did not vanquish them?"

It is a fact that the laws of nature, the rules of "twice two makes four," did not yield before the mystery of Christ. They took hold of the man of miracles as if He had been a simple mortal, and all the power of thought could not prevent the nails from tearing those convulsed hands and the lance from piercing His quivering thigh, or the thorns from pricking the brow that bore the world, and the sweat from running down the divine face.

Thus, in the eyes of Hippolyte, nature takes on "the aspect of a modern machine that has stupidly crushed, slashed, swallowed up, devoured the admirable, infinitely precious being Who alone was worth more than all nature with all her laws—the nature which was perhaps created only to produce Him."

Philosophical systems, Religions, are nothing in the face of matter and number. Christ rose from the dead, they say. But His ignominious end was a defeat for faith. Death reigns over the universe.

Very well, then, since this is so, since there is only an insensitive Prime Mover that crushes both the good and the wicked, the young and the old, the obtuse bourgeois and the pure genius, one must bow before it as Christ Himself did. But to accept the Prime Mover does not mean to worship it. Hippolyte cries, "Can I not be devoured without having to bless that which devours me?"

And if he is mistaken, if he is blasphemous in speaking thus, why should he be held responsible for his error? "If it is so difficult and even completely impossible to understand this, can I be guilty because I am unable to understand something that passes understanding? We cheapen Providence when, unable to understand it, we resentfully attribute to it our own ideas."

This desperate dialectic is the same as that of the underground man: "With clenched mouth and gritting teeth, to sink into inertia brooding over the fact that there is not even anyone to be angry at."

It is not with reasoning that one can counter this attack of logic. Faith is not attained by a series of deductions, like the solution of a problem. It is not attained by intelligence, but by feeling. And several days later, when Hippolyte questions the prince regarding the meaning of life, Myshkin answers him with these admirable words, "Continue on your way and forgive us our happiness." Let those incapable of feeling this happiness beyond and against all reason go on their way and leave the others in peace. Because faith is the foe of "twice two makes four," it is not through application of logical principles that it will be revealed to the heart of the unbeliever. Such is the lesson of the significant episode of Hippolyte.

This overwritten, loosely constructed, unbalanced story unfolds in a nightmarish atmosphere. Every page offers improbabilities intermingled with details derived from actual experience. Throughout the book one can feel the author's desperate effort to keep his feet on the ground while he is being carried away by the current of his ideas.

"That which most people call fantastic and exceptional is for me the most profound reality," wrote Dostoevsky to Strakhov. "I do not value the novel, I value its main idea." The critics were baffled by this inexplicable book that defied all classification. Some did not even mention it. Others were merely indignant. For instance, Burenin wrote, "My God, what has Mr. Dostoevsky not invented in this novel, which is truly the worst of all that he has ever published. . . . In my opinion, this work is a literary compilation of a crowd of characters and events. It is devoid of all artistic merit. Entire pages are incomprehensible."

10. "THE ETERNAL HUSBAND"

"**I** FEEL THAT THE PUBLIC HAS BEEN LESS IMPRESSED BY *The Idiot* than by *Crime and Punishment*," wrote Dostoevsky. "My self-respect is at stake; I want to be in the limelight again." Thus, as soon as he had completed *The Idiot*, he began a new novel, *The Eternal Husband*.

The payment of seven thousand rubles that Dostoevsky received for *The Idiot* was considerably reduced as a result of the advances he had received. A part of the balance went to pay his debts and redeem his furniture and to help his stepson and his brother's family. The little that was left was just sufficient to pay the expenses of the Dostoevskys' stay in Florence.

In January, 1869, Anna Grigorievna discovered that she

was pregnant for the second time. Although this meant new financial difficulties, Dostoevsky was overjoyed. He showered Anna with attentions, and his excessive solicitude amused her. He was convinced that the child would be a girl and decided to name her Lubov. He hid from his wife a copy of *War and Peace*, because of Tolstoy's description of the agonized death of Princess Bolkonskaya in childbirth.

"I await this child with emotion, fear, hope, and humility," Dostoevsky wrote to Strakhov. Fearing that his wife would give birth to her child in Italy, where she knew no one, and where the doctors could not understand her, he decided to leave Florence for Prague, a Slav city par excellence, since it had been the seat of the Slavic congress in 1867. They traveled by way of Venice, where Dostoevsky visited St. Mark's Cathedral and the Doges' Palace, visited Bologna, where he admired Raphael's "St. Cecilia," and passed through Trieste and Vienna. But in Prague the Dostoevskys could not find an apartment nor even a furnished room. They had no choice but to return to Dresden, which at least was familiar to them.

They arrived in Dresden in August; in September, Anna Grigorievna gave birth to a girl. Her father wrote, "Three days ago our daughter Lubov came into the world. Everything went well. The baby is plump, healthy and pretty." But the doctor, the midwife, and the tradesmen were not paid, and there was only ten taler in the family purse. Dostoevsky wrote to the editor of *Dawn* to ask for an advance on his next novel, but the money was long in coming. Every day Dostoevsky went to the window of the bank, and every day was shown the door by the clerks, who made fun of him.

"How can I write at this moment? I walk up and down in

my room, I tear my hair, and at night I cannot sleep. I think
of my distress and am enraged. And I wait! O God! I swear
to you that it is impossible for me to describe my present
misery in detail. I am ashamed of it. . . . And on top of all
this, they demand artistic finish, limpidity, effortless poetry
. . . and they point to Turgenev and Goncharov. Let them
take a look at the conditions in which I work."

A remittance of one hundred rubles finally reached him.
But he spent it almost at once, and in December he did not
even have five taler to send off his manuscript to *Dawn*. "I
do not have and cannot get the money to send my manuscript
to the editor. It is heavy, and the price will be five taler. I
need five taler for the manuscript, but we also must have
something to live on. Ah, how hard everything is!"

Finally *Dawn* granted him another advance, and *The
Eternal Husband*, carefully wrapped and tied, went on its
way from Dresden to Russia.

This novel strikes one as a self-parody. One day Velchaninov, "the seducer," receives a visit from a man who wears a
hat with a mourning band and who has been following him
everywhere for some time. Velchaninov recognizes Trusotsky whose wife was his mistress nine years ago.

"I had no intention of coming in," says Trusotsky, "it
has happened by accident."

"An accident, indeed! I saw you from my window crossing
the street on tiptoe," answers Velchaninov.

Trusotsky's wife is dead. She has left him a daughter named
Lisa, who was born eight months after the "departure" of
Velchaninov. Lisa too dies, but her death does not seem to
affect Trusotsky in the least.

Velchaninov thinks that Trusotsky is a type of the "eternal
husband"—"such a man is born and grows up only to get
married and become a supplement to his wife."

A strange comradeship, born of hate and pity, develops between the two men who indulge in constant quarrels, reproaches, remorse, and pardons accompanied by tears and embracings. Velchaninov cannot escape from these scenes because he feels guilty. Trusotsky is so perverse that he takes his companion to the country to meet his new fiancée and her family. Confronted with Nadia, the young schoolgirl, Velchaninov plays the part of the accomplished seducer. Trusotsky, with a kind of satisfied rage, recognizes the beginnings of a betrayal identical to the one that he endured earlier. Upon his return to St. Petersburg he nurses Velchaninov, who has fallen ill in the meantime.

He runs to the kitchen, lights the fire, wakens the janitor, and Velchaninov, deeply moved, stammers: "You . . . you . . . could you be better than I am? I understand everything, thank you."

The seducer falls asleep, and a short while later is aroused by a painful premonition. He stretches out his arms, and a sharp weapon strikes his left hand. Trusotsky is standing before him holding a razor. But Velchaninov succeeds in overpowering his rival.

Later he meets a fairly pretty young woman in a railroad station and intervenes when a drunken officer who has been traveling with her starts a brawl. The woman, saved from an awkward situation, is effusively grateful and deplores the fact that her husband has vanished, "at the very moment I need him." After some time the husband appears. He is Trusotsky. The two rivals exchange trivialities, then Velchaninov holds out his hand to the "eternal husband," who refuses it.

"And Lisa! And how about little Lisa," Trusotsky stammers, and his lips, his cheeks, his chin begin to tremble, and tears gush from his eyes. The train starts to move. Trusotsky jumps into the compartment. Velchaninov is left alone, standing in perplexity on the platform.

This short tale written in a lively and careful style is very different from *The Idiot*, which is marked by confusion and brilliant flashes of genius. The interesting point about *The Eternal Husband* is that it constitutes a kind of compendium of all the great Dostoevskian themes. These are not developed, they appear only as a succession of ideas summarily jotted down. In this novel Dostoevsky has done only half his usual work. He suggests lines of thought, but does not accompany the reader on these mysterious paths. Such as it is, this book constitutes an admirable summary of all Dostoevsky's motifs. And the scene of the attempted murder is one of his greatest pieces.

When *The Eternal Husband* had been completed, corrected, and sent off, Dostoevsky turned to much vaster projects. He planned to write *The Life of a Great Sinner*, an ambitious work that was to comprise five novels and prove the existence of God. The hero was to be modeled on St. Tikhon Zadonsky. Part of the action was to take place in a monastery, and Feodor Mikhailovich did not want to write it until he was settled in Russia. He used the notes for this book later for the *starets* Zosima in *The Brothers Karamazov*, and some characters in *The Adolescent*.

"This idea is the embodiment of everything for which I have lived. But to write this novel I must return to Russia. . . . I must not only see a monastery, but also live in it for some time," he wrote. "The main question, that will be raised throughout the work, is one that has consciously and unconsciously tormented me all my life—that of the existence of God. In the course of his life, the hero will be successively an atheist, a believer, a fanatic, a heretic, and then again an atheist. The central figure of the second part will be Tikhon Zadonsky—under another name, of course."

In the meantime he made notes for a new novel that was to deal with the social revolution. Anna Grigorievna's brother had come to Dresden during the summer vacations, and this young man, a student in the Petrovsk Agricultural Academy in Moscow, knew a great deal about the nihilistic trends in Russian universities. He spoke with great admiration of a student named Ivanov, "a man of great intelligence and firm character, who had emphatically disavowed his former convictions." This Ivanov was executed as a traitor to the revolutionary cause by Nechaev, leader of a subversive group known as "The People's Avenger," with the help of four wretched accomplices.

Dostoevsky was greatly upset by the news of this ignoble murder. His hatred of the new ideas grew increasingly violent. The stupidity and pretentiousness of university youth filled him with disgust. He resolved to strike a great blow. On the basis of the documents published in the press and Snitkin's accounts, he started a scathing satire entitled *The Possessed*. "The thing I am writing is tendentious. I want to express myself with vehemence. Ah, they will raise a howl, those Nihilists and Occidentalists, they will call me a reactionary. But, devil with them, I will speak my mind!" (Letter of April 6, 1870.)

"One of the main incidents of my story will be the murder of Ivanov by Nechaev, which is well known in Moscow." (Letter of October 20, 1870.) "I want to make known my opinions to present-day youth, without beating about the bush." (Letter of December 14, 1870.)

However, the undertaking proved difficult. The plot grew complicated, and the original heroes were eclipsed by secondary characters. "I like the new hero so much that I have re-written everything." The manuscript of *The Possessed* bears traces of the author's feverish state of mind at that time. It shows a mass of notes jotted down pell-mell with curious drawings, calculations and unintelligible scribblings. "Then N-V [Nechaev] leaves, but he returns and murders Shatov." . . . "Stavrogin, when he believes, does not believe that he believes, and when he does not believe, does not believe that he does not believe." . . . Occasionally the outline of a scene is preceded by words such as "Here," "Fundamental," "Important," "Excellent," "Remarkable variant."

"I know," wrote Dostoevsky, "that if I had two or three years to write this novel in peace—as is the case with Turgenev, Goncharov, or Tolstoy—I too would write a work that would be discussed a hundred years hence."

He attached more importance to this pamphlet than to any of his novels, because he was committing himself as a writer and risked losing a section of his public or winning a world audience. When he sent the first chapters to the *Russian Messenger*, he added a number of instructions, such as, "Please verify the sentences written in French. I think there are no errors, but I may be mistaken," or: "In one passage I use the following expression, 'We have placed wreaths of laurel on louse-ridden heads.' I implore you, for heaven's sake, do not omit the word louse-ridden."

After midnight, when everyone was asleep in the house, Dostoevsky, sitting with his paper and his glass of tea before him, would give vent to his fury. He wrote as though he were striking blows at his enemies. He was fighting the greatest battle of his career.

However, he could not be certain that he would have the

strength to fight to the end. After a long period of respite, he was having a recurrence of epileptic fits. "Isn't this horrible? I am here in my armchair, my head heavy, my limbs worn out, incapable of any serious effort; at my side the baby is crying, and I have not the money to buy medicine at the pharmacy."

He kept a careful record of his epileptic fits: "Violent attack"; "Fairly violent attacks"; "Seizure at six in the morning. . . . Particularly at night, by candlelight, morbid sadness. A red reflection (not a color) on all objects." Another entry noted: "At three o'clock at night, a terribly violent attack in the entrance hall. I fell and scratched my forehead. Without remembering or realizing anything, I brought the lighted candle intact into the room, I shut the windows, and only then guessed that I had just had a seizure. I awakened Anna and told her about it. She cried a great deal when she saw my face. I tried to calm her, and suddenly I had another seizure. When I came to, my head ached agonizingly, I could not speak correctly. Anna spent the night at my side (intense mystical terror)." In order to relax, he went off to Hamburg. There he lost all the money he had with him, suffered a violent epileptic fit in his hotel, fell, and hurt his head. "At the end of the week the bump was still visible."

He returned to Dresden like a beaten dog. On July 17 he wrote in his notebook, "I am grappling with the first parts of the novel and I am in despair. War has been declared. Anna is very tired. Lubov is nervous and unbearable."

The German armies had invaded France, and the whole population of Dresden was in commotion. Transportation facilities were requisitioned by the military authorities. The mail service was suspended. Newspapers from Berlin could no longer be had.

"War! I hope they don't disturb me in my work . . . on the Rhine, on either side, nearly three hundred thousand men are massed. . . . There is a slump on the stock exchange. Prices are going up. . . . Neither one nor the other side can stand a long struggle, and yet they want to fight for a long time. What will be the result of all this? Tomorrow or the day after tomorrow the decisive encounter will take place."

On August 7 he wrote the following laconic sentences, "The novel is definitely given up. (It is dreadful!) The French were defeated on August 6; at present they are re-grouping before Metz, and to my mind, they are hesitating, do not know where to go, what to do, and are losing time."

In his letters one finds evidence of his pro-French attitude during the hostilities: "It is a fine school, this German school that tortures and plunders like a horde of Huns! And the Prussians behave worse than barbarians. It is the professors, doctors, and students who get the most excited and brag most, not the people. I see those fellows every night in the reading halls. The day before yesterday a very influential scholar, whose hair was all white, cried very loudly, 'Let Paris be bombarded, it should be done!' Such is the result of their stupidity, if not of their learning."

A little later he wrote, "No, that which is built by the sword cannot endure. And after that, they cry 'Young Germany!' Quite on the contrary—it is a nation that has exhausted its strength, because it committed itself to the idea of the sword, blood, violence. It has not the least inkling of what a spiritual victory is and ridicules such an idea with a drunken soldier's brutality. No, it is a dead nation, a nation without a future."

The creation of the Paris Commune aroused Dostoevsky's indignation against the socialists. "The men of this movement

only extol paradise on earth (beginning with the phalansteries), but the moment they are in power they display a
loathsome inability to say anything constructive. They cut
off heads. Why? Because there is nothing easier to do. To
say something good is far more difficult. The burning of Paris
is a monstrosity. Our sudden coup did not succeed? Well
then, let the world perish, because the Commune is above the
happiness of the world and of Paris." . . .

"The West has lost Christ (because of Catholicism) and
that is why the West is dying—for no other reason."

Political events reawakened his great anger against French
socialism. Europe seemed to him a prison from which he
would never escape, and to remain another year in Germany
would be an intolerable torture. He had the impression that
he no longer remembered his native land, that he was no
longer stimulated and nourished by it, and that he, like all
uprooted persons, was a lost man.

Previously, in Florence, he had written, "Turgenev, because he lives abroad, is withering and losing his talent as I
have stated in *The Voice*. I am not afraid of Germanization,
because I hate all these Germans, but I need Russia. Without Russia all my strength, all my energies will vanish. I
feel it, I feel it with my whole being."

In Dresden, this complaint continued, "If you knew how
bored I am and how much I long to return to Russia! . . .
It is true that I am going to lose touch—not with the century,
not with the Russian events . . . but with the rapid stream
of life. . . . Quick, quick, to Russia! I must leave this accursed foreign land and all these fancies."

Yet he had no money for the trip. Stellovsky, who had
published *Crime and Punishment* in book form, was asked
for payment, but the swindler refused. Then Maikov applied

to the Literary Fund, requesting a loan of one hundred rubles to enable Dostoevsky to return to Russia. The committee refused in emphatic terms. Dostoevsky wrote, "If the request had come from a nihilist, they would not have answered that way."

On top of everything, Anna Grigorievna was again pregnant. On June 29, Dostoevsky wrote in his notebook, "She is weak, on edge, she sleeps little. Could it be that she is pregnant?" . . .

"I am afraid, I am afraid," he also writes, "I am simply in despair because I will never finish the book."

To soothe him, Anna suggested that he should try his luck at roulette in Wiesbaden. He went, and the eternal comedy began again. Dostoevsky entered the roulette room, followed the game, made a few mental plays, and then risked a stake. He won, won a second time, and wanted to withdraw while he was eighteen taler ahead. But at this moment he was seized with an absurd desire to force chance. He returned to the green table, but the losses followed one another inexorably. At nine o'clock that night he had lost everything. He looked at the green rectangle, the chandeliers, the cadaverous faces, and fled like a madman. He was ashamed; he suffered as he thought of his wife and his little girl waiting for him. "I suffered so much that I ran to find a priest. . . . On the way, running in the darkness down unfamiliar streets, I thought, 'He is a minister of God, I will speak to him not as to a man, but as to a confessor.' "

Through the sleeping city he trotted in a sweat, bareheaded, trying to find his way in the dark alleys. At last he came to a temple which he thought was a Russian church. As he was about to enter it he discovered that it was a synagogue. "This was like a cold shower. I ran to my hotel. Now

it is midnight, and I am writing to you. . . . Send me thirty
taler, I will make that do. Anna, I am at your feet and I embrace you. Do not think that I am mad, Anna. A great work
is being accomplished in me, a stupid and despicable fantasy
that tormented me for ten years has vanished. Now all is
over, it is the very last time. Can you believe it, Anna, my
hands are free at last. I was fettered by gambling. From now
on I will think only of my work and I will not even dream of
gambling as I often did through entire nights. Now my work
will be better and will go faster, and God will bless me."

This time, the promise so often given was not just an
empty phrase. Dostoevsky kept his word and never returned
to roulette.

"He never went back to roulette," writes Anna Grigorievna, "although he was several times at Ems and had
enough money to go as far as Monaco. But he was no longer
attracted by gambling. He not only did not gamble, but he
never spoke of it again. It was as though his passion for
gambling had been a sort of disease, of which there remained
no trace in the last ten years of his life."

Feodor Mikhailovich returned to Dresden. His latest ordeal had calmed him, and he resumed his work. He had only
one thought—to return to Russia before his wife's confinement. The *Russian Messenger* had sent him an advance "for
the holidays," and promised another advance of a thousand
rubles in June. Dostoevsky wrote to Katkov asking him to
speed the sending of the remittance. He also wrote to
Maikov, asking him to resume negotiations with Stellovsky.
He would save himself, he would save his family by his
work. Turgenev, Tolstoy, and Goncharov received important fees—why should he be paid less than they? Had they
so much talent?

"It is a literature of landowners that they give us. It has said all that it had to say (admirably, I admit, in the case of Lev Tolstoy). But it does not alter the fact that these words of the landowners have been their last words." He would be the one to say the new word. He would astonish the world. But for the love of heaven, let him be allowed to work in peace, in his own country!

The money from the *Russian Messenger* came toward the end of June, 1871. The pawned clothes were redeemed, the debts were paid, and preparations for the great journey began. Two days before the departure Dostoevsky gave his wife several rolls of paper and asked her to burn them. He expected to be searched at the Russian border and did not want his rough drafts to fall into the hands of the authorities as they did at the time of his arrest in 1849. Anna Grigorievna lighted the fire, and soon the manuscripts of *The Idiot* and of *The Eternal Husband*, as well as the first version of *The Possessed*, were but a pile of black ashes.

On July 17, Dostoevsky and his family left Dresden for St. Petersburg. Their luggage was thoroughly searched at the frontier. The surly customs officials examined the trunks one by one. Dostoevsky and his wife clamored—a few more minutes and they would miss the train.

"Mummy, give me a roll," whimpered Lubov.

The official shrugged his shoulders and allowed the exiles to get on the train.

Through the dusty windows they could see the Russian landscape flying past them. A little path ran across an embankment and wound through the grass to a thatched hut. A peasant woman near the tracks waved a red handkerchief. On her head was a dirty scarf, on her feet shoes of plaited cord and in her hand a basket of birchbark. She called, she laughed, and she disappeared, enveloped by the swiftly moving smoke of the train. They were coming into Russia, the real Russia—not the Russia of the embittered intellectuals and revolutionaries, the "possessed," but the Russia of land, work, and faith. Dostoevsky was deeply moved.

The compartment was hot, it smelled of rancid oil, of sweat and coal, but Dostoevsky was oblivious to all this. He felt that he was leaving the prison for the second time, that he was being reborn to life. He wondered whether he would feel, as he did upon his return from Siberia, that Russia had become alien to him. But he quickly discarded this fear; he had followed the stream, he had remained Russian, and his books would prove it. *The Possessed* was nothing but a defense of Russia against the demons of whom St. Luke spoke:

"And there was an herd of many swine feeding on the mountain: and they besought him that he would suffer them to enter into them. And he suffered them. Then went the devils out of the man, and entered into the swine: and the herd ran violently down a steep place into the lake, and were drowned."

Whereas *Crime and Punishment* is the story of a man who transgresses the laws of common morality and whose search for freedom leads him to murder, *The Possessed* deals with the experience of a nation that violates the principles of social life in the name of liberty and, as a result, destroys itself. What murder is with regard to the individual, revolution is with regard to the masses. Raskolnikov wants to prove to himself that he is not a worm and to win the right to total independence by committing a reprehensible deed. He wants to become his own God. The demagogues of the revolution claim that they would raise the mob to superhuman dignity;

they want to win emancipation by means of class murder and to replace the cult of God with the cult of the masses. And just as Raskolnikov, because of his crime, becomes the slave of an obsession, so the nation that rebels finds only humiliating slavery and ruin at the end of its ordeal. The temptation of absolute freedom can be both personal and collective; the two experiences are parallel and both must bring the same kind of defeat. There is no freedom without God. Those who seek freedom outside of God must in the end negate themselves. Thus, according to Dostoevsky, socialism is a religious problem, and must be dealt with as such.

Socialism, especially its Russian variety, presents itself not merely as an attempt to ensure the well-being of the working classes, but as a new religion, as the religion of man, as man's ultimate goal. It is not conceived as a duplication of Christianity but as a substitute for it. According to the Russian socialists, there is no God, no immortal soul and no redemption; nor is any happiness possible except tangible material happiness; everything begins and ends on this earth. Such a doctrine implies the transformation of human society into an ant-hill. In the world envisioned by the socialists individual values, spiritual ecstasy and lofty ideals will vanish; the state will supply the wretched herd only with food, shelter and a minimum of everyday comforts.

In such a world, Dostoevsky declared, man cannot be really happy, for man needs more than material well-being; he does not live by bread alone. He yearns to believe that there is a superior happiness which is inconceivably blissful and from which he is not excluded; he yearns for something that cannot be obtained either by labor or cunning—he yearns for the immeasurable, the unimaginable, the infinite.

"The essential condition of human existence," says Stepan

Trofimovich in the last chapter of *The Possessed*, "is that men should always be able to bow down before something infinitely great. If men are deprived of this, they cannot go on living, they will die of despair."

Today one may well wonder if Stepan Trofimovich did not perhaps overestimate mankind.

When Dostoevsky wrote *The Possessed*, the Nihilist Movement was still in its infancy; in the seventies, revolutionaries as fully radical as Stavrogin, Kirilov, Shatov and Verkhovensky did not yet exist; even Nechaev on whom Dostoevsky modeled the sinister character of Verkhovensky lacked breadth. Since the type of the satanic rebel appeared only in the twentieth century, Dostoevsky's brilliant anticipation and frightening prophecy was not really understood by his contemporaries. They thought it was a caricature and were unable to discern in it an appalling forecast of the future. They did not realize that this studio sketch would soon become a terrifyingly exact portrait. The Russian Revolution supplied a sinister conclusion to the novel which foretold that great tragedy.

In *The Possessed*, Dostoevsky points an accusing finger at the liberals of the forties, men such as Turgenev and Belinsky. The responsibility for the inevitable bloodshed of the future is laid at the door of the parlor pinks who "went to the people" without understanding them and without realizing the disastrous implications of their light-headed sermons on freedom. For all revolutions presuppose two factors: the embittered intellectuals, the thinkers who imagine that they have no responsibility, and the benighted masses who, intoxicated with the idea of immediate independence, give free rein to their lowest instincts. "You yourselves said that anything was permissible," they seem to say to the intellectuals. What can the intellectuals answer to that? What was the answer of the Russian intelligentsia after the revolution, of the Stepan Trofimoviches and the Karamazovs of 1917? They fled, and even now are awaiting the national resurrection that Dostoevsky forecast in *The Possessed*. According to him, the demons will not stay forever in the great bleeding body into which they have entered. One day they will be expelled, "enter into the swine . . . and rush down the steep into the lake and be drowned," as it is told in the Gospel of Luke. According to him, "The sick man will be healed and will sit at the feet of Jesus, and we will look at him with surprise."

The main character of *The Possessed* is Verkhovensky. To portray him Dostoevsky, in addition to the newspaper accounts of Nechaev, drew upon his personal recollections of Speshnev, his own fellow conspirator in the "Petrashevsky" plot of whom he used to say, "I have a real Mephistopheles at my side."

Verkhovensky is truly a demonic figure. "At first he charms you, then he offends you because his speech is too clearly articulated and because his words are always studied and prepared in advance." He is alternately obsequious and insolent; he never lets himself go, he always calculates, schemes, and throws out nets to catch the unwary. In the revolutionary group that he has organized everyone hates and fears him. His idea of the revolution is diabolical: "Our partisans are not only those who commit murder and arson, those who let their pistols go off in the traditional manner or bite their superiors. At best such people only embarrass us. . . . The schoolmaster who laughs at God along with his pupils . . . he is one of us. The lawyer who defends an educated murderer on the grounds that he is more cultured than his victim, he, too, is one of us. The schoolboy who kills a peasant in order to experience a thrill also is one of us. . . . We will make an upheaval such as the world has never seen."

After this upheaval, Verkhovensky plans to put into effect the ideas of Shigalev, one of the conspirators, and introduce complete equality among men. He says, "To begin with, the level of education . . . will be lowered. A high scientific and artistic level is accessible only to superior intellects, and we have no use for them. . . . They will have to be exiled or sentenced to death. To tear out Cicero's tongue, gouge out Copernicus's eyes and stone Shakespeare—such is Shigalevism!"

As a result of this organized gagging of thought, man will lose all dignity and all inventiveness, he will become a pawn among other pawns. "The most important force, the cement that will hold everything together, is the shame of holding one's own opinion."

Primitive man fears to be different from his neighbor, to have ideas of his own, to be alone and responsible. With the enslavement of all individuals responsibility will be shared by a countless number of people. Thanks to this leveling, there will no longer be distinct personalities. Even morality will become impersonal, and all life will take place in a world beyond good and evil.

To keep him in this artificial and monstrous condition, man must be protected from everything that might arouse in him a longing for his lost humanity, from love and from the family. "As long as family ties and love exist, the desire for property is innate. We shall destroy that desire, we shall give free rein to drunkenness, slanders, denunciations; we shall permit unrestrained debauchery; we shall stifle every genius in his infancy. Let everything be reduced to the common denominator, let there be complete equality." From time to time, to prevent the herd from being bored, a little local riot will be organized and quickly crushed. A tyrannical minority will rule over this enslaved people: "Slaves must have leaders." The revolution against autocracy will result in a new autocracy. "Starting from boundless freedom I end with boundless despotism." And in the course of this transformation, religion will vanish. Even the existence of God will be denied. But who will be the new master? Verkhovensky says to Stavrogin, "Night will descend upon Russia, the earth will lament its old gods. . . . And then we will call upon . . . Ivan Czarevitch."

This Ivan Czarevitch is none other than Stavrogin. Verkhovensky offers the world to Ivan Stavrogin and asks him to create a myth around his own person whose virile beauty will seduce the mob. "The whole world will resound with the cry, 'a new and just law has been enacted.' The sea will be stirred to its very depths, the old wooden shack will be demolished, and then we will consider building a stone house."

"This is madness," answers Stavrogin. But is not the whole of Russian history a tissue of absurdities?

Toward Stavrogin, Verkhovensky's attitude is one of servile devotion. He follows Stavrogin like a dog, pulls him by the sleeve, and says to him, "You are a pioneer, you are the sun, and I am only a worm." And suddenly he kisses Stavrogin's hand. Thus, the apostle of leveling feels the need of believing in someone superior to himself. The rebel begins by finding a master for himself, the cynic worships the man who despises him. "I am a clown, I know it, but I do not want you, who are the best part of myself, to be a clown also." Or,

"I will follow you everywhere. I will follow you like a dog."

This secret appetite for humiliation and prayer is remarkable in a confirmed atheist. Love must be a vital need if even Verkhovensky experiences it. It matters little that his feeling for Stavrogin is ridiculous, shameful and odious in its human implications; the important thing is that Verkhovensky recognizes the necessity of bowing to someone greater than he. This alone suffices to condemn his social system. As for Stavrogin, Verkhovensky's god, his character remained unexplained for half a century, because Katkov, Dostoevsky's publisher, refused to print an important chapter of *The Possessed* called "Stavrogin's Confession." It remained unpublished until 1927.

Like Raskolnikov, Stavrogin is "a destroyer of walls." Raskolnikov shatters the precepts of old morality, suffers in order to conquer an illusory freedom, and struggles fanatically against himself and against God. He is forgiven in the end because, without realizing it, he has always been in search of Christ. But Stavrogin does not seek anything. Raskolnikov, when he believes, believes that he believes, and when he does not believe, believes that he does not believe. But "Stavrogin when he believes, does not believe that he believes, and when he does not believe, does not believe that he does not believe." Raskolnikov is a passionate negator; Stavrogin, a habitual negator. He does not love his own opinions, because he has not sufficiently suffered for them. They have taken hold of him mysteriously. In his eyes it is a matter of the most elementary common sense that God does not exist, that morality is absurd, that "everything is permissible," and that there is no such thing as punishment by one's own conscience.

The question arises, how is it possible to love, hate, hope, and exist if we are no longer moved by the rejection of any spiritual principle? Stavrogin has allowed the warm springs of life to dry up within him. He does not know why he is in the world and he does not try to find out. He lives by inertia, he drags himself along from day to day and is gradually overcome by boredom. What can he do or say that is worth doing or saying if it is done or said only for his own sake? He tries to shake off his melancholy, and since he respects nothing, all means are legitimate in his eyes. He is horribly grateful to anything that shatters his calm. He receives a slap in the face, but does not retaliate in order to experience the new thrill of fury and humiliation. He steals with a bravado that he considers delightful. He fights a duel only in order to experience the highest degree of rage and shame. He causes a little girl to be whipped by falsely accusing her of theft, then he rapes her, and does nothing to prevent her from committing suicide. He sees her go into a tiny cubicle. He looks at his watch, lets twenty minutes elapse, then looks through a crack in the door. "And I saw what I had to see." The little girl had hanged herself.

"It was then, sitting at tea and chatting with my friends, that for the first time in my life I clearly formulated for myself the idea that I have neither the feeling nor the knowledge of good and evil, and not only that I have lost the sense of good and evil, but that good and evil do not exist." Elsewhere he says, "Life bored me to the point of stupefaction."

This boredom strangles him, and he tosses about like a sick man trying to find a comfortable position in his bed. First he tries to find such a position through the repulsive sacrifice of his love life, by marrying a lame and hideous moron. "The idea that Stavrogin should marry such an abject creature tickled my sensibilities." He does not marry her in a fit of madness or as a result of a drunken wager; no, he does it coldly, cynically, just to see. But the monstrous absurdity of his wedding does not satisfy him, and he quickly tires of his new ignominy. He looks around for another crime as a diversion. For a time he considers bigamy, but eventually rejects this idea. He is haunted by the specter of the little girl whose death he has caused. But the anguish that his daily visions bring him does not cure him of his boredom; instead, the anguish itself becomes boring.

Then he joins the social struggle. Unfortunately, he is ill at ease even among the rebels, because he does not believe in anything. Verkhovensky implores him, "Oh, be more stupid Stavrogin, be more stupid." Stavrogin has faith neither in Christianity nor in the religion of Russian socialism. The organization of paradise on earth, in the style of Shigalev, does not appeal to him at all, and the promise that he will one day become Ivan Czarevitch only makes him shrug his shoulders. What is the good of all that? The massacres, the setting up of a huge workmen's hive on the shambles of civilization, the institution of a new dictatorship over a herd of fools, will not cure him of his boredom. Repentance alone could relieve him. Let him publish his confession, let him brave ridicule, insults, sufferings, then he would find the light. Raskolnikov is saved because he recognizes his error and desires to be forgiven. The very desire for forgiveness is a heavenly reward. But Stavrogin, just when he is on the point of yielding to remorse, returns to his horrible indifference.

Around Stavrogin Verkhovensky groups several seedy-looking, but inflamed, revolutionaries. The conspirators are convinced that their group is only one of hundreds of similar groups scattered throughout Russia. Verkhovensky hints that he has been sent to them by a central committee. He

constantly speaks of secret reports, orders from above, and
the necessity of making contacts. He causes the members of
the plot to suspect one another. He rules over them because
none of them trusts the other.

After a scandal staged by Verkhovensky, a fire and a murder, the members of the group are frightened by their own
actions. To get them back in hand, Verkhovensky tells them
that Shatov, one of their number, is planning to denounce
the whole group, and that he must, therefore, be put out of
the way. Verkhovensky hopes that a collective murder will
cement the union of these cowards. After committing the
crime, they will be bound to each other forever by hatred
and fear.

Shatov, the victim chosen by Verkhovensky, is "one of
those Russian idealists who are suddenly struck by a strong
idea and are crushed by the blow." He was formerly a convinced liberal, but having repudiated the errors of his youth,
has frequent clashes with Verkhovensky. His own aboutface
has so disconcerted him that he no longer knows what to
believe or how to live. Exhausted and lonely, he does not
have the courage to leave Verkhovensky's group, although
he curses it.

"What have I rejected?" he says. "The foes of all true life,
backward libertarians afraid of their own independence, the
flunkeys of thought, the enemies of all freedom and personality, the decadent advocates of death and rottenness. All
they have to offer is senility, glorious mediocrity of the most
bourgeois kind, contemptible shallowness, envious equality,
equality without personal dignity, equality as interpreted by
lackeys or by the French of 1793. . . . But worst of all,
there are swarms of scoundrels among them, nothing but
scoundrels!"

For Shatov, as for Dostoevsky, socialism must be atheistic, because it wishes to build its world according to the laws of science. But peoples are created and live according to other, more mysterious laws. The history of a people is the history of its search for God, or, more accurately, for its own god.

"The object of every popular movement," says Shatov, "is only to find God. . . . Each people has always had its own god. It is a symptom of decay when a nation begins to have gods in common with other nations. . . . If a great people does not believe that truth is to be found in itself alone, if it does not believe that it is the only nation capable of revivifying and saving the world by truth, it ceases to be a great people, and becomes merely ethnographic matter."

According to Shatov, although each people has its own god, there is only one true God. Therefore, all the peoples except one are mistaken. And Shatov thinks that the only really God-bearing people is the Russian people, because it is the only Christian people that has not been contaminated by civilization, the only pure people, the only child-people of the earth.

Thus Shatov-Dostoevsky endows the Russians with a truly Messianic character. Just as the Jewish people considers itself the chosen people, so, according to Dostoevsky, the Russians have been chosen to save the world. Whereas, according to the Christian teaching, the advent of Christ did away with all national Messianic ideas and raised all mankind to the status of a chosen people, Dostoevsky stubbornly insisted on keeping exclusively for the Russians the privilege of being loved by God.

Some have interpreted this idea as a "re-Judaization of Christianity." This criticism is not entirely justified. Dostoevsky did not deny that all nations had been initiated into

God's truth. He did not contend that the revelation had a strictly national character, but claimed that in the course of centuries all the nations, except the Russians, had revealed themselves unworthy of the Messianic role, and that Russia had continued to follow in God's path because she had been untouched by progress. Thus Russia was not alone in having been invested with a Messianic role, but she alone had preserved it. This is a nuance that has often been overlooked by students of Dostoevsky, but it is extremely important and should be stressed.

Nonetheless, the idea of a God-bearing people is dangerous because it leads to the worship of the people for its own sake. Shatov himself commits this very error.

"Do you believe in God or not?" Stavrogin asks him.

And Shatov stammers, "I believe in Russia. . . . I believe in her orthodoxy."

"But in God? In God?" Stavrogin insists.

"I . . . I should believe in God?" says Shatov.

Dostoevsky, like Shatov, came to God through the people. But while for Dostoevsky the people was only a stage in his journey, for Shatov it is the goal. He confuses social and religious elements to such a point that he can no longer distinguish between them. He symbolizes the error of the Russian religious sects that mingled peasant paganism with the evangelical cult of Christ. He is the prototype of the fanatical heresiarchs who confined the Orthodox faith to the boundaries of Russia, who burdened it with strange rites and extra-Biblical mysteries, and stifled it by trying to preserve it. And his anguish stems from his inability to rediscover Christ under this barbarian disguise. Faith is so much simpler and broader than he imagines it to be! And he gropes like a blind man trying to find the happiness that in reality is close to him.

He realizes this when his wife, who once betrayed him with Stavrogin, returns to his house to give birth to a child. He receives her with a kind of timid ecstasy and surrounds her with attentions that surprise him himself. When the child is born and he sees before him a being suddenly come to life, he is shaken by a hitherto unknown joy and exclaims, "The mystery of the coming of a new being into the world is a great mystery."

"What nonsense is he talking? It is simply a further development of the human organism," says the midwife who has been won over to socialistic ideas.

But Shatov does not listen to her—he has seen a miracle, he has been touched by grace, he has faith now and will always have it. For the first time in many years he realizes that he is happy. That same night he is summoned by his group and murdered by Verkhovensky and his companions.

In the meantime Stavrogin has fled. To divert suspicion Verkhovensky decides to make Kirilov, a member of the group, assume the whole responsibility for the crime. This Kirilov is an epileptic who wants to commit suicide in order to prove to himself that he is free. Since he is resolved to die anyway, all he has to do is to sign a confession in which he accuses himself of the murder of Shatov.

Kirilov is certainly one of the most remarkable characters of Dostoevsky's world. Like Stavrogin he is an atheist, but unlike Stavrogin he endows his negation with a passion that others find only in faith. His insane logic makes one's brain reel.

"If God exists," he says, "everything depends on Him, and

I can do nothing against His will. If God does not exist, everything depends on me, and I am obliged to assert my independence." Now, the highest degree of a man's insubordination is to negate his own existence. If man can, by his own will, put an end to his life, he is free, he is God. "If God does not exist, then I myself am God." And Kirilov adds this surprising remark, "Man has invented God only to be able to live without killing himself."

We are thus brought back to the dialectic of the underground man. Man has built an idol for himself and the walls of religion solely to protect himself against freedom which frightens him. He has imprisoned himself because of his fear of independence. He has humiliated himself before his own creation. And Kirilov takes up the theme of the crucifixion that was first expressed by Hippolyte in *The Idiot*: "If the laws of nature did not spare Christ, then the whole planet is nothing but a lie, it rests upon a lie, and corresponds only to a stupid mockery."

Since the divine principle in its old form is absurd, since man himself is God despite his will to be a slave, the world needs proof of the true order of things. Kirilov's suicide, that is not motivated by any external reason, will be the justification of that total freedom which makes man the lord of the universe. "He who is the first must absolutely kill himself, for who else would make a beginning, who else would supply the proof? I will kill myself absolutely, to make a beginning. . . . I will begin, I will open the door." After his sacrifice, men will understand. They will overthrow the walls of Christian morality and become gods. "A happy and proud man will be born who will not care whether he lives or dies."

It is interesting to note to what extent Kirilov remains imbued with the doctrine that he consciously rejects. Like

Christ he sacrifices himself to save mankind. Actually he is obsessed by the figure of Christ. He longs to ascend the cross, to suffer in behalf of others, to pay with his blood for the happiness of others. His ecstatic love for his fellow men transforms this atheist into an almost Christian figure. We say "almost," because Shatov recognizes Christ without recognizing God. We may recall here the letter that Dostoevsky wrote from Siberia to Madame Fonvizin, in which he said, "If someone proved to me that Christ is outside the truth, and if it had been really established that truth is outside Christ, I would prefer to stay with Christ rather than with the truth."

Thus Dostoevsky was torn between Shatov's Messianic orthodoxy and Kirilov's Christian atheism. But Christ remains unassailed. Dostoevsky's problem was only this: Christ with God or Christ without God? This problem tormented him throughout his life. It also torments his characters. "To get out of it," Kirilov shoots himself.

Stavrogin, another libertine, also ends his life by suicide, after grazing redemption. "I wanted to try my strength everywhere. I looked upon our negators with hatred, because I envied their hopes."

Among the other characters of *The Possessed*, the most noteworthy are Stepan Trofimovich, the father of Verkhovensky, a sniveling failure, idealistic and bombastic, modeled on Professor Granovsky, one of the founders of Russian liberalism, and Karmazinov, "the great writer," who is a hideous caricature of Turgenev. Like Turgenev, he is a "Russo-European," and Dostoevsky puts in his mouth Turgenev's own words, "I have become a German, and I am proud of it," or, "I have been living in Karlsruhe for seven years. Last year when the municipality resolved to build a new aqueduct

I felt with all my heart that the question of the canalization of the waters of Karlsruhe was more vital to me than any question relating to my dear fatherland." To emphasize the resemblance between Karmazinov and Turgenev, Dostoevsky gives his hero "a florid face with thick locks of white hair that fell abundantly from under his silk hat and curled around his clean little pink ears." He also gives him a "sweet and somewhat high-pitched voice." Finally, he makes Karmazinov read in public his latest story, entitled "Merci," the text of which was inspired by an article that Turgenev had written for the magazine of the brothers Dostoevsky.

Turgenev recognized himself in this caricature and complained about it in a letter to a friend. "Dostoevsky has indulged in something worse than caricature. He has represented me under the name of K., as secretly favorable to the Nechaev party. It is curious that he should have chosen for his parody the only tale I ever gave to the paper he once published, a tale for which, incidentally, he showered me with compliments and grateful acknowledgments."

Even without this sacrilege, Dostoevsky would have aroused the indignation of the Occidentalists. The publication of *The Possessed* provoked violent reactions in the press and among Leftist readers. This frenzied attack on liberalism seemed to them impious, barbarous, and contrary to the rules of esthetics. They deplored the fact that a former convict had gone over to the camp of the enemy and said it was contemptible for an ex-conspirator to disparage conspiracies.

"Mr. Dostoevsky's novel, *The Possessed*," declared M. Nikitin, "is incontrovertible evidence of a fact, which, incidentally, was obvious upon the publication of his first book, *Poor Folk*, namely, that its author is devoid of creative imagination. . . . *The Possessed* confirms the literary bankruptcy of the author of *Poor Folk*."

The magazine *The Beam* published an article which declared among other things, "If you have patience to read to the end the work of one of our authors who was once quite popular, you will, in addition to your anger, experience a feeling of pity, perhaps even of sadness. You will suffer to see the fall of an author who is doubtless gifted, the fall of a man. . . . Yes, whether one wants to or not, one must recognize that with *Crime and Punishment* we have lost the old Mr. Dostoevsky. . . . At present the critics can only consider him with indifference, contempt or pity." ˙

The editor of *The Russian World* was attacked and ridiculed in the liberal press because he wrote that *The Possessed* ranked "with the most beautiful and brilliant literary productions of recent years."

As for Strakhov, he wrote a beautiful letter to Dostoevsky concerning *The Possessed*, one which deserves to be quoted. "In richness and diversity of ideas, you are manifestly the first writer of Russia. Compared to you, even Tolstoy is monotonous. . . . And yet you overcomplicate your works. If the fabric of your novels were simpler, their effect would be doubly powerful. *The Gambler* and *The Eternal Husband* produced a profound impression but the ideas you put in *The Idiot* were not completely understood. . . . With only one-tenth of your talent, a Frenchman or a shrewd German would have made himself famous in both hemispheres and entered the history of world literature as a star of the first magnitude."

Dostoevsky recognized his faults and criticized them with charming humility. "With me, several separate novels are compressed into one, which as a result lacks harmony and measure. . . . The power of inspiration is always more intense than the means of expression. Such was the case of Victor Hugo; in Pushkin, too, one can find traces of this dualism."

The Possessed is actually a fragment of *The Life of a Great Sinner* which has been mentioned above and which was never written. In Dostoevsky's notebooks of that period one finds the names of people who played a subordinate role in his life, titles of books and recollections of events from the time of his youth. This autobiographical preparation of *The Life of a Great Sinner* led certain critics of Dostoevsky to raise the question whether he had not himself committed a great sin. There is also an oral tradition that one day Dostoevsky confessed to Turgenev that he had committed a most infamous deed.

"Why do you tell me this?" asked Turgenev.

"To show you to what extent I despise you," Dostoevsky is supposed to have answered.

In 1883, Strakhov, referring to "his friend" Dostoevsky, of whom he had become the enthusiastic biographer, wrote to Tolstoy, "He was wicked, envious, vicious. . . . Note that his bestial sensuality did not presuppose any idea of feminine beauty or charm. The characters in his books that are most like him are the hero of *Notes from the Underground*, Svidrigailov in *Crime and Punishment*, and Stavrogin in *The Possessed*."

Strakhov intimated that Dostoevsky had once raped a little girl, and Vengerov and Viskovatov confirm this accusation. According to Turgenev, "Viskovatov told me one day that Dostoevsky boasted of having [had intercourse] in a bath with a little girl brought to him by a governess." And Bulgakov says merely that "Perhaps this is not a slander."

There are not sufficient data to settle this dispute objectively, but Dostoevsky's erotic obsessions certainly entitle one to such suspicions. We have seen him haunted by childish sexuality in Netochka Nezvanova. "Well then, do whatever you want with me. Tyrannize over me, pinch me, I beg of you, pinch me, pinch me just once. My little sweetheart, pinch me." Or, "We kissed one another, we wept, we laughed. Our lips were swollen from kissing." (This scene involves two little girls who have hardly reached puberty.)

In *The Brothers Karamazov* Lisa, at the age of sixteen, is as hysterical as these two girls. "She is sixteen and she offers herself," says Ivan.

"What do you mean, she offers herself?" exclaims Aliosha.

"Well, just like dissipated women."

In *Crime and Punishment*, as we have seen, Svidrigailov rapes a girl of fourteen, and dreams about this child, just as Stavrogin does in *The Possessed*. And in both cases, the victims hang themselves.

One may wonder whether this theme which recurs in Dostoevsky's books at five-year intervals was not dictated by some secret preoccupation or perhaps by a personal recollection. Dostoevsky, as we have seen, even told the story of such a rape in the very prim and formal salon of Madame Korvin-Krukovskaya, and this before young ladies! Little Sonia, then aged fourteen, recorded this incident in her *Recollections*. The hero of Dostoevsky's story awakens from a happy dream and is crushed by the impression of a mysterious responsibility, a remote and unforgivable sin. Sonia writes, "He recalls that after a night of debauch, driven by his drunken companions, he raped a little girl of ten."

Was Dostoevsky an actual pervert like Svidrigailov or Stavrogin, or are we confronted in his case only with a repressed impulse. "It is not himself that he depicts," writes Gide in his *Journal*, referring to Dostoevsky. "But what he depicts he could have become if he had not become himself." Why should we not assume that Dostoevsky did desire a little girl, and that the very idea of this imaginary offense sufficed to poison his life? He evoked the rape he could have perpetrated, in a kind of grandiose hallucination. He accused himself of it with morbid pleasure, and tasted the joy of cynically humiliating himself before another man—and which other man!—a man like Turgenev whom he hated and despised more than anyone else in the world.

"I understand," he writes, "that one can assume responsibility for a crime merely out of conceit, and I can even guess what kind of conceit."

This sentence supplies a clue to the solution of the problem of Dostoevsky's sexual life.

11♦ RETURN

ON JULY 8, 1871, THE DOSTOEVSKYS ARRIVED IN ST. PETERS-
burg at last. As they walked by the Cathedral of the
Holy Trinity, where their marriage had been celebrated, Feodor Mikhailovich turned to his wife and said, "Well, Anna,
despite everything, we have lived happily for these four years.
What has St. Petersburg for us? Before us, everything is a
fog."

After paying his debts and the expenses of the trip, Dostoevsky had only a few rubles left. Moreover, his dishes and
kitchen utensils, which had been entrusted to the keeping of
an old spinster, had disappeared after her death. The pawnbroker with whom he had left his fur coats had sold them

when his interest was not paid. Dostoevsky's books had been sold by his stepson, Pavel, who was short of money.

Within a few days Dostoevsky's relatives came to visit him in an endless procession. There were embraces, questions, gossiping. Pavel had married, and his wife was charming; the eldest son of Emilia Feodorovna, his brother's widow, was a well-known pianist, her second son had a job in a bank and her daughter was a stenographer.

These continuous visits exhausted Anna Grigorievna who wrote in a letter, "Yesterday as I began to have labor pains, my husband prayed for a happy delivery all day and all night." On July 16, she gave birth to a boy who was baptized Feodor. "At this very moment he is being wrapped in his swaddling clothes, and he wails in a vigorous and healthy voice."

At the end of July, Dostoevsky left for Moscow to collect his royalties from the editor of the *Russian Messenger*. Upon his return the family moved to an apartment on Serpukhovskaya Street where he hoped to find enough peace to continue his work. He was mistaken. At the beginning of December a newspaper notice to the effect that the novelist Dostoevsky had recently returned to Russia after a long stay abroad aroused his creditors, one of whom, a certain Ginterstein, even threatened to send Feodor Mikhailovich to prison.

"You see," this creditor declared to him, "you are a talented Russian writer, and I am only a small German businessman, but I want to prove to you that I can have a famous Russian novelist locked up for nonpayment of debts, and be assured that I will do just this.".

Anna Grigorievna, as usual, assumed the task of protecting her husband. She told Ginterstein that Feodor Mikhailovich would not object to going to prison, that he would calmly continue to write in his cell, and added, "Moreover, you will be compelled to provide for his subsistence."

The German took fright and agreed to a compromise.

From then on Anna Grigorievna dealt with her husband's creditors, of whom she wrote later, "What astonishing types came to visit me at that time: professional traders in draft notes, widows of officials, landlords of furnished rooms, retired officers—all of them of the lowest social classes. They had bought these drafts for a song and demanded full payment. All of them threatened me with distraint and imprisonment, but I had learned how to speak to them. My arguments were the same as those I used against Ginterstein."

She turned out to be an excellent business woman. By the side of her dreamy, trusting, sickly husband, young Anna Grigorievna waged her daily battle with the zest of a modern impresario. The burden of the little worries of existence fell upon her, the checking of accounts and regulating of expenses. Nothing was done without her.

In 1873, Anna Grigorievna decided to prepare an edition of *The Idiot* and *The Possessed* in one volume. She herself bought the paper, negotiated with the printer, corrected the proofs, received the booksellers, and held out against them when they asked for discounts amounting to more than twenty per cent. This is her description of a typical scene.

" 'The price of ten copies is thirty-five rubles; since you get a discount of twenty per cent, you owe me twenty-eight rubles.'

" 'Why so little? Can you not give us thirty per cent?' the bookseller's clerk asked me.

" 'Absolutely impossible.'

" 'Make it at least twenty-five per cent.'

" 'I assure you that it is out of the question,' I told him, greatly worried. I thought he would leave and the first buyer would slip from my hands, but he said, 'Well, if it is impossible, that's that.' And he handed me the money. I was so happy that I gave him thirty kopeks for a cab."

The venture was profitable. By the end of the year Anna Grigorievna sold three thousand copies and disposed of the remaining five hundred in the following years.

At the end of 1872, Prince Meshchersky, publisher of *The Citizen*, offered Dostoevsky the position of editor-in-chief of his magazine with a salary of three thousand rubles a year. The fact that *The Possessed* had been a failure rekindled Dostoevsky's desire to engage in a fight to the death against liberal ideas. He had been planning for some time to found a magazine called *A Writer's Diary*, where he would express his opinions on contemporary events. Prince Meshchersky's offer enabled him to realize his dream in a different form. Instead of editing an independent magazine, he was to write an important column in a respectable weekly. He accepted. The board of censorship ratified his appointment as editor-in-chief of *The Citizen*, but "made all possible reservations as regards the ulterior activities of this personage."

The literary staff of *The Citizen* was composed of such writers of the extreme Right as Maikov, Philipov, Strakhov, and Bielov. The spirit of the magazine was distinctly conservative and anti-European, and it became even more so under the editorship of Dostoevsky.

At first Feodor Mikhailovich imagined that his new post would leave him some free time for writing his books, but soon he was compelled to sacrifice his activity as a novelist in favor of his duties as an editor. He received authors, read articles, edited them (particularly those by Prince Meshchersky), corrected proofs, dictated letters, kept up with politics, and wrote his column under the heading, "A Writer's Diary."

In his relations with Prince Meshchersky, Dostoevsky displayed a diplomacy that was surprising in one of his impulsive nature. Prince Meshchersky had literary pretensions, but Dostoevsky was forced to revise all the articles his employer sent him, and he apologized for this with the shrewdness of a courtier. "Dear prince," he wrote once, "your answer to the *St. Petersburg News* is elegant and clearly written, but it is somewhat dry, somewhat challenging (it provokes a quarrel), and perhaps its tone is not quite felicitous. . . . I am enclosing the answer that I have written myself. I have inserted a few passages from your manuscript. But I may have made mistakes; I should be very much obliged to you if you would edit my text. . . ."

One day, however, Feodor Mikhailovich was penalized for a mistake on the part of the noble publisher of *The Citizen*. Prince Meshchersky sent him an article containing quotations from the emperor's speech to a Kirghiz deputation. Dostoevsky, who did not know that it was forbidden to quote the words of the emperor or any members of his family without a special authorization of a minister of the court, published the article without complying with the usual formalities. This omission cost him a fine of twenty-five rubles and two days' imprisonment. But what was that compared with the months of detention in the Alexis Ravelin! Dostoevsky joyously submitted to his imprisonment. His wife brought him linen and food, and his friends came to visit him. He even took advantage of his confinement to reread Victor Hugo's *Les Misérables*, about which he wrote, "It is very lucky for me to have been imprisoned, because otherwise I would never have found the time to reread this masterful work."

With "A Writer's Diary" which three years later was transformed into an independent publication, Dostoevsky inaugurated a new genre, in which intimate confidences were mingled with debates on foreign politics, eternal themes with ephemeral preoccupations, and current news events with fictionalized fantasies. It is a rambling conversation with the reader. Every now and then, Dostoevsky rushes upon his opponent, forestalls his objections, steals the ideas in the back of his mind, and replies with irresistible logic. His column is written in a familiar, loose style, but occasionally it rises to heights of Biblical eloquence. He stands before us entangled in his words and ideas, struggling with his own opinions, marking time, prophesying, making mistakes, and persisting in them with a kind of childish pouting.

Dostoevsky had been editor-in-chief of *The Citizen* for a year when he received a visit from Nicholas Alexeievich Nekrasov, the fatuous poet of the humble, well-to-do friend of the prisoners of damnation, who had been the friend of his youth and had later become his literary enemy. He had not seen Feodor Mikhailovich for several years. Now he urgently needed for the *Annals of the Fatherland* a novel signed by a great name, and having resolved to forget the old quarrels, he came to ask Dostoevsky to write it, offering two hundred and fifty rubles per sheet of sixteen pages, as against the one hundred and fifty rubles paid by Katkov. Dostoevsky was extremely flattered by this proposal. He consulted his wife, and following her advice, agreed to deliver a novel the following year.

This project had only one drawback: the *Annals of the Fatherland* was a magazine of the Left. Most of its contributors were Dostoevsky's enemies, and he feared that they would demand his complete submission to their views. He wrote to his wife, "Nekrasov can seriously annoy me if I write something that goes against their opinions. . . . But even if we are reduced to begging, I will not yield an inch."

He decided to resign from his post as editor-in-chief in order to devote himself entirely to his new book. He even rented a country house at Staraya Russa, a little resort in the Novgorod government, where he had spent the summer of 1872. As Lubov Dostoevskaya remembered it, "Everything was little in this house. The tiny low-ceilinged and narrow rooms were furnished with old empire pieces; green mirrors gave a distorted reflection of the faces that ventured to look into them. Rolls of paper pasted to canvas hung from the walls in lieu of paint and exhibited to our amazed childish eyes monstrous Chinese women with nails several inches long and feet squeezed into baby shoes. A veranda with multi-colored panes of glass was our greatest joy, and the little Chinese billiard table, with its glass balls and little bells, entertained us during the long rainy nights of our northern summer. Behind the house was a garden with ridiculously small flower beds."

Dostoevsky worked at night, as usual, went to bed at five in the morning, rose at eleven, and summoned his children, who ran to tell him about the little incidents of the morning. After his noontime meal he locked himself in his study with Anna Grigorievna and dictated to her the results of his night's work.

"Well, Anna, what do you think of this?"

"I should say it is beautiful!"

Occasionally the young woman even burst out sobbing at some moving passage, and Dostoevsky knew no greater reward than such tears. But he would protest, "Is it possible that you can be so strongly impressed by this reading? How sorry I am, how sorry!"

The book that Dostoevsky wrote in the family retreat at Staraya Russa was a bulky, prolix volume composed from remnants of old notes and seasoned with a novelistic sauce; an unbalanced story that merges ten novels into one and gives the impression that the author has patched together unpublished short stories, fragments of articles, and rudiments of essays on various subjects. The whole is heterogeneous, hasty, yet a work of genius.

Like all Dostoevsky's great novels, *The Adolescent* is the story of a struggle for freedom. Raskolnikov kills to prove to himself that he is free, the idiot finds freedom only in madness, the possessed pursue freedom by way of revolution. The hero of *The Adolescent* wants to buy freedom with his money. The wealth of a Rothschild is the surest guarantee of power and independence.

"My idea is to be Rothschild, to be as rich as Rothschild; not just rich, but rich as Rothschild!" These are the words of young Arkadyi Dolgoruky, illegitimate son of the landowner, Versilov, and a serf. He does not know his father and mother, and it is a kind of orphan who is admitted to the boarding school of an ignorant cruel Frenchman, Monsieur Touchard. This school is an aristocratic establishment, reserved for "princes' and senators' children," and Touchard demands an additional fee for a bastard. Because his demand is not granted, he takes out his resentment on his pupil: "Your place is not here, but over there"—pointing to a kind of closet. "You have no right to sit beside children of the nobility; you are of despicable extraction, nothing more than a lackey."

He beats the child and exposes him to jeers of his comrades. Little Arkadyi, instead of rebelling, strives to disarm Touchard by his patient humility. "He beat me for nearly two months. I recall that I wanted all the time to appease him, I don't know by what means; I threw myself on his hand to kiss it and I kissed it, sobbing." He cherishes his abasement. "You have humbled me; very well, then, I will humble myself even more! Now look and admire!"

Touchard beats the child, desiring to prove to him that he is a lackey and not the son of a senator, and the boy immediately behaves like a lackey. "You wanted me to be a lackey. Very well then, I am a lackey; a scoundrel, I am a scoundrel."

There is a kind of pride in extreme humility. By acknowledging the offense, one surprises the offender. The spectacle of total cowardice is as exceptional as the spectacle of reckless courage. The two attitudes originate in the same concern with the stage effect—one is rarely infamous or proud for one's own recognition.

"As soon as I was really awakened to reason, I began to detest people," Dolgoruky confesses. "I can never confide completely, not even to someone close to me; or rather I can but I do not want to. I mysteriously forbid this to myself. . . . I am distrustful, taciturn, uncommunicative. . . . I often wish to break with society. . . . I do not see any reason for doing good to people. They are not admirable enough for me to bother about them."

One day, yielding to an enthusiastic impulse, he praised his friend, Vasin, but the same night, "felt that I liked him much less. Why? Only because by praising him I had abased myself before him." . . . "Even in the lowest grades at the Gymnasium, as soon as I sensed that one of my schoolmates was surpassing me in his work or in the speed of his repartee or in physical strength, I ceased to associate with or speak to him."

This lackey wants to be a master, or rather, he wants to be both lackey and master, a master in garb of a lackey. The greater his sufferings, the greater the pleasure he derives from imagining a future of joy and valor. He seeks suffering not for its own sake, but because it adds value and brilliance to his idea of future happiness. For him, as for all other Dosto-evskian characters, suffering is not an end but a means. It buys everything and pays for everything. At bottom it is the only currency that Dostoevsky validates, in his novels and in his own mind. How well he knows how to bargain, how to defend himself, how to cheat, when he or a hero of his wants to acquire superior felicity through torment! He is like those horse dealers who do not hesitate to leave the customer but only to return at once, who weep, display indignation, and pretend to yield, when they know they have concluded a profitable deal. He, the "executioner of money," the eternal squanderer, proves to be a first-class businessman whenever the bill must be paid not in cash but in the pounds of flesh.

Little Arkadyi knows at an early stage of his life that wealth has sentimental value only if it has been won the hard way. "As soon as I was in bed, huddled under my blankets and confined to total solitude, far from the bustles of strangers and their noise, I began to reorganize my life on a different basis."

He has his idea. Now, what can be the idea of an injured and insulted personality? He wants to outstrip the world, to break the walls, to explode prejudices, to be feared, respected, obeyed, just as he fears, respects, and obeys. But what will enable him to realize this project? He has only to look about him in order to measure the immense importance of wealth in society. Only a rich man can do what he wants. Only a rich man can buy bodies, consciences, pardons. Everyone's moral code depends on his fortune. Beyond a certain figure, morality does not exist. The moral precepts that Raskolnikov wants to crush under the body of his victims, Arkadyi wants to crush under the weight of gold. Crime for the one and gold for the other are the means of escaping from the herd. Raskolnikov's attempt is tragic; Dolgoruky's is ridiculous; but both pursue the same goal, and both suffer the same failure; both set out to become supermen, and each is stopped on his path because his humanity reasserts itself and because God has mysteriously cast his glance upon him.

Dolgoruky declares, "Do you know to what use I shall put my wealth? What immorality can there be in the fact that these millions will fall from a multitude of dirty and evil Jewish hands into the hand of a steady and reasonable solitary man who turns a piercing look to the world?"

And Raskolnikov: "Of all the lice in the universe I chose the most harmful, and by killing it I intended to take from it exactly what I needed to enable me to take my first steps." . . . "A hundred, a thousand good deeds or excellent initiatives with this old woman's money! Kill her, take her gold, so that you may devote yourself to the good of mankind."

In fact, neither Raskolnikov nor Dolgoruky pursues the general good of mankind. Nor do they pursue their own comfort. What they hope for is power independent of all the material satisfactions it can provide—power for its own sake. Yes, the supreme enjoyment of the adolescent is to remain humble on a pile of gold. What a voluptuous pleasure, to draw aside when one has every right to splendor, to pose as a beggar when one's vaults are crammed with bank notes!

"If I were Rothschild I would walk in a worn coat with an umbrella in my hand. I would not mind being pushed in the street or compelled to crawl in the mud to avoid being run over by a cab. My awareness of being Rothschild would be enough to fill me with joy at such moments. . . . Oh, let this insolent general insult me at the relay post where both of us are waiting for horses; if he knew who I am, he would run to harness them himself and would help me into my unassuming coach."

When he wearies of his power he will distribute his money; he will not need it himself. "The simple realization that I had millions in my hands and that I threw them into the mud will feed me in my desert." Thus, just as Raskolnikov does not need the stolen money, so Dolgoruky does not need the money he has earned. Both merely want to acquire the "calm and solitary consciousness of their strength."

Raskolnikov, however, strives for the goal as a proud man and Dolgoruky as a humble man. Raskolnikov kills and steals, and risks being sent to Siberia in order to achieve power; Dolgoruky chooses a cautious and inglorious method: he accumulates money which he thinks, "is the only means that enables the most obvious ciphers to achieve first place."

But how can he enrich himself? He studies the people around him. All of them hope for wealth, comfort. All of them would do anything to get it. Must one sell oneself? Anna Andrevna light-mindedly sells herself. Must one counterfeit a bank check or a bond? Stebelkov counterfeits. Blackmail? Lambert and Trishatov do not refrain from this method. The boy does not belong to this predatory species. He is humble, although his honesty springs only from fear. He does not earn his money in the dangerous way; he saves it penny by penny. He reduces his diet to bread and water.

After a month it turns out that his experiment has been fully successful, although his stomach is slightly disturbed by this severe regimen. The second ordeal that little Arkadyi imposes on himself consists in saving half his pocket money. In two years he has accumulated twenty rubles. This antlike stubbornness promises well for the future of the boy.

Unfortunately, man is not merely a directed will. Just as Raskolnikov during his rise to the status of superman realizes of a sudden that he is "vermin like the others," so Arkadyi is made to stumble over humble feelings. The "grand idea" of Raskolnikov or the adolescent is not defeated by another idea, but by life.

Arkadyi's first check arises from his meeting with Rynochka, an abandoned child discovered at the door of Nicholas Semyonovich, in whose house Arkadyi lives. The child is about to be sent to a foundling home, when Dolgoruky takes a hand in the situation, pays the nurse, and declares himself ready to defray all other expenses. But soon Rynochka dies. Half of Arkadyi's capital is lost in this venture.

This first eclipse of the "idea" is followed by other, less honorable eclipses. "Why shouldn't I have some fun and amuse myself? Life is long and the idea will always stay with me, I cannot drop it. Thus all I have to do is to forget it for a quarter of an hour." And the "idea" waits, while the hero spends the money he has earned on stupid entertainment, betting, gambling, clothes, horses. He plunges into intrigues, associates with scoundrels, and finally accepts the bankruptcy of the dream that once intoxicated him in the solitude of his underground. The future Rothschild gives up being a superman. His renunciation is less moving than Raskolnikov's, because he has not paid for it with as much suffering, but it proceeds from an analogous moral conflict.

Beside this shriveled creature, Dostoevsky placed the broad and terrible figure of Versilov, Arkadyi's father. Versilov is, so to speak, a composite of all Dostoevskian types. He is a character as mysterious for the writer as for the reader. Like most of Dostoevsky's heroes, Versilov knows the split of love. He loves Catherine Nicolaevna with passion and Arkadyi's mother with pity. He is sensual—a "prophet for women"—but his love is without hope, because it is impossible for Versilov to escape from himself to another person, to forget himself for the sake of another. Neither sensuality nor pity can bring two beings close together, neither of them is true love, although both are a part of that emotion. Love is first of all gift of oneself, but pity presupposes superiority of one over the other, and sensuality presupposes absolute selfishness. For the debauched the union is only a means for obtaining pleasure. In voluptuousness he thinks only of himself. Lust is the most total isolation into which a being can fall.

In this isolation man is lost and split. Versilov exclaims, "My heart is full of words and I do not know how to say them. It is as though I were divided in two. . . . Yes, verily, I am divided in two, and that I really fear. It as though your double stood beside you. You are intelligent and reasonable, and the other, your double, wants absolutely to commit some absurdity."

Arbitrariness leads to the destruction of personality, to the appearance of the double, the demon, the grimacing Golyadkin who is a forerunner of madness. Versilov, the inconstant phrasemonger, wastes his strength on speeches about the role of Russia, about the general well-being of mankind, about love without God. "The deserted humans will soon unite with one and another more closely and more tenderly. . . .

They will cherish the earth and life with frenzy as they gradually accustom themselves to seeing their origin and end here." He talks and talks but in fact does not believe in anything. Arkadyi says that "Versilov strove for no definite goal. A whirlwind of contrary emotions bewildered his understanding." But Arkadyi himself is also unable to achieve a definite goal. He gives up his "idea" and writes his confession: "The old life is finished, and the new one is only beginning."

One is reminded of the conclusion of *Crime and Punishment*: "Already the dawn of a new future, of a complete resurrection to life, shone on their harried faces."

The reviewers gave a favorable reception to Dostoevsky's latest work. One columnist wrote, "Having read this novel, you are forced into this inescapable obligation—to think, to think, to think. . . ."

Nekrasov himself, according to Dostoevsky, read the book in one night and declared, "What freshness is yours! Such a freshness is very rare at your age, and no other writer has anything like it. In his last novel Tolstoy more or less repeats his previous works, but they were better!"

Turgenev, Dostoevsky's old enemy, confided to Saltykov, "I cast a glance at that chaos; my God, what a sour soup, what a morbid stench, what useless gibberish, what psychological gratification in scratching his own scabs!" This did not prevent Turgenev, two years later, from writing to Dostoevsky in the following terms: "Monsieur Emile Durand has been commissioned by the *Revue des Deux Mondes* to write a monograph about the most important Russian writers. . . . It goes without saying that you are among the first."

During these years of work Feodor Mikhailovich lived at Staraya Russa with his wife and children, leaving them only to see his publishers in St. Petersburg or Moscow and to take the waters at Ems for his throat catarrh. He was happy. He spoke of his children with genuine ecstasy: "They have settled in the parlor, confiscated the chairs to play. . . . The children ate veal and biscuits, drank milk, and went for a walk. Then they went to gather snow. . . . I dreamed that Fedya climbed up on a chair, fell, and hurt himself. For the love of God, do not let him climb up on chairs, and tell the nurse to be more careful!"

Feodor loves his wife as in the first days of his marriage. His letters to her were signed, "Your eternal husband," after the title of his novel. He wrote to her, "Incidentally, my love, you are indispensable to me at this moment. Do you understand me? Is it true that you see me in your dreams? Perhaps it is someone else, you see? I kiss your little feet and everything. I kiss them very much." Or again, "Annushka, my idol, my darling . . . don't forget me. It is true that you are my idol, my god. I adore every atom of your body and of your soul, and I kiss you *all, all,* because everything is *mine, mine!*"

He attends to Anna's dresses with moving tenderness. "Incidentally the Shtakenschneiders told me that faille is no longer fashionable in Paris and is worn little. It is alleged that it breaks, forms folds that wear out, and that the new fashionable black material is called broadcloth—everyone rushes to get it. I was shown broadcloth that is very much like faille, but even more like the old poult-de-soie."

In 1875, Dostoevsky went to St. Petersburg to correct his proofs. There he met Nekrasov, who complimented him on the last book, and Maikov and Strakhov, who cold-shouldered him. Of the latter he writes, "Yes, Anna, he is a bad seminarist and nothing more. He dropped me once before, after the suspension of the *Epoch,* and he returned to me only after the success of *Crime and Punishment.*"

The trip to Ems, he wrote to Anna, was particularly unpleasant. He took the waters in microscopic doses, and listened to the orchestra in the park. He read. "I am reading the Book of Job. It arouses in me a morbid enthusiasm. I interrupt my reading and pace in my room for an hour, almost crying . . . I am bored to death."

In the same period, the *Russian Messenger* published the following notice: "We learn that our famous writer, Feodor Mikhailovich Dostoevsky, is seriously ill." Anna Grigorievna, panic-stricken, wired to Ems. Dostoevsky reassured her at once, "Ah, it is a misfortune to be a great man!"

He hastened his return to Staraya Russa, overjoyed to be at home again in this little resort, with its houses built of second-hand boards, its spacious garden and its casino for idle bathers. He joined the children's games, took long walks along the banks of the river and clumsily cared for Anna Grigorievna who was again pregnant.

One month later, on August 10, 1875, Anna gave birth to a boy, Aliosha, "a vigorous and healthy baby with," as his sister noted, "a curious oval-shaped, almost angular forehead."

Immediately afterward the Dostoevskys decided to leave Staraya Russa for St. Petersburg where Feodor Mikhailovich, having completed *The Adolescent,* planned to start independent publication of *A Writer's Diary.* At the beginning of October he prepared the first issue of this periodical, in which he intended to publish exclusively his own writings. On December 22, he petitioned for authorization to publish "a monthly organ . . . that would record all my impressions, as a Russian writer, before everything that I see, hear, and read." The authorization was granted to him on condition that the articles were not to be printed before being passed by the censor.

The first issue that appeared in January, 1876, opened a new phase in Dostoevsky's life.

The articles of *A Writer's Diary* are a continuation of those published by Dostoevsky in Prince Meshchersky's *Citizen*. In the words of their author, they form "a diary, in the full meaning of this term, that is to say, a record of what I was most interested in personally."

He was uncertain as to the tone that he should adopt. "Would you believe me, that now with the first issue already out, I have still not found the form of the diary, and I do not know whether I shall ever find it. . . . Thus, I have ten or fifteen subjects when I sit down to write. However, I unwittingly discard my preferred subjects. They would take up too much space, they would demand too much ardor on my part . . . and as a result I do not write what I please. On the other hand, I was too naïve imagining that I could write a real diary. A real diary is impossible; one can only write a sham diary for the public. . . ."

This simulated diary, this diary for the public, nevertheless contains the quintessence of Dostoevsky's ideas. In it he reasserts his "territorialist" doctrine attacking the Occidentalists for attempting to transform Russia into a dependency of European countries, and attacking the Slavophiles for hypnotizing themselves with a vision of Russia as she was before the time of Peter the Great.

He raises the question whether Russian progress must have

the same meaning as European progress. Is Russia really faced
with the alternative of servility to the West or servility to her
own past? Can she enter upon an individual path, and enter
upon it at once?

Dostoevsky's answer to this question is affirmative. Russia
can follow her own contemporary path, and it is her people
that must make the road. Russian people, Dostoevsky says,
will save Russia, because the muzhiks have preserved their
simplicity, their ignorance, their belief in the truth of Christ,
because their very backwardness protects them from infection by the European disease.

"It is alleged," he writes, "that the Russian people is ignorant of the Gospels, and even of the Commandments, which
are the very foundation of our faith. Indeed, this is so, but
the Russian people knows Christ and bears Him in its heart
through all time."

Knowledge is not a prerequisite of faith. Belief is not the
result of reasoning but of a "physical" disposition that has
nothing to do with intellectual functioning. It comes from
the heart, one might say, from the body. The Russian has an
appetite for suffering that brings him close to Christ, that
gives him Christ. "The Russian people experiences a sort of
voluptuousness in pain, I believe the Russian's deepest spiritual need is a need of endless, ubiquitous, perpetual suffering."

The Russian is always dissatisfied with himself, he hates
and despises himself. There is no trace in him of that "candid
satisfaction that makes for radiant faces." And for just the
reason that he renounces moral complacency, that "he forgets all measure in all things," that he is restless, vulnerable,
lost in the center of the world, the soul of the Russian, the
Russian muzhik, is loved by God.

Even the muzhik's drunkenness, his criminality and cynicism, his misery and indignity, his lies, should not arouse fear. They derive from the propensity to go to extremes that is his eternal characteristic. They are like the convulsions of a wounded beast. They are the signs of his mission. "The Russian muzhik will save himself and he will save us along with him, because once again light will come from below."

This formula which the revolutionaries have seized upon is turned against the revolution by Dostoevsky. The idea of the Russian Christ that Shatov proclaims in *The Possessed* is reasserted in the *Diary*: "I believe in Russia . . . I believe in her orthodoxy. One cannot have faith in the one without having faith in the other."

The Messianic function of the Russian people is not confined to Russia. The Russian people will save not only Russia but the world. Why? Because "the Russian spirit, the genius of the Russian people, is perhaps more susceptible than that of any other people to the idea of universal union and brotherhood. . . . In the eyes of a true Russian, Europe, as the domain of the great Aryan tribe, is as precious as Russia herself. . . . The destination of the Russian is indisputably pan-European, universal," and the hour when the peasant Marei will heavily enter world history is close at hand.

Russia has begun to organize in the face of an inert Europe, deprived of God, spiritually killed by progress. The abolition of serfdom and the institution of jury trials testify to the respect in which the people's beliefs are held in Russia. The growth of the Russian feminist movement is also a symptom of renovation. "One of our great hopes, one of the guarantees of our resurrection, is the Russian woman. . . . The character of her claims is clear, unequivocal, and dauntless."

The Russo-Turkish War brought Dostoevsky's patriotic

exaltation to its highest pitch. "Yes, the Golden Horn and Constantinople, all this will be ours." He even sanctions the shedding of blood. "War refreshes the air that we breathe and that chokes us who are spiritually diseased and disintegrating." Again, "What can be holier, what can be purer than this war that Russia is waging today. . . . Ask the people, ask the soldiers why they rise, why they leave, and what they expect of the present war. All will tell you in one voice that they will serve Christ and deliver their oppressed brothers."

He actually sees in this war a confirmation of his conception of the Messianic character of the Russian people. The Russians, according to him, are warring against the enemies of Christ, and those who resist Christ do not know that He brings them joy in truth.

But what about the massacres on the battlefields, what about the dead? Such questions do not bother Dostoevsky. Yet he writes, referring to the war of 1870: "No, what has been built by the sword cannot endure." Confronted with this, he might answer, like Raskolnikov, that he was killing not human beings but "principles." In his eyes, the great idea of a universal alliance in Christ justified the means employed to achieve it.

Nevertheless, this slaughter in the name of Christianity is a dangerous sophism. Christ shed His blood to save us. But are we entitled to shed the blood of others to save Christ? "May civilization be accursed if, to preserve it, human beings must be skinned," Dostoevsky wrote. What can we say of Christianity if people must be killed in order to ensure its reign on earth? Dostoevsky is evasive on this point: "It is perhaps revolting if one thinks of it abstractly, but it is so in practice." He is too much obsessed by his vision of Russia's future to waste time on metaphysical discussions: "May the echo of our victory resound throughout Asia, as far as India! May the belief in the invincibility of the White Czar spread among these millions of human beings!"

So much for Asia. And how about Europe? According to Dostoevsky, Europe too must be saved by the Russians. "Europe is tottering," he writes, "and perhaps tomorrow it will founder without leaving a trace. . . ." Germany, he thinks, is "a dead nation without a future. . . ." The French "ruin themselves. . . ." The English are "the shopkeepers of rationalism." All Europe is nothing but a graveyard, the resting place of "precious dead." And the Russian Christ will resurrect these legions of men like Lazarus. But Europe hates Russia: "Europe is ready to scald out all the Slavs like a nest of bedbugs in the mattress of an old woman." A new happiness in Europe must be imposed by force.

It might be objected that Catholicism brings about that desired union in Christ. But Dostoevsky replies that Catholicism betrayed Christ. The Roman Papacy was the first to proclaim the necessity of temporal control of nations and countries. This attitude, which is not religious but political, led to "the establishment of a Roman monarchy that was to be headed by the Pope." In contrast to this, the Orthodox ideal demands that mankind should first effect a religious union in Christ, "and only then the political and social union that is the normal result of this spiritual union." In brief, the Catholic Church reverses the order that Dostoevsky considers to be the right one, and this reversal is in his eyes a sufficient ground for attacking it bitterly.

He does not realize that in proclaiming the advent of the Russian Christ he is further from Christian teachings than the Catholics he condemns. He does not see that he diminishes the significance of Christ by tying him to a specific nation. He appropriates the specious arguments of Shatov in *The Possessed*, although in the novel they are referred to as foolish. He admits that in the eyes of Christ all mankind is the chosen people, but he maintains that all mankind, except the Russian people, has forgotten the word of God, and that the role of the Russian people is to remind mankind of it, and that the whole world will spiritually belong to Russia for the greater glory of God. Thus the third kingdom, pan-Slavism, will be established.

In Dostoevsky's mind, politics and religion are inextricably confused. His passion prevents him from dissociating them. He attacks Europe, that new Babylon, science, democracy, pacifism. He goes into trances, he has visions, he makes forecasts, and his eloquence carries him far beyond his own thought. As a result, *A Writer's Diary* often strikes the reader as a mass of extravagant anticipations; and today, the passages concerning the Christian mission of the Russian people can only make one smile.

The *Diary* also includes two delightful short stories, *The Dream of a Ridiculous Man* and *The Gentle Girl*. In each of them, a "man of St. Petersburg," apprehensive, embittered, and proud, ruins his own and other people's happiness by refusing to accept life as it is. To be a child, to love—such were Dostoevsky's precepts.

Gradually his readers began to understand him. The success of this publication exceeded all expectations. At the end of the first year it had two thousand subscribers, and as many people bought it on the stands. In the following year these figures rose respectively to three and four thousand. Some of the issues were reprinted two, three, five times. Dostoevsky's moral ascendancy grew by leaps and bounds. In the eyes of a

considerable section of the educated young people, he became a kind of spiritual healer, a prophet. In his mail he received a constant stream of personal confessions, questions
about love and religion and despair. "I received hundreds of
letters from all over Russia, and I learned many things that
I had never known before. I would never have believed that
so many people in our society shared my ideas."

Although Dostoevsky had little leisure, he answered all
his letters, and even did various favors for his correspondents.
One young girl wrote him that she did not love her fiancé
and that she wanted to continue her studies. He immediately
secured for her the protection of an influential person and
wrote to her, "Considering your aspirations, you must not
become the wife of a businessman. . . . Under no circumstances must you mutilate your existence. If you do not love
him, do not marry him. Write to me again, if you wish."

To another young woman he wrote, "One should not
marry without love. But consider this carefully: Perhaps he
is one of those men whom one can love *afterward*. Now here
is my advice. . . . Ask your mother to give you some time
to think the thing over without promising her anything, and
use this time to study the man, to get accurate information
about him."

A girl student wrote that she had failed her exams, and he
did not hesitate to comfort her. "I am very sorry that you
failed in your examination in geography, but this is such a
trifle that one must not exaggerate its importance. Yet you
have written me a desperate letter." He sent his blessings to
a young girl who was going to Siberia as a nurse. He shared
the joy of a young mother: "How fortunate it is that you
have children! How they humanize our existence, how they

elevate it! Children are a burden, but an indispensable burden."

To a Jewish correspondent he declared, "Now I will tell you that I am not an enemy of the Jews and have never been one. But their forty centuries of existence, as you say, prove that this tribe has a prodigious vitality, and that throughout its history it has been unable to avoid constituting various states within states." He sent a long message of sympathy to the Moscow students. "Gentlemen, you ask me: 'To what extent are we, students, guilty?' Here is my answer. You are not guilty of anything. You are merely the children of this society which you abandon at present, and which is a tissue of lies. Yet, as our students wrest themselves from this society and desert it, they do not go to the people, but somewhere abroad, to Europeanism. . . . And yet our salvation is with the people."

Dostoevsky's new authority was revealed not only by the volume of his correspondence but also by his extended social life. He was invited everywhere and accepted most of the invitations. His wife, worn out by her bookkeeping work and the distribution of the periodical, seldom accompanied him on his visits. In a few years this woman had lost all coquetry, all ambition. She neglected herself and wore patched dresses, hoping to be attractive to her husband only by reason of her "soul." He clumsily tried to restore her liking for elegant clothes by writing to her details of the latest fashions. "Do you know, dear Anna, so and so wore a splendid dress. It was simply tailored, the right side raised, the back low, but not dragging on the floor; I forget about the left side, but I think it too was raised. You *must* order a similar dress. You will see how becoming it will be!" Another time he wrote,

"You do not know what marvels your eyes are, your smile, and your sudden inspired flights of inspiration when you converse. Your only mistake is that you do not go out often enough. . . . But if you will begin to see people a little, if you will dress a little more carefully, you yourself will be surprised at seeing yourself so young and so extraordinarily beautiful."

She did not understand him. He had so completely driven her into the fleshless world of his books that she was no longer able to keep a foothold in the real world. She lacked Dostoevsky's flexibility—he could shuttle between the prosaic world and the supernatural world without deserting one for the sake of the other. And in the salons, just as of old, Dostoevsky was alternately amiable and embittered, patronizing and resentful.

"I have always been surprised by his excessive modesty," wrote E. A. Shtakenschneider. "It was as though he did not realize his own worth. Incidentally, this explained his extreme touchiness or, more accurately, his constant expectation of being insulted. He often saw an insult where someone with a high opinion of himself would notice nothing of the kind. . . . Occasionally it was as though a drop of bile had formed in his chest and burst suddenly, and he was compelled to free himself of this bile, against his own will. As for myself, I always knew by a certain wrinkle around his lips, a guilty expression of his eyes, that he was about to say something nasty. Sometimes he controlled himself and swallowed his bile, but then he would grow somber, silent, and ill-tempered."

In the eyes of the world, Dostoevsky's genius excused his ill nature which came almost to be regarded as a permanent feature, indispensable in the make-up of a genius. Far from harming him, it helped him, brought him closer to his readers.

In 1878, the former convict received the following letter from the Academy of Science: "The Imperial Academy of Science, desirous of expressing its esteem for your literary work, has elected you a corresponding member of the section of Russian language and literature." Shortly afterward, the tutor of the grand dukes Sergey and Pavel asked him, in the name of the emperor, to visit the eminent pupils. Thus Dostoevsky enjoyed the pleasure of fame and recognition. He had succeeded in paying most of his debts. Thanks to his wife's brother, he had the use of a country house at Staraya Russa, and *A Writer's Diary* brought in a good income.

What else could he wish for? His daughter drew a charming picture of her father at this period. He slept in his study on a sofa. Above it on the wall hung a photographic reproduction of Raphael's "Sistine Madonna," and his first glance upon awakening fell on this graceful effigy. He would rise, wash himself, "using a great deal of water, soap and eau de cologne," and then dress from tip to toe, for he disapproved of wrappers and slippers. "From morning on he was correctly dressed, with shoes and tie, and wearing a handsome white shirt with a hard collar." He took good care of his coats. "Spots bother me," he used to say, "I cannot work as long as they are there."

After dressing, Feodor Mikhailovich would go to the dining room to take tea. He drank two glasses and took a third one to his study. On his desk everything was in perfect order—cigarette box, letters, books, newspapers. Anna Grigorievna joined her husband, arranged her notebook, pencils, and her erasers on a little table, and took down in shorthand what Dostoevsky had written during the night. After she copied it, Feodor Mikhailovich would correct the copies.

Later he had lunch, went out for a walk, bought tidbits for his children, ate dinner, drank tea, and again returned to his study to work. He greatly enjoyed this regular and productive life, and it seemed that nothing could spoil its sweetness. But it was written that fate should persecute Dostoevsky till the end of his life.

On May 16, 1878, young Aliosha had a violent epileptic fit that lasted for three hours and ten minutes, and he died without regaining consciousness. Dostoevsky was crushed by this death, of which he felt guilty, because the child had succumbed to a hereditary disease. The idea of universal responsibility re-emerged in him, more clearly defined than before. Innocence is only a vain word. "Every one of us is guilty before all, for all, and for everything."

On the day of the burial, the family sat in a landau, with the little coffin placed between the parents. The daughter wrote, "There was a great deal of weeping, the little white coffin was caressed, covered with flowers, and the favorite words of the child were recalled." At the cemetery, grass had grown between the graves, the trees were in bloom, the birds were singing. "Tears rolled down my father's cheeks. He supported his wife, who sobbed. She could not wrest her eyes from the little box that slowly disappeared into the ground."

Dostoevsky overcame this last ordeal as he had the others. He saved himself by work—and the price of his salvation was *The Brothers Karamazov*.

12. "THE BROTHERS KARAMAZOV"

DOSTOEVSKY INFORMED HIS READERS, IN THE ISSUE OF *A Writer's Diary* for December, 1877, that he had decided to suspend his publication for some time in order to devote himself to "a work of literature that I have imperceptibly and involuntarily conceived in the course of the last two years." The new book was to be, like *The Adolescent*, a fragment of the vast cycle entitled *The Life of a Great Sinner*, and would deal with the existence of God, "the problem that has consciously and unconsciously tormented me all my life."

Dostoevsky knew that his literary work was still incomplete. It was high time for him to come forward with an ultimate statement of his views that would be his "very last word." He meditated, gathered notes and material. It took him three years to complete this project.

"I have conceived and soon will begin a great novel, in which, among other characters, there will be many children," he wrote on March 16, 1878. The first entry in his notebook for *The Brothers Karamazov* is with the following memorandum, "Find out whether it is possible to lie between railroad tracks while a train goes by above you at full speed. . . . Get information concerning children's labor in factories, and concerning schools. Visit a school. . . . In a foundling asylum."

At about this time Dostoevsky discovered a kinship between himself and Vladimir Soloviov, the son of the historian, a brilliant young professor. "The Crisis of Western Philosophy," Soloviov's doctoral thesis, was a searching criticism of European positivism, and proclaimed the advent of a new metaphysics. The young philosopher's person, his inspiring beauty, impressed even his stanchest opponents, and Dostoevsky asserted that his face was like that of Annibal Caracci's "Young Christ."

In this strange friendship between the elderly writer and the young philosopher Dostoevsky was the disciple. Thanks to his interminable discussions with Soloviov, he was able to formulate, order, and illumine his own ideas. With the help of his young friend he translated into abstract terms the philosophical problems in which he had struggled chaotically for so many years.

Concerning the problems of Orthodox doctrine, Dostoevsky consulted Constantin Pobedonostsev, procurator of the Holy Synod, but he also showed interest in Fedorov's theory of common action and read the work of the eighteenth-century bishop, Tikhon Zadonsky. As early as 1870 he wrote to Maikov, "I intend to make Tikhon Zadonsky the central character of my new novel."

After the death of little Aliosha, Anna Grigorievna urged her husband to accompany Soloviov to Optina Pustin, hoping the change of scene would have a beneficial effect on Feodor Mikhailovich, all the more so because he had always wished to visit this monastery, where Gogol, Leontiev, and Tolstoy had taken refuge. Dostoevsky followed his wife's advice, and after a short stay in Moscow, the two friends took the train to Sergeevo. The remaining fifty miles they traveled in a coach that jolted them over stony paths and after two days brought them to Optina Pustin. The monks received them cordially and the *starets* Ambrosius granted Dostoevsky two private interviews. This visit supplied him with details for the character of Zosima in *The Brothers Karamazov*.

It should be noted that as early as 1877, one year before his trip to Optina Pustin, Dostoevsky had visited Darovoe, his father's estate, its woods and ravine, and the village of Cheremashny. He had chatted with the wrinkled old peasants who had once been his playmates, and laughed with them, refreshing his inspiration at its very source.

Yet, his work on his new book proved more arduous than that on any of his previous novels. He did not want to botch this book which was to be his crowning production. But he feared that age had weakened his creative ability, that sickness had distorted his memory, and that he would die before he had said everything.

"I have noticed," he writes, "that the more I advance, the harder it is for me to work. . . ." In a letter to his wife, he said: "I think constantly of my death . . . and I wonder what I will leave to the children and you." But his driving purpose was the completion of the *Karamazov*. "It is important that it should be a work of art, and this is a difficult and risky thing, a fatal thing—it must place my name very high, give it a firm foundation, for otherwise there is no more hope."

The Karamazov family live in a little provincial town. Karamazov *père*, a cynical and lewd old buffoon, has ruined his life with mysterious debauchery. From his first wife who beat him unmercifully, he had a son Dmitri, a savage brute with sudden impulses to honesty and metaphysical preoccupations. From his second wife, a peevish and hysterical woman, he had a son Ivan, an irritable intellectual with a tormented and destructive mind—a hero and martyr of negation. But Aliosha, his youngest son, seems to be untouched by the hereditary curse of the Karamazovs. His disposition is characterized by male kindness, the opposite of the asexual kindness of the hero of *The Idiot*. He is the positive principle of the book, the luminous axis around which the other characters whirl like black midges. In addition to the three brothers, there is the infamous Smerdiakov, a son of old Karamazov by a feebleminded deaf-mute whom he had raped one night for sheer bravado. This epileptic bastard serves as a lackey in his father's house. He is stolid, pretentious, cunning, admires Ivan who is annoyed by him because in Smerdiakov he recognizes a caricature of himself.

Old Karamazov and his four sons quarrel with one another about a woman named Grushenka. Smerdiakov, thinking that he is obeying Ivan's secret wish, murders his father. Dmitri is accused of the crime, sentenced to hard labor, and leaves for Siberia. This is the story.

The book is dominated by two problems—the problem of

seduction, and the problem of God. It is the conflict between the idea of Grushenka and the idea of Christ. The other characters are placed between these two poles. Some, like the old Karamazov, are symbols of sensuality; others, like the *starets* Zosima, are symbols of religious faith. Between these extremes the souls of the other characters are arranged skillfully in a hierarchical order. Smerdiakov, Dmitri, Ivan, and Aliosha are, so to speak, progressive embodiments of the same character—the individual who shakes himself free of the beast and is realized in the "new man." These four brothers are one and the same being; each represents a different stage of the single personality development. "The ladder of vice is the same for all," Aliosha says to Dmitri. "I am on the first rung, you are a little higher—at the thirteenth, for instance. In my opinion, it's absolutely the same thing."

Grushenka too is on this "thirteenth rung." This prostitute, the mistress of an old merchant who has rescued her from poverty, is a courtesan, says old Karamazov, but probably a "greater saint" than all the nuns in the convent. "This woman is a beast," "this woman is an angel," retort the other characters. And Dmitri exclaims, "Yes, that's what she is—a tigress. The queen of immodesty, the completely infernal woman, the queen of all fiendish women unleashed in the world." But what strikes Aliosha is "the naïve and kind expression of her face."

Whom are we to believe? All of them are right, for Grushenka has earned all of these opinions. Grushenka, the young girl, the slut, the beast, the saint, embodies the multiple contradictions of woman. She is woman on the model of Polina Suslova. Woman is folly become flesh, women are worn out by waiting and are disconsolate when their desires are gratified, they yearn to give themselves and reproach men

for having taken them. They are cruel for the pleasure of
being gentle afterward, then they are gentle for the pleasure
of being cruel afterward. They are perversely modest and
voluptuously innocent. They lie to God, to men, to themselves. They are not caught in life, they toy with life, they
pose before life as before a mirror. And they make faces and
change their expressions to give themselves the sensation of
existing. While permanence is for men the proof of their
reality, woman asserts her existence through change. Man
wants to be one, woman wants to be multiple. Man feels his
strength only in the full consciousness of his virtues and defects; woman feels strong only in total unconsciousness of
herself. Man is the organized world, woman the formless
universe. Everything is possible with her, nothing is certain
with her. One must flee from her or else renounce dominion
over her.

Grushenka's beauty has bewitched old Karamazov. This
drunken, stingy, lying, and vicious old man seems to be a
portrait of Dostoevsky's own father, painted with pitch. "He
was sentimental, yes, he was sentimental and wicked." Lubov
Dostoevskaya notes, "I have always been convinced that
Feodor Mikhailovich was thinking of his father when he
created the character of the elder Karamazov."

In the presence of the beautiful Grushenka, old Karamazov
is nothing but a stammering and slobbering buffoon. He
gives her the portion of his estate that was to be Dmitri's
inheritance. Every day he hopes that she will visit him, and
wanders from room to room befuddled with lust, waiting
endlessly; but Grushenka does not yield to him, nor to Dmitri
when he falls in love with her. She laughs at father and son,
and as the days go by the two men hate each other more and

more intensely. "They scrutinized each other, with their knives ready in the sheaths."

Raskolnikov is obsessed by an idea to such an extent that he loses all freedom; Dmitri and his father are so obsessed by a human being that they become slaves of their desire. "Beauty is a terrible and horrible thing," says Dmitri. Its power over men equals and sometimes exceeds that of ideas. The erotic madness of the Karamazovs is comparable to the political madness of the protagonists of *The Possessed*. In both cases, the desire for an earthly gratification reduces man to the status of beast, and the claim to the right of defying all moral limits leads him to depravity and murder.

"As for Dmitri," says his father, "I will crush him like a cockroach."

And Dmitri says of his father: "I don't know—perhaps I will kill him, perhaps I won't. I fear that I shall be unable to endure his face at such a moment. I hate his Adam's apple, his nose, his eyes, his impudent smile. He disgusts me. That is what frightens me."

Nevertheless, he spies upon his father, lest Grushenka, lured by promises of money, should yield to the old man. One night Grigori, the servant, surprises Dmitri in the garden. Dmitri strikes him on the head with a pestle and runs away. He finds Grushenka at the inn. "Then an orgy began, a mad party," with wine, songs, dancing. Grushenka, completely drunk, admits to Dmitri that she is in love with him and wants to marry him. "Although you are a savage," she says to him, "I know that you are noble. From now on we must live honestly. . . . Let us be good and honest, let us not be like beasts. . . . Take me far away from here. . . . I don't want to stay here, I want to be far, far away."

It is as though a looming disaster were intensifying the emotions of these sensual characters. The foreknowledge of a terrible fate drives them to intensify their transient pleasures. They are cheerful because they feel that they have no right to be cheerful. And it is a fact that in Dostoevsky's characters all joys that are not strictly spiritual ones seem strangely fragile. At the very moment when we witness sudden happiness in an individual, we are perturbed, because we know that he is doomed. With the refinement of a sadist, Dostoevsky nurses the happiness of his hero before punishing him. He does not strike a tired, sick body; he gives the blow on a day when the individual is in his prime, when his hopes are being fulfilled. Dmitri is arrested at the height of amorous intoxication. He is charged with parricide, and his protestations of innocence are of no avail; all the evidence points to him as the criminal.

Smerdiakov, the actual murderer of their father, plays the role of the diabolical double that is so dear to Dostoevsky. What torture for an honest man to meet the embodiment of everything dirty, unavowed, forgotten, beastly, and cowardly that is buried in himself! You are serene, you accept yourself—and then suddenly you are confronted with an individual whose soul is made of everything that you have cast away, an individual who is the offal, the cesspool of yourself, who is yourself in what is most vicious in yourself. In his corrupt mouth, your noblest words sound like obvious stupidities; in his narrow mind, your noblest ideas are turned against you.

Thus Ivan Karamazov walks his own alter ego like an ape on a leash. He hates Smerdiakov; Smerdiakov is gratified by this hatred, and commits murder because he believes that he is thereby obeying a secret order from his master. What has been only a vague hope in the heart of Ivan Karamazov is suddenly transformed into a monstrous actuality that horrifies him. Because of Smerdiakov who realizes the criminal intention of his master, Ivan is guilty no longer of a dream but of a deed. Smerdiakov stands for the fusion of the idea and the act, he symbolizes the negation of spiritual irresponsibility, the punishment of the freethinker.

"You yourself," he says to Ivan, "have strongly desired your father's death. . . . You were incapable of killing him yourself, but you hoped that someone else would do it."

Ivan questions himself, tries to be reasonable, is troubled. "Yes, I have been waiting for this, and if so, it is true that I wanted to kill him." And he asks his conscience, "Did I desire my father's death to this extent?"

Ivan is guilty because of this thought, this intention.

"You have killed him, you are the chief murderer. I was only your helper," Smerdiakov insists. The lackey proceeds to reveal the origin of his crime to his master. The truth is that he committed murder because there was nothing to stop him. Thanks to the speeches of Ivan, the intellectual, Smerdiakov understood that "everything is permissible" in this world. If there is no God, there is no hell. "If God does not exist, there is no such thing as being virtuous, virtue is useless. That is the way I reasoned."

Having thus negated the rules of common morality, having jumped over the wall, Smerdiakov confuses freedom with license. He commits murder and his act involves Ivan who declared that "everything is permissible," and Dmitri, who said, "Why does such a man exist?"

Ivan is innocent before human justice, but nothing can justify himself in his own eyes. Because he negates God, he is faced with Smerdiakov. Instead of superman, he discovers

the ape; instead of the luminous ladder, he perceives the
abyss; instead of defying superior reason, he is faced with
madness. This intelligent, educated, gifted man begins to
suffer from hallucinations; he undergoes a split of personality, he sees the devil, and this devil is himself. "It is myself,
but with a different face. . . . You express my own
thoughts. . . . Only you have chosen my most foolish
thoughts; you are stupid and trivial."

Ivan Karamazov is Dostoevsky, whom "God has tortured
all his life." Ivan's blasphemous negations are Dostoevsky's
own negations in his moments of doubt. "These fools have
not even dreamed of the power of negation that I have overcome," he writes. And when Ivan Karamazov says, "Can one
accept universal harmony at the price of the tears of one
little martyred child?" it is Dostoevsky himself who speaks.

Ivan was to Dostoevsky what Smerdiakov is to Ivan—the
embodiment of all that was odious in himself. Ivan was that
part of the author's soul which he wanted to cast away, and
the masterful punishment of his author.

Shining above these wretched beings are two luminous
figures, Aliosha and the *starets* Zosima. The youngest of the
brothers Karamazov is a novice in a peaceful monastery with
big white walls, but he is not a real mystic. Dostoevsky writes
of him, "Aliosha was in no way a fanatic nor even, I think,
a mystic. He was simply a philanthropist ahead of his time."

This boy is perfectly balanced, perfectly adjusted to reality and he has a healthy and serene confidence in God. To
be sure, he believes in miracles but he is not troubled by
them; they are the crowning of his faith, not its foundation.
"For a realist faith is not born of miracles; miracles are born
of faith."

Thus Aliosha is a "realist," a complete human being. Unlike Myshkin, he is of this world, he is capable of understanding the views of his brothers and father; he is not a stranger in relation to the sinners around him. Therefore his merit in resisting all temptations is the greater. The *starets* Zosima tells him, "This is what I think of you: You will go forth from these walls and live like a monk in the world. You will have many adversaries, but even your enemies will love you. Life will bring you many misfortunes, but you will find happiness in misfortune; you will bless life, and you will make others bless it, and this is what matters most."

Aliosha was doubtless modeled on Shidlovsky, Dostoevsky's childhood friend, and Soloviov, the philosopher with the face of Christ. As for Zosima, we have seen that this character was inspired by Tikhon Zadonsky and Father Ambrosius of the Optina Pustin monastery.

"The *starets*," writes Dostoevsky, "is a man who absorbs your soul and your will in his own." He is a powerful confessor who rules the monastery by virtue of his extreme clairvoyance and the serene shrewdness of his advice. "Many say that as a result of receiving, for many years, all those who came to pour out their hearts to him, eager for advice and consolation, he finally acquired great perspicacity. He would cast one glance at a stranger and guess why he had come, what he needed, and even what tormented his conscience."

Like Aliosha, Zosima was a man before becoming a saint. He lived among his fellow men and served in the army. When he decided to become a monk he was motivated not by despair or intellectual conviction, but by love. Zosima's doctrine is a doctrine of love and joy.

The *starets* repeats the words of his young brother, "Life is a paradise in which we all dwell, but we refuse to recognize this." He says also, "Everyone of us is guilty before all men,

for all men, for everything." All men are united by universal
sympathy, and the villainy of any one man has repercussions
on the rest. Evil is not confined to single criminal and his
direct victim; it spreads like a grease spot. Those who unconsciously desire evil are affected by it even if they do no
evil, and those who have realized such desires in themselves
without condemning them also suffer. Even those who know
nothing of crime are mysteriously accomplices in it.

We are all responsible, defiled, unhappy. We have stolen
with the burglar whose face we do not know, we have murdered with the parricide about whom we read in the newspapers, raped with the lewd, cursed with the blasphemous.
Each of us bends under the sin of the world. And yet all of
us will be saved. Zosima says, "Man cannot commit a sin that
can exhaust God's infinite love. Believe that God loves you
more than you can conceive, that He loves you in your sin
and with your sin. . . . If you love, you belong to God. Love
redeems everything, saves everything."

Zosima does not summon the believer to embrace rigorous
monastic rule, to practice asceticism, to whimper with con-
trition. He asks men only to admit their faults and to love.
What matters is not the result achieved, but the effort to
achieve it. When the proud man bows his head, he is closer
to God than the lackey who falls on his knees, because the
proud man has had to struggle with himself in order to offer
to God this sign of human modesty, while the lackey prostrates himself by habit.

"Do what you can, and it will be taken into account. . . .
That which seems to you wicked in you is purified by the
very fact that you have realized it. . . . At the moment
when you realize with horror that despite your efforts you
are not only no closer to your goal, but have moved away

from it, at that moment you will achieve your goal, and you will behold . . . the Savior who, without you knowing it, has lovingly guided you."

Zosima and Aliosha are bathed in the same blessed light. They love, and this is sufficient to gain the sympathy of simple people and children. (Book X of the novel is entirely devoted to Aliosha's friendship for the children of the region.)

The intellectual attacks this serene philosophy. Ivan Karamazov fights the serene faith of his brother with the diabolical arguments of the Grand Inquisitor. The legend that Ivan relates to Aliosha is the culmination of *The Brothers Karamazov*, and probably the testament of Dostoevsky's literary career. It sums up everything, illumines everything, and is truly Dostoevsky's last word.

In Seville, during the Inquisition, Christ appears among the crowd. He is recognized at once. People throng around Him and beg Him for miracles. Jesus performs the miracles asked of Him. Then the Grand Inquisitor, a man of ninety with a dried up face and hollow eyes, orders the arrest of the Savior. At night, the Grand Inquisitor visits Jesus in the dungeon. "Why have you come to disturb us," he says. "For You do disturb us." The old man proceeds to read a terrible indictment against Jesus. The Grand Inquisitor does not believe in God or man. He does not believe in God because he refuses to heed the Savior's words, "You have no right to add one word to what you have said." He does not believe in man because he maintains that the Christian doctrine goes beyond the moral strength of mankind.

He rejects the synthesis of the human and divine principle in freedom. "I want to make you free," Jesus had said. But by proclaiming the freedom of choice between good and evil, Jesus proclaimed man's responsibility, condemned man to the torments of his conscience, and made him the object of a whole machinery of suffering, in which remorse, temptation, and hope are inextricably mixed. Freedom is inconceivable without suffering. Freedom can be bought only at the price of suffering. And Christianity is above all a religion of suffering.

Thus man is confronted with a dilemma: on the one hand, independence with moral torture, on the other, well-being through submission. What will be his choice?

The Grand Inquisitor chooses for him. Christ, he maintains, has overestimated the strength of His creatures in imposing the ordeal of freedom on them. "Have you forgotten that man prefers peace, even death, to the freedom of choosing between good and evil?" Man's great goal is happiness, and the task of the church is to organize his happiness on earth. Thus the church loves man better than Christ loves him since Christ has placed an excessively heavy burden on his shoulders.

"Because You placed man too high, You acted pitilessly toward him, You demanded too much of him." The ideal of Jesus in the form that it assumes in the Gospels can be realized only by a few chosen spirits. Christianity is an aristocratic religion, and as such impossible. Religion is intended for the masses, and it must propose a way of life that can be followed by the masses. It must bring comfort to fools, cowards, perverts, and the sick. It must be accessible to the lowest of mankind; it must be vulgar. In the place of freedom, uncertainty, and spiritual suffering, the Grand Inquisitor wants to give man a Euclidean organization of the world. At this point the Grand Inquisitor embraces Shigalev's doctrine. He takes care of the crowd and defends the hungry and the weak. He promises them not heavenly bread but earthly bread. "You have promised them heavenly bread, but can it compare with earthly bread, in the eyes of this weak human race, eternally wicked and eternally ungrateful? . . . To us, it is the weak who are precious." This religion of earthly bread is identical with the atheist socialism of *The Possessed*.

The Grand Inquisitor proclaims the ideal of mediocre happiness, as against great spiritual aspirations: "We shall give them the quiet happiness of weak creatures, such as they are by nature. . . . Yes, we shall set them to work, but in their leisure hours we shall organize their life like a child's game, with childish songs, choruses, and innocent dances. Oh, we shall allow them even sin, because they are weak and helpless."

It was in the name of man's freedom that Christ in the desert refused to succumb to the first temptation, that of earthly bread. According to the Grand Inquisitor, this was his first error.

His second error was his wish to be loved freely. Men cannot believe when guided by their hearts alone. They need a certainty. The divine promise is unintelligible to them, it is enveloped in too much mystery, too much silence, too many allusions. "You have chosen the strangest, most enigmatic, most indeterminate things—everything that exceeds man's strength." Man wants to be terrorized, enslaved, he wants to be convinced of the inexorable *necessity* of worshiping.

Christ allowed himself to be crucified like a thief, he bled on the cross, and his death was witnessed by women in tears. Because he desired that man's love should not be won by miracles, he moved away from man and lost him. "You wanted a freely accorded love, not the servile passion of a terrified slave. Here again You overestimated man."

Thus the second temptation, that of authority, is complemented by the third temptation, that of the miracle.

The Grand Inquisitor accepts these three temptations that Christ rejected. He corrects the work of Christ by basing it on earthly bread, on authority, and on miracles. "And men rejoiced at being led again in a herd and delivered from the fatal gift that caused them such torment."

Thus, Christianity is no longer the religion of the elite but the religion of all. The church betrays God out of love for man. It uses Christ to symbolize not a spiritual but a social order. It sets up "Christian communism." It formulates rigid duties, bourgeois theories, and gives promises of absolution, pardon, and eternal life to reassure its lamentable flock. Rites, festivals, and professions of faith are the official pageantry of the Divine Presence. Supernatural mystery is transformed into fairy tales for young persons who partake of the sacrament for the first time. It multiplies bells, incense, pictures and sculptures. It mobilizes all the arts, all the senses, to dazzle the masses. It diminishes God, offering him for sale like a commodity. And its triple lie, its triple blasphemy, is so cleverly contrived that no one dreams of denouncing it. The church disavows Christ while extolling his work. It is the last refuge of atheism. And men will burn Christ rather than renounce the facile dogmas that the Grand Inquisitor has forged for them. "They will cling to us with terror, like a young brood under their mother's wing. . . ."

"If anyone deserves the stake more than all others, it is You," says the Inquisitor to Christ. "Tomorrow I shall order You to be burned."

Christ approaches the Inquisitor and kisses his bloodless lips. The old man shivers, opens the door, and says, "Go away, and don't come back."

It is noteworthy that Ivan, the atheist, exemplifies the divorce between religion and the church. He attacks not Christ but the church, he defends not atheism, but, unwittingly, the true faith. He, more than anyone else, stresses the supreme moral beauty of Christ, his wish to be loved for his own sake.

According to Dostoevsky, the Catholic theocracy alone is guilty of having stolen the word of Christ for imperialistic purposes. Yet the Byzantine orthodoxy can be accused of the same crime; in fact any ecclesiastical system incurs the reproach of Caesarism. Throughout its history the church has fought against the temptation of denying spiritual freedom. For nothing is less suited to the human nature than this freedom. And yet the true mystery of Christ is the mystery of freedom. The meaning of Calvary is the assertion of man's perfect freedom of choice. Victorious divine truth would have compelled the allegiance of human souls apart from love. Crucified divine truth, truth humiliated, lacerated, covered with spittle and pus, does not impose itself on man. Man believes not *because* but *notwithstanding*. The act of faith in the presence of this corpse that is like any other corpse is perfectly free. And Dostoevsky invites us to this free faith that is incomprehensible and logically inadmissible.

Faced with the problem of God, Ivan Karamazov rejects the theological explanation of the world. He evokes the memory of all human suffering. In his eyes the expiation of wrongdoers in eternity does not redeem the horrors for which they were responsible during their earthly existence: "What is the use of all the hellish sufferings of the doomed, if a child has been tortured to death?" Moreover, he asks,

"Where is harmony, if there is still a hell? I want to forgive and to reconcile myself. I do not desire that there should be more suffering." The explanation supplied by the church is oversimplified. Something more than the give-and-take principle is needed. But what? "How can I conceive anything about a God who is too high for me?" he says.

Thus this atheist does not deny God; he rejects the possibility of conceiving him. To want God is not to be an atheist any longer. To insult God, is to believe in God. Ivan's passionate negation is directed against the God of the church, against the administrative, factitious, familiar God of the Grand Inquisitor. Ivan refuses to admit a God comprehensible to the human mind, justified by human syllogisms, and brought down to earth by humans. "God is not of this world." He can only be a riddle, a hope. The church spoils this hope by making it specific.

Having thus reached the threshold of true faith, Ivan withdraws. He is filled with admiration because the idea of God could germinate in man's obtuse mind. Did God create man or did man create God? Ivan does not want to know the answer to this question. Before this world that is a failure, before this God who does not even illumine his work, Ivan "returns his entrance ticket," saying: "I do not accept it, I refuse to accept it." And he renounces God out of love for mankind, as did the Grand Inquisitor in the legend.

Having refused God, Ivan becomes satanic. Ivan Karamazov is the devil. He sees the devil in a delirium, and this devil is himself. The devil knows God, yet rejects Him. "I was there," he says to Ivan, "when the Word expiring on the cross ascended to heaven taking with him the soul of the good thief who was crucified. . . . At that moment I should have liked to join all the choirs and cry hosannah with them.

. . . But in view of my duties . . . I was compelled to repress a beautiful gesture and remain in my ignominy."

Thanks to the devil, Ivan at last discovers the reasons for his own atheism. Because of his desire to measure himself against God, to do without God, to replace God, he refuses the faith that pursues him. Here we find the theme of the superman, the concept so dear to Dostoevsky: "The human mind will grow great, it will rise as high as satanic pride, and this will be the era of deified mankind." But Ivan is not at ease in his atheism. He hurls a cup of tea at the devil, "like a woman." He drives out the devil, he drives himself out. For it is difficult to deny a presence that one perceives inwardly to be necessary. He is one of those who voluntarily take the path to hell. He is sick with God. Will he die of this sickness?

Aliosha looks upon his brother with horror and pity and in the end gently kisses his mouth, just as Christ kissed the Grand Inquisitor. Such an answer is the only possible answer of a Christian to an atheist. For he can oppose only love to logic. Faith cannot be explained, cannot be imposed at order. Myshkin, the idiot, says to Hippolyte, the unbeliever, "Go your way, and forgive us our happiness."

"God will be victorious," thinks Aliosha. "Either Ivan will be resurrected in the light of truth or he will succumb in hatred." And he prays for his brother, because there is no other way of saving him.

This tremendous book sums up not only Dostoevsky's ideas but also his method. Nowhere does the author's shuttling between the fantastic and the real appear more clearly than in *The Brothers Karamazov*. The reader hardly thinks of the setting. There is little information about the physical appearance of the characters. To be sure, the elder Karamazov has

bags under his small, distrustful eyes and an Adam's apple
that gives him a hideously sensual appearance; and we are
told that Aliosha "has a slender build, brown hair, a regular
although oblong face, pink cheeks, dark-gray brilliant eyes,
a pensive and calm appearance"; but that is all. Ten pages
farther on, the reader forgets these rapid sketches; these faces,
these bodies completely sacrificed to an abstraction. The passions of the heroes consume their flesh. We are confronted
with a conflict of ideas; we are introduced into a world in
which people do not eat or drink or sleep, in which multiple
events are squeezed into the space of a few hours, in which
terrible foreknowledge haunts the heart of man, in which
night and day are merged, and in which everyone speaks to
convince himself rather than to convince others.

Amid this disorder and restlessness these beings are tormented not by sickness or the fear of the day to come but
by God. By a dispensation of their author, they are free of
ordinary everyday concerns and placed naked in the face
of mystery. Their mundane life corresponds to our inner life.

They are ourselves observed from the inside. Because of
this method of "taking shots," the phenomenon nearest to the
cameraman is the most unconscious suffering, and that far-
thest for him is the flesh, the clothing, the light of day. The
camera is focused on the inner world, and the external world
remains blurred like a dream. And when we are shown this
negative of ourselves, we do not recognize ourselves in it,
just as we cannot see ourselves in an X-ray plate.

This optics of the underground man is conditioned by the
author's feverish sympathy for his creations. It is as though
we were hurled into the midst of his creation by a fit, almost
an epileptic seizure. He suddenly penetrates the visceral
shadows of the inner world; his eyes become accustomed to

the darkness, and he sees and understands. And just as an entire lifetime can be compressed into the few seconds of a dream, so he lives in one flash a total spiritual experience, with its searching, its failures, its hopes. But when he re-emerges to the surface with his booty of ideas, and attempts to put order, according to artistic laws, into a story that he has lived outside of time, space, and causality, he is the prey of the artist's anguish. He is faced with the problem of making a tragedy of profound life intelligible to readers who are familiar only with superficial life. He must impose the unconscious on the common consciousness, translate the unconscious in terms of the conscious and interest his readers in something which is truly themselves.

Caught between the fantastic and the real, Dostoevsky strives to insert the fluid matter of his observation into the solid framework of logic. But it is an arduous task. As a result, the novel teems with implausibilities. The enormous mass of the events that constitute the story of *The Brothers Karamazov* is compressed into the space of a few days. The characters make speeches ten pages long and meet to discuss God in the Russian manner. Smerdiakov, the flunkey, speaks elegantly. Dmitri, the boor, exclaims, "No man is big, too big. I would reduce him." As is usual with Dostoevsky, the heroes have prophetic knowledge about each other: Zosima tells Aliosha that Dmitri's fate will be a tragic one; Aliosha kisses his father's shoulder on taking leave, because he senses an imminent disaster; Ivan goes to Cheremashny because he foresees the murder that is being prepared.

Hallucinations, dreams, crime are the small change of this allegorical world. To explain the actions of his heroes, Dostoevsky naïvely invokes heredity or pathology, as though to say to the reader, "These people are not like you or me, they are neurotics, of course." He deceives the reader as to the identity of his creations, and in his desire to be plausible, piles on material details. He relates the crime of old Karamazov with the care of a specialist. The cross-examination and the counsel's speech at the trial of Dmitri strike one as having been written by a frequent visitor to courtrooms. "I don't think that I have made any technical errors in my story," writes Dostoevsky. "I discussed matters with the public prosecutors in St. Petersburg."

Just as Dostoevsky refused to choose between revolution and czarism, so he refused to choose between the fantastic and the real. He shuttles from one to the other, he tries to reconcile the irreconcilable. And it took him forty years of toil to impose this hybrid cosmogony on the public. But impose it he did with *The Brothers Karamazov*.

13. FINIS

DOSTOEVSKY WAS AS MUCH ADMIRED AS TURGENEV AND Tolstoy after the publication of *The Brothers Karamazov;* indeed, he inspired more faith than Turgenev and Tolstoy. Behind him were a joyless childhood, an undeserved conviction, the penal colony, sickness, gambling, debts, privations, work on commission. He had passed through all these ordeals as through a morass, and now emerged on the plain, exhausted, bleeding, but saved.

Now he was old and weak. In his eyes, this sudden calm heralded death. For the last seven years Dostoevsky had suffered from an emphysema in the lungs, which he had contracted as a result of his catarrh in spite of his frequent trips to the waters at Ems. At first this illness seemed trifling to him, but now it worried him, and in his letters he mentioned it with as much apprehension as pleasure.

"A certain part of my lungs has been displaced," he wrote, "as well as my heart which is at present in a different position, and all this because of my emphysema." Or, "I still think of the future, and especially of buying an estate. Would you believe that I have gone insane? I tremble at the thought of my children's future." Or, "Everyone thinks we have money, but we have nothing."

His tremendous labors served only to pay his creditors. He needed money, urgently, very urgently. His wife opened a bookshop which brought in a fair income. As for himself, he planned to resume *A Writer's Diary* and to write the second part of *The Brothers Karamazov*. This was supposed to deal with Aliosha, the personification of the new Russia, as contrasted with Dmitri, the symbol of the old Russia, and Ivan, the European. The new type of Russian was to achieve his salvation in the world, following the advice of the *starets* Zosima. In the course of a heated discussion with Count Melchior de Voguë, Dostoevsky declared that the Russian people had the same spirit as every other people and its own genius in addition. That was why the Russian people could understand every other people without being understood by them.

This intense nationalism was recognized by the authorities. Upon Dostoevsky's request the Minister of the Interior suspended the secret police surveillance of which the great novelist had been the object ever since his release from prison.

On December 24, 1877, Dostoevsky made the following entry in his notebook:

(1) Write the Russian *Candide*.
(2) Write a book on Jesus.
(3) Write my memoirs.
(4) Write a poem about Sorokovin.

N.B. All this represents ten years of activity, and I am at present fixty-six years of age.

In May, 1880, the Society of the Friends of Russian Literature invited Dostoevsky to make a speech at the unveiling of the Pushkin monument in Moscow. Along with Gogol, Dostoevsky had always recognized Pushkin as his master. Hermann in the *Queen of Spades* gave Dostoevsky the idea for his Raskolnikov; the great poet's *Demons* supplied the title and the motto for *The Possessed* (the Russian title of this novel is *Demons*); and it was the monologue of the *Avaricious Knight* that awakened the thirst for money and boundless power in Dolgoruky of *The Adolescent*.

Dostoevsky's attitude toward Pushkin was one of jealous love. He feared that other orators might show themselves treacherous or cowardly with regard to his idol. The Occidentalists praised Pushkin as a great European; the Slavophiles did not dare proclaim him a great Russian. The public wanted a definitive appreciation of the poet that would reconcile the two camps, and Dostoevsky felt that it was his prophetic mission to accomplish this task.

However, his wife feared the effects of the trip from Staraya Russa to Moscow. Feodor Mikhailovich was tired and, in the opinion of his doctors, his emphysema had made terrible progress, threatening his very life. Anna Grigorievna wrote, "My cousin Snitkin told me, that the little arteries had become so thin and brittle that they could break at any moment as a result of physical exertion."

Dostoevsky would have liked his wife to accompany him,

but the couple could not afford the expense. Anna Grigorievna agreed to let her husband go alone on condition that he
send her news of his health every day.

Upon his arrival in Moscow Dostoevsky was welcomed
and entertained by the Slavophiles. The intellectual circles
awaited with feverish impatience the opening of the parlia-
ment of letters that was set for May 26, Pushkin's birthday,
but the death of the empress shortly before this date postponed it for a two-week period of official mourning. Dostoevsky wanted to return to Staraya Russa to work and attend
to his family affairs, but his friends told him that his departure would be regarded as desertion. "People would say
that I lack the civic courage to neglect my personal affairs in
the face of such an important event," he wrote to his wife.

His presence was all the more indispensable because it gave
him the opportunity of defending publicly the idea of a
"European Russia," for which he had fought for thirty years.
"The other camp (Turgenev, Kovalevsky and almost all the
members of the university)," he wrote, "are bent upon diminishing the importance of Pushkin as the personification
of Russia by rejecting the very idea of nationality. On our
side we have only I. S. Aksakov to take up the challenge.
. . . But Aksakov is old, and Moscow has had enough of
him." Thus Dostoevsky decided to stay, but he was not sure
that he would have enough money to pay his hotel bill. He
was told that the municipality would pay all his expenses, but
this suggestion upset him. "And I, who dissatisfied with my
coffee, have sent it back twice to ask for a stronger brew!
In the restaurant they must have said I can afford to be difficult, considering that it doesn't cost me anything."

News came from St. Petersburg that the dedication of the
monument had been postponed till the beginning of June.

Meanwhile, the delegates spent their time visiting each other, planning dinners and speeches. Dostoevsky was received and honored everywhere. He was surprised at his own popularity. "They spoke of my great importance as an artist, as a universal mind, as a publicist and as a Russian," he wrote. He naïvely admired the luxurious salons and lavish banqueting. "The dinner was very luxurious. It was served in a separate parlor (which must have involved considerable expense), and with such refinement that after the meal, along with coffee and liqueurs, two hundred excellent and very expensive cigars were brought in. Yes, the picture here is quite different from that in St. Petersburg. . . . Six speeches were made in my honor, some of them were very long."

As the date of the opening approached, the literary groups grew more and more animated, the antagonism between the Slavophiles and the Occidentalists, sharper. Katkov, the leader of the Rightist movement, was excluded from the celebrations because he had failed to advertise the ceremony in his newspaper, the *Moscow News*. The partisans of Turgenev worked hard to ensure the triumph of their leader, recruiting a considerable claque and shrewdly distributing the invitations at their disposal. Dostoevsky wrote, "I fear, that as a result of the many clashes of opinion a real fight will develop in the end."

On June 5 the Pushkin celebrations opened with a solemn mass. After the service, Dostoevsky approached Madame Suvorin and asked her, "When I die, will you attend my funeral and pray for me as you prayed today for Pushkin?"

The following day, the representatives of the Russian writers placed wreaths at the foot of the poet's monument, then they went to an academic meeting at the university, where the Rector announced that Turgenev had been elected

Firebrand

an honorary member of the faculty. The students acclaimed
the old novelist in whom they recognized "a worthy and
direct successor of Pushkin."

"Since Turgenev was the most important representative of
Occidentalism at the meeting," wrote Strakhov, "it could be
expected that this literary movement would play the greatest
role and be victorious in the intellectual tournament that was
to follow."

After the session at the university, the delegates went to
the banquet organized by the municipality at the Nobles'
Club. All the toasts and speeches contained allusions to Pushkin but no one dared to define the significance of this poet
for the Russian nation. At night, Dostoevsky publicly recited
the scene of the monk Pimen, and his voice was drowned in
applause. "But Turgenev," he noted, "who read very badly,
was recalled more often than I."

During the intermission, the ladies thronged around Dostoevsky, exclaiming, "You are a prophet. We have become
better human beings since reading *The Brothers Karamazov*."

On June 7 the solemn assembly of the Society of the
Friends of Russian Literature took place at the Nobles' Club.
Turgenev took the floor before an audience that was determined to be enthusiastic at any price. How could anyone
dislike this heavy giant with his white beard and gentle,
weary face? His gestures were elegant, his speech was beautiful, studied, polished. But he avoided all embarrassing questions. Was Pushkin a national poet epitomizing the peculiar
genius of his race?

"I do not say that he was," said Turgenev, "but I would
not permit myself to deny it either." He concluded with a
panegyric to Nekrasov, the poet of rebellion.

This clever maneuver exasperated Dostoevsky who was

beside himself with rage when he heard the wild ovation that welcomed the speech of his rival. For Turgenev was indeed his rival now as he had been of old. It was as though the Pushkin celebrations were reduced to a duel between two men, with Pushkin as a pretext.

"Turgenev diminished Pushkin by refusing him the title of national poet," wrote Dostoevsky. And referring to the admirers of his enemy, he added: "They are only hired clappers, while mine are real enthusiasts." He comforted himself by uttering a few, much applauded remarks on his own idea of Pushkin. But he hoped to take his real revenge the following day.

The second session was set for June 8. Aksakov was scheduled to speak before Dostoevsky, but the program was suddenly changed and Dostoevsky took the floor first. The hall was packed full. It was hot. After the first outburst of excitement, the majority of the audience had realized that Turgenev had been noncommittal about the poet. What would Dostoevsky have to say? Would he be able to explain Pushkin's real significance? Tense minutes passed. The platform was empty. Then suddenly Dostoevsky stepped onto it and faced the crowd that acclaimed him. His tired, gray wrinkled face seemed to bend under the weight of the surging applause. His body was so small and thin that it seemed to be supported by the armature of his dress coat. Holding the sheets of his notes in his big hands with their knotty fingers, he waited. As the applause continued, he made an awkward gesture asking for silence, bowed and passed his hands through his ruddy beard. As he wrote to Anna, "What are my successes in St. Petersburg in comparison? Nothing!"

Finally the assembly was still, and Dostoevsky began his speech in a breathless voice which gradually gained amplitude and in the end dominated the hall. Where did this sick and exhausted old man find the energy to shout from the platform? What miraculous power electrified this body, illumined these eyes, inspired these words? Unlike Turgenev, he did not dodge the essential problem of Pushkin's meaning for Russia.

What is Pushkin? He is the embodiment of the national spirit, explained Dostoevsky. Thanks to his extraordinary ability to grasp the genius of other nations, Pushkin is Russia in her most universal aspect. Shakespeare's Italians speak like Englishmen, but Pushkin, is he not Spanish in his *Don Juan*, English in his *Feast During the Plague*, German in his *Fragment of Faust*, Arab in his *Imitation of the Koran*, and Russian in *Boris Godunov*? Yes, he is all that, and because he is all that, because he can be all that, he is Russian. For the hundredth time, Dostoevsky took up the old theme that he had developed in his novels and in *A Writer's Diary*: "The significance of Russia is patently European and universal. To be a real Russian, to be fully Russian, means only (remember this well) to be the brother of all men, to be panhuman if I may say so."

All the old peoples of the West are dear to the young Russian people, and the young Russian people will save them because thanks to its admirable purity it remains the ultimate refuge of Christ. "Why should it not be we who will embody Christ's last word?"

This speech is interesting not so much for its argument as for the emotion that it reveals in its author. It was written to be spoken, rather than to be read. And Dostoevsky spoke it marvelously. Every oratorical period was completed amidst thunderous applause. When he spoke of Pushkin's

Tatiana, the Russian young girl par excellence, the women shouted with joy. When he recited Pushkin's summons:

> Humble yourself, proud man,
> First of all, break your pride!
> Humble yourself, lowly man,
> First of all, toil on your land!

the men lowered their heads, as though listening to a sermon.

Dostoevsky experienced the intoxication of being understood, admired and chosen as a spiritual leader by all these strangers with anxious faces. He ruled over them. "All this because of the Karamazov."

Finally he reached his peroration. "Pushkin died in the full flowering of his powers, and there is no doubt that he carried with him to his tomb a great secret. Now we must strive to penetrate it without him."

Dostoevsky stopped. His face was pale, sweat rolled down his wrinkles and his eyes were red from exhaustion. And suddenly a frantic roar rose toward this broken body. Men and women rose up from their seats, clapped their hands, yelled and sobbed. Enemies embraced and swore to each other that they would be better human beings and forget their old quarrels. Young people clamored: "The prophet, the prophet!" Pushing aside the ushers the audience climbed up to the platform, and Dostoevsky, jostled and bewildered, saw a surging wave of tailcoats, faces and arms coming toward him. People fell at his feet, kissed his hands.

"You are a genius! You are more than a genius!" For half an hour he was again and again recalled on the stage.

Finally the committee in charge suspended the session. But the public had forced their way backstage. A group of students shouting with enthusiasm rushed in, and one of them, shaken with sobs, fell at Dostoevsky's feet and lost consciousness. Turgenev embraced his rival with tears in his eyes. Aksakov spluttered with joy. Yuriev, in a sonorous voice, announced that the Society of the Friends of Russian Literature had unanimously elected Dostoevsky an honorary member. Dostoevsky, broken with emotion and fatigue, smiled, wept and wrung the hands of the people who thronged around him. His knees were shaking. He felt somewhat dizzy in the smell and heat of the crowd but was buoyed up by his joyful excitement.

After an hour's interruption the session resumed. Aksakov appeared on the stage and declared that he would not read his speech. "I cannot speak after Feodor Mikhailovich Dostoevsky. Everything I have prepared is only a weak variation on some of the themes developed in his allocution of genius." His voice was drowned in thunderous applause. He continued, "In my opinion, Dostoevsky's speech is a great event in our literature. . . . The true meaning of Pushkin has at last been revealed to us and there is nothing more to say. . . ."

Aksakov was about to leave the stage, but the public protested and forced him to read his address. While he spoke, the ladies quietly collected some funds and sent a delegation to the nearest flower shop. At the end of the meeting the crowd recalled Dostoevsky, and when he appeared on the stage, about a hundred women rushed toward him and placed a tremendous wreath of laurels behind him. "In the name of Russia's women of whom you said such great things," was the inscription on the ribbon. The spectators rose to their feet and applauded frantically. Many wiped their eyes. Hats were waved. Tears filled Dostoevsky's eyes.

Thus, thanks to him, there were no longer Occidentalists and Slavophiles, but only Russians. A whole nation, once divided, was now united in brotherly love and pride in itself. A whole nation was saved by his faith, his words. "You must admit, Anna, that it was worth while to stay. This is a pledge for the future, a pledge of everything, even if I die."

At the night session, Dostoevsky, despite his exhaustion, recited Pushkin's *Prophet*. Once again he was on the platform, thin, with a hollow chest, all shriveled up. But once again he was visited by the miracle of inspiration. His dull voice gradually grew stronger, it became trenchant and vigorous. One of the spectators wrote, "His right hand was stretched downwards, as though he forbade himself to make the obvious gesture and his tone was forced to the point of shouting." When he read the last quatrain:

> Arise, oh prophet! Behold and listen.
> Let my will possess you,
> Wander o'er land and sea
> And burn the hearts of men with your word.

a formidable ovation shook the assembly. In the eyes of these strangers who listened, Dostoevsky was truly the prophet.

He returned to his hotel exhausted, with a heavy head and smarting eyes. He lay down, seeking sleep, but an almost physical sensation of happiness prevented him from sleeping. He rose, dressed, took the wreath of laurels that had been presented to him and drove in a cab to Pushkin's monument.

The night was hot, blue, without a breeze. The streets were deserted. At Spaskaya Square, Dostoevsky alighted from his cab and approached the statue which rose high and black on its granite column. He gazed at the face of bronze and the dead eyes that looked down on the earth. Then with a great effort he lifted the wreath and placed it against the pedestal. He stood near his master and for a little while collected his thoughts. Mentally he measured the road he had traveled since the day when, as a child, he had learned of the poet's death, until the present moment when he stood before Pushkin's monument, so old, so tired, so close to death himself.

He evoked the little rooms of the Hospital of the Poor, the linden trees of Darovoe, the long corridors of the Engineering School, Petrashevsky's den, the dark casemates, and the three posts stuck in the snow before the troops. He recalled the wind, the cold, the night—Siberia, Semipalatinsk—the trip to Zmiev in Wrangel's coach—Polina's haughty laughter—the roulette wheel that turned, turned, turned—Anna Grigorievna's tears—a little grave in an unknown cemetery—cities, voices, eyes—a lamp on a desk—the scowling face of a pawnbroker—the roar of a train—the pale sky of Russia that moved toward him, inspired him, took him to itself. A surging tide rose from an invisible crowd: "You are a genius, you are more than a genius!" He had struggled so much, he had suffered so much. And now the great joy of being understood—he experienced it so late! Would he have time to enjoy it?

He straightened himself. The moon shone gently on the roofs and the pavements. The silence was soothing. Dostoevsky turned his back to the monument and walked toward the cab that waited for him at the corner.

On June 10, 1880, at the height of his triumph Feodor Mikhailovich left Moscow. His brief stay there had worn him out more than a year of work, but he felt confident, relaxed, happy. Yet he was not deceived as to the true proportions of the miracle. Upon his return to Staraya Russa he wrote to his friend Countess Tolstoy, the aunt of the novelist, "You can be sure that soon you will hear the jeerings of the crowd. In the various literary cliques and blind alleys I will not be forgiven for what I have done."

And true enough, when the exaltation subsided, his enemies recovered; it was as though they resented the fact that the speaker had bewitched them. Saltykov wrote to Ostrovsky, "It is obvious that the shrewd Turgenev and Dostoevsky, that madman, succeeded in diverting the Pushkin celebrations to their own profit."

Critical articles were published on Dostoevsky. "Mr. Dostoevsky's speech . . . affects one's nerves more than one's intelligence," wrote the columnist of *Action*. And, "The hero and final champion of this absurd affair was Mr. Dostoevsky. It is not the first time that he has got off the right track and imagined himself to be a publicist. But he lacks the education, intellectual development, political knowledge, and finally, the most elementary notions of tact that are necessary in a publicist."

"How absurd, this tirade!" wrote the *European Messenger*. "It would be desirable if in his future divagations Mr. Dostoevsky did not forget elementary historical facts and the rules of common sense."

Dostoevsky was so shaken by this sudden aboutface of public opinion that he had two successive epileptic fits and stayed in bed for two weeks. On August 26 he wrote to O. F. Miller: "Regarding my speech in Moscow, you see how almost the whole press treated me: one might think that I had committed a theft or a fraud or counterfeited a check." He decided to answer his most virulent detractor, Professor Gradovsky whose article "Dream and Reality" was pub-

lished in *The Voice*. His reply, as well as his speech on Pushkin, were published in the single issue of *A Writer's Diary*
for 1880. This issue had an unprecedented success. Six thousand copies were sold in a few days and a second printing
was sold out during the fall.

Dostoevsky was somewhat comforted by the obvious popularity of his works. He worked to complete *The Brothers
Karamazov*, the fourth section of which had not yet been
written. "From June 15 to October 1 I wrote twenty printed
sheets of my novel, and published *A Writer's Diary* which
amounts to three sheets." In November he sent the epilogue
of *The Brothers Karamazov* to the *Russian Messenger*, with
the following note, "Here is the end of this novel. I worked
on it for three years and took two years to publish it. This
is a solemn moment for me."

He returned to St. Petersburg at the beginning of the
winter, revisited his friends and took part in several public
readings. "Today the Literary Fund gave a matinee in a hall
where it is difficult to read, and where the readers cannot be
heard from every seat," wrote Shtakenschneider. "Nevertheless, Dostoevsky, sick, with his tired throat and his emphysema, once again was heard better than the others. What a
miracle! It seems that there is no soul left in his body; he is
thin, with a hollow chest and a whispering voice, but as soon
as he begins to speak, he seems to grow in stature and vigor.
Whence come his energy, his power?"

In January, 1881, Dostoevsky began to write the first issue
of *A Writer's Diary* for that year. He was in good health,
saw his friends frequently and even agreed to play the part
of the ascetic in A. K. Tolstoy's *Death of Ivan the Terrible*
at an artistic gathering scheduled for February. He also

promised to recite a passage from Pushkin's work on January 29, the anniversary of the poet's death. But four days before that meeting a slight accident made him apprehensive.

On the night of January 25, while working at his desk, his pen fell on the floor and rolled under a shelf. Dostoevsky tried to get it out, but at the first effort he felt a hot paste mounting to his mouth. He wiped his lips; it was blood. But the hemorrhage was mild, he did not ascribe any importance to it, and did not even awaken his wife to tell her about it.

The following day he felt very well. He had invited to dinner his sister Vera who had recently arrived in St. Petersburg, and expected to evoke with her memories of his childhood in Moscow and Darovoe. The meal began in a cheerful atmosphere. Dostoevsky reminded his sister of the children's games at the Hospital of the Poor, the feverish preparations for the vacations and his literary discussions with Mikhail. He was gay and laughed at his own jokes.

However, "Aunt Vera" seemed embarrassed. Her sister had sent her to St. Petersburg to discuss a financial matter with her brother. The liquidation of the Kumanin estate had provoked dissensions in the family, and Vera was impatient to attack the subject. She interrupted Dostoevsky, became excited, accused him of "cruelty" toward his sisters and finally burst into tears. Dostoevsky left the dining room and took refuge in his study, while his wife escorted Vera to the door.

Dostoevsky sat at his desk holding his head, conscious of the whispering of the two women in the hall. With an immense disgust, an infinite weariness, he thought of this spoiled evening, these tears and reproaches. Suddenly a hot liquid fell on his hands. He looked at them—they were covered with blood. He touched his mouth, his mustache—they were wet and sticky. At his cry, Anna Grigorievna rushed in and found him standing, his face pale, his beard soiled.

"Call a doctor, at once!"

Before the doctor came, the hemorrhage had stopped. Dostoevsky washed his hands and face, and called in his children to show them some cartoons in a humorous magazine. When the doctor came, he found a calm and smiling patient who asked only for a careful auscultation. During the examination, however, a new hemorrhage began and Dostoevsky lost consciousness. When he came to, he murmured, "Anna, please, summon a priest at once. I want to receive absolution and communion."

After confession and communion, the patient seemed to improve. He gave his blessings to his wife and children, then lay down on a couch and fell asleep, with Anna Grigorievna and Dr. von Bretzel at his side. Meanwhile his wife had sent for Professor Kochlakov and Dr. Pfeiffer. The fact that Dostoevsky had lost only a small amount of blood reassured them.

"He will recover," the doctors said. The following day seemed to confirm this prognosis. Dostoevsky awakened in good spirits, asked for the proofs of *A Writer's Diary* and discussed its make-up with his wife.

The news of his illness spread in the city, and his friends began to visit him. It proved necessary to tie the bell cord, for the noise disturbed Dostoevsky. Further, Anna Grigorievna asked the tenants on the floor above to remove their shoes in their apartment.

Dostoevsky ate a little caviar and drank a glass of milk.

"I am thinking of the children when they grow up," he said.

During the night of January 27, he awakened his wife.

"Well? How do you feel, my darling?" she asked.

"You know, Anna," he said in a low voice, "I have not been sleeping for three hours, and I have been thinking all this time. It is obvious to me that I will die today."

"My darling, why do you think that? You are better now, you are not bleeding any longer, a 'stopper' has probably formed, as Kochlakov said. For God's sake, don't torment yourself with doubts; I assure you, you will live!"

"No, I know it, I must die today. Light a candle, Anna, and give me the Gospel."

Often, when unable to make a decision, Dostoevsky opened at random the old Bible he had brought from the penitentiary, and read the first lines he saw. This time again he took the thick book bound in black leather and handed it to his wife, saying, "Read."

"It is the Gospel according to St. Matthew, chapter III, verse 14," said Anna Grigorievna, and she read, "I have need to be baptized of thee, yet comest thou to me? And Jesus answering said unto him, Suffer it to be so now, for thus it becometh us to fulfill all righteousness."

Feodor Mikhailovich smiled.

"You have heard," he said, "Suffer it to be so now. That means I will die."

Anna Grigorievna burst into tears, and he comforted her. Then he fell asleep holding his wife's hand in his. He awakened at eleven in the morning, sat up and had a brief hemorrhage.

"Poor darling, I leave you so worried. . . . How difficult it will be for you to live!"

He summoned his children to give them his last counsels.

"Have absolute trust in God, and never despair of His pardon. I love you, but my love is nothing in comparison with

God's immense love for man, His creation." He kissed them, gave them his blessing and handed his Bible to his son Fedya.

Dostoevsky now declined rapidly. At sunset he again sat up on his couch, but he choked, and a stream of blood ran from his mouth onto his sheets. Anna Grigorievna gave him little pieces of ice to eat, but the hemorrhage did not stop. The doctor was summoned. Dostoevsky murmured incoherent words that his wife wrote down on a slip of paper: "I am ruining you with my illness. . . . Cross out what you think is unnecessary. . . . What are they saying about me? . . . The end, the end, I shall be submerged."

He fell unconscious on his pillow. His wife and his children knelt around his bedside and sobbed. Friends and relatives waited in the parlor for the latest news of the patient. Telegrams of sympathy came from everywhere.

At seven at night visitors were admitted to his room. It was dim, lighted only by a candle. Dostoevsky lay fully dressed on his couch, his head thrown back on the pillow, only his face could be seen, white and dry as a paper mask. A red spot glowed on his beard. His closed lids showed the exact curve of his pupils. A strange gurgle came from his throat. His breathing stopped, then resumed, whistling, choking. He tried to speak, but no one could understand him.

The doctor came at eight o'clock, and he could do nothing except to listen to the last heart beats of the dying man. Feodor Mikhailovich died at 8:36 P.M. without having regained consciousness.

His body was washed, dressed in fresh linen and laid out on the table, covered up to the belt with a gold-embroidered coverlet from the parish church. A candlestick was placed on each side. The dead man's hands were crossed on his breast and an icon placed on them. A night light burned in the corner. The air smelled of incense, wax, and eau de cologne. A painter sat beside the dead man, drawing him.

Meanwhile religious services followed one another. Delegations, accompanied by a chaplain and a choir, came one after the other to ask permission to celebrate a mass in Dostoevsky's honor—they represented the students, the Navy cadets, and many others. The priest recited prayers and the attendants chanted in chorus.

It was hot. The air was so heavy that the flame of the night light occasionally went out. Wreaths, bouquets and sheaves with streamers piled up in the room. Admirers kissed the hands of the corpse and implored Dostoevsky's children to give them a flower as a souvenir.

Anna Grigorievna wandered from room to room like a madwoman. The continual procession of strangers in her apartment was more than she could bear. They streamed through the front door and the back door, and crossed each other before the bier. Who were these strangers? Why were they admitted? Anna Grigorievna felt that all these people stood between her and Feodor Mikhailovich. He was no longer the man whom she had cherished, who was irritable, sentimental, ridiculous, sickly and loving. He no longer belonged to her. He had been taken away from her. He belonged to the crowd.

Grand Duke Dmitri Constantinovich, scholars, students, great ladies of the court, and a representative of the Ministry of the Interior visited the small apartment. N. S. Abasa, the steward of the imperial household, presented Anna Grigorievna with a letter from the Ministry of Finance, informing her that the emperor had granted an annual pension of two thousand rubles to the great writer's widow and children. This news so overjoyed Anna Grigorievna that she rushed to the study in order to tell her husband. "It was only upon entering the room where his body rested that I realized he was no longer of this world, and I began to weep bitterly."

The monks of the Alexander Nevsky monastery offered to bury Dostoevsky in their own graveyard and to pay the expenses of the funeral mass in honor of "the jealous guardian of the true Orthodox faith." Anna Grigorievna recalled that one day she had joked with Dostoevsky about his burial. "I should like to bury you in the Alexander Nevsky monastery," she had said.

"But I thought only infantry and cavalry generals were buried there," he had answered laughing.

"Are you not a general of literature?" she had answered.

The funeral took place on Saturday, January 31. Early in the morning an enormous crowd filled the street. A hearse had been ordered, but Dostoevsky's admirers carried the coffin to the monastery on their shoulders. Thirty thousand people accompanied his remains; seventy-two deputations presented wreaths; fifteen choral societies followed the cortege, intoning canticles; and a double garland sixty yards long, made of laurels and fresh flowers, separated the procession from the rest of the crowd.

The head of the column reached the monastery after two hours of marching. The coffin was placed in the Chapel of the Holy Ghost. The following day, February 1, 1881, such a crowd of friends and curious strangers invaded the monastery that the police were forced to close the gates. Even Anna Grigorievna had great difficulty in penetrating into the church. When she said that she was the widow of Dostoevsky and that her daughter was with her, she was told that a certain number of Dostoevsky's widows had already been there, some alone and some with children.

Finally Anna Grigorievna succeeded in getting in, and the religious service began. The coffin in the center of the nave was covered with flowers. An archbishop officiated, and the rector of the Ecclesiastical Academy and a representative of Archimandrite Simeon attended the final benediction. Before the absolution, Bishop Ianichev pronounced a sermon extoling Dostoevsky's Christian virtues.

After the ceremony, the coffin was again carried out of the church by the writer's admirers. The graveyard was covered with snow and the branches of the trees bent over, and all the noise seemed purified by the snow. Sightseers who had perched on the monuments bared their heads at the approach of the cortege.

The vault intended for Dostoevsky was next to that of Zhukovsky. The writers Palm, Miller, Gaydeburov and Solovyov made speeches before the open grave. "He had faith in the infinite and divine strength of the human soul which triumphs over all external violence and all internal weakness," said Solovyov. "United here by our love for him, let us try to remain bound to one another by a similar love. Only thus can we pay our debt—for his great achievements and his great sufferings—to the spiritual guide of Russia."

Strangers threw flowers on the coffin. The vault was too small for this forest of leaves and petals. A stealthy reader broke off laurel branches and hid them under his coat. It was cold. Night fell. At four o'clock in the afternoon, Anna Grigorievna, exhausted from strain and hunger, left the cemetery. But among the crosses there still roved strange black silhouettes, with raised collars, faces red from the frost, and

figures like the queer characters of Dostoevsky's own novels.
They, too, left soon. The gates were closed, and further
down, at the end of the alley, the guard's windows were
lighted.

Then began the real life of Feodor Mikhailovich Dostoevsky, a life outside of time and space, in the hearts of those
who loved him.